Children, Race, and Power

Children, Race, and Power

Kenneth and Mamie Clark's Northside Center

Gerald Markowitz and David Rosner

University Press of Virginia
Charlottesville and London

The University Press of Virginia
© 1996 by Gerald Markowitz and David Rosner

First published 1996

∞ The paper used in this publication meets the minimum requirements of
the American National Standard for Information Sciences—Permanence of
Paper for Printed Library Materials, ANSI Z39.48-1984.

Library of Congress Cataloging-in-Publication Data
Markowitz, Gerald E.
      Children, race, and power : Kenneth and Mamie Clark's Northside
Center / Gerald Markowitz and David Rosner.
          p.   cm.
      Includes bibliographical references and index.
      ISBN 0-8139-1687-9 (alk. paper)
          1. Northside Center for Child Development.   2. Social work with
Afro-American children—New York (State)—New York—Case studies.
3. Social work with minorities—New York (State)—New York—Case
studies.   4. Community mental health services for children—New York
(State)—New York—Case studies.   5. Afro-American children—Services
for—New York (State)—New York—Case studies.   6. Harlem (New
York, N.Y.)—Social conditions.   7. Clark, Kenneth Bancroft, 1914– .
8. Clark, Mamie Phipps.   I. Rosner, David, 1947– .   II. Title.
HV3185.N7M37   1996
362.7'9796073'097471—dc20   96-7614
                                                                            CIP

ISBN 0-8139-1687-9 (cloth)

"Tribute to Mamie Phipps Clark" excerpted with the kind permission of
the poet.

Printed in the United States of America

Contents

Illustrations

Preface

In late fall 1989, as we were completing our last book, we received a call from George Smith, an old friend and president of the Winthrop Group, a historical research and consulting firm. George posed a simple question: did we know any historians who might be interested in writing a history of a small clinic in Harlem, the Northside Center for Child Development? We knew of the center and its founders, and we knew that this center was well-respected among those seriously involved in race, mental health, and urban politics in New York. In fact, we told George we might be interested in such a project ourselves.

In part, our knowledge of the center was rooted in our own backgrounds and interests. One of us had been a student of Kenneth B. Clark, a cofounder of the center, in a City College class on human motivation in 1965, a time of heightened optimism about the future of race relations and the possibilities for eliminating racial and economic inequalities. Aware that the Clarks' famous "doll studies" had been crucial to the 1954 U.S. Supreme Court decision, *Brown* v. *Board of Education*, David had taken the course anticipating an examination of the inevitability of progress and racial equality. But Kenneth Clark's class was anything but sanguine. The reading list was loaded with memoirs of German concentration-camp survivors, philosophical and theological examinations of the predicament of the human condition, novels that explored human capacity to endure pain and suffering, and reports of psychological experiments showing people's willingness to torture other humans when ordered to do so. Kenneth Clark's just-published and widely reviewed book, *Dark Ghetto: Dilemmas of Social Power*, was not on the list. Only Ralph Ellison's *Invisible Man* bore any apparent connection to civil rights or urban poverty. At the time, David considered this course a scholarly and academic exercise, unrelated to Kenneth Clark's broader involvement in the political and social movements shaking the country in the mid-1960s.

Thirty years later, it seems to us that Kenneth Clark's 1965 course on human motivation was much more than an academic exercise: it was profoundly concerned with the crisis of race and racism in mid-twentieth-century America. While writing this book, we learned that the optimism of white students at the time was fundamentally misplaced. It is clear now that

Clark's doubt, and what had seemed to David almost melancholia, was rooted in his understanding of the broader culture's resistance to racial integration and to social, political, and economic equality. He could not share the optimism of his white students.

As we considered writing a history of Northside, we saw it as an opportunity to explore Northside not only as a clinic serving Harlem's children but also as the institutional base for Kenneth and Mamie Clark. We spoke at length with people central to the Center: Kenneth Clark (Mamie Clark, cofounder of Northside, had died in 1983); their daughter, Kate Harris, then director of Northside; Jeanne Karp, its long-time remedial education director; and others. The vision shared by the people at the heart of Northside, then nearing its fiftieth anniversary, was that a serious history of the Center could provide the staff, the board, and the larger public a way to comprehend the crises affecting African-American youth today.

Northside Center had been established on the northern edge of Harlem just after World War II, when African-American migration to New York City was accelerating. Founded by and headed jointly for much of its history by Kenneth and Mamie Clark, it began life as a mental-health center. Its history has reflected the continuing controversies not only about racial justice but also community psychiatry, deinstitutionalization, and community action. Members of the Rosenwald and Stern families and other leading white, principally Jewish, philanthropists, have served on the board, as have leading figures, among them Judge Robert Carter and James Dumpson, in African-American legal worlds and social service. For nearly all of Northside's fifty years, the center was a base for Kenneth Clark's varied activities in education and in psychology, and in antipoverty and urban renewal programs. It seemed inevitable that such a center would be a lens through which to view the history not only of Harlem and New York urban politics, but of black-white relations, the War on Poverty, and academic disputes on "the culture of poverty" and the IQ controversies.

The widening circle of people we spoke with at Northside understood, as we did, that a serious history would require considerable research. We formulated plans for a comprehensive series of oral histories and for processing Northside's extant records and a vast array of archival materials from outside funding agencies and from personal and university archives. Northside committed itself to raising funds from its own board of directors and to gaining adequate foundation and other support.

Our proposal in hand, Northside approached the Ford Foundation, the Lilly Endowment, and the New York Times Fund, all of which gave generously in the early months of the project, largely to support the oral histories we considered essential to our research. The National Endowment for the Humanities provided an Interpretive Research grant that allowed us time off from our teaching responsibilities to travel to distant collections to photocopy and process material and to write the first drafts of the book. A number of smaller grants from the PSC-CUNY Research grant program at the City University of New York provided photocopying and some travel funds. John Jay College and Baruch College provided each of us released time.

Such support allowed us the freedom to pursue documents in places ranging from Minnesota to Cambridge to Washington, D.C., and enabled us to write an independent and critical history that would attempt to place Northside in a broad context of urban, professional, racial, and political history. Northside granted access to administrative and program files, excepting, of course, the personal or clinical records of their clients, maintained as confidential for professional, ethical, and legal reasons. They agreed that the research and the editorial control of the manuscript would be our responsibility, and they have been helpful, supportive, and unobtrusive even when aspects of the story we have told have not been wholly to their liking.

Initially, we all believed that the bulk of the institution's early historical records were simply unavailable as a result of moves and changes in administration. It seemed that little else was available beyond the minutes of some board meetings and some of Mamie Clark's files, stored at the New York Public Library's manuscript division. In light of this, our strategy of research emphasized first the need for oral histories of more than fifty former staff, board members, and parents of Northside's children, and the collection of materials from a variety of manuscript and archival sources outside Northside itself. We worked with the staff of the Columbia Oral History Research Office to establish a set of research questions and topics. We developed a list of archives and records of the antipoverty programs Northside participated in, minutes of organizations and foundations that funded Northside at different times or that worked with it in various programs, records of professional associations that accredited the organization or that represented psychologists, psychiatrists, social workers, and other mental health workers.

This strategy well underway, we discovered a set of locked file cabinets at Northside. No one had the keys and no one knew what was in the files. After an intense search, keys were found and the cabinets opened: inside were uncataloged and sometimes unlabeled folders with thousands of documents going back to the center's earliest days. Word went out among the staff that two historians were poking around in search of old files; soon, another set of boxes was discovered by Gladson Hudson, the maintenance man, and staff uncovered other boxes and records in closets, under tables, and in file cabinets. The collection of materials gathered is now so immense that Northside has made arrangements for the New York Public Library Manuscript Division to catalog, process, and house the collection.

The files reveal not just a mental-health center, but an institution whose functions and reach were far greater than what we could have imagined. Northside had been deeply involved in the critical historical events of the past half-century: the struggle for integration of northern public education; Harlem's and New York's Wars on Poverty; the Model Cities and urban renewal efforts of the late 1960s; crises in Jewish and black relations; decentralization and community control; community action; and community mental health. Center psychotherapists, educators, physicians, and philanthropists had struggled to provide effective aid for children in need. And, beyond Northside, as the world in which these children lived disintegrated, the Clarks sought to reshape and reorient the worlds of the professions, social services, and the city, state, and federal governments' activities.

At the center, some of the city's and nation's most important child welfare advocates, black political leaders, academics, and philanthropists had sought common ground. The center attracted to its staff, board, and administration a host of others whose names would become commonplace in the city's and the nation's history: James Dumpson, New York City's first African-American welfare commissioner; J. Raymond Jones, the first African-American Tammany Hall boss; Robert Carter, leader, with Thurgood Marshall of the NAACP's *Brown* v. *Board of Education* lawsuit to desegregate the nation's schools; Richard Cloward, a leader in the National Welfare Rights Organization; Viola Bernard, a founder of Columbia University's Psychiatric Institute; Stella Chess and Alexander Thomas, two of the nation's top child analysts; Marion Rosenwald Ascoli, daughter of Sears's magnate, Julius Rosenwald; Judge Justine Wise Polier, one of the most important reformers in the juvenile justice system and daughter of Rabbi Stephen Wise. There were many others.

In the context of the 1990s, with its deep racial divides and suspicions, it may seem incongruous that an institution devoted to the needs of African-American and Hispanic children and rooted in the Harlem community would ask two white, Jewish, academics to write their history. Yet, Northside was in this way—as in other ways—the embodiment of the Clarks' vision of an integrated society where a person's worth is measured by what each can contribute, not by ethnicity, race, or religion. Nevertheless, we as authors did have to address our own assumptions and preconceptions on race and racism. We were compelled to become more fully sensitive to the insidiousness of race and racism during a time in New York's and the nation's history when many, especially in the white scholarly community, preferred to believe that racism had been eliminated or honestly—and adequately—addressed.

Acknowledgments

Historians rarely have the chance to meet, interview, and get to know the individuals about whom they write. But, from the moment we began this project we have been fortunate to meet many of the principals in this story. Further, we have had a unique—and unforgettable—opportunity to enter into a world of ideals and idealism that seems all but vanquished by the sour political and intellectual environment of the 1990s. Of course, getting to know Kenneth B. Clark and working with him has been a special highlight. He has been called an "uncompromising integrationist" and, even now, in the twilight of his career and after many in the black and white intellectual and political communities have turned away from integration, his insights into the tragic consequences of racism for white and black Americans are profound.

We were aided enormously by the help, the support, the intellectual stimulation, and the warmth of a host of people who played a role in keeping Northside alive for half a century. When we began this project, Kate Harris, the daughter of Kenneth and Mamie Clark, was the executive director of the center. Her early support literally made our project possible. Hilton Clark, the son of Kenneth and Mamie, has been extremely supportive. Sharon Johnson and Thelma Dye, the two executive directors who followed Harris, were also extremely encouraging, forthcoming, and enthusiastic about this project. Jeanne Karp, the long-time remedial reading department head, deserves special thanks for her unwavering commitment to this effort and her many hours helping us locate Northside's organizational records. Also, she was essential in organizing meetings with current and former staff members, board members, and former clients. It is difficult to overstate her importance in helping us complete this work, and we thank her most sincerely.

Others on Northside's staff and board were also helpful in a variety of ways. Bea Levison, Bruno Quinson, and Joanne Stern, among others, provided insight into Northside's history. George Smith, the President of the Winthrop Group, was essential in initiating the project and in supporting the research. Ron Grele, director of the Columbia Oral History Research Office, was knowledgeable, enthusiastic, and helpful from the beginning and was essential in organizing the dozens of oral histories that his office produced. Celia Alvarez, Jonathan Lee, Lisa Miller, and Wanda Phipps conducted the various interviews, and we are grateful to them for their sensitivity to the issues that we discussed with them. Joanne Glenn and Tobias Markowitz provided us with timely and intelligent research assistance at various phases of the project.

This project could not have been completed without the support of the Interpretive Research Grants Division of the National Endowment for the Humanities. This federal agency provided us with essential research assistance that allowed us to take a leave and devote full time to this book. Also, the Ford Foundation, the Lilly Endowment, the New York Times Fund, and the PSC-CUNY Research Award program of the City University of New York provided funds for the oral history project, travel expenses to archives, photocopying, and research assistance.

Richard Cloward, professor of social work at Columbia University and one of the organizers of Mobilization for Youth, was invaluable in providing us with his extraordinary collection of newspaper articles and other documents relating to Mobilization for Youth. Frances Fox Piven, professor of political science at the Graduate Center of the City University of New York, was also extremely helpful in providing us with documents and with the benefit of her experiences as a participant in the early antipoverty programs.

Numerous librarians and archivists were very helpful. At the Library of Congress, where we spent weeks plowing through the Kenneth B. Clark Manuscripts, Fred Bauman, Rick Bickel, Jeffrey Flannery, and Debra Newman Hamm were always friendly, cooperative, and knowledgeable. At the National Archives, Bill Creech and Aloha South, two archivists who we have known through our previous work, once again proved to be valuable resources. At the American Civil Liberties Union, Marcia Lowry gave us access to their enormous and rich collection of depositions, documents, and briefs. Gail Nayowith, executive director of the Citizens' Committee for Children, was kind enough to give us unrestricted access to the committee's library and organizational minutes. Librarians and archivists at the Columbia University Manuscript Division, the Jewish Historical Society in Waltham, the New York Public Library Manuscript Division, the Rockefeller Family Archives in Tarrytown, the Schlesinger Library of Radcliffe, the Schomburg Collection in New York, and the University of Minnesota Social Welfare History Archives also provided valuable assistance.

Jeannette Hopkins deserves special mention. She has been an invaluable critic, source of encouragement, and task-master from the earliest days of this project. She brought to editing our manuscript a special affection for the subject and a special knowledge of Kenneth B. Clark, with whom she worked as both an editor and colleague. Our work together was not without tension—as well it could not have been with a good editor—but we know that the book is richer because of the many days we spent in Portsmouth, New Hampshire.

Our colleagues and staff at the John Jay College, Baruch College, and the Graduate Center of the City University of New York have been supportive throughout this effort. We thank Jackie Ayala, Carol Berkin, Jane Bond, Stanley Buder, Myrna Chase, Blanche Cook, Ines Dominguez, Henry Feingold, Tom Frazier, Betsy Gitter, Carol Groneman, Bert Hansen, Billie Kotlowitz, Sondra Leftoff, David Nasaw, Veena Oldenburg, Murray Rubinstein, Dennis Sherman, Doris Torres, and Cynthia Whittaker. We would also like to thank Richard Holway, our editor at the University Press of Virginia, for his enthusiastic support, and Deborah A. Oliver, the managing editor; and Faith Famlin, for guiding us to Virginia.

Jerry would like to express his love for Andrea Vasquez and thank her for taking time from her documentary filmmaking to share in the excitement of this book. David would like to thank Kathy Conway, who, despite real-life crises and work on her own book, continued to read, comment, listen, and love. Of course, a book like this makes us think about the future in store for our children. To Billy, Toby, and Elena Markowitz, Isa and Anton Vasquez, and Molly and Zachary Rosner, we can only hope that the vision of the Clarks can prevail over today's mean-spirited cynicism.

Excerpt from Tribute to Mamie Phipps Clark

Mamie Phipps Clark
A melody among us
Presence beyond intellect among us
Wife entwined with loving man among us
Mother, sister, friend among us
Volumes on love among us
Was with us. Is with us still.
Like a prompter in the wings
Urging us to reach out with love to
The children. The children.
The children who
Hold in their hearts and hands
Our measure, our future
Ourselves.

—RUBY DEE

Children, Race, and Power

1. The Abandonment of Harlem's Children

Shelters Like a Juvenile Jail

On 6 October 1943, a pillow fight broke out in the Shelter of the New York Society for the Prevention of Cruelty to Children, a temporary home for neglected and delinquent children aged two through sixteen, on Fifth Avenue at 105th Street. At about 10 o'clock that night, the rough-housing had escalated; sixty or so children were hurling furniture about and, in the words of the *New York Times* the next day, causing a "general wild disorder."[1] The "resident custodians" called the police, who carted some of the children off to jail.

Other, similar, disturbances had occurred in the shelter within recent years. For at least three years, the juvenile courts and Mayor Fiorello H. La Guardia's administration had focused public attention on the Dickensian conditions at the shelter. Severe overcrowding and inadequate educational, vocational, and physical-education programs had made the shelter little more than a prison for children dispatched there by the city's juvenile courts.

An investigation later that year headed by Justine Wise Polier, daughter of the noted Reform rabbi Stephen Wise, and a justice of New York City's Domestic Relations Court, reported that shelter staff were wrapping children's feet in cloth instead of providing shoes. Children were routinely punished by isolation for a few hours or even several days in two dark basement rooms, one "a triangular room without a window or means of ventilation," the other with "cement walls and ceiling, a heavy door with a peephole, a small barred window." Children confined in a cell overnight or longer had only a mattress on the floor; there was no furniture, and "a strong stench of urine penetrate[d] the air."[2]

Children in the shelter had little more to eat than cold cereal, milk, and soup. "At supper time tonight," one child complained, "I found three little roaches in my milk so I could not drink it and they did not want to give me another cup." "Sunday night for supper we get cornflakes," said another. They complained of meals of rotted leaves of lettuce, limp carrots, and bowls of thin, saltless soup with scraps of fat floating on top.[3]

In a building meant to house fewer than two hundred, between two hundred and three hundred were herded together for days, weeks, and some-times months. Children were required to adhere to a strict, often pointless schedule, awakened at 5:50 A.M. and sent to their dormitory beds at 6:00 P.M. They had to line up at certain hours to go to the bathroom and wash under staff supervision. With so little recreational space, children spent many hours cooped up in classrooms with few organized activities.[4] The child in-mates had the use of a caged-in rooftop playground but could not venture out to the street or play in Central Park, where they might disturb whites strolling in the conservatory gardens or along Fifth Avenue. A few months af-ter the October 1943 disturbance, the acting president of the Society said, "this is an institution, and is not run to be attractive."[5]

The *New York Times* reported that the staff and administration segre-gated children according to labels of "good," "redeemable" or "bad." For ex-ample, to the ward for "bad" children, which housed the most violent and "unreachable," the shelter routinely assigned girls as young as eleven who were victims of sexual abuse or who the shelter found to be sexually active. Boys of widely varying ages were grouped according to an arbitrary, ad hoc set of criteria devised by the administrator. Apparently no attention was paid to the actual reason that a child had been assigned to the shelter, nor did the administrators see any reason to tailor the shelter's programs to meet indi-vidual needs.[6]

About half of the children in the shelter were African American in a city where fewer than one in twenty persons were black. The appalling situation at the shelter was part of a broader crisis for African-American youth that had been brewing over at least the two previous decades. When the police ar-rived to stop trouble, "the majority sent to prison were thought to be Ne-groes." Justine Polier pointed out, in 1943, that "many feel there is a Negro issue involved."[7] Poor and minority children had been abandoned, in ef-fect, by organizations charged with protecting and caring for them. Albert Deutsch, a journalist and advocate of reform in children's psychiatric ser-vices, pointed out in the liberal tabloid *PM*, "the very name 'shelter,' as ap-plied to the insanitary, crowded, gloom-ridden detention homes maintained by the SPCC [New York Society for the Prevention of Cruelty to Children], is a mere euphemism for a juvenile jail. . . . The shelters . . . are harsher on their wards than are most modern reformatories." The "conditions in the SPCC shelters in Manhattan and other boroughs . . . [were] more apt to promote than to prevent cruelty to children." Yet the Society was the only child ser-vice agency in Manhattan required to accept all children sent to it by the city's juvenile court system.[8] It was perceived and operated as a dumping ground for children—primarily African-American children—other private agencies refused to accept.

In the years before Northside was founded, a number of philanthropists, Domestic Court judges, reform advocates, and psychiatrists who analyzed the inadequacies of the child welfare system saw the dehumanizing treatment at the shelter as a reflection of a total absence of personal attention to each child's individuality and unique problems. During the 1930s, this coalition of philanthropists and other liberal New Yorkers, black and white, had begun to address the systematic segregation of children and the isolation of the growing population of African Americans. In the depression years and during World War II, this coalition had begun to search for an alternative to the shelter and to the foster-care system generally. When the Northside Center was established, in 1946, at the end of the war, its founders, two young African-American psychologists, both with doctorate degrees from Columbia University, Mamie Phipps Clark and Kenneth Bancroft Clark, envisioned the center as a potential alternative to the harsh and alienating and destructive child welfare system of New York City.

Harlem and "Institutionalized Racism"

In New York City there had been an African-American community, slave and free, since colonial times, but from the 1890s into the 1920s a dynamic community was emerging in Harlem. Nathan Huggins's 1971 book, *Harlem Renaissance*, warns against projecting upon the past present assumptions and "our own frustrations." "Harlem now connotes violence, crime, and poverty. . . . 'Ghetto' and 'Harlem' have become, to most, interchangeable words." But in the years before the Great Depression, "Harlem . . . represented for many the aspirations and possibilities of a people in the midst of one of the greatest migrations in American history."[9] The Harlem of writers like Countee Cullen, Langston Hughes, Zora Neale Hurston, and James Weldon Johnson and artists like Aaron Douglas, was a community of extraordinary vibrancy, not only a ghetto of poverty and suffering. James Weldon Johnson in 1925 saw Harlem this way:

> In the make-up of New York Harlem is not merely a Negro colony or community, it is a city within a city, the greatest Negro city in the world. It is not a slum or a fringe, it is located in the heart of Manhattan and

occupies one of the most beautiful and healthful sections of the city. It is not a "quarter" of dilapidated tenements, but is made up of new-law apartments and handsome dwellings, with well-paved and well-lighted streets. It has its own churches, social and civic centers, shops, theaters and other places of amusement. And it contains more Negroes to the square mile than any other spot on earth. A stranger who rides up magnificent [S]eventh [A]venue on a bus or in an automobile must be struck with surprise at the transformation which takes place after he crosses One Hundred and Twenty-fifth Street. Beginning there, the population suddenly darkens and he rides through twenty-seven solid blocks where the passers-by, the shoppers, those sitting in restaurants, coming out of theaters, standing in doorways and looking out of windows are practically all Negroes; and then he emerges where the population as suddenly becomes white again. There is nothing just like it in any other city in the country, for there is no preparation for it; no change in the character of the houses and streets; no change, indeed, in the appearance of the people, except their color.[10]

More recently, Ann Douglas reiterated the special meaning of Harlem to African Americans in the 1920s. "What, then, were the sources of black optimism [during that moment]? . . . What was new, as [W. E. B.] Du Bois, James Weldon Johnson, [Alain] Locke, and Charles Johnson were aware, was that American Negroes now had in Harlem, however precarious its economic status, a haven and a stomping ground, the first 'race capital,' in Locke's words, 'the first concentration in history of so many diverse elements of Negro life.'"[11]

During the depression the entire country suffered but blacks disproportionately far more so both in the South and in northern cities. With millions unemployed, men and women, white and black, were forced to abandon their families in search of work far from home; young blacks left southern and rural communities to travel to distant cities to work as domestics, cooks, and porters; long hours in harsh, unhealthy work environments combined with abysmal pay to undermine families and communities.

Between 1910 and 1930, the African-American population of Manhattan increased nearly tenfold, from about 23,000 to 204,000.[12] Seven in ten lived in Harlem, about one in four of them immigrants from the Caribbean—Kenneth Bancroft Clark, his sister, and their mother, Miriam Clark, came from Panama in 1918. The new migrants were crowded into a segregated center of Harlem, straining housing and social services. Harlem of the 1930s was as crowded as the Lower East Side, with a population density of 150 to 450 persons per acre. The square block from 138th to 139th Streets and from Lenox to Seventh Avenues in Harlem had the highest density in the city, 620 people per acre.[13] The deterioration of housing, along with growing rates of unemployment and infant mortality, were overt manifestations of the depression's impact on the black community. The fragmented voluntary services offered by black churches, Y's, and African-American fraternal organizations in Harlem were overwhelmed by the community's needs during the depression.

In 1935, when a Puerto Rican youngster was arrested and accused of shoplifting, rumors spread throughout Harlem that the police had beaten and possibly killed him in the basement of Kress's department store on 125th Street. Such rumors led to the Harlem Riot of 1935; Mayor La Guardia appointed an investigatory commission of whites, among them journalist Oswald Garrison Villard and lawyer Arthur Garfield Hays, and African Americans, among them jurist Hubert Delany, poet Countee Cullen, and labor leader A. Phillip Randolph of the Sleeping Car Porters. E. Franklin Frazier, of Howard University, the Commission's research director in 1935, produced one of the first comprehensive studies documenting the social, economic, health, and housing conditions in the "capital of Negro America."[14]

But Mayor La Guardia considered the report of this renowned African-American sociologist too controversial to publish: "The Mayor, embarrassed by [the Report's] criticism of institutionalized racism in city agencies, refused to endorse or implement its recommendations," as Frazier's biographer, Anthony Platt, put it.[15] Following leaks and partial publication of the report in the *Amsterdam News*, social reformers and activists were spurred to confront the legacy and impact of racism in the city's institutions. The "precarious economic conditions and poor housing" contributed, Frazier had concluded, to a "Negro death rate . . . exorbitantly high in the very diseases in which lack of sanitation and medical care, and poverty are important factors."[16] In 1910, the death rate from tuberculosis for Harlem residents was 175 percent above that for whites, but it was four times greater than the white death rate for tuberculosis in all of New York City. Yet despite—or because of—Harlem's alarming rates of infectious disease and venereal diseases and high infant and adult mortality rates, Harlem had few clinics or private physicians.[17] A 1942 study charged that "the diseases that thrive in Harlem are for the most part those usually rampant in an environment of poverty, overcrowding, ignorance and lack of adequate health facilities. It will also be noticed that these diseases thrive even more than in the usual ghetto, due to indirect ramifications of racial prejudice. It is significant that the three greatest killers in. Harlem are tuberculosis, cancer and accidents." [18]

Central Harlem, from 125th Street on the south to 155th Street on the north and from the Harlem River on the east to St. Nicholas Avenue and Edgecomb Avenue on the west, had three small proprietary hospitals, three marginally larger voluntary hospitals, and an overcrowded, understaffed, and under-budgeted municipal Harlem Hospital. Harlem Hospital often had to squeeze 450 or more patients into a building intended for 325, on cots in hallways, on litters squeezed between beds, and even in chairs. With "the elevator . . . out of order for more than a year," Frazier had reported, "patients are carried up and down on the elevator that is used for garbage," a point whose symbolism was not lost on the people of Harlem. Reports of staff abuse of patients were common. It was "an unbelievable situation in a civilized community." By the 1930s Harlem Hospital was serving a predominantly African-American clientele but had only recently hired a few African-American professional staff after bitter struggles with the hospital's administration, doctors, and nurses.[19]

By the 1930s, of nine schools in one Harlem district, eight ran on double sessions; children eight and older had to crunch down into seats "suited to kindergarten children." [20] Harlem had no academic high schools but did have two vocational high schools, an annex of Straubemuller Textile High School and the Manhattan Industrial Trade School for Boys. "Harlem is the only section of the city without nursery schools, although no section needs them more than this area of broken homes and with a large proportion of mothers who must work," Frazier reported. "Moreover, if a Negro child is on the verge of delinquency, the school principals do not have the assistance of psychologists and psychiatrists." An African-American child neglected or seriously disturbed had no foster home or group home to go to: "Usually, the child is dismissed from school without any other provision since there are no juvenile homes to which it can be sent." [21]

Nearly pervasive racial discrimination and segregation existed throughout the city. During the war, the City-Wide Citizens' Committee on Harlem, a coalition of black and white civic leaders, politicians, professionals, civil rights leaders, social-service spokespersons, and court personnel, challenged, for example, the segregated hiring practices of the Chase National Bank, headed by John D. Rockefeller Jr. After protracted negotiations, the bank "agreed to take four or five well-equipped Negroes in their Mailing Department," but even this modest deal fell through after City-Wide Committee members discovered that the new workers "would not be allowed to eat in the restaurant where all other employees have their lunch." [22]

The lack of housing for African Americans elsewhere, the limitations of Harlem's schools, and the refusal of employers to provide jobs in downtown businesses made the abandonment of Harlem by white social-service agencies devastating. The City-Wide Citizens' Committee on Harlem sought to address the effects of discrimination from its organization in 1941 after Magistrate Anna Kross, who presided over a court in Harlem, pointed to the numerous cases of crime and delinquency appearing before her as "symptomatic of a dangerous social situation." At her urging, a meeting of 250 "leading citizens of the white and Negro community" was convened at her court. Although "they who were to solve the problem, almost came to blows," the meeting ended with agreement among prominent African Americans like Reverend Adam Clayton Powell Sr. of the Abyssinian Baptist Church; Lester Granger, social worker and director of the National Urban League; Walter White, executive director of the NAACP; A. Phillip Randolph; M. Moran Weston, later minister of St. Philip's Protestant Episcopal Church; Justice Hubert T. Delany, one of the two black judges on New York City's Domestic Relations Court (Jane Bolin was the other); and some of the white community's political and civic leaders, among them Robert Wagner Jr., later mayor of New York, Councilman Stanley M. Isaacs, Judge Polier, and psychiatrist Dr. Max Winsor. [23] Many would come to play a crucial role in challenging and attempting to reform New York's social service and educational services for children, and in creation of the New York Citizens' Committee for Children, an advocacy group of the postwar years and of the Northside Center itself.

Sectarian Agencies and the Race Discrimination Amendment of 1942

"An upsurge in crime is an after-cost of all wars," noted a New York State committee evaluating the need for future services for incarcerated youth in 1944. "All wars threaten family life, but this total war has blasted many of our families in every direction." With millions in the armed forces, and "mass migrations of unparalleled dimensions," "more than 17 million people left home and moved into industrial centers; 16 million women, of whom six million have children under 14 years of age, are in factories and other essential industries." The prospect of "an epidemic of youthful crime, delinquency and truancy" in city after city frightened the public. Newspaper columnists, radio personalities, and members of the criminal justice establishment raised the alarm. The New York State Committee on the Youth Correction Authority Plan predicted that "all the evidence points to the gravest behavior problem in our history after this war, particularly among adolescents and young adults."[24] In New York City, the problem was perceived as grave in light of the rapid increase in the number of children brought before the juvenile courts—in 1941, 4438 appeared in Domestic Relations Court, by 1945, 6975.[25]

The City-Wide Citizens' Committee pointed to the "much higher" rate of delinquency "among the Negroes of New York than among the whites." That is, African Americans were, proportionately, five times as likely as whites to be in jail,[26] and by the early 1940s, they numbered about one-third of the city's prison population, compared to only 6.5 percent of the city's general population.[27] Juvenile delinquency rates for white children rose 7 percent in 1941; for Harlem's children, they rose 34 percent.[28] Newspapers proclaimed a sensational "crime wave" in Harlem, though the City-Wide Citizens' Committee countered that Harlem's increase in delinquency and adult crime was "not as high as the increase in the Negro population."[29]

During the war, with its increase in employment and easing of the depression, services for youth were cut back everywhere. Viola Bernard, a psychiatrist and a member of the City-Wide Citizens' Committee, pointed out in 1942 that budget-cutting "affects all children in the community, [but] it particularly involves the Negro children, because their needs for this kind of service are greater, and the resources to meet them, less. . . . Privately financed treatment resources for Negro problem children are endangered by partial extinction, due to discontinuance of funds."[30]

The African-American migrant to the city faced hardships of adjustment similar to those faced by immigrants from Europe, but hardships "accentuated by the discrimination against color." The City-Wide Committee argued that the crisis the press was focusing on—"juvenile delinquency"—was aggravated by abandonment of the most vulnerable children in the African-American community, those dependent on the white-led social service institutions. With the foster-care system of New York dominated by sectarian agencies in the nineteenth and early twentieth centuries, the old Protestant welfare agencies had played a central role in organizing settlement houses, foster care services, and relief services specifically for white ethnic emigrants, not for blacks. White Protestants were then the principal population group in the city. In the twentieth century, Jewish and Catholic charities assumed an increasing responsibility for serving members of those faiths, and few of these were African American; by the 1930s and 1940s, Italian and Irish Catholics and Eastern European Jews comprised the majority of the city's needy white population. As the city's Protestant population became increasingly African American, old-line Protestant agencies' understanding of their mission was increasingly out-of-date.

By 1942, the Sub-Committee on Crime and Delinquency of the City-Wide Citizens' Committee on Harlem had brought together many persons who, several years later, would form the core of the support for the Clarks' work at Northside. In addition to Bernard, Judge Polier, and Dr. Winsor, there were Judge Jane Bolin, of the Domestic Relations Court; Herschel Alt, president of the Jewish Board of Guardians; and Dr. Caroline Zachry, a prominent child psychiatrist. The sub-committee, surveying the causes of crime among Harlem's youth, argued that it could not "be substantially decreased by any remedies short of large-scale social reconstruction both in New York and in those underprivileged areas of the South which now pour a flood of racial emigres into New York." Substantial progress would require an end to discrimination in employment ("more important than all the other remedies combined"), additional low-rent housing, better probationary and psychiatric care in courts and schools, better utilization of playgrounds and parks, and an enlarged police force.[31]

They were convinced that the delinquency problem was enhanced by the refusal of voluntary agencies to serve African-American youth in the way they had served the young people of earlier, white, European immigrant populations. "Hundreds of neglected and delinquent Negro children who should be given institutional care cannot be committed to institutions because of racial discrimination." Eighteen Protestant and two nonsectarian institutions with space for 3200 neglected and delinquent children "refuse to accept Negro children." It was noted that "the city contributes more than $1,000,000" to Protestant agencies, yet these agencies maintained all-white schools and the New York State Board of Regents licensed them. Indeed, Wiltwyck, in upstate New York, since the 1930s known as a facility for "Negro Protestant boys," was now threatened with closure "for lack of sufficient funds."[32]

The Sub-Committee on Crime and Delinquency observed that segregation and discrimination pervasive in the foster-care system was responsible for the lack of services to black children. Judges, educators, and guidance counselors either provided no services at all for African-American children or placed neglected children in city-run shelters, prisons, and reformatories, instead of in the virtually segregated sectarian institutions. The refusal of voluntary agencies "to take Negro children has meant that several hundred such children each year have been returned to unfit homes or handled more severely than they should be because of lack of proper facilities for their rehabilitation." The Sub-Committee determined that "more private and public money is needed to place several hundred Negro children in foster homes and institutions if they are to be saved from a life of delinquency and crime."[33] The Riverdale Children's Association, founded in the nineteenth century as the Colored Orphan Asylum, complained: "Placement has been difficult for many Protestant children and frequently they were known to as many as six public agencies . . . for a period of sometimes as long as six or eight years before receiving placement or adequate home guidance in its place. This has been particularly true for the Negro child and children needing specialized services. Agencies caring for neglected and dependent children frequently are unable to serve them and after a long Shelter period they are sent to correctional institutions."[34]

The Sub-Committee pushed for a relatively radical solution to the racism of the system, urging that "the State Department of Social Welfare, the City of New York and the Greater New York Fund should refuse licenses and money to any charitable institutions that practices race discrimination." It drafted, advocated, and lobbied for enactment of a "Race Discrimination Amendment" to the Board of Estimate budget for fiscal year 1942-43 to prohibit the city's comptroller from giving money to private agencies that continued to discriminate on the basis of race. Because private agencies were permitted to continue to employ religion as a criterion for service without loss of financial support, Jewish and Catholic agencies were virtually exempted from provisions of the Race Discrimination Amendment because, as stated above, the vast majority of the black children were Protestants.[35] No doubt the limited reach of the amendment contributed to its passage, by unanimous vote, on 27 April 1942.

Response to the new law among most Protestant institutions was token at best. Catholic agencies were beginning to respond to new demands from a growing Puerto Rican Catholic population, but almost all Protestant welfare agencies resisted racial integration of services.[36] Immediately after the law's passage, Polier, Kross, and members of the City-Wide Committee learned that some Federation of Protestant Welfare agencies refused city funds rather than integrate their services.[37]

Services to minority children through the voluntary system actually deteriorated in the war years. By 1944, five Protestant institutions that had refused to comply with the Race Discriminations Amendment were removed from the city list of those eligible for public subsidies. In the entire foster-care system, only 113 African-American children were admitted by 1947 to previously all-white institutions.[38] The chairman of the Sub-Committee on Crime and Delinquency of the Citizens' Committee, Edwin J. Lukas, suggested that "perhaps we must make a choice between being at the mercy of private agencies or expanding a State-wide system of care." Herschel Alt advocated establishment of a state-run system as "the only solution to the problem." Another committee member, however, Miss Esther Hilton, was worried about alienating the sectarian agencies by revealing their token response to a child care crisis. She expressed concern about bringing pressure against such institutions by threatening to challenge their tax-exempt status.[39]

Agencies willing to take African-American youth faced other, more subtle, problems. Judge Polier elicited the facts in 1945 from the Hopewell Society of Brooklyn representatives in court about one African-American child. The superintendent of the society related, "one Sunday Shirley was invited by our former cook to attend her church . . . but the following Sunday Shirley would not go to the same church alone, and . . . she became very morose and said everyone had a place to go but her, because she is colored."[40] The Classon Avenue Presbyterian Church the other children attended "would not permit them to bring a Negro child."[41] Other black foster children experienced similar problems in segregated YMCAs and YWCAs, as one Y executive explained: "For many years our girls have used the community resources for recreation. Our main source is the Bedford Y.M.C.A. which has an excellent co-education program. As you know, the Y.M.C.A. and the Y.W.C.A. segregate Negroes from Whites, and here again we find difficulties."[42]

City officials accommodated the existing patterns of segregation by seeking public sector alternatives to the private institutions that resisted taking black children. Judges in the Domestic Relations Court, faced with a child in need of shelter, made its decisions about placement on the basis of race, assigning most white "dependent" children to private foster care or to child guidance services of the Jewish Board of Guardians, Catholic Charities, or Protestant Welfare Council. In the absence of resources for black children, the same judges labeled these children "delinquent" instead of "dependent" and sent many to city prisons.[43] "The Department of Welfare also admits regretfully that in the case of Negro children it often seeks to have what ordinarily would be a case of dependency transferred to neglect or delin-

quency so that the Court might have an opportunity to use its power to de-
clare delinquency and give the child shelter at least in a State Institution." [44]
Boys from those "institutions of intermediate class [intended] to handle the
less serious offenders" had to be identified as dangerous delinquents in order
to be sheltered at all. For African-American adolescent girls charged with
"sex incorrigibility" there was a similar lack of appropriate facilities. The
City-Wide Citizens' Committee charged that, "with few exceptions there is
no intermediate place to which a Negro girl can be committed who is not yet
a full-blown sex criminal." [45]

By the mid-1940s, the extensive demands for care on the courts, schools,
and voluntary agencies had brought many of the agencies to the verge of
collapse. One such was Youth House, a publicly funded detention center on
East 12th Street that opened in 1944 after the closing of Manhattan's Shelter of
the New York Society for the Prevention of Cruelty to Children, the scene of
the earlier disturbance. Youth House had been established as "a more enlightened and expanded service with emphasis on meeting the needs of the
child while in custody, through the assistance of a professionally-trained staff
of social workers," but, almost immediately, faced with almost overwhelming demand for services, it abandoned these goals of individualized treatment. Pressed by the courts to accept scores of boys and girls, it became
little more than a detention center similar to the reformatories of old and the
shelter it had replaced. [46]

One survey of problem youth in New York concluded that services for
African-American children in difficulty were, by 1948, as bad, if not worse,
than ever: "In New York, and elsewhere too, it is practically impossible
to find a placement for a Protestant child offender, especially if he is a
Negro. Consequently, either he is returned to an unwholesome home where
conditions are conducive to further delinquency, or he is committed to a
correctional institution. This is a sad commentary on our present welfare
structure." [47]

Child Guidance for Neglected and Delinquent Children

Mayor William O'Dwyer's Committee on Juvenile Delinquency, organized
at the end of the war, concluded that most problems of the city's youth could
be traced to a rise in truancy and behavior disorders in the schools. Truant
officers referred such students to the courts because schools themselves had
limited facilities for treatment of troubled children: "With the exception of

court proceedings," the Committee explained, "there are few diagnostic and treatment facilities available to the Bureau of Attendance after it has exhausted its own resources." Truant officers who considered psychological or counseling services necessary could refer students only to the Bureau of Child Guidance or to a city hospital. The Mayor's Committee urged the city to provide more "psychological and child guidance facilities to which the Bureau of Attendance may refer its cases for diagnosis and treatment." [48]

Judge Polier had been in the forefront of efforts to introduce psychiatry into the courts, schools, and institutions as a means of forcing professionals to address the individual humanity of black children. She had become convinced that serious work had to be done in the schools to treat antisocial behavior before children reached the courts. In 1940 she had informed Mayor La Guardia of her struggle of the past several years, undertaken at his request, to secure "adequate facilities for neglected and delinquent Negro children." She described the conversion of Wiltwyck to a nonsectarian agency, now "an excellent school . . . for 8 to 12 year old boys who present behavior problems." She identified what she considered other improvements in services for children previously locked out of the system: "a growing foster home service through the Children's Aid Society, and the Colored Orphan Asylum [was now available]. Brace Farms has been expanded for older neglected boys who need a period of group care prior to foster home placement in the country, and New Paltz has recently been opened for older Negro girls." The next step, she said, was provision of services in African-American communities "to prevent the necessity of removal, wherever possible." She had begun to consult with the director of the Bureau of Child Guidance, and with Dr. Max Winsor, Bureau representative in the Harlem area, about the situation in four Harlem schools where "almost 60% of the boys who are committed to the New York State Training School from New York County come from those four schools (P.S. 37, 139, 171, 184)." [49]

Out of these consultations came a three-year experimental program sponsored and funded by the Foundation to Further Child Guidance in the Field of Public Education, a small group of philanthropists. Its Board of Directors included Marion Ascoli, the daughter of Julius Rosenwald of the Sears fortune, Marshall Field, the Chicago Department store magnate and publisher of *PM*, the liberal New York daily newspaper, Adele Levy, Marion Ascoli's sister, and her husband, David Levy, a leading psychoanalyst, and Justine Wise Polier.[50] It agreed "to provide, without cost to the schools, the services of a psychiatrist, a psychiatric social worker, a clinical psychologist and two clerks . . . [who] would be satisfactory to the Bureau of Child Guidance, and would work in conjunction with the bureau" within the schools. The New York School of Social Work agreed to assign graduate students to work with the children.[51]

At the first meeting of the experimental program's Joint Advisory Committee in 1940 Judge Polier had "voiced the hope that by means of the new clinic we may find it possible not only to give more clinical service but also in a broader way to find out what larger needs there were that might be met by focussing attention on them."[52] Dr. Viola Bernard, whose third year of psychiatric residence was spent at the program under the supervision of Dr. Winsor, was one of the two part-time psychiatrists; Dr. Samuel Jenkins was the sole pediatrician, and he was part-time. In 1942 the Joint Advisory Committee of the Foundation and the Board of Education reported, "the fact is that the needs for service in all these schools is much greater than anticipated"; the numbers participating indicated a "tremendous need" for guidance in the schools. In Public School 139, one out of every five boys "manifested some definite overt misbehavior or maladjustment." Not only was diagnostic therapy needed, but teachers also must be enlisted: "The clinical staff can act not only for the diagnosis and treatment but to educate the teaching personnel to take a greater share in the treatment approach."[53]

At the same time, Bernard, Winsor, and Zachry, working through the City-Wide Citizens' Committee's Sub-Committee on Crime and Delinquency, urged additional mental-health services for the youth of Harlem. The delinquency problem was exacerbated "because fewer community agencies are available to them than to the white group. Accordingly, the Negro children are particularly dependent on the clinical facilities attached to the Court [Adjustment Bureau and Psychiatric Clinic of Children's Court], which are insufficiently staffed." Existing agencies should "expand their psychiatric services"; the need far exceeded the availability. "Our concept of psychiatric service," Bernard and her colleagues wrote, "includes not only psychiatrists, but the work of related professional groups, such as social workers, pediatricians, teachers, and psychologists, when operating as part of a mental hygiene program." They praised a new pilot program of the Bureau of Child Guidance to provide therapeutic services in a few Harlem schools but warned that the need far exceeded the supply. A psychiatric clinic was needed, too, in the outpatient department of Harlem Hospital where treatment resources for parents were meager.[54]

The focus on psychiatry as a tool of reform of children in trouble received wider legitimacy in a 1942 report by the American Council on Education after a three-year study. "The inquiry disclosed . . . that 'of all Negro youth, only an occasional one ever comes into contact with a professionally trained social worker. In many communities private social agencies do not welcome, and certainly do not solicit, colored clients. Public agencies generally receive them, but in many such organizations the worker is a dispenser of relief or a determiner of eligibility—and not a sympathetic counselor with the time, patience, and training to give low class Negro youth the encouragement and continued counsel they need.'" "Social work is as unable as education to claim credit for saving" African-American youth. It was "increasingly urgent" that "a foundation, a state department of education, a private college for Negro education, a group of social agencies, or a combination of these agencies should establish a new type of guidance center for Negro youth in which the complete personality development and adjustment of the individual is the center of interest." [55]

The Sub-Committee on Crime and Delinquency of the City-Wide Citizens' Committee agreed that the emotional problems of Harlem's poor ought to be addressed by mental health professionals. But both "public and private institutions have failed to provide them with anything approaching adequate services." Bellevue Hospital, below midtown on Manhattan's East Side, offered outpatient mental-health services, but "there is great need of supplementary services especially in Harlem itself." The sub-committee recommended a psychiatric clinic for the outpatient department of Harlem Hospital, expansion of the Children's Court Psychiatric Clinic on East 22nd Street, and "special efforts . . . to train Negro physicians at Bellevue Hospital for careers in psychiatric service." [56]

The three-year "Harlem project," an "experiment aimed at checking delinquency and maladjustment," opened in June 1943 in three Harlem schools, with a grant of $120,000 from the New York Foundation. Its final report, prepared by Polier, Marion Kenworthy, a philanthropist, and others, issued in December 1947, concluded that "punitive methods, discriminatory attitudes and the lack of adequate staff, supervision and materials" had created a depressing educational environment for the children and staff at these Harlem schools. The report detailed the treatment of young children by Board of Education personnel: "Observers saw children pushed around by teachers, and gang methods by [school] monitors condoned." [57] The project had introduced services their sponsors believed held out the hope of real change: "mental hygiene and modern teaching techniques succeeded in rehabilitating problem children where the old-fashioned way [of corporal punishment] failed." The study's description of the harsh treatment by teachers, guidance counselors, and others was damning.[58]

The "crisis of youth" was the product of war and the depression, racism and the related abandonment of care by the voluntary welfare agencies. By 1945, child dependency had become linked to varying causes other than delinquency, such as poor mental health, stresses in home life, emotional trauma, and inadequate education. In the December 1945 "Report on the Critical Situation Facing the Children's Court of the City of New York in Regard to the Placement of Neglected and Delinquent Children for Temporary and Long-Term Care," three judges, Joseph F. McGuire, Delany, an author of the "Report on Truancy," and Judge Polier, soon to become a board member at Northside, described the tragic situation faced by children in the city's criminal-justice system. Among the most urgent needs was lack of "facilities for Negro neglected and delinquent children for whom none exist because of non-compliance or token compliance of Protestant institutions with the Race Discrimination Amendment." Almost no facilities existed "for emotionally disturbed children over twelve years of age," for groups of "adolescents in need of individualized care and psychiatric treatment," or for "children of normal intelligence with problems of school retardation." The three judges criticized the "failure of private agencies to develop special services need[ed] by children such as remedial teaching and mental hygiene." They said "continuing discrimination of some agencies by reason of race or color further narrows the number of places available for children."[59]

In 1946, Channing H. Tobias, an African American who was director of the Phelps-Stokes Fund and a member of the newly formed New York Citizens' Committee for Children—upon whose board sat some of New York's most prominent and progressive women reformers—saw the "almost totally neglected field of psychological and psychiatric examinations and treatments" as a source of crime and juvenile delinquency.[60] The new committee noted that lack of facilities placed inordinate burdens on the community and on the court system, which—in the absence of a voluntary system willing to assume some of the burdens of care—had been forced to send many children and adolescents back to the community. A committee of judges composed of Polier, Delany, and McGuire (who had just written the report on the crisis in the children's court) joined the Mayor's Committee on Juvenile Delinquency to request delineation of the responsibilities of the public and voluntary sectors. They asked city and state agencies to expand their long-term care services and voluntary agencies to increase outpatient and community-based care.[61]

By the end of the war, Judge Polier summarized the thinking of a rising group of philanthropists and professionals in psychiatry and social welfare: "the great majority of children who reach mental hospitals, courts, and correctional institutions" had been "burdened for years by emotional insecurity." These children needed an "adequate program for the diagnosis and treatment" as well as "intensive care if they are not to be permanently lost to the community." Yet, clinics for child guidance, especially in the black community, were so scarce that agency heads were "prone to accept defeat without even attempting referral."[62]

Growing out of the broad attention among social welfare reformers, progressive psychiatrists, and educators in the immediate postwar years were two mental-health clinics. The first, a relatively short-lived experiment, was the Lafargue Clinic, housed in the basement of Harlem's St. Philip's Episcopal Church at 131st Street and Convent Avenue. It was established by Frederic Wertham, a German-Jewish émigré who had trained in psychiatry in Vienna, Paris, London, and Munich. Wertham, who had joined Adolf Meyer at the Phipps Psychiatric Clinic at Johns Hopkins Hospital in 1922, in the 1930s moved to New York City, where he served as director of psychiatric clinics of the Court of General Sessions, as professor of clinical psychiatry at New York University, and as senior psychiatrist at Bellevue Hospital. Failing to secure financial backing for the clinic from established social-service agencies and philanthropic sources, Wertham consulted with novelist Richard Wright and *Life* magazine reporter Earl Brown, and opened the clinic in March 1946 on a part-time basis with a volunteer staff of young psychiatrists. The three saw in the clinic an opportunity to remove the barriers that had effectively limited psychiatric services to a wealthy white clientele. Organized as a general "drop-in" center, the Lafargue Clinic served ex-GIs, adults, and children alike, but ultimately succumbed to financial pressures in the early 1950s.[63]

The second mental-health clinic, established at virtually the same time as the Lafargue Clinic, was the Northside Testing and Consultation Center.

2. The Northside Center for Child Development

At the end of the war, two young psychologists with doctorate degrees from Columbia University, one an assistant professor at the City College of New York and the other a psychological consultant doing psychological testing at the Riverdale Children's Association, decided to try to do something about the lack of services for troubled youth in Harlem. Kenneth Bancroft Clark and Mamie Phipps Clark approached nearly every social service agency in New York City with a modest proposal. They urged the established agencies to expand their programs to provide social work, psychological evaluation, and remediation for youth in Harlem, since there were virtually no mental-health services in the community.[1] Each agency they explored the proposal with rejected it, as Kenneth Clark later charged, with "indifference, insensitivity, [and] lack of understanding of what we were trying to say."[2] Representatives of social-service organizations, such as the Urban League, the YMCA, the YWCA, and the Community Service Society, and ministers of a few local churches told the Clarks that their proposed initiative was unnecessary because, after all, these organizations were already taking care of it. The Clarks "realized that we weren't going to get [a child guidance clinic] opened that way. So we decided to open it ourselves."[3]

The Community Service Society, just formed after the recent merger of the New York Association for the Improvement of the Conditions of the Poor and the Charity Organization Society, two of the city's oldest social welfare agencies, was an obvious possibility. But, as Kenneth Clark would report, on 8 April 1946, at the first Board of Directors' meeting of Northside Center, Jane Judge, the Community Service Society representative in the Harlem office, had responded to their plan with "a 'cold' one [reaction] when she had first been informed about the center and that she had stated that 'people in this area are adequately being taken care of.'" She objected that psychologists (i.e., the Clarks) were "in charge of an institute, such as this, when it should be . . . in the hands of psychiatrists."[4] It was an issue that would emerge and reemerge in various guises in Northside's future.

In the winter months of January and February 1946, Kenneth and Mamie Clark called together a small group of friends and associates to form the Northside Testing and Consultation Center, (a year later it was reorganized as the Northside Center for Child Development). Although they had no backing, their center would undertake to provide the most up-to-date ethnically and racially integrated psychological and counseling services for children of Harlem and northern Manhattan. The Clarks sought to avoid the label of a charity service for poor African Americans. Their goal was to match or surpass the quality of service offered by the best and most sophisticated centers in the city.

The Clarks celebrated the opening of their new center with a two-day open house on 28 February and 1 March 1946. The center opened for business on 1 March in a small office on the ground floor of the Paul Lawrence Dunbar apartments (named for the renowned African-American poet and built in 1928 by John D. Rockefeller Jr. to provide housing for middle-class African Americans at a reasonable rent) on West 150th Street between Seventh and Eighth Avenues in Harlem, then the northern edge of Manhattan's black community; it was from this northern edge that Northside took its name. The Clarks paid a monthly rent of $30; they turned to Mamie Clark's father, Harold Phipps, one of the few black physicians in Arkansas, for a $936-loan to furnish and renovate the one large room into five "little cubby holes" and a small adjoining room. Dr. Miriam Weston, who joined Northside as a psychological assistant to the center's director, Mamie Clark, recalls: "I can see it now: we entered through a playground area. From the street you'd go down some steps and then you'd go in a playground and then from the playground, you'd go into the clinic." The secretary sat in the waiting room, and Mamie Clark shared her own office with staff members who interviewed clients and administered psychological tests. The center "used a carriage room or a trunk storage room as a playroom for the kids."[5]

Mamie and Kenneth Clark met often with PTA and women's groups, spoke on radio, and granted newspaper interviews to spread the word of the services available to the community. For the first year or so, only the remedial teacher and secretary could be paid.[6] Northside was otherwise staffed by volunteers, four psychiatrists, four psychologists, three pediatricians, and four psychiatric social workers, all part-time.[7] Professionals, black and white, were attracted by the prospect of working with the Clarks, who were beginning to be recognized as important African-American professionals in the city. No other mental-health clinic in the city was headed by black professionals with credentials matching those of the Clarks. The center was unique also because it intended to have an integrated staff dedicated to providing services not only to the growing population of Harlem but also to whites and Hispanics of upper Manhattan.[8] At the time, segregation was not only the law in the South and sanctioned by the U.S. Supreme Court, but accepted social practice throughout the North as well. When the Clarks initiated Northside, Jackie Robinson had not yet been allowed to play baseball in Brooklyn; the Yankees would not even consider integrating their team until another decade had passed. It is scarcely surprising that Northside faced enormous obstacles that, in retrospect, seem overwhelming.

With a modest ground-floor suite of offices and no funds except the small loan from Mamie Clark's father, Northside nonetheless served sixty children in its first year. In its first nine months, March through December 1946, it provided diagnostic services and treatment to forty-six black, white, and Puerto Rican children, one third referred by private physicians and another third by private schools. The psychology staff administered and interpreted 392 psychological tests for clients aged two to forty-six years, most of them school-age children. By the end of the first year, remedial reading and math tutoring were attracting almost as many clients as the psychological counseling services, thirty-two boys and four girls.[9]

"Each of the individuals associated with the Northside Center," as the Clarks announced in a brochure to neighborhood professionals, "is not only well-trained professionally but also brings to his work a broad understanding of our community and its people and a sympathetic insight into our peculiar constellation of personal problems."[10] An early staff member, Stella Chess, a young psychiatrist recently graduated from New York University Medical School, had met Mamie Clark when they shared an office in 1946 at the Riverdale Children's Association.[11] Known as the Colored Orphan Asylum until 1944, the asylum had been organized for black children in 1836 by Quakers[12] and was the oldest such institution in the state. With benefactors such as Winthrop Rockefeller, Marian Anderson, Mrs. John D. Rockefeller Jr., and Mrs. Edward S. Harkness providing financial support, by the time the nation went to war, the asylum was offering institutional care for approximately 175 children in cottages and about 350 children had been placed in foster homes throughout New York State. A period of fiscal crisis in the late years of the depression and the war altered the program; by 1945, fewer than 10 percent of children at the institution were orphans; the majority were there because of delinquency, emotional disorders, learning disabilities, abuse and neglect by parents, or referral by the courts, the schools, and the police department. But, like other agencies, Riverdale found that its mission to serve black children was undermined by the lack of adequate outside services in the community. Riverdale was overcrowded, understaffed, and poorly financed precisely because other voluntary agencies were abandoning black children.

"To Build a Child's Self Esteem"

When the Clarks opened Northside, they wrote to Harlem's professionals that the clinic was one of only ten such institutions in New York and that it had the "distinction of being the first one opened for the concentration of its services for Negro patients." But, from the start the Clarks made clear that theirs was to be a socially and economically integrated facility, open to "people from all localities." They pointed out that, before Northside was established, "people in the community had only public hospitals to visit when problems arose." There was nowhere that "the average family could inexpensively and comfortably seek the guidance of a qualified staff. The opening of this center was the answer to a community need in the solution of mental hygiene problems." "Up to the present, there has been no private child guidance service for those individuals in the middle income group who would be not only ineligible but also reluctant to obtain services from 'free' clinics," the Clarks wrote. "In order to maintain our service on the highest professional level we plan to accept for diagnostic and extensive consultation service only those clients who are referred to us by physicians, ministers, principals, or responsible officers of private schools and recognized social agencies. A few physicians of our community, the Riverdale Children's Association, and the Little Brown School House, have already referred cases for testing and consultation." [13]

The center attracted attention in the white press and in the African-American press, each describing the goals and underlying philosophy of the center from its special perspective. In the *New York Herald-Tribune*'s story, for example, the emphasis was on pathology of the children and their families and on the Clarks' interest in using psychology and psychiatry to cure sick children and help their families. The Clarks, the *Tribune* reported, "have passed several months convincing civic leaders that many of the maladjustments from which the Negro suffers have their roots in psychological drawbacks." Because "the average Negro child . . . is seldom safeguarded from the ill effects of the oppressive environment in which his parents live," psychological problems result, and "a sense of frustration . . . is handed down from one generation to another." The *Tribune* quoted Mamie Clark's opinion that this "ingrained frustration . . . breeds the kind of resentment which undoes the work of white liberals who are trying to help us solve the race problem." For the *Tribune* reporter, the new clinic was a private psychological service to treat this youthful "resentment" that gave rise to "community annoyances, and city-wide problems." The newspaper told its readership that "the new center has a staff of Negro physicians, psychologists and social workers who will be assisted by a staff of three white psychiatrists."[14]

Ebony magazine also quoted the Clarks' view that "ingrained frustration, . . . an unseen, little-recognized disease" was corroding "Negro children in ghettos the country over." But, it described the causes differently. In addition to "the worries that plague youth of all colors—career and sex fears, cold parents and impossible school work," the magazine quoted the Clarks as saying that "the scourge of Jim Crow" caused much of the problem. "The Clarks know they cannot change the larger Jim Crow environment which twists young personalities," but they "have shown that applied psychology can modify home and school environments, can unburden sick emotions and guide children to new interests." Even the photographs of the clinic at work sent a message to *Ebony's* readers about the importance of integration, showing both black and white children being helped at the center. The text sought to counter the prevailing view of professionals as aloof from the children they served or the community of which they were a part. "Despite too many Harlemites' notion that psychology implies straight jackets and barred windows, no clammy clinical hush prevails here," it noted, "from the remedial reading room comes scuffles and laughter, along with faltering words as children once tagged as 'dull' learn to read by playing word-games." Despite the appearance of informality and caring, "psychologically speaking, none of this is time wasted. While new 'patients' are losing their fears enough to hug 'Mamie' or wrestle with 'Kenneth' or any of the other staff, fifteen young colored and white pediatricians, psychologists, social workers and psychiatrists are learning things about the children which may help diagnose and cure their emotional disturbances."[15]

The *Tribune* had focused on the pathology of the child and the community; *Ebony* had emphasized the Clarks' broader environmental understanding of the origins of the children's problems. "Our biggest job is to build a child's self esteem so that he can bear life in spite of slums, lack of privacy, discrimination and ugliness all around him," *Ebony* quoted Kenneth Clark as saying. The *Herald-Tribune* emphasized that the Clarks had spent much of their time "convincing civic leaders" of the need for the clinic; *Ebony* reminded its readers that the Clarks had grown weary "of waiting for wealthy institutions to understand the importance of aid to Harlem's tortured young nerves," and had "financed the Northside Center from their own pockets." *Ebony* explored the human and philosophic ideals of the Clarks through a brief portrait of their daughter, the elder of their two children. "Kate has a truly cosmopolitan sophistication about race at the age of 6, thanks to her growing doll collection, which has always included dolls of every color and nation." It told its readers of the Clarks' recent joint Rosenwald-supported research on racial awareness among black children, a study that used black and white dolls to test the impact of segregation on the self-awareness and identity and self-image of black children.[16]

Ebony had caught the perspective of the Clarks more accurately than had the *Herald-Tribune*. The new model that the Clarks developed would employ psychological counseling in part to seek to heal the injuries of racism in a largely segregated city. Northside's philosophy and program necessarily reflected what Kenneth Clark called the "realities of a community that would make any sensitive human being mad, angry, and acting out."[17] The esprit de corp of the young, mostly volunteer, staff committed to the principles of racial justice and integration was critical to Northside's survival. Staff members refer to the sense of purpose, friendship, and community that existed at the center.

The clinic, as noted, sought to provide individual testing, therapy, and remedial services for children referred from a variety of primarily private sources: doctors, private schools, and social-service agencies. But the very fact that the center was sensitive to the needs of the African-American community almost immediately shaped the program. One morning, a young mother traveling from Jamaica, Queens, "came to the Center and tearfully related the fact that the principal of the school attended by her child had told her that the child was feebleminded and that she could not hope for her to do anything other than 'learn to wash dishes and maybe read a newspaper.'" The school principal had placed the child in a class for children with retarded mental development (CRMD). The mother wanted to know if her daughter was indeed retarded "because if this is true I'll not pester her to learn if she doesn't have the ability to learn." When Northside tested the child they found that the girl was not at all feebleminded but, rather, "dull normal"; and she could learn if "given both remedial reading help and guidance to help overcome some of the emotional difficulties which were blocking her development." Indeed, after Northside's contact with the school, and following reevaluation by the school psychologist, "the child made such remarkable progress that . . . she was removed from the CRMD class, placed in a regular class where she is receiving special help and encouragement." The mother was "overjoyed" and "insisted upon bringing her case before a parents' group in her neighborhood."[18] This, in turn, led to a surge of referrals to the clinic from other mothers whose children had been placed in CRMD classes. "Without any big fanfare, or without a context of community involvement or moving into the community," Kenneth Clark recalled, "we just started testing those children, and found that these parents were right: that 80% of those children were being condemned to classes for retarded children illegally. . . . This was common practice."[19]

When the news of Northside's findings got out, the parents demanded a reexamination of referrals of children to CRMD classes. The school authorities in Jamaica were forced to retest all the children Northside had evaluated. "In every case, the retest by the school psychologists supported our findings and the seven children were placed in a regular class."[20] Kenneth Clark recalls that "Adam Powell was publishing a newspaper in those days, called the 'People's Voice,' and you know Adam Powell has a sense not only of news, [but also] the sense of justice, and somehow the—that's true by the way—somehow, somebody on the staff leaked this information to Adam's paper, and Northside was in business on the side of justice."[21]

Kenneth B. Clark and Mamie Phipps Clark

The principles of Northside Center reflected broad support within a wider community for integration. Yet, they also reflected the experiences, backgrounds, and personal beliefs of the founders themselves. Kenneth Bancroft Clark was born in 1914 in the Canal Zone of Panama where his father, Arthur, a Jamaican by birth, was a supervisor for the United Fruit Company and, later, chief timekeeper for the Panama Agencies Company and the Grace Steamship Company.[22] His mother, Miriam Clark, also Jamaican, brought Kenneth and his sister Beulah to New York City when they were four and a half and two, respectively, determined to provide the best possible schooling and life for her children, even if it meant leaving her husband. In the early 1920s, Kenneth grew up in a sequence of apartments in the northern edge of Harlem near his elementary school at 140th Street and Edgecomb Avenue, a predominantly white community. Speaking both English and Spanish, Kenneth was known by both African-American and Irish children in his new neighborhood as "Spanie." He attended a predominantly white elementary school with Irish children from the neighborhood, Jewish children from the West Side, and a handful of African-American youngsters. The school staff expected performance from all students, black or white. In fact, Kenneth Clark doesn't "remember color being a factor in [his] relationship with [his] classmates, up through the fifth grade." Not until a black student teacher, Hubert Delany—the same Delany who was to become an attorney and New York Domestic Relations Court justice—came to teach in his school did Kenneth Clark realize how central racial awareness was in his own life. "[Delany] was apparently at City College, and had come down to do his practice teaching at P.S. 5, and I remember one of my classmates telling me that there was a colored teacher, and I went to the door to look at him. I was so proud . . . I remember the joy, the pride, the thrill I had, and I think I went home and told my mother that I saw a colored teacher."[23]

By the mid-1920s, with the neighborhood above 135th Street increasingly black, the schools rapidly lost their white students. Kenneth Clark recalls that "junior high school was the beginning of [his] segregated educational experience." When he entered Junior High School 139, on 139th Street between Seventh and Lenox Avenues, the school that was to become a focus of reform efforts during World War II because of its high delinquency rates, it was already predominantly black. In his graduating class was only one white, an Italian-American student. Even so, the teachers were committed to teaching all students:

> No one of those teachers at that time—this is in the 1920s—gave a damn about the fact that I came from a broken home, or that my mother was a labor organizer [one of the only blacks to be a shop steward in the ILGWU at the time and hence, subjected to various forms of discrimination by both employers and the union itself] in the garment industry. Those were absolutely irrelevant things, in terms of what they saw as their responsibility and their goals in the classroom, and there were kids in my classes at 139 who were poorer than I, . . . but everybody was poor. It didn't matter a damn, you know.[24]

Only when he was considering high schools did Kenneth Clark experience the pain of racism in the city's school system: his guidance counselor urged him to attend one of Harlem's vocational schools, rather than to pursue an academic track. Kenneth rejected this advice and entered George Washington High School in Washington Heights. He once again entered a predominantly white school, one of ten African Americans in his graduating class. He was one of the best students in a school that during the 1930s graduated a wide range of scholars and writers, among them Henry Kissinger and Kenneth's classmate, Howard Fast.

The options for college for an extraordinary black high-school graduate were limited in the early 1930s. Ivy League colleges admitted few if any black students in those years and, with the exception of Oberlin (which the Clarks' daughter Kate later attended—their son Hilton went to Columbia), most colleges practiced open discrimination. Kenneth never considered applying to predominantly white schools, instead choosing Howard University, the elite African-American university in Washington. Even though it was 1931 with the depression worsening, Kenneth's mother found a way to save enough money to allow him to attend.

An African-American intellectual community that believed in the possibilities of a nonracist America thrived at Howard during the late 1920s and 1930s, at a time when the Ku Klux Klan held real political power throughout the South and Midwest, and social custom and practice kept blacks and whites apart in the North. A gifted group of Howard professors and students helped lay the groundwork for the flowering of the civil rights movement of the 1950s and early 1960s. Scholars such as E. Franklin Frazier, Alain Locke, Ralph Bunche, Charles Houston, Sterling Brown, and psychologist Francis Cecil Sumner (whom Clark considered his "intellectual father"[25]) inspired and taught a new generation of black leaders, academics, and activists. Convinced that racism could and would be overcome and that an integrated society was both necessary and possible, they held a basically optimistic view of the possibilities of America—that integration was achievable and that equal opportunity, coupled to an expanding economy, could lessen—even abolish—the virulence of America's racism.

Kenneth Clark was profoundly influenced by his professors: many became close friends during his Howard years. By his junior year, he was "integrated into an informal small group of professors and fairly selected students, who met and talked. . . . [and] were teaching not only their subject matter, but values. They were teaching the perspective of life and race. This was when I started really to become concerned with racial injustices in America, because these men were putting this in their relationship with you." Kenneth became convinced that "there was a possibility that disciplined intelligence can be an instrument for racial justice, social and economic justice." The talks with this inspiring group of black intellectuals—

"outside the classroom, drinking beer, in their homes, in the halls"—were, for Kenneth, "intellectual and ideological ferment." [26]

The experience at Howard had a direct impact on Kenneth not only as an academic but also as a social activist. At the height of the depression, he and twenty or so other students picketed the Capitol Building "because the restaurant in Congress did not serve Negroes." They were all arrested in an incident reported in both the *New York Times* and the *Washington Post*. Clark remembers his astonishment that a police sergeant, when told why they were arrested, told the arresting officer, in a thick Irish brogue, "Let these young men go! Take their names off the books." On campus, these events created a maelstrom of controversy since Howard was largely dependent on congressional appropriations for financial support. Kenneth Clark recalls that the president of Howard, Mordecai Johnson, "hauled us up before the disciplinary committee, and it was clear that we had to pay for our sins." Johnson threatened Kenneth with suspension but was overruled by a disciplinary committee that included Ralph Bunche and Sterling Brown. Indeed, Kenneth overheard Bunche say to the other committee members, "we ought to be giving these young men medals." [27]

Mamie Phipps had come from a quite different background, born in 1917 in the resort spa of Hot Springs, Arkansas. There her father, Dr. Harold H. Phipps, an immigrant from St. Kitts in the British West Indies, maintained a private medical practice and managed a hotel and spa for black patrons. She grew up in a middle-class household, part of a small elite of African Americans in a relatively liberal southern town. Although the community's economy was based upon tourism, much of it from the North and Midwest, all public services were segregated and the vast majority of African Americans in Hot Springs were excluded from public facilities. Despite her family's social prominence, Mamie Phipps attended a segregated school and was "always aware of which way you could go, which way you couldn't go, and what you could do and what you couldn't do." At football games or public functions, Mamie Clark had to know the location of "Colored Only" bathrooms or food stands. There "was a real chasm . . . between the races," but because of her father's privileged position, her family was able "to cross certain lines," with "access to certain kinds of things, like merchandise stores, drug stores, variety stores, that other [African-American] people didn't have." Her parents sought to protect her from the worst aspects of racism and taught her how to protect herself and to negotiate within a segregated society. When she went to Howard University, her father reserved a compartment on the train from Hot Springs to protect her from possible racial incidents during the trip; he warned her "to keep the shades down all the way, and never to go out of the compartment," and he "made arrangements with the [train] porters, whom he knew . . . to protect us and see that we got fed and, you know, and that we were never to go out." [28] Thus, from early in her life, Mamie Phipps had learned how to negotiate the boundaries white society imposed.

Mamie Phipps entered Howard in 1934 at sixteen, planning to major in mathematics and eventually teach, but, in her sophomore year, the intellectual environment at Howard convinced her that the social sciences were more intellectually challenging when "juxtaposed against the detached and impersonal approach of the mathematics teachers (and, I believe particularly toward female students)." By that time she had met Kenneth Clark, then a graduate student and teaching assistant in the psychology master's program and well known on the campus as editor and writer for the school newspaper, the *Hilltop*. Kenneth reinforced Mamie's growing interest in the social sciences and, as they started to date, convinced her that psychology had scientific rigor and could satisfy her desire to work with children. [29]

By the end of Mamie Phipps's junior year, in the summer of 1937, Kenneth Clark had been accepted at Columbia University in the psychology department, the first African-American student permitted to enroll in its graduate program. He had applied to one other Ivy League campus, Cornell in Ithaca, but had been rejected because, as they wrote him, "PhD work was very intimate and involved close . . . working [and] social relationships with faculty and a . . . small number of students." [30] He would be "unhappy" there, he was told. He went to Columbia, in the more urbane and familiar environment of New York City.

Mamie Phipps's parents worried that she would sacrifice her own education by leaving Howard to marry. In response to a letter from Kenneth formally introducing himself to the family, Mamie's father wrote back in no uncertain terms of his concern: "Our objective with regard to Mamie is to have her complete her education and to be equipped to earn her own living if that should ever become necessary." He warned Kenneth that he "would not countenance anything that would interrupt that course." Not until Mamie Phipps graduated would the family consider the possibility of her marriage. [31]

In fall 1937, Dr. Phipps, learning of their engagement, wrote his daughter in dismay that she had "contracted a marriage that I cannot approve." She had ignored "the advice offered to you on numerous occasions," which in his judgment constituted "contempt of parental advice." He wrote that he "had envisaged an entirely different programme for you; a brilliant scholastic career; equal brilliance in your chosen field of endeavor and then for me the honor and pleasure of giving you away in marriage. Such a course would have capped off the interest and pride I have always had in . . . you. But all of these hopes have been dashed to pieces." At a time of extreme economic hardship resulting from a diminished practice, he could see this action by Mamie and Kenneth only as disrespectful to him.[32]

For much of the academic year, Kenneth Clark and Mamie Phipps corresponded virtually every day and from time to time commuted between New York and Washington, Mamie sometimes hitching a ride with E. Franklin Frazier[33] and Kenneth taking the train down to Washington when he could afford it. After one weekend together, Mamie wrote, "Really Kenneth I am happier than I ever dared imagine. Those two days with you were like a grand holiday where you just revel in deliciousness. . . . All of it was so very nice—you'll never know what it meant to me."[34]

The separation became too painful for them and, during the 1938 spring break, they eloped, to be married by a justice of the peace in Virginia. Since Mamie was not graduating until the end of May and because school rules prohibited marriage for undergraduates (Mamie would have been forced to leave school for a year, thus sacrificing her chance for a fellowship for graduate study at Howard), the marriage was kept secret, not the least from Mamie's parents.[35] As Kenneth recalled, Mamie "had already been elected May Queen, which meant she was virginal. And we didn't want to mess up the May Queen affair. So we kept our marriage secret—except for my parents."[36]

During the summer of 1938, just after graduation and before the beginning of graduate school, Mamie Phipps Clark took a job in Washington in the law offices of Charles Houston, a pioneering black civil rights attorney and "the virtual 'hub' of early planning for the civil rights cases which challenged the laws requiring or permitting racial segregation." Among those preparing the various legal challenges and coming in and out of the office that summer were William Hastie (whom Felix Frankfurter had called "one of the finest students who ever studied at Harvard"[37]), Thurgood Marshall, and others, Kenneth recalled, whose assault on legal segregation "made a deep impression on me."[38] At about the same time, reflecting on possible topics for her master's thesis, Mamie became interested in a series of studies by Ruth and Gene Horowitz on "self-identification" in nursery school children, and considered how she might merge her own interest in children with her broadening perspectives on racism and segregation. She wrote to Kenneth, "The most wonderful thing happened today"; a doctor at Freedman's Hospital in Washington, still a segregated facility, "made it possible . . . to have access to the 300 Negro nursery school children under W.P.A. school projects." [39] She could observe the children for a thesis on "The Development of Consciousness of Self in Negro Pre-school Children." [40]

Over the course of that academic year the Clarks discussed and refined the central theses Mamie would test through her preschool sample. By the spring of 1939, it was clear that they were on the verge of developing a ground-breaking study on racial identity in young children. In April, Mamie wrote to Kenneth, still at Columbia, that a white professor of psychology at Howard, Dr. Max Meenes, had recognized the importance of her work: "he would like to 'have' my thesis presented in a paper at the meeting of the American Psychological Association (this summer)." She understood what this meant: "*he* will give this paper," effectively taking credit for work she and Kenneth had conceived of and carried out: "It was such a shock to me that I couldn't refuse him point blank and I knew better than to say yes. I told him I would have to think about that in view of the fact that I could get it published with you," she wrote to Kenneth. Francis Sumner, not only the Clarks' mentor but also their close friend, advised her "to try to rush the acceptance of my article for publication through (within the next 3 months)" for "this would prevent Dr. Meenes from pressing the matter." [41]

In a matter of months, the Clarks prepared four papers, all of which were accepted in prestigious academic journals of the period. The first, written by Mamie Clark, appeared in the *Archives of Psychology*. The latter three were coauthored with Kenneth B. Clark and appeared in the *Journal of Social Psychology* and the *Journal of Experimental Education*. The Clarks developed a joint proposal, submitted to the Julius Rosenwald Foundation, to develop "newer methods of a coloring test and a doll's test" to continue their research on identity and race. Awarded to them just after Mamie Clark graduated in 1940, the fellowship meant that Mamie and Kenneth could now work together in New York and that Mamie could enter Columbia University. [42]

At the time the Clarks did their graduate study at Columbia University, the psychology department was largely "experimental" in its approach, emphasizing empirical research rather than qualitative social theory. But the psychology and other social science departments at Columbia were home to more socially oriented social scientists—Ruth Benedict, Franz Boas, Otto Klineberg, and Gardner Murphy (Klineberg and Murphy had earlier studied with Boas)—who had joined with other white intellectuals to challenge some of the most regressive currents of psychological and biological theory. Klineberg, in particular, attacked eugenics, long the cornerstone of many social scientists' research and beliefs. For these white intellectuals watching the perverse use of laws of heredity among Nazi social scientists in Germany, the fight against racism in American social thought took on a new importance, leading them to argue in favor of admitting Kenneth Clark to the department.[43] Klineberg told Kenneth, as the latter recalled, that when he entered Columbia "the majority of the people in the department—the psychology department—[had] accepted [him] on an experimental basis because they did not believe any Negro had the intellectual equipment to meet the high standards of a Columbia University Doctor of Philosophy degree in psychology."[44]

Despite the wide range of scholars and the relatively liberal academic department, Clark recalls that Columbia was not as "exciting as my period at Howard," but a "necessary and inescapable step toward the credentials" even if "not particularly intellectually stimulating."[45] He developed close personal and intellectual relationships with Klineberg and Murphy, and by the time he earned his doctorate in 1942 he and Klineberg were so close that "we even got to know each other's thoughts." Still, race always imposed limitations in subtle and not very subtle ways. After his oral defense of his dissertation, Kenneth went into Klineberg's office to reflect with him on his three years at Columbia. Klineberg pointed to a copy of the dissertation and told Kenneth that he had done "an excellent job." As Clark said later, "I felt just wonderful—all my anxieties were now beginning to dissolve." But he became rudely aware of the limits of even his close friend and most important intellectual mentor at Columbia when Klineberg told him, "'You know, you are the best Negro student I have ever seen.' All of my feathers dropped—I said 'Otto, what did you say?' and he repeated 'You are the best Negro student I have ever seen.' I told him we were the closest of friends and I had come to Columbia because he was there. I said I had read everything on race he had ever written, and up until that point I did not know he saw me as a Negro student. He said 'Kenneth, you misunderstood me.' I said I did not think so; somewhere in his unconscious he had me categorized as a fine Negro student."[46]

Yet, in the sophisticated, well-mannered environment of the psychology

32

department at Columbia, the faculty treated Kenneth Clark as they did any other graduate student. "I could not see any of their feelings, because they did not give me the impression of my being special." Even his "chief opponent," Henry Garrett, a professor of psychology, a former president of the American Psychological Association, and a leading academic advocate of the view that African Americans were intellectually inferior to whites, "could not have been more fair or gracious. He gave me fair treatment." When he received his degree, it was, for Klineberg, "a vindication of his original position" to urge Columbia to admit Clark, but that "was the reason the aspect of my color remained in his mind." As Clark put it later, "what fascinated me was this was 1937–40, five years before the atomic era, that civilized highly intelligent human beings were still having this kind of discussion among themselves in the cloistered halls of Columbia University."[47]

Years later, Klineberg's and Clark's relationship would be tested once more during the communist witch hunts of the mid-1950s. This time it was Klineberg who depended upon Clark's loyalty and friendship. In July 1954, Klineberg, then a UNESCO employee in Paris, was being investigated for communist sympathies as a result of pressure from U.S. government agencies. Two months after the Supreme Court's *Brown* v. *Board of Education* desegregation decision that catapulted Kenneth Clark to national attention, Klineberg wrote asking Clark to write on his behalf. Clark wrote a long, detailed letter for Klineberg's use, pointing out the hypocrisy of a government investigation of someone who was "a loyal American who ha[d] dedicated his life to the strengthening of American democratic ideals." After Clark had written the statement, he showed it to Ralph Bunche, who had worked with both Clark and Klineberg on Gunnar Myrdal's *American Dilemma* and who, a year later, would become the United Nations' undersecretary general. Bunche supported Clark's efforts for their mutual friend but cautioned Clark that "there was a strong chance that the mere writing of that statement might subject [Clark] to similar investigations." Clark told Bunche that "there was not the slightest chance of my not sending it no matter what the consequences." Soon Klineberg was "cleared" and allowed to keep his post at UNESCO.[48]

The same year Kenneth Clark was completing his doctoral degree, Mamie Clark entered Columbia's psychology department as its second African-American student and gave birth to their first child, Kate. Mamie had opted to work with Henry Garrett precisely because, as she put it, he was "not by any means a liberal on racial matters."[49] Kenneth tried to convince her to become a student of his own mentors, Klineberg or Murphy, but she told him "that's too easy. I want to work with the man who had these racial attitudes."[50] She carried out her dissertation, "The Development of Primary Mental Abilities with Age," under Garrett's direction, studying children from the public school system in New York. In 1943, their second child, Hilton, was born, and the next year Mamie Clark received her doctorate degree.

Two summers before, the nation's African-American community learned of a remarkable breakthrough through a story in the *Chicago Defender*. Kenneth B. Clark had become the first African-American instructor appointed to the City College of New York. Beneath a banner headline reporting Paul Robeson's appearance before 50,000 cheering unionists, another story on Clark's appointment to teach a City College summer session course called it "precedent setting."[51] In October 1942, Clark was appointed instructor in the psychology department of City College's evening session, at $3,200 per year, a victory for which many promptly sought credit. "Dr. Clark's appointment climaxed the long and bitter fight of the *Amsterdam Star-News*, the New York State Temporary Commission on the Condition of the Urban Colored Population, The Greater New York Coordinating Committee and other organizations and individuals," reported one African-American paper.[52] How these entities had achieved their goal was not explained. The newspaper *PM* and Adam Clayton Powell Jr.'s *People's Voice* also claimed credit for this accomplishment. So too did the young Powell himself, then a City Council member, attributing Clark's appointment to his own role in introducing "a measure to [the] City Council to have Qualified Blacks appointed to staffs of city colleges." The *People's Voice* proclaimed, "Democracy in Action was observed as City College opened here last week. For the first time in history a Negro was added to the regular faculty."[53]

At home one day in 1942, Mamie Clark was hanging up the wash—Kate's diapers and baby clothes—in the kitchen, when the doorbell rang. She opened the door to find Adam Clayton Powell Jr. "and a couple of other entourage people, including a photographer." Powell proposed to wait for Kenneth to come home so that he could take a photograph of the Clarks and Powell together. "I'll never forget, he said to me, 'Of course, I was responsible for your husband's appointment. Did you know that?'" She was frantic at the thought that he would come into the house to wait in the midst of all the baby clothes and confusion. But she was also angry that he "wanted to get into the newspaper, so that he would take responsibility for that appointment. And fortunately, that picture never got taken."[54]

Mamie and Kenneth Clark saw the latter's post at City College not as an enormous victory for civil rights but rather as a grudging acknowledgment by the white academic community of scholarly achievement. In graduate school Kenneth Clark had been an outstanding student—black or white—and had won his degree, as he put it years later, "on a single standard of competition." Nonetheless, the faculty at Columbia assumed that he would teach at one of the southern black colleges, not in New York, although students far below him in grades and class standing were being offered jobs at Ivy League schools. One teacher asked him "which one of the black schools [he] was going to [teach at], in order to help [his] people" to which Kenneth replied that he was not planning to go to a black college but to "go wherever Columbia PhD's go." [55] The response he got was "a raised eyebrow." [56] He had hoped to get a fellowship or a junior appointment at Columbia itself, but "Columbia was not ready to have any black person, even as an assistant or fellow." [57] Despite his intention of teaching in a northern college, the summer after his graduation Clark was offered a teaching position at Hampton Institute, a predominantly black college in Virginia. "I went to Hampton largely out of residual guilt, I think, because I had not yet worked out this problem of was I doing right in insisting upon being in a northern, white college, or did I owe something to the Negro college." His experience at Hampton convinced him that he need not worry over that issue. He was "required to function as a Negro psychologist, rather than a psychologist." The president of the college called Clark to his home to make it clear that he wanted him to "help the Negro student adjust to the reality of his lot in life," and he "offered to make me the best known Negro psychologist in the country if I would operate on his philosophy." [58] Kenneth Clark told him "politely" this was not acceptable. The president suggested that "no one person can change the situation no matter how badly he wants to," indeed, if the president were Clark "he would adjust. Hampton was a nice, comfortable place. I could have a nice home, they would raise my salary, provided I functioned within their terms." Instead, Clark left Hampton in the middle of the year and applied for a job at City College, where Gardner Murphy had moved from Columbia to chair the psychology department. [59]

By the mid-1940s, Mamie Clark had completed her own doctoral degree. At the same time, the Clarks had together completed collecting data for the Rosenwald-sponsored study of identity in black children and were beginning to write their conclusions. The principal finding of the study, that "Negro children [became] aware of their racial identity at about the age of three years" and that "simultaneously, they acquire a negative self-image" because of "society's negative and rejecting definition of them"[60] was soon to play a central role in reshaping race relations in the nation. It would also have a significant impact on the emerging civil rights struggle a decade later and would significantly extend Kenneth Clark's influence in *Brown* v. *Board of Education* and subsequent desegregation cases. It played an important role in shaping Mamie Clark's own career plans. In considering why so many black children developed negative self-images and what could be done about it, Mamie Clark said, "I began to think that a crucial part of children's lives, no matter what happens, has to be a degree of security and acceptance, on the part of your parents, and I had had that. Many children have that. Not everyone, but a number of children have security and they are loved and accepted, so they can accept themselves."[61] It became more important to decide what to do to help provide acceptance for other children.

Mamie Clark had been sobered by some of the experiences that forced her to confront the limitations that her race and also gender forced upon her. "It soon became apparent to [me] that [a] black female with a Ph.D. in psychology was an unwanted anomaly in New York City in the early 1940s." When she applied for a research position at CBS,[62] then still a radio network, she was "rejected without explanation" even though "white men and women with far less qualifications were hired at relatively high salaries."[63] One of her first jobs at the American Public Health Association was, in her words, "absolutely the most ghastly experience I'd ever had in my life." She told her husband that there was no way she could work with "these kinds of people," that she would "have to do something by myself." From September to June 1946 she conducted psychological tests at the Riverdale Children's Association. For the first time, she became aware of the vast number of problems deserted and neglected children faced in New York.[64]

By 1945, Mamie Clark decided to strike out on her own and abandon her plans to work in the white social service system. One evening at home, she said "Kenneth, I've come to the conclusion that I can't work for anyone else. I have to work for myself. I have to do something for myself. And there's a need for help for children."[65] She considered organizing a child guidance clinic that would address an obvious need in the growing Harlem community. "One thing leads to another, and you begin to think about the security in children, and you begin to wonder, how can you give these children security? The next stage is, what to do about it? What kinds of remedies are there for children?" The Clarks agreed that they should seek to organize such a service. "We spoke to a great many individuals. We had groups of people to our home, to discuss the establishment of it." [66]

Alliance with Philanthropy for an Integrated Service

During Northside's first year, the Clarks sought to put the center on a more stable financial footing, but it was difficult at best for the small cadre of young African-American professionals to meet white benefactors capable of and willing to support their programs. M. Moran Weston, an African-American graduate student in his mid-thirties, working toward his doctorate in political science at the New School for Social Research, found a way into this white world of money and influence through the New School. A native of North Carolina who in 1957 would become rector at St. Philip's Episcopal Church on West 134th St., Weston came to New York in 1928 to finish college at Columbia (he received his degree in 1930). By the early 1940s, Weston had met the Clarks, two of the small group of black graduate students in the city. On a visit to Northside in 1946, he learned that the Clarks were supporting the institution with their personal and family funds: "This didn't make sense," he said later, "because they could never finance it alone." [67] The Clarks had hoped to become self-sustaining from patient fees but quickly found out that it was not possible, "largely because of the general economic condition of the community and in part because the community has not been sufficiently educated to the need for such a service." [68]

Weston had become a protégé of Max Ascoli, a professor at the New School and a refugee from Mussolini's Italy. Widely known as the "University in Exile," the school was a haven for Jewish intellectuals and other academic refugees escaping from Europe and was one of the few environments in which black and white intellectuals had a chance to meet. Ascoli had established himself as an important social critic, starting both literary and political journals, and, through Ascoli, Weston became friends with his wife, Marion Rosenwald Ascoli, daughter of Julius Rosenwald of Chicago, who long had been involved in health and philanthropic endeavors in the black community. In fact, the Rosenwald Fund Marion's father had founded had supported many programs in African-American higher education in the South, including programs at Meharry Medical College, Howard University, and Fisk, in addition to the Clarks' own fellowships. Marion Ascoli had worked with her sister, Adele Rosenwald Levy, to found New York's Citizens' Committee for Children, with some of the city's leading liberal white philanthropists, politicians, and social welfare activists comprising the board. Weston told Marion Ascoli of the "pioneering program" the Clarks were initiating and asked if she would consider supporting their efforts.[69]

From members of the newly formed New York Citizens' Committee for Children and especially from her colleagues on the Committee's Mental Health Section, Viola Bernard, the chair of the section, and Justine Polier, Marion Ascoli sought counsel on whether to support the Clarks' innovative undertaking.[70] Organized in 1944 as one of the few integrated social policy organizations in the city, the New York Citizens' Committee for Children as a body shared much of the Clarks' own analysis of the crisis of youth in New York City and Harlem, and in particular, on the importance of psychiatry and psychology in addressing the needs of children. Although the Committee for Children itself did not formally link up with the Clarks or the center, "Mrs. Ascoli decided to help the Center, and Dr. Bernard, Miss [Charlotte] Carr [who had been Director of Jane Addams's Hull House in Chicago] and Mrs. [Trude] Lash [the CCC's Executive Director] assisted in setting up a temporary association to be in existence until the Center could be fully developed."[71]

Ascoli and the Clarks recruited a reconstituted board of directors at Northside, and on 1 April 1947, thirteen months after its founding, the reorganized and renamed Northside Center for Child Development was in business. Ascoli was elected president of the board of directors and her fellow Committee for Children board member, Charlotte Carr, secretary-treasurer. Others on the Northside board were Justine Polier, Trude Lash (a close friend of Eleanor Roosevelt), and the psychiatrist Viola Bernard, all of whom had also been on the City-Wide Citizens' Committee; Dr. Robert Cooper; Mrs. Louis (Honi) Weiss; and, shortly afterward, Dr. John Johnson; Edward Lewis, director of the New York Urban League; and Dr. John Moseley (who was on the original board).[72] Judge Polier's husband, Shad Polier, became Northside's attorney. This very well-connected and politically active group of mostly white reformist benefactors threw themselves whole-heartedly behind the Clarks' efforts, recognizing, as Bernard recalled, that "this was a unique and very valuable undertaking with its goals . . . to really give services to those who needed them and were lacking in them and to demonstrate that an interracial program of this kind could work and did work."[73]

The board set a broad agenda: to found a professional advisory committee, to develop relationships to the state and city, to establish the center as a non-profit, tax-exempt corporation able to solicit large-scale contributions, and to stimulate development of professional relationships necessary for a growing agency. They sought to provide a stable financial foundation that would allow Northside to grow and flourish in the years ahead. They provided access to "downtown" power that the Clarks lacked in the early years and, over the next decade, members became involved in a series of activities aimed at shoring up city and state support. They were instrumental, for example, in getting a "dispensary license" from the State Department of Charities—a means of securing state and professional accreditation, and a help in gaining tax exemption as a nonprofit institution. When, in late 1949, New York City established a Youth Board to plan, fund, and administer services for delinquent, abused, and troubled children, Northside was "among the first agencies to enter into a contract . . . to provide out-patient psychiatric services for specially referred children." [74] The contract with the Youth Board, in turn, allowed Northside to expand its services to include training, consultation with nursery schools, and community education. The Clarks gradually added Spanish-speaking staff to each department. In 1951, congressional passage of the National Mental Health Act gave the center additional financial stability to expand services. A few years later, the new New York City Community Mental Health Board, which "supplemented and consolidated previous mental health funds to agencies," [75] provided further support for the center. The support from its powerful board allowed board members and the Clarks to cultivate financial support from city, state, and federal agencies. [76]

Dr. Viola Bernard recalls the tremendous enthusiasm with which Ascoli and other members of the Committee for Children worked for the new center. They saw it as potentially the most up-to-date psychological and psychiatric service for children in New York City, a model for the psychiatric profession and a service to a community in need. [77] In 1947 the board appointed a Professional Advisory Committee of mostly outside, mostly white, advisors from the fields of social work, education, and psychiatry. Bernard served as chair of the committee, and with the help of Ascoli, recruited Herschel Alt, executive secretary of the Jewish Board of Guardians, Winifred Arrington, field secretary of the New York City Committee on Mental Hygiene of the State Charities Aid Association, Dr. Louis J. Gilbert, a psychiatrist with the Board of Education's Bureau of Child Guidance, Mabel Jenkins, a psychiatric social worker with the Board of Education's Bureau of Child Guidance, and Dr. Morris Krugman, an assistant superintendent at the Board of Education. [78] Jenkins was the only member of the Harlem community. During the late 1940s, when the system of youth services, in general, in Harlem was so inadequate, this group of civic and professional representatives sought to bring new psychiatric insights into the clinic. Dr. Bernard, for her part, was, to some extent, critical of Northside's service: "there was an unevenness, we felt, in the competence as we could evaluate it in the actual programmatic aspects, the clinical aspects." The very qualities of social purpose and commitment that had attracted so many of the early staff members to the clinic and were, from the Clarks' perspective, an integral part of the center's effectiveness, were seen by at least some of the new board members as possibly at odds with competence. "The Clarks were limited to some extent," Bernard says, "in welcoming the volunteer help of those willing to, out of their own value system and their motivations, to be useful in such a thing, so that they couldn't be choosy about the actual competencies and I think, maybe rightly, put the attitudes and motivations ahead of certain kinds of technical competencies."[79]

The Clarks and other of the original staff understood Bernard's and Ascoli's desire to establish order and organization in the center, and shared their desire to establish a "state-of-the-art" service. But they disagreed on exactly what was meant by this. The Clarks conceived of Northside's purpose as seeking to meet the needs of "parents in the Harlem area" as well as "the prevention and treatment of emotional maladjustment of [their] children,"[80] but not by means of psychiatric therapy alone and never for children of the African-American community alone. Clara Rabinowitz, one of the first volunteer psychiatric social workers, originally went to the Northside Center expecting to serve black children. Indeed, in a society suffused with segregation, few professionals could conceive of anything else other than a center "for" black children. But, "Mamie helped me understand that Northside was not a black clinic but one that knew no color."[81] It was to include children from the entire Harlem area, and Harlem had historically been home to Italian Americans, Jewish Americans, German Americans, Irish Americans, Puerto Ricans, and African Americans.

In its first years, the center was located a few blocks to the south of the Polo Grounds, home of the New York Giants baseball team. Just to the west across Broadway was a large neighborhood of Jewish immigrants and their children, and to the north were the Irish and Jewish neighborhoods of Washington Heights and Inwood. Northside was almost perfectly situated to become a model of a racially and socioeconomically integrated clinic the Clarks envisioned. It sought "to demonstrate that such centers can be operated on an integrated community basis." For "troubled" children, yes, but the Clarks saw the center as serving intellectually gifted children as well because "in the Harlem area little or no emphasis had been placed on the discovery and development of the fullest potentialities of above normal and gifted children."[82]

During the second year of its operation, between 1 April 1947 and 1 December 1948, three-fourths of the clinic's clients were black and one fourth were white. One hundred and fifty-six clients came through the doors of the clinic, 94 percent of them under the age of sixteen: "65 received some form of psychiatric service, 69 received psychological testing only, 15 received psychiatric service and remedial treatment in reading and arithmetic, and 7 received remedial service only." The staff had expanded in one year from a mostly volunteer to a paid staff of one "executive director, one psychologist, two case workers and two clerical workers employed on a full-time basis, and 17 other professional persons (psychiatrists, medical social service workers, case workers, psychologists, pediatricians and recreational workers) working on a part-time basis. Only 27 percent of the present staff [as of 1948] is on a volunteer basis."[83] In contrast to the first year, when the center's major activity was psychological testing, Northside now provided a range of therapeutic and remedial services.

The center quickly outgrew its space in the Dunbar Houses and sought new facilities at the southern edge of the Harlem community on 110th Street immediately above Central Park, where it moved in December 1948. For only $150 a month, the center rented a light and airy half floor of well-partitioned office space in a relatively new seven-story building: "Instead of being in cramped quarters, we had on 110th Street a wing of a whole floor and a spacious waiting room and maybe about ten offices."[84] Northside could now serve many more children; in 1948-49 257 received care. The staff also expanded, by 1949, with ten part-time psychiatrists, two full-time psychologists and three part-time psychologists, three full-time and one part-time psychiatric social workers, three part-time pediatricians, and four full-time secretaries. It continued to expand modestly, and not until 1960 was it large enough to warrant renting the entire top floor of the building.[85]

The new facility offered Mamie Clark, or "Dr. Mamie" as many on the staff called her (Kenneth was "Dr. Clark"), an opportunity to create a physical and aesthetic environment that would complement and reinforce the emotional and intellectual support to the children served. Staff members remember that Dr. Mamie "had a sense of beauty"; "she wanted the kids and the families to come into a place that was visually stimulating and beautiful, a little oasis in the middle of all this ugliness that they sometimes lived in." [86] She herself was always impeccably groomed, and she sought to bring beauty into the work place itself. In a sense the center's atmosphere was crucial to its treatment.

The move to a new location had compelled members of the board to consider their differing motivations for supporting Northside. The first, northern, location at 150th Street, close to a number of white communities and in the midst of a cooperative housing development, could meet its important mandate to serve a diverse group of middle-class—and working-class—black and white youngsters. The move to 110th Street, at the southern edge of Harlem and the northern edge of Central Park, into a neighborhood community center that served primarily lower-income black youth and to a building only a block away from the Harlem neighborhood with the second highest delinquency rate in the city,[87] challenged the board to confront the center's priorities. Dr. John Moseley, a physician and one of the original members of the Northside board, was less than enthusiastic. Convinced that "Northside had done a very good educational job on middle-income groups in Harlem up to this point," he thought that the 110th Street facility would alienate this clientele "with the resultant emphasis on treatment of the lower income groups." He feared that the center could all too quickly become a segregated charity service for black poor. Mamie Clark, on the other hand, thought Northside at 110th could be a magnet to attract people of all social classes and racial groups without minimizing its identification with the community. After all, across Fifth Avenue to the east and south were Puerto Rican, Italian, and wealthy white communities. Her assessment was partially borne out a few years later when the New Lincoln School, a primarily white, progressive private school, moved into the same building, leasing the five lower floors.[88]

In the first two years, the Clarks had begun to develop a program built around both integration and service to minorities, one that would stand in stark relief to other child guidance centers. They were able to find a detour around the resistance of the established social welfare system to provide services for a community in desperate need. They succeeded in enlisting a virtually-unheard-of working alliance between a group of white philanthropists committed to supporting black and white professionals in providing the most up-to-date services to an integrated clientele previously defined as outside the scope of any such individualized care.

Yet, in the evolving relationship between the Clarks and some of the board members, there were omens of future conflicts over direction, purposes, and ideological orientation. An elite board, a professional staff, and the Clarks themselves would, over the next ten years, become engaged in a profound and extended discourse and struggle over the meaning of Northside, which would endanger the existence of the center. This contention reflected broader political and ethnic struggles between blacks and whites, philanthropists and professionals, and the battle for the conscience of the nation as a whole.

3. Philanthropy and Psychiatry, an Exercise in White Power

Any Day, Spring 1954

On a late April morning in 1954, a few minutes before 9 o'clock, Stella Chess, a young psychiatrist, who was white, arrived from her home on Manhattan's West Side, at the brick building on the southern edge of Harlem and the northern boundary of Central Park. The Northside Center for Child Development was now leasing space from the building's principal occupant, the New Lincoln School. In the playroom on the sixth-floor head-quarters of the center she found a mess scattered over the floor—blocks, dolls, paper and pencils, finger paints, old shirts used as smocks. It was nei-ther the first nor the last time that her first duty of the day was to clean up. Although expected to tidy up the evening before, therapists often worked too late with the children or were too exhausted to take the extra twenty minutes or so putting things away in the cabinets that lined the walls. Then she moved to Mamie Clark's office, where she shared a desk with Kenneth Clark, who would come in the afternoon after his classes at City College.

At about the same time, two young African-American boys and their mother stepped out of the elevator into the center's open reception area. They could see from the wide windows Central Park to the south with its newly budded trees and the azaleas blooming in the Conservatory Gardens a few blocks away at 105th Street (across from the old Manhattan SPCC Shel-ter, now the Children's Center). They could see as far as the buildings on Central Park South at 59th Street, two and a half miles downtown at the heart of Manhattan. On the center's freshly painted, brightly colored walls were paintings by Stanley Austin and Norman Lewis and a sculpture of a child's head. Opposite the secretaries' desks was the director's office, identified by a name plate, "Dr. Mamie Clark." Within minutes, Dr. Ruther-ford Stevens, a psychiatrist, later chief psychiatrist at Children's Village, came out to welcome the boys and their mother. The mother entered an office to speak with Victor Carter, a social worker, who, like Stevens, was an African American. Stevens took the boys to a large airy playroom flooded with morning light from the corner window overlooking the Park and East

Harlem. It was crowded with punching bags, a soft-dart game, a puppet theater, and shelves and closets with toys, games, and arts and crafts materials. One boy, a short and pudgy eight-year-old, began to race around the room, trying out everything available and gabbing nonstop at his brother and the therapist. The brother, a slender, silent eleven-year-old, stood pensive and removed.

After Stevens observed the scene, he rolled up his sleeves and asked the older boy if he wanted to play ball. The boy ran to hunt in the closet for square blocks to use as bases and a long block to use as a bat. He called balls and strikes, ran around the bases, slid into home. As the hour came to an end, both boys left reluctantly to join their mother in the waiting room. The operator pulled open the grates of the old elevator, and the therapist waved goodbye; the boys reminded him that they would probably see him tomorrow after school when they came in for their reading lesson.[1]

Jeanne Karp, a remedial reading specialist, who, like Chess, was white, was now in her own small office with one of the eighteen children she saw for forty-five minutes twice a week. On this particular day, Karp had picked out a book for the child who, though he had never missed a session, had consistently refused to read anything there. Karp described the story, read a couple of pages aloud; she also mentioned the many children on the "Waiting List" who wanted to work with her. She brandished a pad filled with the names of the waiting children. The boy walked to the bookshelf, without saying a word, picked up the book she had read from, and hesitantly, with Karp's help, started to read aloud.

By eleven o'clock, Chess was back in the waiting room to greet a ten-year-old-boy here for his regular appointment. In the playroom she asked how things were going in school and at home. It was clear that something was bothering him. Later, he told Chess, reluctantly, that he and some friends had been playing on a barge on the Harlem River and had found a pile of hidden guns. They had divided up the guns. He hid his in the bottom drawer of the dresser in his room. He had told no one about this, not even his mother. Chess was in conflict between her concern for his safety, her professional and legal responsibilities, and her relationship with the boy. She explained that she must phone his mother to tell her the gun was there; she urged her to put it in a plain paper bag, take it outside to the closest sewer grating, and drop it through. The boy began to smile in obvious relief.

In the office next door, Olga Taylor, a young African American who was a social worker from Atlanta University and a new, official Northside staff member after a year as an intern, was working with a thirteen-year-old girl. When Taylor had arrived that morning, she had found a copy of *Peyton Place* on the table with a knife inserted to mark a page. A portion of the page had been scored so violently that it was cut. It was about a girl who had been raped by her mother's boyfriend. Had this happened to her, Taylor asked? Yes, she said, it had.

Later that morning, Olivia Edwards, a social worker, also African-American, was at her desk when Thelma Morrell, the receptionist, called her to the waiting room to meet an Italian girl with whom Edwards had been working. The girl's clothes were rumpled, her hair in disarray. She had had a tiff with her mother, stormed out of the house, and spent the night nodding off on the subway. Edwards called in Stella Chess, and they took her to the bathroom to wash up and help disentangle her hair. When she looked presentable, Edwards took her home, where she reconciled with her mother.

By a quarter past twelve, the last of the children with morning appointments had returned to their school classrooms. The staff, from Mamie Clark to the therapists and the secretaries, locked up the office for the lunch hour, went down the elevator and over to Lenox Avenue, to a small Chinese restaurant where they exchanged their stories of the day.[2]

That evening, after most of the staff had left, Mamie Clark was still in her office. Kenneth Clark, who had arrived at mid-afternoon, pulled open the accordion door that separated his desk from hers, and related his activities of the day. He had been on the phone virtually the entire afternoon with representatives of the New York Urban League, the American Jewish Congress, the NAACP, the United Neighborhood Houses, judges from the Domestic Relations Court, parents from local schools, representatives of various teachers' unions and organizations and the Board of Education. The conference on the segregation of New York's public schools they were planning to hold at the center the following weekend was bound to attract wide attention, and any week now the U.S. Supreme Court was due to rule on the constitutionality of segregated schools. The Northside conference, "Children Apart," was sure to awaken New York to the fact that racism existed not only in the South. With several hundred people probably arriving on Saturday, how would they fit into the New Lincoln School's small auditorium, which they had borrowed for the occasion?

These scenes—a composite from a number of spring 1954 days—embody the program and the purpose of the Northside Center: it was at once a center for service to individual children and parents of the community, with both staff and children racially integrated, and also a base for actions and activities, led by the Clarks, aimed at addressing larger social crises centered around racial injustice and affecting Harlem, the city, and the nation.

The Culture of Northside

The culture of Northside had been established in the first year by the Clarks, who set the tone and established the atmosphere. Kenneth Clark, who came to the center every afternoon after his college classes, was the public, often controversial, spokesperson, working within the center as its research director and outside the center in the wider world of academia, politics, and public policy. For him Northside was, in a sense, a laboratory for testing concepts and for organizing educational programs he hoped would become models for the city and the nation. Mamie Clark arrived before nine every day to assume day-to-day administrative functions. On the boards of the ABC network, the Museum of Modern Art, and a variety of agencies and community groups, Dr. Mamie's style of involvement was quite different from that of her husband. She concentrated on implementing their joint vision in a particular setting, seeking to provide security, stability, motivation, and experiences of success for children and parents, concrete examples of how reforms could be effected. To most outside the center it seemed that the Clarks existed in separate spheres. But for each other and those who knew them well, they worked as "partners," as Kenneth Clark put it, looking back a half-century later. She was less confrontational, less emotionally expressive, more diplomatic, cooler, more private. He was more candid and expressive, openly charming, more volatile, more public. Both, in their own ways, were combative when they needed to be.

As Bea Levison, a reading specialist whose husband, Stanley, was Martin Luther King Jr.'s close confidant, put it, Mamie Phipps and Kenneth B. were an extremely effective and charismatic team whose personal and intellectual characteristics complemented each other's. Mamie Clark's background in Arkansas had prepared her to negotiate the boundaries of race in board rooms and professional settings. "She knew what was going on. She was cool, you know. She was not an emotional person. Mamie always contained her composure and her calm but very much knew what was going on with everything." Joanne Stern, a Northside board member for more than forty years and whose mother-in-law, Marion Ascoli, was the financial mainstay and board chair in its first decade, remembers Clark's public face, "completely feminine and charming—charming looking, charming manners, beautifully dressed, very poised." She "looked frail and kind of like a doll," which could be mistaken for softness or lack of will. But Mamie, like Kenneth, understood how to navigate in the white-dominated professional and philanthropic worlds. Stern recalls that the casual observer "would have no idea of [her] grit . . . or the really strong and determined person. . . . she was like a rock and she was very tough, . . . she was a very complex woman." Miriam Weston, a social worker from an elite black Alabama family, recalls that Mamie Clark was "the silent, strong force that kept all this going, that made it work." [3]

Kenneth Clark's own personal sense of mission and authority served him well, not only during the first two decades of the center's existence, when he directed research, but in his impact on the center and its staff as well, of course, as on the outside world of Harlem, New York, and the United States. He knew how to make friends in and negotiate the white arenas of philanthropy, government, the academy, and wealth. And he knew how to get and hold public attention. A social worker during Northside's first decade, Cathy Lombard recalls that, when she first went to visit the center in the Dunbar Houses, she saw a "guy running back and forth, that was Dr. Kenneth, a high-energy level guy, and it was just a basement . . . but it was beautiful." [4] Bea Levison describes Kenneth Clark arriving at Northside, often "bubbling over." Miriam Weston told of early weekly staff meetings, for her the highlight of the week, when "we discussed all of the children and families . . . a time of real staff exchange. . . . Kenneth always threw in something that stirred up a lot of conversation and excitement. . . . It really was a sense of family feeling where all of the workers felt they were part of something bigger and thought that what we were doing was important." [5] The Clarks, in the 1940s and 1950s, like the rest of the staff, were young—in their twenties and thirties—idealistic, full of energy, convinced that they could affect a social-service system whose primary function, in their mind, had come to be to rationalize its failure to help Harlem's children.

The early culture of the center was decidedly informal, almost egalitarian, though the Clarks' core authority was never in question. Stella Chess says that "there was no question of rank." After one particularly distressing incident in which a child left the clinic, went home, and threatened his mother, Mamie Clark told Chess, "you know, we've got to have someone who's responsible." She meant legally. "So that's how I took on that job,"

Chess said, "and I forget what my title was called. She [Mamie Clark] was director of the clinic and I think I was medical director or psychiatric director. . . . It had to fit in, whatever the qualifying agencies demanded, that was what my title was." She herself accepted the position in 1947 as the first medical director of Northside because the center needed someone who could be held accountable in order to obtain a state dispensary license and professional accreditation. Jeanne Karp recalls Chess's own "philosophy" as "quite eclectic and flexible," allowing for a "very open, free atmosphere." As a result "there were frequently heated discussions and sometimes disagreements among psychologists, psychiatrists, and social workers about treatment and diagnosis."[6]

Mamie and Kenneth "created a close-knit 'family' feeling at Northside," in Karp's words. "Kenneth frequently invited us to his house for work sessions, Dr. Stella Chess had an annual party at her home for staff . . . and at lunchtime, the entire staff ate together, with Mamie usually joining us" at a neighborhood restaurant. "The result was that a very close strong bond developed among staff members."[7] This was at a time when many professionals elsewhere were seeking to bureaucratize institutions and impose status distinctions in the name of efficiency and professionalism.

The nonhierarchical spirit of the early center reached every worker, without regard for job description. Mildred Stevens, the wife of Rutherford Stevens, one of the staff psychiatrists, started as secretary and became office manager when the center moved to 110th Street. She recalls, "I was never so inspired in all my life. I'm serious. And as a matter of fact I felt that my . . . six or seven years at Northside was the greatest education I had in my whole life for many reasons."[8] This sense of purpose and community, critical to the survival of the center in its formative years, would allay some serious tensions of the later years. The Clarks and staff fostered a culture of "commitment and caring" that was, ultimately, as central to their treatment of the children as was the quality of service, and both were more fundamental than professional credentials and formal training.[9]

A small clinic, Northside could handle only a tiny percentage of Harlem's children in need of help. Therefore, from the start, the Clarks and staff decided to develop a program that could serve as a model for other private or voluntary agencies if and when they chose to return to Harlem or even to serve Harlem from an outside base. They consciously rejected professional ideas and techniques that they saw as reinforcing a sense of hopelessness and despair among minority children and parents. Mamie Clark viewed traditional psychoanalysis and other standard therapies as starting, as she later said, "with the weaknesses or the pathology of the family," rather than with the child's difficulties. Northside would "start with what's strong in this family, and pick it up and work with it." Any preconceived notions of what was the "best" or the most appropriate form of therapy for the children were not to determine treatment.[10]

In this spirit, the Clarks fostered an atmosphere of experimentation and innovation. For the first decade, the staff and the Clarks' center successfully balanced the differing approaches of psychologists, social workers, psychiatrists, and physicians by focusing on the center's goals and programs and on the needs of the changing clientele. Over the years, it resisted multiple pressures—from state licensing boards, from city agencies providing funding, from professional organizations, and from some of Northside's principal benefactors—to impose upon the center a formal organizational and professional structure that elevated the power and status of physician-psychiatrist authority.

The unique interracial composition of the staff, committed black and white professionals, often with eclectic backgrounds in psychology, social work, and education, reinforced this model. Miriam Weston, for example, had been raised in Montgomery, Alabama, the daughter of the president of Alabama A&M. She had attended both Spelman College, an elite black women's institution supported by the Rockefeller family, and Oberlin College, which in the nineteenth century became the first white college to admit African Americans. Weston came to Columbia University intending to become a social worker, but she majored in psychology and took courses in remedial reading. Edna Meyers came from a quite different background. Meyers had grown up white and Jewish in Harlem when Irish, Jews, and Italians lived in close proximity to the growing African-American population. Always politically progressive, Meyers, whose first love was music and, particularly, modern dance, considered herself a "left-wing dancer," but she supported herself as a remedial teacher. Her husband, Sidney Meyers, was a filmmaker who directed and edited *The Quiet One*, a film about a child at the Wiltwyck School. A number of persons and events had led her to Northside: Her analyst, Alexander Thomas, was the husband of Northside's Stella Chess and himself actively involved in the center, as a member of the board in the 1960s and 1970s. He had encouraged her to go into psychology. When her son needed guidance she was led to Northside, where she met Victor Carter, with whom she was to enjoy a life-long friendship. After starting as a remedial tutor, in which capacity she occasionally administered a few tests to the children, she decided to enter the City College of New York; there she received a master's degree and went on, later, to Teachers College, where she received a doctorate. She became chief of psychology at the center in the late 1960s.[11]

Carter, who had joined the staff as a psychiatric social worker in 1948 and remained at Northside for three decades, had met Kenneth Clark at George Washington High School in the early 1930s, when the two were among the handful of black students. West Indian by birth, he and his family were so close to Clark that he accompanied Kenneth when he went to Howard to look the campus over. We "had never been out of New York . . . so we thought we were world travelers when we got on the bus and got to Philadelphia and Baltimore and Washington." A pianist by training, Carter attended City College, then earned a master's degree in social work from Columbia. His first job at Northside was as a social worker, and, as was true of early jobs of Mamie Clark, Stella Chess, and others of Northside's original staff, his had been in the disintegrating foster-care system of New York. He had worked for two years at Youth House, the city-run shelter on 12th Street, established in 1947 in response to the 1943 disturbances at the New York Society for the Prevention of Cruelty to Children shelter on Fifth Avenue.[12]

Other members of this inclusive staff came from diverse backgrounds in and outside of the United States. Teodora Abramovich, one of the center's first therapists, was an Argentinean Jew whose family had emigrated to South America from Romania; Clara Rabinowitz, Jewish, and a lay therapist for many years, worked as a social worker before her studies at the Washington (D.C.) School of Psychiatry, an integrated clinic. Others, black and white, came to the center attracted by the Clarks and the opportunity to work in a setting dedicated to the ideals of integration in a country and a city that were largely segregated. The culture and philosophy of Northside attracted to it a remarkable group of psychiatrists, social workers, psychologists, and educators.

Stella Chess shared with Mamie Clark a common perspective on treatment. In many ways, Chess herself was at odds with the psychiatric profession of the time, which was increasingly drawn to European-based, largely Freudian psychoanalysis. She was born in New York City, graduated from Smith College and received her medical degree from the New York University College of Medicine in 1939. She trained in psychoanalysis at the New York Medical College in the early 1940s, but she did not consider herself an analyst, seeking rather a more multifaceted explanation for individual personality development in young children. Jeanne Karp remembers Dr. Chess's eclectic and nonideological approach: "She was always willing to listen to others, and give other approaches a fair trial." For Chess, individual psychotherapy and particularly psychoanalysis ought to take a back seat to urgent, practical problems that directly affected the lives of the children at the center. Karp observed that Chess recognized that "these families were so overwhelmed with housing and welfare problems, lack of jobs, and problems with the school system that . . . they had to start practical interventions in helping the families with their everyday frustrations and that traditional therapy was unrealistic."[13] Chess's perspective was a fit for the young center, and the center's focus on social as well as psychological factors that shaped a child's personality was a fit for Chess. She, along with Alexander Thomas, were to become leaders in the developing field of child psychiatry, emphasizing the individuality of children's personalities and the importance of their experiences as forces in shaping personality. (In the years after her 1959 departure from Northside, Chess would publish sixteen books and 150 articles, receiving numerous awards for her work.) Northside's flexibility in doctrine and approach allowed it to escape the often fierce struggle for dominance in the professional cultures of psychology, psychiatry, and psychotherapy, and that eventually tested Northside as well.

Freed by the Clarks' rejection of professional orthodoxy, Chess discerned that Northside was a place "where I got to have my outlandish ideas about what a psychiatrist did." At Pleasantville Cottage School, where she worked during World War II, she functioned as a traditional analyst. But at Northside, she often took on decidedly nontraditional roles, and not only ones of cleaning away playroom debris. If a patient was "worried about a test the next day, I'd tutor him. I felt this was good mental hygiene and this would raise the kid's self-esteem if he could pass that test." "Early on," says Victor Carter, who was promoted to head of social work in 1954, "Northside—and when I say that I mean Kenneth and Mamie and all of [the staff]—realized that a clinic in the Harlem community had to be more than a psychiatric clinic for children as put on that paper by the state. . . . It had to be more." For Carter, "Northside was not just a clinic for children," but "a family agency . . . a community agency in a very broad sense." Norman Wyloge, who joined the center in the 1960s as a social worker, explains that "certainly, to have a Northside parent come in and lie on the couch or sit in a chair and talk about a dream they had would not be helpful if they can't pay their rent."[14]

Carter's description of Northside's service and family model encapsulates much of the early character of its program. The staff's first objective was to establish trust. A mother at the agency for the first time is scared and distrustful: "all she knows is something terrible [is happening], and she's afraid someone thinks her kid's crazy." Carter knew that it would be too easy to frighten and alienate her further by treating her condescendingly or assuming a traditional, professional stance that blamed a child's deviant behavior or delinquency principally on the parent-child relationship: "If you start asking her about the Oedipal situation and ask her about her father and grandfather, first, she won't know what the hell you're talking about, and she doesn't care. Her stomach's growling, she needs food. Second, her husband's left her. . . . Kids are giving her hell." Carter, like Chess, often used techniques very different from those of prevailing practice. For example, Carter assumed that a client's past history with social service professionals, if indeed there had been such a history, had been negative and would have to be overcome during the first encounter if a successful relationship were to be established. "These parents are very sharp. They may not make Phi Beta because they didn't go to college, but they're sharp." Not only would the professional diagnose the patient or client, employing a particular set of assumptions and professional interpretations, but the patient-client and their parents would evaluate the professional from their own experience. A mutual process of evaluation and interpretation was underway. "If you think [clients are] not diagnosing you, forget it." [15]

Abramovich had received her medical degree and specialization in child psychiatry in Argentina, fleeing Argentina during the Perón dictatorship, and like many emigrant medical professionals was denied certification to practice in the United States; instead, she found work as a lay therapist at Northside. She had come to the United States intending to remain "only one year, to observe their psychiatry, to study the differences in problems and their solutions," but stayed at Northside as a therapist for nearly thirty years, finding the atmosphere and philosophy of the center consistent with her own training and beliefs. U.S. psychiatry may "have more theories, more medicines, more probabilities. But, I will tell you the truth: some American psychiatrists do not have enough depth of feeling." Many times she gave her home phone number to patients and told them, "if you need something, call me." It was not unusual for her to get emergency calls in the middle of the night. Abramovich described one such incident that happened shortly after she began working at Northside. "I received a call from a patient about 11:30 at night. 'Doctor! Come! Come! Come!' I said, 'my goodness, what is happening?' 'Mother wants to send me to Bellevue.' . . . I left my apartment [on West 12th Street]—asked the doorman how to get [to the address], and took the subway. I didn't know if Harlem was good or bad or what was there. Well, I arrived and took the situation in hand." Some of her Northside colleagues were startled by her traveling in the middle of the night to an unknown locale in central Harlem, but none seemed to find it either inappropriate or unprofessional. Over the years, many on the staff found themselves in similar situations in which personal commitment crossed ordinary boundaries of professional responsibilities.[16]

Abramovich treated the center's location on Central Park as an opportunity for therapy. She used the park in the treatment of her patients, taking some on runs through the park, "pretending that the Indians were there." She found the Harlem Meer, the lake in Central Park's northeastern corner, virtually across the street from the center, a favorite spot to interview and work with the children. "I always believed that my children needed contact with nature." When she first arrived at Northside, she rowed a twelve-year-old boy who had been diagnosed as schizophrenic across the lake. When they reached the other side, she said, " 'You know what you will do now? You will row back by yourself.' Without a doubt, I was a little audacious, [but] *he did it*! He was so happy because he did it." Abramovich wanted him "to be in touch with the beautiful and healthful elements of nature rather than his sordid and ugly environment." [17]

From its earliest days, the goal of the center was to address "the whole child," placing the child's needs in the broadest context. Miriam Weston describes the process that evolved: "So you had the family work, the work with the parents. You had the psychotherapy. You had the remedial reading, . . . and you had the medical part, the physical exams." Many child guidance clinics were, in effect, narrowing their focus to concentrate on intrapsychic treatment; Northside's staff was seeking to broaden its own. In addition to working with parents, Northside was the only agency—certainly in New York—to integrate remedial reading into its treatment. "So here was a new struggling clinic that somehow had a vision that if you're going to work with children you need to have all of these pieces in place, and I think that was the genius of Northside." [18] Northside simultaneously sought to educate the broader professional community and political world to understand these children as needing not only mental-health services but also remediation to reverse educational and social neglect.

Northside's program was aimed as much at the professional community as at the children themselves. It introduced into the social science and psychological literature an attention to race and racism as forces that shape all children's experiences, of black children, especially, in profoundly destructive ways, and that racial integration could be a powerful factor in healing the deep wounds of racism.

Written in 1957, a nine-year study of patient treatment records from 1948 to 1956, undergirded Northside's conviction that poor blacks and whites were as amenable to psychiatric treatment as middle-class whites and blacks. But the study found that the key to successful treatment was not whether the individual therapist was white, black, or Hispanic; successful treatment was a consequence of the interracial nature of the team working with the patient and the family. "There is a strong trend for more children to improve when the clinic team is of mixed ethnic background or when the ethnic background of the clinic team is entirely *different* from that of the child." Mamie Clark speculated that the critical variable was the team's motivation: "One might infer that the mixed ethnic teams afford a greater intercultural stimulation and possibly higher motivation on the part of team members." [19]

"A Certain Kind of Power"

While the staff was developing an eclectic approach to its children's problems, the Northside board itself was evolving from a different perspective but to similar ends. The liberal philanthropists—most of them Jewish—on the founding board advocated a greater sensitivity to the suffering in the black community. Given the tragic history of Jews in Nazi Germany and central Europe so recently revealed, board members felt strongly that all racial stereotyping was repugnant and all racial oppression abhorrent. During the 1930s, the continual stream of Jewish refugees had brought stories of ghetto confinement, anti-Semitism, the cruelties of Hitler Youth, the horrors of Krystal Nacht, the confiscation of Jewish property, the disappearance of merchants and families, and the persecution of Jewish scholars and rabbis. Rumors, then testimony, of concentration camp torture and genocide began to reach the United States. In the United States itself, anti-Semitism among the blatantly racist Ku Klux Klan and nativist organizations and awareness of the oppressive experience of African Americans in the South, especially the denial of the right to vote, the dehumanizing pattern of segregation, the beatings and lynchings, had laid the foundation for an alliance of the oppressed, of Jews and blacks.

Marion Rosenwald Ascoli, Northside's president of the board from 1947, had long believed, as her influential father, Julius Rosenwald, had, that U.S. Jewry had a special duty to support African-American institutions. She herself had married Max Ascoli, a Jewish refugee from Mussolini's Fascist Italy. In European-based psychoanalysis, in which Jewish physicians predominated, she saw a therapeutic approach whose emphasis on the individuality of the patient could counter racial stigmatization and racism. Her brother-in-law, David Levy, a founder of the New York Psychoanalytic Institute, influenced her efforts to shape Northside Center to assume a larger role for psychoanalytic psychiatry.

As founders of Northside, both Mamie and Kenneth Clark—and both psychologists, after all—agreed with assumptions of the philanthropic and psychiatric canon that, for example, personality is shaped by intrapsychic forces, but they saw limitations in what they understood as psychoanalysis's deemphasis of social environment—hence also of racism itself—as a central force in shaping lives and in determining behavior. At Northside, Ascoli's and the Clarks' differing perspectives on the role of psychiatry and, indeed, on the relevance in a racist society of a medical model of disease, therapy, and care more broadly, provoked a fierce dispute that for some time masked a deeper struggle over control of the center that, to some degree, paralleled the general relationship of white philanthropy to the black community. On one level, the struggle at Northside was over professional credentials and program, and public prestige (to which financial support was tied). On another level, the struggle was about power. Who should decide what was "best" for black children or for poor children? Who should control the center? Quite simply, should the upper-class, wealthy, primarily white, and predominantly Jewish board be in charge, or should black professionals of an intellectual elite, with little independent financial resources of their own, be in charge?

The struggles at the center anticipated broader conflicts between Jews and blacks that, in the 1960s, would overtake these erstwhile allies of the 1950s civil rights movement. As early as 1946, despite—or perhaps *because* of—Kenneth Clark's long standing friendships with leading Jewish intellectuals, such as his mentor at Columbia, Otto Klineberg, he had foreseen a coming disintegration of that relationship in light of the enormous disparity in power and wealth that marked these two oppressed groups and in light of their differing perspectives on the causes of racism. In the journal of the American Jewish Committee, *Commentary*, and, in succeeding years in other intellectual journals that reached the Jewish community, Clark discussed the potential for a breakdown in the alliance between these American minorities.

At Northside, despite the board's good intentions, social commitment to equality, and mutual goodwill, the board and the staff did not share wholly coinciding agendas—personal, philanthropic, professional, or political. Although the board's goals were often consistent with the original perspective of the Clarks and of the staff on how best to serve the children of Harlem, sometimes they were not.

Marion Ascoli's involvement with Northside had begun in the winter of 1947, when she called Viola Bernard, the psychiatrist who headed the New York Citizens' Committee for Children's mental health section, to ask Bernard to help her come to a decision. Ascoli had been approached by Moran Weston, one of a small group of African-American graduate students in New York, who told her of two "Negro" psychologists who had begun what was clearly the most unusual child guidance center in the city. Ascoli's own support of the New York City Board of Education's child guidance clinic in Harlem during World War II had heightened her understanding of the need of Harlem's children for psychological services. Here now were two young professionals, Mamie and Kenneth Clark, who were seeking to provide such service. Ascoli hoped Bernard would help her decide whether or not to give the Clarks her support. "She felt," as Bernard has put it, "that she needed advice . . . on the worthwhileness of this undertaking—whether it was valid or whether it was something to invest in or not because they needed quite a lot of money." Ascoli, Bernard said, "was receptive to this because she was, as part of the Rosenwald family, concerned with the welfare of children and with race relations in the way that the Rosenwald family were." [20]

Bernard, fresh from her own efforts with the City-Wide Citizens' Committee on Harlem's Sub-Committee on Crime and Delinquency and the New York City Board of Education's Bureau of Child Guidance pilot program in Harlem, arranged an exploratory meeting with the Clarks at her penthouse apartment at Fifth Avenue and East 74th Street. In 1947, Fifth Avenue doormen routinely routed African Americans who came to their buildings to the service entrance; Bernard, to ward off such an awkward encounter, alerted the doorman and the elevator operator that they were to expect the Clarks and that they were to treat them courteously. [21] When the doorman announced their arrival, Bernard took the elevator down herself to meet them and "to avoid any embarrassment." [22]

Bernard says the relationship was obviously unequal almost from the first. Whatever her own personal good will, she recalls, she "had power . . . lived on Fifth Avenue." The Clarks had indeed established Northside independently of any outside philanthropic help, but it had become obvious that outside financial support was essential if the center were to survive. Should the Clarks get such support from Marion Ascoli?[23] Bernard felt she herself "was invested . . . with a certain kind of power. . . . I had power to persuade Marion to either do it or not do it."[24]

This initial meeting led to other meetings with an expanded group drawn primarily from Ascoli's and Bernard's associates of the mental health section of the new Citizens' Committee for Children, itself organized by Ascoli's sister, Adele Levy. (Her husband, David Levy, was the prominent psychoanalyst who would play a key role later in Northside's conflict over the role of psychoanalysis). Bernard was "struck . . . that [the Clarks] were attempting to do something very much needed and very valuable [that would] meet an unmet need." Further, "the staff was interracial" and its leaders were African Americans with doctoral degrees from Columbia. It was clearly deserving of support from the philanthropic liberal elite of the city and could greatly benefit, in Bernard's view, from the leadership a well-selected board could provide.

For Bernard, Ascoli, and others at the Citizens' Committee for Children, because the Clarks were "relatively inexperienced in the area of such organizations," they needed a board of trustees to guide the center, providing it with professional stature as well as tax-exempt status, which depended on meeting certain licensing requirements. "We met a lot and I did bring in my allies—Justine Polier and Shad Polier." Justine Polier, a judge in the Domestic Relations Court, and for years a leader in child welfare reform, had, along with Moran Weston, called Ascoli's attention to the Clarks in the first place. Shad Polier, her husband, a civil rights lawyer, was attorney for the New York Citizens' Committee for Children and headed a committee for the liberal American Jewish Congress, which in turn had been started by Justine's father, Rabbi Stephen Wise. "We met several times in my living room . . . to make a recommendation about [Ascoli] investing in this or not." The Poliers, Bernard, and other members of the mental-health section of the Citizens' Committee for Children agreed that although Northside had "drawbacks," as Bernard recalls, "there was absolutely nothing in New York City like it." "Here were two really rather respected, well-trained black professionals with an already ongoing state of affairs, and so we made a recommendation to

Marion—for God's sake, go ahead with this. [We said that] it does need probably to go and develop more professionally than it has with its beginnings, but it is an extremely invaluable beginning, and it has a lot of people in it who care and it ought to be supported." [25]

The Poliers, Ascoli, Bernard, and the members of the Citizens' Committee for Children were committed to working with African-American professionals to change the existing social service system. Born in Chicago and one of five children who were heirs to the Sears fortune, Marion Ascoli had been reared by their father, Julius Rosenwald, to be active in philanthropies that were pioneering for their time. Like virtually all the daughters of America's upper classes, the three Rosenwald daughters were not expected to enter the family business as managers or owners; unlike many privileged young women of their era, many of whom chose a socially prominent and prestigious museum or library involvement, all three Rosenwald sisters engaged in socially progressive philanthropic endeavors. Living in New Orleans, Edith, the oldest daughter, participated in voter registration drives at a time when blacks were openly and violently excluded as voters. Adele founded the New York City Citizens' Committee for Children. The youngest, Marion, came to New York shortly after her divorce from her first husband, Alfred Stern Sr. When Adele founded the Citizens' Committee for Children in 1946, Marion Ascoli joined.

Marion Ascoli was first and foremost a philanthropist who was deeply influenced by her family's half-century commitment to supporting institutions and programs that served African-American communities in the segregated South. When she arrived in New York from Chicago in the early 1940s, she encountered a well-established philanthropic community that all but ignored the growing black population. Through her work at Northside she hoped to remedy that neglect. The Citizens' Committee for Children and many of Northside's early board members were interconnected, but Northside became Ascoli's personal project. As her daughter-in-law and fellow Northside board member, Joanne Stern—still on the board after forty years—explains it, given the daughters' control over part of the Rosenwald fortune, "the three girls were used to being listened to." Both at the Citizens' Committee for Children and at the Northside Center, Ascoli expected to have "her own way." [26]

Bernard, Ascoli's confidant, also from a wealthy German-Jewish background, had set out to become a professional rather than a philanthropist.

She established herself in the emerging psychiatric and psychoanalytic community in New York, where she made a point of pressing for the inclusion of African Americans, both as practitioners of psychiatry and as clients. Early in the 1940s, she tried to organize a mental-health clinic in Harlem but found that "the chief difficulty lies in the shortage of suitable Negro psychiatrists to head it up." [27] Aware of the inadequacy of services for black children through her year-long residency in the Harlem unit of the Bureau of Child Guidance, she, too, was drawn to Northside.[28]

Judge Polier, Marion Ascoli's first link to the Clarks, was also of German-Jewish background, part of the reformist New York elite. Polier's father, the noted Reform rabbi Stephen Wise, had been in the forefront of various labor, religious, and social movements since the Progressive era. Justine Polier's activities as a judge in the Domestic Relations Court had highlighted for her the need to challenge the existing order within the social service sector of the city. Two of her colleagues on the court were African Americans, Hubert Delany, the first African American to graduate from Yale Law School, and Jane Bolin, the first African-American woman judge in the country. Both Delany and Bolin focused Polier's attention on the centrality of race as a social and political issue; she saw Northside as fulfilling a vital need for the neglected youth that came before her every day. An integrated agency like Northside, headed by two African-American professionals, seemed to Polier an opportunity to compel the established agencies to confront their own racism.

Ascoli's presidency of the new Northside board, which began in 1947 when she was in her early forties, was her first experience in chairing an organization. Moran Weston remembers her as "very gracious" and "as warm and generous a person as one would expect growing up in [such] wealth." Though most philanthropists, he said, wanted to give their money but not themselves, she "had a sense of involvement that many [didn't] have." [29] She visited the center virtually every week, attending staff meetings, visiting classrooms for the tutoring sessions, and following the progress of individual children.[30] She was immensely enthusiastic about the Clarks, in whom she had a "real belief," as Joanne Stern recalls. "If you look over that early board, you'll see that nobody was on this board for prestige or anything fancy. I can't think of anyone who was. They were just there because of a real belief in the Clarks. You simply cannot underestimate Mamie's charisma and Kenneth's charisma." [31] Indeed, Ascoli's concern was not with social prestige. The two organizations to which she devoted her energies and money, the Citizens' Committee and Northside, both, Stern says, "had zero prestige" among New York's social elite.[32]

Although the Clarks looked to Ascoli and the board for advice, as well as funding, Ascoli viewed the Clarks, as Bernard saw it, as "sort of supplicants in a way or, rather, people who needed to be assisted." She saw "the rest of us [on the board as] kind of advisers in whom she had confidence to help her carry out this mission."[33] The class differences were, of course, reinforced by the unmistakable signs of wealth that distinguished Ascoli's life from that of the Clarks and the staff. Some of the early meetings of the Northside board were held in Ascoli's townhouse living room on elegant Gramercy Park, and, for some on the staff, Ascoli's graciousness could only partly overcome the sense of social distance.[34] Her wealth reinforced the sense of class difference that no one, in Bernard's words, could "be too open about expressing."[35]

For the Clarks, dealing with Ascoli and certain other members of the early board entailed constant and deft negotiation. The "power people on the Board were friendly, overtly respectful, but we knew what the limits were," Kenneth Clark recalls. Still, he and Mamie "would not accept paternalism . . . [in this we] made it clear that there was something about [us] that was peculiar" in the context of race relations in the 1940s. Both Clarks "demanded respect." "Here were two blacks—very professional . . . and their professionalism at moments would not permit [the board] to be patronizing." As a consequence, the Clarks expected to deal with Marion Ascoli and all others on their board as equals. The Clarks' styles balanced each other; as Kenneth Clark later described it, he tended to be "overtly confrontational" in style, whereas Mamie was more "diplomatic," employing, in Kenneth's words, "her manners" to demonstrate to the Northside board what their limits were.[36]

But, with the support from the affluent white community came professional, legal, and financial agendas that, over time, challenged the objectives and strategies of the Clarks. To attain tax-exempt status and certification as a mental-health center—goals the Clarks, Ascoli, the Poliers, Bernard, and others knew were central—was an objective on which all could agree. In putting the Northside Center on a firmer financial ground, state certification as a "charity dispensary," that is, as a tax-exempt, nonprofit organization approved for any available public funding, was requisite. And, from the perspective of professionals, acceptance by standard accrediting associations was an essential goal if the center was to become a training ground for badly needed black psychiatrists and professional staff.

Tensions were inherent in this pursuit of affirmation, stability, and status that would require constraints for such an unorthodox center as Northside. Yet, over the next decade, professional accreditation and a priority for psychiatry among disciplines at Northside would come to symbolize a struggle, with racial overtones, between the board, outside professional advisors, and the Clarks and their core staff, black and white. The Clarks made sure that Northside's children and parents themselves were sheltered from involvement in what became an intense battle of wills.

Psychoanalytic Theory and Practice in a Racist Society

The program Northside developed for Harlem's children and their families was a response to shifting terrain in child guidance theory and practice that had been evolving since 1900 in the United States. Early in the century, the growing attention to child labor, the place of children in an industrial and highly urbanized society, alarm at high infant and child mortality rates, and the dislocation caused by massive migration from Europe and rural America helped spur a broadly based social movement focused on child welfare reform. Settlement house workers, labor reformers, social welfare advocates, and government officials pondered how to "save" children. Following World War I (a similar anxiety would arise after World War II), the focus of public concern about children was an apparent rise in juvenile delinquency. In response, the Commonwealth Fund, the Rockefeller Foundation, and the Laura Spelman Rockefeller Memorial began to provide grants to establish child guidance clinics. By the 1920s, institutional and governmental programs to limit child labor, improve children's health services, reform juvenile justice systems, and humanize corrections facilities were also in process. The early child guidance movement itself, however, took on a "behaviorist" orientation, focusing on reversing misconduct and other problems in school and the community through negative and positive reinforcements. Clinics were largely staffed by social workers drawn from older settlement houses and from newer professional social work programs. During the 1930s, as psychoanalytic theory, particularly Freudianism, gained greater credibility in the United States, psychiatry and psychiatrists began to shape the programs and orientation of many guidance clinics.[37]

The concentrated attention of the psychoanalytically oriented psychiatrists to individual pathology substantially transformed programs and affected social class and the makeup of clinic clienteles. By the end of the Great Depression, as clinics tended to distance themselves from traditional social welfare functions in order "to keep child guidance distinct from the work of social welfare agencies," child guidance as a movement was "shaped and constrained by professionalization," in the language of historian Margo Horn. It "enhanced the status of mental health professionals, reinforced the middle-class family and conformity to middle-class standards of behavior, and left out children in great need of help."[38] Among the most prominent psychiatrists in the movement was David Levy, Marion Ascoli's brother-in-law, who had come from Chicago to Manhattan in the early 1940s when psychiatrists were pressing to establish themselves in the field by excluding—through control of the accrediting agencies—lay therapists from work with children. The New York Psychoanalytic Institute, in which Levy was a leader, sought standards that would ensure that medically trained analysts would shape and lead care in child guidance clinics. The New York City psychoanalytic movement encountered, however, a strong and well-established social service industry, whose leaders were unwilling to cede control of therapy to the medical profession. New York's established agencies supported incorporation of intrapsychic and psychiatric techniques into the work of child guidance centers, but not at the cost of loss of place for social workers. Herschel Alt, executive director of New York's Jewish Board of Guardians and one of the first members Bernard has said she recruited for Northside's Professional Advisory Committee, pointed to the changing focus of his own agency as psychiatric theory became "the core of the agency's treatment program." The staff of agencies of the Jewish Board of Guardians gradually began "to accept psychiatric concepts of the development of human behavior and to recognize . . . the multiple destructive drives operating in the children coming to the child guidance department," as Frederika Neumann, a Board of Guardians staff member, put it. These agencies "gropingly accepted psychiatric concepts," and with the help of their psychiatrists, they "began slowly to arrive at a dynamic concept of diagnosis," as a result becoming "clinically oriented" agencies.[39]

Northside's board of directors found the new model of treatment emerging from the medical and social welfare communities attractive. For one thing, psychoanalytically oriented treatment represented the latest and presumably the most "scientific" approach to child delinquency and malad-justment. Also, from the perspective of sophisticated philanthropists in the postwar era, it was also the most humane treatment offered because of its attention to the individual child and to therapy, not punishment.

Interest in psychoanalysis and psychiatry in child guidance was growing at a pivotal time. Voluntary agencies abandoned their traditional mission just as the old immigrant communities of Italians, Irish, and Eastern European Jews began to leave the city for the suburbs and as African Americans arrived in record numbers from the South. Private agencies, who had previously defined their roles as charities providing services to the *poor*, increasingly focused on services for the "whole" community, thus on ethnic white and suburban populations and even the wealthy. The agencies explained that they were now serving people according to need rather than according to class, but it looked as if the agencies were abandoning responsibility for the city's growing poor population of African Americans. Agencies concentrated their services on troubled youth, but the class served was increasingly in the outer boroughs and in Westchester and Long Island, where few blacks lived.

The new-found prosperity of the nation in the post-war era also led institutions once dedicated to serving only the poor of differing religious backgrounds to expand into new missions. Richard Cloward—one of the organizers of Mobilization for Youth, a mid-1960s antipoverty agency on New York's Lower East Side and professor of social work at Columbia—and Erwin Epstein explain that many social-service administrators identified poverty as an anomaly rooted in the cultural and the psychological experiences of the individual. Agencies that had provided food, clothing, and relief to needy families through a variety of charity mechanisms by the 1950s had begun to serve what they saw as the previously unrecognized, unmet need of society: the fulfillment of individual ability through the use of a variety of introspective, psychotherapeutic programs.[40] Poverty was being pathologized, and social change to redirect social and economic resources was necessarily downplayed.

Throughout the nineteenth and twentieth centuries, the balance between understanding poverty as an inevitable result of social change, explaining it as a reflection of characteristics of the poor themselves, or interpreting it as evidence of remediable injustice shifted dramatically as the society industrialized and experienced massive and chronic periods of child labor, sweatshop employment, and unemployment.[41] During the depression, the impact of economic dislocation and its concrete manifestation in bread-lines, Hooverville packing case housing on city dumps, strikes, and strike-breaking and social unrest forced the public government and the private agencies to recognize through the New Deal that poverty was best under-stood as a social and economic consequence, not as a moral or individual problem. By the 1950s, however, the postwar boom and a growing political conservatism once again allowed a shift toward individual blame and respon-sibility. For some psychiatrists and psychologists, and for a newly emerging generation of social workers, the real problems of the affluent society were principally "intrapsychic": individual adjustment and personality limited an individual's full potential, irrespective of class; middle-class "underachievers" and poor "delinquents" shared a common weakness that could be modified only through therapy. Generally, race itself was not taken directly into ac-count as a determining factor. A number of psychoanalytically oriented pro-fessionals came to believe that the poor, white and black, were incapable of benefiting from psychotherapy, given what the professionals deemed to be a lack of cognitive skills, of reflection, and of a willingness to postpone imme-diate satisfactions in behalf of long-term goals.[42]

Further complicating the picture was a prevailing racism in much of the social science and psychiatric literature of the 1950s. For the most part, the legacy of eugenics theory of the early decades of the twentieth century and the reality of stated and unstated racist assumptions among many academics and professionals (let alone political leadership and the general public) con-tinued to act now as a serious barrier to the adaptation of psychoanalysis to African-American clients. If psychoanalysis was indeed a highly intellectual endeavor, on the part of therapist and patient, and if, in the United States of the 1940s and 1950s, certain psychiatrists could conclude that blacks as a group were as cognitively inferior as the earlier poor were assumed to be, then it could follow that African Americans as a group would generally not benefit from psychoanalysis. Even as late as 1970, only a small group of psy-chiatrists seemed to question that belief in the published literature. Five black psychiatrists, critiquing prevailing views, wrote that psychoanalytic theory "stresses that those people who will benefit from intensive psy-chotherapy are those whose ego strengths of motivation, intelligence, intro-spection, delay of gratification, and repudiation of action in favor of think-ing are rated highly. Invariably, a black person is rated as having few of the desired ego strengths and is therefore not a good candidate for anything more than the supportive therapies."[43] The rise of the psychoanalytic movement, backed by the prestige of medicine and the cult of presumed scientific "objectivity," came to form a powerful rationalization for the effective abandonment of Harlem's youth by members of the "helping" professions.

Ascoli, Bernard, and others on Northside's board of directors joined the Clarks and the staff in rejecting such professional racism. Indeed, the new board of 1947, and later boards, hoped to use Northside itself in a broader attempt to prove that black children were just as appropriate as white middle-class youngsters for the new psychiatric treatment. They believed that Northside's children deserved the most up-to-date techniques available. The Clarks, committed to the conviction that their children deserved the best, differed with Ascoli and Bernard, however, about what "the best" was. The Clarks believed that much was to be learned from psychiatric insights, but they were suspicious of any doctrinaire approach, including any methodology that depended primarily on physicians and an orthodox Freudianism that tolerated little dissent within its ranks. The Clarks also questioned an approach oriented principally, even if unconsciously, to the white middle-class and any that seemed insensitive to the social environmental causes of lack of achievement or of problematic behavior, especially in a poor, black community for which racism was the central reality. Thus, they sought to incorporate psychiatry selectively into a broadly psychosocial approach: "the traditional psychiatric, medical approach to emotional and behavioral disorders of children—while it might be all right for middle-class white children, and affluent—had to undergo rather serious reexamination and modification, if one were trying to help children who were suffering from economic, social, and racial deprivation." [44] Children would see therapists, yes, but they would also be evaluated for reading difficulties, family dislocation, or other problems of poverty that social workers, educators, or family counselors could address.

The Clarks were engaged in a struggle on two fronts. On one side, they sought to convince the social-service community that black children could benefit from and must not be denied up-to-date therapeutic diagnosis and intervention. On the other side, they sought to convince psychiatry and psychology to incorporate race and ethnicity more rigorously into their paradigms. Thus, at the White House Mid-Century Conference on Children in 1950, Kenneth Clark outlined the argument that later undergirded his testimony in the NAACP's legal challenge to school segregation in Virginia and in other southern and midwestern states and that, on appeal, became the basis of the social scientists' brief which he compiled, and prepared, cited in the

1954 U.S. Supreme Court's unanimous *Brown* v. *Board of Education* decision. Clark argued that "segregation, prejudice and discriminations, and their social concomitants potentially damage the personality of all children." Afterward, he proposed that Northside sponsor a conference to educate and to mobilize New York's professional community in support of integration.[45] Clark and Viola Bernard set about planning such a meeting, to coincide with Northside's fifth anniversary, to focus on effective programs that dealt with the "harmful [effect of racism] on [the] personality of minority group kids." They wanted also to address the limitations of liberal theories that tried to avoid race altogether by "denying racial factors as relevant."[46]

Northside's staff continually prodded the therapeutic professions to reexamine psychoanalytic (and other limiting) assumptions and to adapt methods and theories to the realities of race and class in U.S. life. Stella Chess, Kenneth Clark, and Alexander Thomas wrote in *Psychiatric Quarterly* in 1953 that they had "come to feel that unless the social milieu in which the patient functions is understood and given adequate consideration, significant errors in psychiatric diagnosis, prognosis and evaluation in treatment will occur." They described, for example, the case of "Edward," an eight-year-old black child who exhibited a "variety of symptoms and fears in his school situation," including wetting, fear of his teacher, and refusal to play with other children. Edward's symptoms could "have been considered evidence of serious emotional disturbance." But, Northside's staff saw his symptoms as reflective of a social experience. His family had recently migrated from the South, where they had been poor sharecroppers. During Edward's early years, he and his family "had had a number of fear-inspiring experiences with white people in which they were cheated, threatened, intimidated and terrorized." The family, in order to help their children survive, had taught Edward "not to fight back with white people, and to exercise the greatest care not even to express his thoughts and feelings to them." In Harlem, where, for the first time Edward had a white teacher, the three reported, "it was normal for him to be fearful, afraid to ask questions, and even afraid to ask permission to go to the toilet." Without Northside's intervention, Edward would have been diagnosed as emotionally disturbed. Northside's staff taught the school officials that Edward was "an essentially normal boy" reacting appropriately to a specific situation. When Edward had a chance to adjust to his new environment and when it was explained to the teacher what was troubling him, Edward made "rapid strides."[47]

"Arnold," a twelve-year-old, had engaged in activities that traditional therapists would label antisocial. The article in *Psychiatric Quarterly* pointed out that Arnold's involvement with gangs was a common survival strategy for many youth in poorer communities. Chess, Clark, and Thomas said that their own experience with such children "grew inevitably out of work with patients whose social environments differed sharply from those of the white middle class groups who have provided the dominant source for psychiatric studies." [48] Northside, therefore, sought to address virtually all relevant needs of children they served. Among Northside's patients, of course, there were cases of passive or rebellious behavior common to all adolescents, black and white. But Northside provided family-oriented, not only individual-oriented, therapy.

Thus, "Joanne" came to the center with her mother, who "desired only advice concerning someplace to send her for corrective or punitive purposes." The staff's first task was to convince the mother that the child "needed psychological and psychiatric help." They assigned a social worker to work with the mother and a psychiatrist to work with the daughter. The "job of the social worker was to attempt to modify the unconscious attitudes of rejection and other negative feelings which the mother revealed in her initial interview." The psychiatrist

> soon discovered that this child had a deep-seated feeling of being rejected by her mother. . . . Further she felt resentful of the fact that her friends her age had a father in the home and she had none. This manifested itself in a most drastic fashion when in one of her first contacts at the Center she was given paper and pencil and asked to draw anything she cared to. The result was one big word: "FATHER."
>
> With painstaking work over a period of months [Joanne's] overt symptoms began to disappear. Her mother became more tolerant, if not completely positive in her attitudes towards the child, and finally said she had observed marked behavior improvements both in school and at home. The child no longer stays out—she seems more interested in constructive work and recreational activities and in general seems to have modified a strong tendency toward pre-delinquency. [49]

Members of the professional staff at Northside were continually confronted by the need to argue and to demonstrate that their strategies for commitment to their clients were legitimate and appropriate. At one American Orthopsychiatric Association special symposium in 1955 on the subject of the treatment of children "from socially and economically deprived areas," two Northside staff members, Clara Rabinowitz and Olivia Edwards, presented papers, later reproduced by the U.S. Children's Bureau with the notation about this innovative attempt to adapt therapeutic services to children who had been "too long rejected by many child-guidance and social-casework agencies as not amenable to treatment." In her article, Edwards pointed to the sociologist Sol Ginsburg's criticism of the tendency of therapists to avoid direct human involvement with their clients: "We have been hampered by the erroneous prestige which has come to be associated with dynamic therapy as opposed to what seems to be looked upon as the more humble desire and skill of 'merely' helping people." [50]

The prestige of "dynamic therapy" rooted in a psychiatric-psychoanalytic model had many sources. Broad public awareness of the gains made in controlling disease as in the introduction of antibiotics and, later in the decade, in the development of polio vaccines, had given a new aura of success to medicine. Also, with the rising acceptance of psychotherapy in the 1940s and 1950s, psychiatrists were seen as providing a significant new model that could help corrections officials, social workers, and educators understand and respond to the problems of deviant or troubled youth. In the postwar years, U.S. psychoanalysis experienced an enormous infusion of energy and prestige as European analysts came to the United States to escape Hitler. New York, the center of the psychoanalytic movement, with the New York Psychoanalytic Institute its core, weathered any number of schisms and internal battles during the late 1940s and early 1950s between theoretical factions and personalities, and, in the aftermath, developed a number of training institutes, including the Horney, William Allison White, and New York Psychiatric. Eric Fromm, Karen Horney, and followers of Harry Stack Sullivan among others, formed their own institutes to broaden psychoanalytic theory and practice so that it included social and cultural factors in personality development. In 1945, Columbia University organized a Psychiatric Institute with a group of academic psychiatrists, among them Abram Kardiner, Sandor Rado, and others who sought to adapt psychoanalysis to the insights of anthropological and social-science literature.

During the mid-1950s, the medical model began to assume great importance at Northside as the board brought to policy discussions a deepening fascination with medicine and psychiatry as crucial to the center's program. But the board leadership, especially as represented by Ascoli, did not derive its own perspective on psychology and psychiatry from the more socially oriented schools within New York City's psychiatric professional community but rather from the more orthodox Freudian and psychoanalytic schools which the Clarks found less persuasive.

The Price of Control

The conflict on these matters that arose at Northside in the late 1950s had its origin in the formation in 1947 of the Professional Advisory Committee. That committee, which included several Northside staff, was dominated by outside consultants from New York's psychoanalytic and psychiatric communities. Headed by Viola Bernard, the committee held most of its meetings at her apartment at East 74th Street and Fifth Avenue. Bernard personally was deeply committed to integrating social and behavioral science approaches with psychoanalytic theory and practice; her central commitment to medicine and the medical model, with the biological—which she saw as the domain of the physician—integrated with the anthropological and cultural establishing the psychiatrist in the key and central role. "My sense of professional identity was . . . to be a doctor," she recalls. Her involvement with the Psychiatric Institute had put her in the midst of academic and professional controversies on the role of physicians in psychotherapy.[51] The psychiatrists on the committee saw Northside from the perspective of struggles in their own field to win and advance professionalism, legitimacy, and status within the social welfare community. Herschel Alt, for example, had been deeply involved in transforming the program and treatment model of the Jewish Board of Guardians into a paradigm for the social-welfare agencies in the city. In 1947, the Northside Professional Advisory Committee sought state certification under a dispensary law that required a heavy emphasis on psychiatric evaluation and approval of all treatment techniques employed by an agency.[52] Early that year the committee had contacted the State Board of Social Welfare to begin the process of licensure, and in July the state board dispatched a representative to Northside to evaluate its program and to suggest any necessary reorganization. Bernard was chosen by Northside as liaison with the State Board. As one of the formal requirements for attaining a "Dispensary License" from the State Department of Mental Hygiene, the committee urged Northside to appoint a psychiatrist as director of treatment. The committee also promoted an administrative reorganization of the center, with four professional service centers to be designated as follows: psychiatric treatment, psychological testing, remedial education, and social casework. Under this plan, Stella Chess would be appointed as coordinating psychiatrist, with responsibility for the conduct of all therapy; Kenneth Clark was to be coordinating psychologist; Miriam Weston was to continue as co-ordinator of the Remedial Program; and Diana Tendler would become coordinating case worker.[53]

There was little initial disagreement within Northside on the necessity of achieving outside recognition. A license would, after all, make financial stability more possible and it would not, per se, disrupt Northside's unique culture and administration. Yet, over the next years, the priorities of the board's Professional Advisory Committee, under its chair, Viola Bernard, began to diverge from the priorities of the staff and of the Clarks themselves. Conflicts arose, ostensibly on issues of professionalism and credentials, that can best be understood as a struggle over power and control. Therapeutic strategy debates camouflaged issues over the place of predominantly white psychiatrists in positions of dominance within an integrated staff of therapists and other professionals, and, at the core, the appropriate roles of philanthropists in assuming preeminence over professionals and staff, and of white philanthropy in a black-run institution.

The white philanthropic tradition in U.S. society was rooted in a concept of noblesse oblige, generous in intent, and of enlightened benevolence, but whose financial largesse often guided and directed groups it supported. It was, essentially, paternalistic in style. Marion Ascoli exemplified that tradition at Northside. Also, because of her close associations with David Levy and Viola Bernard she saw excellence at Northside as properly to be evaluated by the standards of psychoanalysis and psychiatry. The standard psychoanalytic model focused on the person as the problem; it did not give critical place, as the Clarks intended, to the damaging consequences of poverty and racial oppression in defining both cause and remedy. Northside, under the Clarks, meanwhile had evolved its own therapeutic ethos, one that, while borrowing from the new therapies, declined to identify with any particular school or sect within the contentious world of psychoanalytic politics then dominating psychiatry in New York and Chicago. Ascoli's and the advisory committee's push to establish Northside as a premier or cutting-edge training institution within New York's professional world owed more to questions of prestige, the Clarks believed, than to the needs of the children served. The Clarks maintained an eclectic and diverse set of programs and approaches; neither Mamie nor Kenneth Clark were doctrinaire in style or ideological in approach, but pragmatic and adaptive. In the end, the struggle between board and staff became a conflict essentially between fascination with ideology and strategies based on experience and need.

By the early 1950s, the outside professional world intervened directly in this emerging conflict in withholding full recognition of Northside's work. Northside had applied to become a member of the American Association of Psychiatric Clinics for Children, an accrediting agency that sought to promote the growing discipline of child guidance and psychiatry, but the association wrote back in 1950 that, in light of "remedial deficiencies," Northside could not be granted full membership. It was offered "associate membership" instead.[54]

The AAPCC representative who had made a site visit in 1950 was irked that now, in its fourth year, the center lacked full-time psychiatric staff. It had full-time psychologists and social caseworkers, but only part-time psychiatrists who, in effect, donated a few hours a week. To the association, this "fractionated psychiatric time" interfered with Northside's ability to provide intensive analysis. Northside, in response, increased Stella Chess's hours, but explained why a diverse group of practitioners could serve Northside best— in a small agency, staff diversity could be attained only through the employment of part-time medical personnel. In a letter protesting the accrediting agency's denial of full membership, Bernard supported Northside's perspective: "in view of our diverse population of children we have been very careful to maintain a diversified staff," heterogeneous both racially and professionally. With the field of child psychiatry quite new, it was, furthermore, "very difficult to secure therapists with specific training and experience in child psychiatry for as much as 20 hours or more." Even more important, Northside itself could offer a model for this developing field of child psychiatry if the AAPCC would allow the center to develop its own training program: "one of our objectives [is] to offer training with children particularly with those therapists who find it difficult to achieve such training." She pointed also to the lack of such training opportunities for African-American psychiatrists in New York and the nation as a whole. Bernard did agree with some of the objections raised by the AAPCC, that is, that Northside needed to schedule more conference and consultation time. But she "stressed again that an interracial clinic such as Northside is in some ways unique and, therefore, some aspects of functioning though different from orthodox procedures, have positive value for us."[55]

To Stella Chess, "the interracial character of the [Northside] clinic has carried with it the conviction that the professional interchange has enriched the knowledge and skills of the staff in the treatment of children." Chess, for example, saw Northside as a "unique" child guidance center precisely because of its interracial staff and its clients' multi-cultural origins. As Northside's newly named part-time coordinating psychiatrist, Chess tried to explain to the AAPCC Northside's special character. Relating her own experience with anti-Semitism and her difficulties in finding psychiatric placements only ten years before, she pointed out that "a Negro psychiatrist would meet the same negative possibilities in the usual child guidance" training centers. "If no deliberate attempts are made to create situations which give dignity to minority cultural groups who need professional aid and opportunities for professional training . . . then deliberate thought and effort is needed to fulfill these needs." She argued that "Northside provides opportunities for experience in child guidance to individuals who might otherwise find great difficulty in seeking training on a similar level, or possibly might find all such opportunities closed to them." [56]

Northside's frustrating experience with application for accreditation convinced the staff, the board, and the professional advisory committee that it needed to prepare on its own for what Mamie Clark called the "development of an accredited training center for child psychiatrists." But Bernard herself, according to Clark, considered Northside "not at present ready for recognition as a training center for child psychiatrists." [57]

Judge Justine Wise Polier had campaigned in 1945 for the development of clinical services in her own and the other domestic relations courts, to provide evaluations of delinquents by psychiatrists, psychologists, and case workers. But, by the mid-1950s, Polier saw "only limited and lagging efforts to apply this new knowledge either within the community by schools, social agencies or the courts, or within the institutions that were to deal with the children sent away from home." She was increasingly disturbed by the distortion of what she considered an essentially humanistic discipline. Agencies, both public and private, she said, were now using individualized treatment methods to label and effectively to exclude children. Foster-care agencies and schools employed projective tests and psychiatric evaluations as a rationale for rejecting referrals by city agencies and courts. Polier observed a "growing gap" between diagnostic services and availability of treatment services. "All of us have witnessed the growing number of cases where a child has been diagnosed repeatedly—but has never been admitted to treatment." [58]

In early 1956 Marion Ascoli approached the Avalon Foundation for a grant to underwrite a training program for psychiatrists. It would be "a wonderful thing for Northside Center—the answer to a long felt need," she wrote. The first step was to "engage a top psychiatrist to work on the planning of the program." The Foundation, in March, agreed to sponsor the initial planning for such a step, and Ascoli and Bernard approached their fellow Professional Advisory Committee member, Exie Welsch, a psychiatrist at Columbia University, to conduct the study.[59] The committee agreed that "an initial exploration is desirable . . . to determine the need for a study." "An effective training program must not only meet the established standards, but must also come out of the needs of the agency," the committee decided. It determined that an effective program would directly benefit "the larger community, the field of child psychiatry, and the individual psychiatrists who were being trained." The Clarks and Victor Carter, who, as a psychiatric social worker represented the staff on the committee, seemed skeptical about whether the plan would be cost-effective, and, as the minutes of the advisory committee meeting reported: "Kenneth Clark cautioned that the training program not be at the expense of service to children or add an unrealistic administrative burden."[60]

This expression of a mild sense of caution masked an acceleration of tension between the committee and the staff. Several months later, Welsch, anticipating her preliminary recommendations, expressed concern that word of pending changes would leak to the staff; she requested that the "first report . . . be made only to PAC [advisory committee]."[61] When the first draft was presented at the committee meeting of 29 November 1956, it was accompanied by a scathing rebuttal from Mamie Clark, who saw it as an attack on Northside's program and especially on its leadership. Ostensibly about training possibilities at Northside, its underlying message, she said, was really that "the quality of work with the children is poor." Yet, "it is my firm belief that one cannot find a staff more dedicated to self-development and more conscious of increasing the effectiveness of its services to children." The Welsch report, Clark said, praised Northside's "basic philosophy and beliefs," its "inter-cultural aspects," and the "warmth of the staff," but faulted the administration, diagnostic procedures, admissions procedures, psychotherapy, the degree and quality of supervision, and other aspects of the treatment program. She concluded, "weighing the nature of the defects and the nature of the assets, one could only conclude that service to the children is substandard. The strengths cannot be equated with professional competence." How could the immense expense of Northside be justified in light of such apparent failure to provide quality service? With what clinics had Northside been compared to have been found so wanting? What could explain the numerous earlier studies by foundations and federal, state, and city agencies that already found Northside's service competent? "How does one reconcile the present evaluation with the effectiveness of treatment of children?" Clark criticized Welsch's disapproval of her own performance: "The suggestion of an 'administrative consultant' to train the director is an insultingly interesting concept." She dismissed the report's call for further "study" of this idea: "If incompetence is the issue, then an 'administrative consultant' is not the answer." [62]

In an appendix to Mamie Clark's response, Kenneth Clark seconded her points and underlined the implications of Welsch's critique. The major thrust of the report, he said, was that "Northside Center does not now function on that minimum level of competence which would justify" its budget. "Conscientiousness is not a substitute for competence in evaluating the work of professionals. To suggest this is either condescending or a serious, even though merciful, indictment of professional performance." To accept this view would mean that everyone associated with Northside—administration, staff, board, and the advisory committee itself—"is guilty of the most gross and inexcusable form of negligence." The report reflected "fundamental differences in the philosophy and operation of a clinic." If Welsch's recommendations were to be followed, Northside would be remade "into the image of an 'efficient' psychiatric clinic, with a strong, prestige father figure of a psychiatrist from whom all wisdom flows." Kenneth Clark posed his own image: "An effective clinic is one in which each professional group gropes competently toward some solution of the important problem of how can we help a child. We do not have the answers ready made. Each child is an individual human being. We must seek to understand him and respect him as such." [63]

By April 1957, Mamie Clark was expressing alarm that the advisory committee was seeking to implement sections of the report unilaterally and without meetings with the staff. She made clear she would strongly oppose any such attempt. Through the various department heads, the staff promptly directed a memo to the board protesting that what had begun as a joint board–advisory committee–staff effort to initiate training had broken down, with Welsch having canceled scheduled meetings with staff "without explanation." The staff was "left . . . affronted." The memo from the heads of departments concluded that there was "a lack of genuine respect for our experience, knowledge, and cooperative efforts." [64]

Submitted to the board in May 1957, the final Welsch Report, as it came to be known, called for a dramatic restructuring of Northside and administrative reorganization. It drew immediate and intense criticism from the staff. A psychiatrist was to head Northside's clinical operations, coequal to— that is, not supervised by—an administrative director, who was to be Mamie Clark. The report recommended that a significantly greater share of available resources be assigned to psychiatric therapy.

The staff responded to the report as a direct challenge to Northside's central and unique mission and as a threat to power relations at the center. The proposed changes in administrative structure would lead to professional dominance by the psychiatrist, with subordination of remediation, social-work services for families, interaction with schools and child-welfare groups, and other community services, all of which the staff saw as critical to the center as psychiatric psychotherapy itself. As they saw it, Northside approached "the problems of emotionally disturbed children not only in terms of its clinical and psychiatric aspects but also in terms of the larger social and community context of these problems." The staff put forward an alternative plan for training that would "prepare psychiatrists for service in all-purpose mental health clinics" and "also serve as a basis for further work in career child psychiatry." [65] The staff interpreted the effort to place psychiatry and psychoanalysis at Northside's core as a way to wrest control from its founders, the Clarks (both psychologists with doctorates, not psychiatrists with medical degrees, and thus considered by the medical profession to be of lower prestige), and to turn it over to the board and, especially, to board members who were physicians.

Ascoli and her allies on the board and the advisory committee themselves did not espouse directly a change of Northside's direction or purpose. The language it employed in memos, board meetings, and letters referred to service, quality, efficiency, and excellence, objectives no one could oppose. Ascoli simply sought the "best" quality. In a letter to her close friend Viola Bernard, however, she was less euphemistic: "We cannot sacrifice quality of service even to preserve the morale of a dedicated staff. This is too high a price to pay for the intangibles which I realize are important and strong at Northside." In effect, she did not see tangible excellence in Northside's performance. She, therefore, backed the proposed reorganization of the administrative and professional hierarchy, confiding to Bernard that once the new structure was in place "Mamie and Ken could find their niche." [66]

In the same year, Ascoli set up an ad-hoc committee of the board, composed of herself, Bernard, and Alt, and charged to offer specific recommendations to strengthen the position of psychiatry at Northside. This ad-hoc group proposed a formal division of responsibilities between administrative and clinical directors. This meant, of course, that Mamie Clark would not have authority over any treatment regimen, hence neither of program nor quality of performance. It postponed a decision to train psychiatrists pending appointment of the proposed clinical director. Northside's medical director, Stella Chess, an accredited and increasingly prominent psychiatrist, would not be eligible for that position, since the proposal included mandates that the new clinical director be someone not presently on staff and that the new director be a diplomate of the American Board of Psychiatry, which Chess was not. The board adopted these proposals on 16 January 1958 and Chess was forced to resign.[67] She had been at Northside since its founding in 1946.

The board's new agenda was captured after an exchange between Ascoli and Mrs. Mary Kingsbury in which the latter inquired how the changes would affect Northside's budget. "Mrs. Ascoli expressed that some cuts might have to be made in the number of children served but that the goal was to give the children the best possible psychiatric treatment." Staff members promptly wrote to Ascoli, cautioning that service based principally on a disease-care model could destroy exactly what made Northside unique. Ascoli's swift response was not encouraging, noting only that board members would "certainly" pay attention to staff concerns.[68]

A year later, in February 1959, Albert Bryt, an elegant, dapper, and articulate refugee from Hitler's Germany, then a part-time psychiatrist on the staff, agreed to become the new Clinical Director.[69] For many on the board, Bryt was the embodiment of the characteristics they admired in a psychiatric professional. He had been trained in Europe in psychoanalysis and represented, culturally, the European, upper-middle-class German-Jewish traditions with which many of the most influential board members identified.

In his first meeting with the board, Bryt focused on what influential board members had identified to him as "problem areas," particularly that the form of treatment at the center was not state-of-the-art. Children were treated for too short a time to allow for adequate analysis of their difficulties. Remedial reading should not be provided except as an adjunct of psychotherapy. Bryt wanted more discrimination in the selection of clients in line with the center's primary mission as a psychotherapy clinic. In sum, he held that Northside's existing eclectic program focus was incompatible with its goals.[70]

At the next meeting, Bernard praised the innovations and changes Bryt was advocating, noting that "it was very heartening to hear of the increased attention being given to quality, focus, and clarity in treatment plans and

goals." She found it particularly encouraging that "supervision seemed better organized in as much as it was more intensive." She and others voiced
their disagreement with Bryt's deemphasis on remedial reading, but the
board's support for his plan, on balance, was solid.[71]

If the board was increasingly delighted with Bryt's style and his vision,
the staff experienced him differently. When he had started at the center two
years before as a part-time consulting psychiatrist, his demeanor had rankled
other professionals on the staff. Chess recalled that during his first months at
Northside "he began to pull rank" at the staff meetings: "He began to give
neurologic discussions with a whole lot of medical terminology that were a
put-down [to the nonmedical staff]. And they were things that could have
been easily explained in ordinary prose. You don't have to use the word *gyrus*.
You can say a specific area of the brain that has to do with such-and-such.
Everybody can understand that. And if you can't talk plain English, you don't
know what you're talking about if you can only talk in jargon." With Bryt in
the new post of clinical director, by the winter of 1959–60 a wave of staff resignations demonstrated low morale. Bryt acknowledged that there was "friction . . . between supervisors and therapists," but it was an inevitable consequence of a "period of transition and reorganization."[72]

At the 4 February 1960 board meeting, a verbal skirmish erupted that
proved a precursor to greater difficulties. Bryt reported that he had discovered "a number of distressing findings" in his review of "the total professional structure." In response to a board member asking if these unspecified
findings "were so distressing as to interfere with the Clinic's operation," Bryt
said that he would rather not discuss the issue further, and he tried to move
on. Kenneth Clark refused to let the issue drop. What exactly had Bryt meant
by "distressing"? Such an "evaluative term leads to a variety of interpretations and this is dangerous," Clark pointed out. A prolonged discussion ensued, only to be ended when Ascoli stepped in: she would accept "full responsibility for Dr. Bryt mentioning" any problems "at the present time . . .
without going into detail."[73]

In mid-February a staff memo, representing the views of all but one of
the members of the psychology, social work, and therapy departments, and
presenting the staff's objections to Bryt and the direction of the board as
well, was delivered to Ascoli as board president. It noted that "since Dr. Bryt's
official appointment as Clinical Director, the total operation of the agency
has become increasingly affected by his negativistic and destructive attitude."
It pointed to the resignations in all three departments and the disastrous state

of staff morale. Treatment was affected as well. "Usurpation by Dr. Bryt of authority" had "intensified the friction." Bryt had used supervisory sessions to berate the social workers and psychotherapists "rather than offering constructive help." Ascoli dismissed the staff's complaint. Where a word was misspelled in the memo, she wrote in the margin, "Can't they spell?", and a few lines later, next to a typo, "can't they type?" and at the end of the page, "can't they think?"[74] (Her notations, not seen by the staff, appeared on the copy she sent to Bernard.)

Mamie Clark's letter of response to Ascoli defended the staff. In sharp terms she reminded Ascoli that Teodora Abramovich, one of the most dedicated and effective therapists on the staff, had resigned after a Bryt tirade, and another staff member felt "so assaulted, verbally of course, as to announce that she would not continue at Northside." Bryt, she said, did not understand Northside. "The situation has been aggravated by virtue of a dedicated interracial staff witnessing the most acute intimidations and verbal assaults directed at its professionally respected Spanish-speaking staff members." Clark explained Bryt's behavior as reflecting insecurity—he was "working in a new and tenuous field," yet behaved as if he "knows all and others know nothing." She reminded Ascoli that Bryt refused to acknowledge the staff's accumulated body of knowledge and technique. "In a period where no clear philosophy or framework of psychotherapy has yet been defined, individual staff members have been severely 'criticized' for not adhering to some expected but undefined level of performance." He had demeaned and humiliated professionals—among them Stella Chess, Alexander Thomas, Clara Rabinowitz, and Olivia Edwards—who had published widely and participated as panelists and presenters in countless conferences and colloquia. In sum, Clark told Ascoli, "We cannot achieve the goal of the best possible psychiatric [care] for our children in a situation where a staff is constantly made to feel inferior, worthless, incompetent, and incapable."[75]

In early March 1960, at a meeting with the personnel committee of the staff and the personnel practices committee of the board, the staff made clear its united dissatisfaction with Bryt. It criticized what it saw as his arrogance, condescension, and authoritarianism in an area where honest differences about appropriate treatment should be respected. "His constant approach is that staff has nothing to offer," that its role was solely "to learn" from him. He was given to "constant fault-finding and sadistic types of attack." The executive committee of the board gave Bryt a vote of confidence, whereupon the staff went to the full board to demand Bryt's resignation, threatening a wave of resignations if the board refused. The staff could not and would not work with Bryt. Ascoli recognized the united and determined staff action, with the wholehearted backing of the Clarks, themselves, as the ultimatum it was, and immediately after the meeting she tendered her own resignation as board president, to take effect three months later, on 1 July 1960.[76] Her resignation was to cost Northside $100,000 over a year in lost contributions from Ascoli.

The Dilemma of African-American–Jewish Relations

Years earlier, by the opening of the Northside Center in 1946, the Clarks and some of the first board members were already aware of the complexity of the relationship between Jews and blacks. On the one hand, they understood and needed each other: both groups had been hurt by racism and bigotry, in the United States and in Nazi-dominated Europe. On the other hand, the relationship between the two groups in respect to resources and status in American life was unequal. The board as Ascoli reconstituted it after her 1947 arrival at Northside brought the problem of inequality between blacks and Jews in U.S. society into the center itself.

Today, at a time of heightened tensions in the culture between African Americans and Jews, there is a tendency to see the period before 1960 as a golden era of empathetic and effective alliance. But the imbalance in political power and financial resources and the real differences in histories and experiences often strained black-Jewish relations long before and even during the civil rights movement itself.[77] Liberal Jews, for example Rabbi Stephen Wise, Polier's father, remained stalwart supporters of civil liberties and civil rights for African Americans, and in the terrible period of the Nazi era the two groups often made common cause. Yet, even then, as Murray Friedman has documented, tensions between the two were high. Jews were most concerned about what was happening in Germany, whereas some black leaders wondered why equal or greater attention was not being paid to the lynchings, economic and social exploitation, and the cruelties of segregation in the American South. But even when blacks and Jews were in alliance, as in various civil rights organizations, African-American leaders often felt that white liberals, Jewish leadership not excluded, were condescending.

Kenneth Clark was one of a handful of intellectuals to talk candidly in those years about the stresses in Jewish-black relations. Acknowledging that "many personal relationships between Negroes and Jews" were close and free of overt hostility, he identified many underlying tensions that had to be acknowledged if they were to be effectively addressed. Kenneth Clark's *Commentary* article in February 1946, the same month that Northside opened, took issue with the prevailing view among Jewish intellectuals that Jews and African Americans viewed their struggle against racism and anti-Semitism as identical. Such views ignored "the very wide difference between Jewish and Negro social, political, and economic status." "Many Negroes, rightly or wrongly, see the struggle of Jews in American society as primarily a conservative one, to consolidate gains already made; and secondarily to expand these gains to a higher level of economic, political, educational and social integration with the dominant group." Clark observed that, for their part, "many Negroes are disinclined to view [American Jews'] struggles as fundamental or as critical as their own—the struggle of the Jew [in America itself] is after all not one of life and death, to wring from society the bare necessities of life." [78]

In late 1945, Kenneth Clark had participated in a forum, organized by the Central Conference of American Rabbis, on "Judaism and Race Relations," its purpose to "secure justice for the Negro." On a panel on "the problems of 'the Negro in the United States,'" he pointed out that, imbedded in the prospectus and program of the conference was the assumption that few of these problems affected relations between Jews and African Americans themselves. "It is significant that in neither the original statement nor the one finally released was any mention made of the specific problems of Jewish-Negro relations as such." At the conference, one rabbi who urged the group to issue a statement opposing "anti-Negro practices in Jewish hospitals and certain department stores" had met denial and resistance. Why should Jewish institutions be singled out, he was asked, when "they were not the only ones guilty of discrimination against Negroes"? To Kenneth Clark, the conference "reflected the dilemma of Jewish-Negro relations in contemporary American society." Despite the best intentions, Jewish leaders were "unable to free themselves from prevailing American attitudes toward the Negro." Most problematic was the implicit and explicit inequality in status and position. "On the face of it, it appears commendable that one minority group should be concerned with the status of another oppressed group," he noted. "But the question arises as to what Jews and others would think if a conference of Negro leaders were to devote a roundtable to the problem of 'The Jew in the United States.'" When Jewish leaders addressed the issue of race, he said, "Most typically perhaps this attitude reveals itself in condescension." [79]

Kenneth Clark, an astute student of American society, like other black intellectuals and professionals, had found his own role circumscribed by the prevailing racism of the forties. He was seldom asked to venture beyond racial themes and issues in his intellectual pursuits despite the fact that he had become a social psychologist, not solely a student of race; neither he nor Mamie Clark had written their doctoral theses on subjects even tangentially racial. In December 1944, after he had worked as part of the team conducting research for Gunnar Myrdal's *An American Dilemma*, the Commission on Community Inter-relationships of the American Jewish Congress, perhaps the most liberal of Jewish associations, had invited him to join its staff. But, despite his Columbia doctorate and his post as an assistant professor at the City College of New York, he was not permitted the freedom to develop his own programs or to write up his own findings. He remained, in his words, "the professional 'manservant' or 'office boy' to those who have the dignity of assigned primary responsibility." He wrote to the American Jewish Congress director that he could only conclude that he was "being employed on a token, rather than genuine basis. It would also be necessary for me to state frankly that the idea of racial or personal discrimination as a possible explanation of this patently confused and distorted situation has occurred to me." The immediate stimulus to his expression of outrage was his experience at the office one morning when he arrived to find that a colleague with whom he was in conflict had had Clark's desk removed from the office they shared and "moved to the hall." The AJC office manager observed that it was indeed an "awkward" situation, but it had been necessary. Clark wondered, as he said in a memorandum he wrote to himself at the time about the incident, if other members of the "staff [could] expect this type of high-handed, arbitrary, capricious manipulation." He expected not.[80]

During the same period, Clark had been recruited, as a "junior professional," by the Council on Democracy, to participate in a workshop on race relations organized by the all-white, primarily wealthy and Protestant, Women's Clubs. He had assumed it was intended to be an open and honest discourse on the relationship between whites and blacks until a member of the council staff told him, as he reported in a memo to the council, she was disappointed in him because "Negroes are usually much more agreeable and conciliatory than you are." In fact, he was informed that he was "just as defensive as the Jews." Clark responded that he had naturally believed that he had been asked to participate because the council thought he had something worthwhile to contribute as an academic and perhaps, especially, to convey a

scholarly understanding of "the basic and psychological function of stereotyping of cultural and racial groups." If the group had wanted "a job of com-
forting ('making these women feel good') . . . then it was a mistake to have
invited technically trained people for that purpose." The staff member with
whom Clark conversed was "even more convinced that I was not a 'typical
Negro' and even more undesirable than she at first suspected." [81]

A decade and a half later, Marion Ascoli's abrupt resignation statement
of 1960 as chair of Northside's board further revealed the unresolved complexity of Jewish-black relations. On one level, the crisis at Northside was
part of a serious and profound evaluation and reevaluation of the center's
mission and purpose. Medicine, with its promise of a method of addressing
human disease through scientific methods that applied to all human beings,
irrespective of race, religion, or ethnicity, fit neatly into the nonracist, assim-
ilationist model of U.S. democracy that Americans, and particularly Jews,
held out as the hope of America. Psychoanalysis, too, fit the optimistic mood
of a generation of social reformers who saw in it the possibility of individual
growth and healing. Psychoanalysis, with its emphasis on intrapsychic phe-
nomena and its virtual blindness to social forces, was well-suited to those
who promoted a vision of America as a classless and nonracist society. Yet,
on another level, as events at Northside demonstrated, the crisis was, at its
heart, about power and authority. When it was clear that Ascoli would lose
in the contest for control of Northside, after a period of winning, she told
the board at its March 1960 meeting that "she had lost faith in the ability of
Northside to become the type of clinic she could be proud of." She noted "a
gap between what Northside should be and can be" and what it was. Directly
linking the crisis to her earlier promotion of psychiatry and psychiatric training there, she saw the effort to strip the new power she had gained for the
clinical director (with the consequent diminution of the Clarks' control) as a
direct assault on her own authority as board chair, and, no doubt, as principal
benefactor, to shape the center and its programs. [82]

For Kenneth Clark, however, the struggle with Ascoli had a different,
and perhaps more troubling, meaning, one that was part of the larger history
of Jews and blacks. Writing in 1957 in the Anti-Defamation League's *Bulletin*
three years before Marion Ascoli's dramatic departure, he said that relationships between African Americans and Jews had improved over the last decade
as the civil rights movement had raised the morale and self-respect of blacks,
with Jews in the forefront of white support. But, he said, the real test of

Jewish-black relations lay in the future when, as he hoped and expected, blacks would have attained greater and greater equality. Presently, "Jews who help Negroes in the struggle for equality do so from a position of unquestioned economic and political superiority." Clark wondered what the basis of the relationship would be "if the Negro attains the position where he no longer requires or desires the help of benefactors," and he speculated that "it may require a restructuring of the total pattern of this relationship."[83]

In 1960, just as Kenneth and Mamie Clark were insisting upon their right to define Northside's mission without regard to the supporting power of white liberal allies, Kenneth Clark published another telling essay on the impact of the civil rights movement upon white-black relations. The movement to desegregate the schools in the South and the gathering intensity of the students' sit-ins that had begun in Greensboro, North Carolina, in February, had upset not only Southern segregationists, but also white benefactors who had previously felt entitled to speak on the behalf of African Americans. "In effect, the present assertive pattern of the Negro necessarily involves a change in the role of his friends." He urged that in order "to minimize the intensity and duration of the inevitable disturbances which come with social transition, it is necessary for the friends of the Negro to understand these significant dynamic changes." Rather than see such a transition as the end of a relationship, Kenneth Clark maintained that if the dynamic were understood, then "for the first time since the Reconstruction period" it could be "the basis for genuine and honest communication between Negroes and whites."[84]

A Broader Base of Benefactors

Ascoli may not have perceived the broader significance of the confrontation at Northside, but neither did she intend to destroy an institution whose history she was part of and that was one of the few models for professional integration in the city and the nation. She did not, for example, use her social position and influence to drain the board of its philanthropic support. Except for Ascoli and Bernard, the white board members would remain with the Clarks and Northside, continuing to seek common ground and to begin the process of defining a new, more egalitarian relationship. Indeed, it was Ascoli herself, Kenneth Clark would later discover, who urged Joanne Stern, Ascoli's daughter-in-law, to stay on the Northside board and, thereby, maintain a family connection and commitment to the ideals it represented. Kenneth Clark notes that Joanne Stern "understood . . . what our goals were" and rejected the "patronizing" values that he felt had led Ascoli to withdraw when her will was challenged.[85]

The board called in Professors Clara Kaiser and Saul Scheidlinger from the Columbia University School of Social Work to conduct an independent evaluation of Northside over the course of the next month. Scheidlinger recalls that they concluded that all parties bore some responsibility for the impasse but that Bryt's position had become untenable and he should now resign. Scheidlinger recalls that it took the prestige and the powerful personality of Clara Kaiser to counteract the will of the board and particularly of Bernard. After hearing their recommendation, "Viola very angrily rose up and said, 'Well, I'm going to take this further now to the board and finish the whole thing.'" He remembers that Clara Kaiser "wasn't going to be threatened, so she rose, too,'" telling Bernard "Okay! You go and try it and we'll see who wins out." Shortly after, the board acted upon Kaiser's and Scheidlinger's recommendation, requesting Bryt's resignation.[86] Scheidlinger remembers the circumstances that framed his involvement in writing the evaluation. A young professor at the time (and, like Kaiser, Jewish himself), he had quickly caught on that "Bryt was just a symptomatic issue. . . . The issue was the issue of control and power between an old guard, well-to-do, mostly Jewish and some not Jewish ladies . . . who had already been active in the Jewish philanthropy field. . . . And the issue really was whether the minority people, particularly the Clarks, would get the power, or would the board people who felt that they deserved the power because they gave the money. And it was as strictly as that a power issue."[87]

Viola Bernard wrote a thoughtful letter of resignation in early April, reviewing her long history of involvement with the board and the professional advisory committee, noting why she had been attracted to Northside in the first place. Northside had been "fruitful and satisfying" to her because it had long dedicated itself to providing "more and better mental health services to a population of children that was grossly underserviced." Unique, in her view, was its interracial quality "at the Board, staff and clientele levels." Because "the Clarks are synonymous with Northside," she said, "of all the . . . components in the Northside partnership, they are the least expendable." She was resigning "in the spirit of helping, not hindering, the maximum prospering in the next phase of Northside."[88] Looking back on this time from the perspective of thirty-two years, Bernard suggests that "it might have been wiser to have gone along with the kind of psychiatry that Stella [Chess] managed to do," if the board had "let some of these standards of mine that I was so excited about drop by the wayside." "Maybe in the long run, more would have evolved positively, if I had been more Stellaish than I was."[89] Ironically, Chess, of course, had been compelled to resign in the course of the revaluation the board—and Bernard herself—had endorsed.

With Marion Ascoli's departure, Northside lost an annual contribution that generally amounted to between 10 and 35 percent of its annual budget. In 1976, Mamie Clark commented in retrospect on this critical juncture:

[Marion Ascoli] deserted us literally, taking $100,000 with her. And I think if Kenneth and I had been "good people" and, you know, done what they wanted us to do, we would not have had the crisis—nor would we be as strong as we are today. The specific issue was over psychiatry, believe it or not. This agency has always been untraditional. The traditional model is the psychiatric one, with the psychiatrist in control of everything, and we've never, never, been that, so that as we were evolving in our program, we were moving, as I told you, educationally—heavily educationally. And it came a point where the board wanted to fire the chief psychiatrist [Stella Chess], my friend from Riverdale, who was very good and very social minded, very eclectic herself. She wasn't bound by Freudian principles or anything like that.

So they wanted to get rid of her, and they wanted to make this place really psychiatric, and at that time, Dr. David Levy [Marion Ascoli's brother-in-law] had been very critical of us because we were not psychiatric enough. In the end, Stella Chess did go. Our chief psychiatrist [Bryt] did go. But in the end, we won the battle, because Marion quit.

We were never bound by the Freudian psychoanalytic approach. Never. But at that time, this was the thing, and if you weren't a psychoanalytically oriented psychiatrist, you weren't a psychiatrist. I mean, it just wasn't tolerated in this field. And all the schools were geared to it. Everything was geared to it. But we had always known that for our particular population of children, this wasn't going to work. . . . You know, they have an immediate need. And we always knew that, but some of the Board people did not. People like Dr. David Levy never knew what it meant to offer psychiatric services to poor children.[90]

At the May 1960 board meeting, the first after Ascoli's and Bernard's departure, Kenneth Clark summarized what he saw as the core cause of the crisis, only now emerging clearly and unambiguously. The Northside Center was more than just a psychiatric clinic; it had to be understood within the context of the community which it served. "A strict and exclusively psychiatric structure might be more appropriate for a predominately middle-class community." Northside should "make the maximum contribution to the problems of this community."[91]

Northside emerged from the Ascoli-Bryt crisis to face immediate problems of survival. Marion Ascoli, as board president for nearly fifteen years, had been the financial linchpin of the center in annual contributions and, immediately before the crisis, she had also committed the board to finance the expansion and renovation of their space at the New Lincoln School, personally pledging $50,000 to this effort. (That small, progressive private school was expanding its enrollment and needed some of the space being rented to Northside. Northside was asked to move to the seventh floor of the building, where more space was available.) When Ascoli resigned, she withdrew her pledge for the space renovation: "A crisis has developed at Northside Center which makes it impossible for us to formulate plans for the future structure and size of the agency. Therefore, I cannot contribute the $50,000 as I had intended for the remodelling of the New Lincoln School to include a floor for Northside."[92] Kenneth and Mamie Clark, in search of alternative funding, approached four foundations—the Rockefeller Brothers Fund, the Taconic Foundation, the New York Foundation, and the Field Foundation—with direct appeals to save Northside. Without new sources of funds, "Northside Center will have no base from which to operate. In effect, Northside Center would be dissolved."[93] The staff of the Rockefeller Brothers Fund considered the Ascoli episode a personality clash rather than a substantive disagreement over Northside's direction and program and they, along with the New York Foundation, proffered funds to complete the renovation program.[94] The Clarks turned to the city, too, for support, building on the history of city mental health and Youth Board contracts that had provided funds periodically over the past decade. Kenneth Clark went directly to his friend James Dumpson, recently named New York City Commissioner of Welfare, and to John Theobold, New York City School Superintendent, with whom Clark had worked in the 1950s on the New York City Board of Education's Commission on Integration. Dumpson remembers that Clark told them "you two public officials really have to help Mamie and me and Northside Center. You're committed to doing what is right by children. You're committed to particularly black children in the Harlem Community and I know both of you professionally and socially, and I need your help." Dumpson and

Theobold worked together to "network with our commission of mental health and began to turn the funding thing around." The Community Mental Health Board began to provide operating expenses, and, in addition, Northside received from it a grant of $50,000. Shortly after, Dumpson joined the Northside board, making explicit a relationship that would continue for more than thirty years.[95]

New York City provided nearly half of Northside's income over the next decade. In effect, the Ascoli crisis had forced Northside to reconstruct its financial base and to turn for support, on the one hand, to the black community, in which Dumpson was a prominent figure, and, on the other, to the public sector. At that very time, the local and federal governments were both paying greater attention to juvenile delinquency and poverty in the black community. Northside, in consequence, and in need of new allies, turned away from a focus on paternalistic philanthropy and toward government. Its reliance on private philanthropy diminished proportionately if not in actual dollars.

The issue of race and power at Northside would become multifaceted in the coming years as Kenneth and Mamie Clark placed on the board African Americans from Harlem with real power who could effectively balance the downtown benefactors. In New York of the 1950s, few African Americans had either the financial or political clout to offset the power of affluent benefactors. But in the 1960s Harlem was to become more important politically to New York's Democratic party, and Harlem's politicians were to gain a new stature and centrality in the broader city as the number of blacks entering the city during the 1950s expanded dramatically. African-American politicians, such as Adam Clayton Powell Jr. and Hulan Jack, who was elected Manhattan borough president in 1954, presaged the coming to power of black political leaders nationally in the 1960s and 1970s.[96] The Clarks brought onto the Northside board, for example, their friend J. Raymond Jones, known as the "Harlem Fox," who in December 1964 became the first African-American Tammany Hall leader. Jones "played a very intricate part in Northside. . . . I think he helped the Board to understand that we were serious." Jones provided a type of political protection that wealthy patrons did not underestimate. As the Democratic leader in Manhattan, he had instant access to Mayor Robert F. Wagner and other pols who controlled patronage and city contracts.[97]

Over the next few years, a new drive was made to identify other individuals whose commitment to Northside's goals was matched by a commitment to broader needs of the larger Harlem community. In April 1966, board president Howard Sloan, who had succeeded Ascoli in 1960—and without whom Northside might have lost its connections to the older philanthropic community that had long supported it—stepped down from the position (though not from the board), to be succeeded by James Dumpson. Dumpson had Harlem roots, a broad knowledge of the city's social welfare programs and administration, and connections at City Hall. In an "emotional" meeting, Sloan thanked the board for its support and "assured" Dumpson "that he would receive as much help as he did and perhaps more" from board members who would "recommit themselves to move forward." Dumpson's initial statement after his election as the board president summarized the transformation overtaking Northside. He lauded Sloan's leadership in navigating Northside in the six years after Marion Ascoli's resignation as board president. Now, Dumpson observed, it was necessary "to move ahead and develop a new model . . . of service to a community which is in need." He emphasized that "what happens in the next six months, or year, or two should not only be the provision of services to this community but involvement of the community and the recipients" in Northside itself.[98]

The coming decade was not without struggles within the board and between the staff and board, but the issue of control of Northside would not again center around the power and personality of one person of means, although conflicts between black and white board members would again become an issue in the late 1960s and early 1970s. A larger number of African Americans, with greatly enhanced political and social position, joined white philanthropists to engage in thoughtful and sometimes heated, substantive debates on the program and goals of Northside. In the years following the 1954 Supreme Court decision, Kenneth Clark himself had become a nationally and internationally known and respected scholar and social analyst, and then in 1964 had written the noted study of Harlem, *Dark Ghetto: Dilemmas of Social Power*, and numerous scholarly articles.

The debates at Northside now were not framed by the earlier inequality in power and status. After Howard Sloan's tenure as board president, Dumpson was a natural and logical choice, and it is significant that his election caused so little notice after a period of so much dissention. It marked a major step for a board so recently dominated by a powerful representative of traditional white philanthropy. Changes in financing also signaled the implementation of Kenneth Clark's own vision of a more egalitarian relationship between committed leaders in the white, especially Jewish, community and in the African-American community. By October 1966, Kenneth Clark felt confident enough in the integrity and strength of the new board to resign his post as research director at Northside and to establish and serve as president of the new Metropolitan Applied Research Center. He became a member of the Northside board and followed its activities and fortunes assiduously.

Dumpson, in a poignant remembrance, traces Northside's uniqueness to Kenneth Clark's vision: "What [an integrated board] meant to me of course was that this was a way that Kenneth would have created the world if Kenneth had been the creator of the world. He would have brought all kinds of people into his world to collaborate, to work together for a common end. And he would have made no distinctions whether they were white or black, whether they were Jew or Gentile, whether they had Ph.D.'s or they had a fourth grade education, as long as they had something to contribute to the well-being of people—that would be Kenneth's world." Yet, Kenneth and Mamie Clark understood that the realities of interracial and interclass relationships could destroy or at least endanger even the most idealistic programs and plans. Although the differences in power and authority between educated, wealthy, white benefactors and African-American professionals were very real, the Clarks were determined that the imbalance in power not be the critical variable in the shaping and control of the program. Dumpson remembers that "part of Kenneth's commitment [was] that when we have people from Park Avenue with money who are white, they're not going to control, they're going to be partners but they're not going to determine the policy and the procedure." [99]

4. Children Apart: Education and the Uses of Power

"Separate and Unequal" in New York City

It was Monday, 17 May 1954; Kenneth Clark was preparing to speak on relationships between blacks and Jews to an organization of Jewish social workers. At Northside, a radio was on in Mamie Clark's office when the news bulletin came through that changed their lives: the U.S. Supreme Court had unanimously decided, in *Brown* v. *Board of Education*, that the segregation of children by race in public schools was unconstitutional. A spontaneous party broke out as the Northside staff celebrated the momentous nature of the long-sought victory. Staff members brought in the children they were working with, saying later, "this was going to change everything," "everything was going to be different." Kenneth and Mamie Clark's work had been crucial to the landmark decision and Northside's staff felt they, too, had shared a small but critical part in shaping the nation's future.[1]

This moment was the culmination of fifteen years' effort of the Clarks. In the late 1930s, they had set out to study race and self-awareness in children, studies that were the foundation for the social-science brief cited in the Court's now famous "footnote 11." In 1939, Mamie had written her master's thesis, "The Development of Consciousness of Self in Negro Pre-School Children," and later, with the aid of the Rosenwald Fund, developed the dolls' tests that asked black children to pick out the doll they liked and that most resembled them. She also participated in a larger effort organized by Kenneth Clark as part of his work with Ralph Bunche for Gunnar Myrdal's monumental Carnegie-sponsored undertaking, *An American Dilemma*. Other social scientists, including E. Franklin Frazier and John Dollard of Yale, and psychiatrists, including Abram Kardiner and Lionel Ovesey, who together would write the influential *The Mark of Oppression* in 1951, had been part of a broader scholarly movement that won respect for studies demonstrating the destructive impacts of segregation and white supremacy. In 1951, the NAACP Legal Defense Fund had turned to social scientists in an unorthodox and innovative attempt to marshal expert testimony for a systematic fight against school segregation. Thurgood Marshal, the general counsel for the NAACP, who had led the team of lawyers in arguing the *Brown* decision, and his colleagues were unable to find senior academics willing to testify publicly. Robert Carter, later a federal judge in New York and board member of Northside, asked Otto Klineberg at Columbia for advice. Klineberg led him to Kenneth Clark, then still in his thirties. Clark recalls the beginning of that story:

> Around February or March of 1951 I got a call from Bob Carter of the NAACP. . . . and they wanted help from the psychologists to prove that segregated education could never be equal and that segregation, in it-self, was harmful, without regard to whether facilities were equal or not. Otto [Klineberg] had told him I had this manuscript which I had pre-pared for the [Mid-Century] White House Conference [on Children, 1950] and whatever help psychologists could give would be found in this manuscript.
>
> So Bob Carter and I met for the first time. He told me the problem they faced; . . . that segregation, in itself, damaged the personality of the Negro child. They had come upon this question themselves. They had formulated their legal approach and the only thing they didn't know was whether they could get any support for it from psychologists. . . . So they went back to Otto, and he said your man is Kenneth Clark. . . .
>
> [But] he took the manuscript and read it and called me about a week later, all excited, I'll never forget his words. He said, "This couldn't have been better if it had been done for us." [2]

Clark, then an assistant professor at City College, marshaled other so-cial and behavioral scientists, including Northside board member and psy-chiatrist Viola Bernard, to prepare and support an appendix to the NAACP brief "summarizing the evidence on the effects of segregation and the con-sequence of desegregation." [3] "It was necessary for us to be very skillful because we had to recognize that we were asking people—scholars, psychol-ogists and research people—to step into an uncharted road, into a controver-sial area, to step into an area which might be detrimental to their academic prestige and status." [4]

Both he and Mamie Clark testified in NAACP cases in South Carolina and Virginia about the results of the doll test and the negative impact of pub-lic school segregation. Mamie Clark said she was asked to testify in the Prince Edward County desegregation case in order to rebut directly the testi-mony offered in that court in support of inherent racial differences presented by Henry Garrett, former president of the American Psychological Association, because he had been her advisor at Columbia (see chapter 2). Her testimony and Kenneth's would provide an important rationale relied on by the Court in its final opinion declaring that "separate education facilities are inherently unequal," and hence, unconstitutional.[5] Kenneth Clark later reflected, "if I had been aware of the extent of the commitment and the nature of the involvement when Bob Carter first came to talk with me, I probably wouldn't have assumed it as easily as I did. I don't say I would have rejected it, but if there had been any way to see all the problems, all the complications, how much of my life that would have actually taken, and that's not professional life but personal life, I would have been more deliberative in pursuing it."[6]

The changes that would come to the nation and the city in the wake of *Brown* could hardly have been predicted in those first exciting moments of triumph. It would take a massive civil rights struggle the better part of two decades before de jure segregation of public accommodations—from buses to swimming pools, lunch counters to schools—would crumble. But, in northern cities, New York in particular, where informal but pervasive customs and extralegal practice had forced black children into segregated neighborhoods and poorly funded, inferior schools, de facto segregation resisted popular activism and legal assault. While the nation focused on the more dramatic desegregation struggles in the South, this more insidious, but no less insistent, form of urban segregation continued in the North without remedy.

Since the early 1940s, both Mamie and Kenneth Clark had seen two issues as interrelated: the problems of troubled youth and the impact of segregation on the education of children in New York City. Buoyed by the Supreme Court decision, the Clarks saw in *Brown* a unique moment neither the city nor the country could afford to miss. For the first time since Reconstruction, a significant part of the nation's leadership had thrown its political and moral weight behind integration, exactly the precondition the Clarks believed necessary for a revolution in race relations. New York, in particular, appeared well-positioned to become a model for a northern effort to address de facto segregation. Its traditions of liberalism, its strong labor movement, its historical mission of acculturating new immigrants, and the growing political importance of Harlem in the new Democratic coalition seemed to augur well for a sustained attack on inferior education and segregated schools.

Segregation in the New York City educational system appeared to be a relatively recent phenomenon, dating from the 1930s. It is true that in the late eighteenth and early nineteenth centuries, the New York Manumission Society, whose members included Alexander Hamilton and John Jay, had established New York African Free Schools specifically and exclusively for African-American children. These schools actually preceded the establishment of free public schools for white children by nineteen years. In 1834, the then-seven African Free schools were incorporated into the evolving public school system and, in 1858, were taken over by the newly created New York City Board of Education. In the city, shortly before the outbreak of the Civil War, most of the relatively small population of African-American children began to attend integrated public schools, and, by 1884, Governor Grover Cleveland signed a bill that proclaimed schools "open for the education of pupils . . . without regard to race or color." [7]

From the beginning of the twentieth century to the Great Depression, African Americans had been able to attend integrated schools in their local communities but, as urban residential segregation became more prevalent with accelerated black migration from the South, schools had become more segregated, especially in Harlem. By the depression, Harlem's schools lacked adequate funds for academic programs and for renovation of deteriorating buildings. The African-American population of Manhattan had increased from 23,000 in 1910 to more than 200,000 only twenty years later, but virtually no new school buildings had been erected in Harlem since the turn of the century. There were twenty-one elementary schools, but only one high school, an annex of a larger vocational training school for the textile industry. The worst of these schools was PS 89 at 135th Street and Lenox Avenue, where "the classrooms are dark and stuffy; the blackboards are old and defective and the wooden floors are dirty and offensive." Like most other schools in the area, it ran double sessions to accommodate the growing population, but even so, between forty and fifty pupils were packed into each classroom. Morale among the teaching staff was so low that "many of the white teachers appointed to the schools of Harlem regard the appointment as a sort of punishment" and, not surprisingly, there was a "great deal of turnover." The 1935 report on the Harlem disturbances by E. Franklin Frazier had showed that schools lacked libraries, gyms, and basic educational resources available elsewhere in white communities. Schools routinely steered Harlem's children away from the academic high school programs and into the vocational training programs. Indeed, Kenneth Clark himself was told by the white guidance counselor that he should attend a vocational school, rather than the academic program at George Washington, and might have done so but for the intervention of his mother, who, Clark recalls, "got me out of my classroom and took me with her to the guidance counselor's office. I will never forget the scene; I was so embarrassed by my mother's confrontation with the guidance counselor. She said, 'I don't care where you send your child. You can send him to a vocational school if you want to, but my son is going to go to George Washington High School.' My mother had attended night classes at George Washington High School and she knew where she wanted her son to go." [8] By the early 1950s, the process of school deterioration in Harlem had accelerated despite the relative prosperity of the postwar years. Clark's immediate intervention in New York public-school desegregation politics resulted directly from the challenges of southern attorneys, during the school desegregation lawsuits in Virginia and elsewhere. One attorney asked Clark why he was focusing so much on southern segregation when the schools in his own city were just as segregated.[9] In response, in a speech to the New York Urban League in February 1954, at Harlem's Hotel Theresa, Kenneth Clark challenged New York's political leadership to acknowledge its own role in perpetuating a segregated system. He called upon the city's board of education to cooperate in a "study of the extent and effects of segregation in the public schools of New York City's Harlem." Only a concerted and honest confrontation of the facts would allow "our children and all children [to be] provided with a more democratic education." [10] Mayor Robert F. Wagner, who attended the Urban League dinner, phoned William Jansen, superintendent of schools, after the meeting to inquire whether there was substance to Kenneth Clark's accusations. Jansen denied them: Clark's accusations against the board of education were unfounded, and his speech had been merely an attempt to blame board officials for a pattern of school segregation that was simply a consequence of segregated housing.[11]

In April 1954, shortly after his speech at the Hotel Theresa and a month before the Court's decision in *Brown*, Clark organized a conference at Northside Center called "Children Apart." More than two hundred representatives of sixty schools, social-welfare agencies, religious organizations, unions, parents' organizations, and Harlem community groups attended. So did B'nai B'rith and the NAACP. The meeting attracted wide media coverage because of its implicit and explicit condemnation of the resistance of the city's governmental and educational leadership to acknowledging, much less confronting, the "increasing segregation" of the city's school system and the continued denial of an equal education to its African-American and Puerto Rican children. In the conference's principal address, Clark noted the subtle and not-so-subtle impact of educational policies, social theory, and housing patterns on the education of African-American children. Segregation was a fact of life no less real in New York than in Mississippi. He described the implicit racism in the "discrepancy between 103 classes for retarded children and six classes for gifted children in the Harlem schools." He pointed to the self-fulfilling prophecy of an educational system that so reduced academic standards in the lower grades that African-American children were unprepared to enter academic programs or to compete with better-prepared whites for places in the city's respected specialized high schools.[12] After the meeting, an Intergroup Committee of New York's Public Schools was organized, its founding meeting held at 31 West 110th Street, not coincidentally, Northside's headquarters. Its stated purpose was to press the New York City Board of Education to desegregate and improve Harlem's schools.[13] A month later came the *Brown* decision. At the 3 June 1954 Northside board meeting, Kenneth Clark reported on the Intergroup Committee's activities. "The Board voted unanimously that Northside be a participating agency in the effort to improve educational standards in all underprivileged areas of the city."[14]

Also in June, Kenneth Clark delivered an even more pointed and detailed speech at another New York Urban League meeting, warning against assuming that segregation was confined to the South. Northerners had to confront the reality of de facto segregation. Responding to Arthur Leavitt (the president of the New York City Board of Education, who also spoke at the meeting), who rejected charges of school segregation, Clark pointed to three instances in which, he said, racist assumptions were implicit in board of education policy. Facilities were poor, curriculum diluted, academic standards weak or nonexistent; indeed, the systematic and destructive impact of de facto segregation could be demonstrated. First, he noted, no white pupils had been assigned to the one high school in Harlem, despite the fact that it offered a vocational course of study unavailable elsewhere in the city. Second, Harlem teachers were often substitutes who had neither teaching credentials nor classroom experience. Third, he pointed out, as he had earlier, there were 103 classes for retarded children in Harlem, whereas the board of education had established only six for gifted children. Kenneth Clark's point was that these were fragmentary, but suggestive, data; what was needed was a comprehensive and objective study of the conditions of Harlem's schools.[15]

Leavitt took up Clark's suggestion that an independent group be asked to gather such data. In mid-July, the Public Education Association announced that it would conduct a study of whether "the city's primary and secondary schools in Negro neighborhoods receive inferior teaching, guidance and counseling." At a news conference at Northside, Clark announced that the Intergroup Committee of New York Public Schools had "confidence in the objectivity and integrity of the study of these schools which Mr. Leavitt has requested."[16]

Kenneth Clark kept up the pressure at forums throughout the city and in the newspapers. At the Annual *New York Herald-Tribune* Forum at Hunter College in fall 1954, he described one case in which gerrymandering had led to the creation of one all-white and one all-black school in upper Manhattan. Between West 155th and 160th Streets, Broadway had developed as an informal demarcation between the largely white, Jewish community on the West Side and the largely African-American and Hispanic communities on the East Side. The closest elementary school was PS 46 at West 156th Street, between Amsterdam and St. Nicholas Avenues, yet white children on the west side of Broadway were steered by the local principal to PS 169, nearly a mile away. This must have been arranged with the knowledge of the board of education, Clark noted, since special school buses were assigned to carry the white children uptown.[17]

Six months later, in April 1955, on the first anniversary of the Intergroup Committee's founding, Thurgood Marshall and Kenneth Clark chaired a meeting held at the Community Church on East 35th Street near Park Avenue. Clark recounted the history of the group, reporting that two of its three goals were already accomplished: "arousing public interest about the problems of segregated schools in New York City and obtaining a systematic and objective study of these problems." What remained, however, was "probably [the] most difficult goal . . . of eliminating every vestige of racism and segregation from the public schools of the city of New York." To accomplish that task, the board of education had agreed to create a commission "directly responsible to the Board" to "recommend to the Board a plan of action which would prevent the further development of such segregated schools and to integrate the existing ones as quickly as practical." At the April meeting, Clark announced his resignation as the chair of the Intergroup Committee; shortly thereafter, he accepted appointment to a new commission established by the incoming president of the board of education, Charles Silver, its mandate "to accept the challenge implicit in the language and spirit of the [*Brown*] decision of the Supreme Court" and to implement the recommendations of the Public Education Association's forthcoming report on segregation in New York City's schools.[18]

The association's report, "The Quality of Education Offered to Majority and Minority (Negro, Puerto Rican) Children in New York City's Public Schools," drafted by the Research Center for Human Relations at New York University, was completed in August 1955, just before the beginning of the new school year. The issue of segregation and inferior education went beyond the moral and political issues of inequality in a democratic society to impact the economy. It noted the economic transformation of the postwar city in transition from an industrial and commercial center to a city with a service economy. New York's future depended on an educated and skilled labor force and it could not "afford educationally underprivileged minority groups." Inadequate education and underemployment were likely to lead to an increase in "crime and other forms of social pathology."[19]

The report compared predominantly white and minority schools at the elementary and junior high school levels. New York's minority schools fared poorly by nearly every measure: space allocated per child; amount spent per child; average class size and age of buildings; maintenance and equipment; and, not surprisingly, in student achievement levels. The capital expenditure per child in white elementary schools was $65.50, in the minority schools only $21.10. Ten times more white schools had 80 percent experienced tenured teachers; class sizes in predominantly minority schools were larger and school buildings were much older. At the junior high level, the average age of the predominantly white school buildings was fifteen years, most erected after the beginning of World War II; the minority schools were on average thirty-five-years old, and most predated World War I.[20]

The report addressed Jansen's claim that there was no school segregation as such in New York because unequal conditions were the result not of legal or intentional planning as in the South, but of "the City's pattern of residential segregation. . . . [the] prejudice against ethnic groups among some of the City's population . . . [and] the social and economic conditions under which ethnic minority groups live." The board of education would have to deal with the school consequences of inequality whatever the causes; it could no longer hide behind a facade of ignorance of these consequences. The report argued that the "very act of making unintended consequences explicit . . . [meant that] they can no longer be called unintended." It acknowledged that it might well be true that no one was to blame. But, "the facts speak for themselves and must be changed lest we be all suspected of approving them." Three primary means could address inequality. First, a program to spur long-term integration would need to enlist the cooperation of housing administrators in readdressing residential segregation, and, to spur more immediate results, zoning changes of school districts must be implemented so as to encourage school integration. Second, "an emergency plan" must be adopted to raise "the quality of education of [minority] children." Third, teachers and administrators in primarily African-American and Puerto Rican schools, in order to take their jobs as educators seriously, must demand from the city greater resources and improved programs.[21]

To Kenneth Clark, the "most significant finding" of the report was its direct linkage of low achievement of minority youth to the inadequacies of the school system. The report noted, for example, that test scores in minority schools "decreased as [children] went from the lower to the higher grades." Clark concluded that "the school [system of New York] not only does not help these children, but as far as their intelligence is concerned appears to impair them."[22]

The Commission on Integration versus the Board of Education

By May 1956, the Commission on Integration, on which Kenneth Clark now sat (chairing its sub-commission on curriculum and standards), came out with its recommendations, the most controversial of which was a rezoning of school districts to achieve integration. Soon, rumors began to circulate that the commission was recommending massive bussing of white children from as far away as Staten Island into schools in the heart of Harlem. The rumors, in turn, set into motion a confrontation between the board and parents in some of the city's white ethnic neighborhoods. Community groups in Queens were especially vocal in opposition, the president of the Queens Chamber of Commerce stating that "maybe parents in other boroughs in the city favor forced integration of their school children, but we don't want it in Queens." White parents in Brooklyn threatened violence if their children were forced to attend JHS 258, a predominantly black school, whereupon the board of education delayed its integration. Then Kenneth Clark wrote to board president Silver that desegregation "must proceed" and that "anticipations of violence, real or fancied, cannot be accepted as a valid excuse for inaction."[23]

The core of the second proposal, that "every public school in the New York system should have a proportionate number of experienced teachers," [24] would require rotation of experienced teachers into schools with predominantly minority children. While parents were mobilizing to oppose integration by zones, teachers now began to organize to fight "forced" transfers and reassignments to mostly black schools. New York's *Amsterdam News* reported that teachers were charging that the plan would tend to "destroy teacher morale and cause mass resignations from the school system." [25] Clark says that, at one public hearing, representatives of a teachers' group "stated that to require experienced teachers to serve in these underprivileged schools would be 'like sentencing them to Siberia.'" For Clark, the insidious racism that led teachers to see the schools of African-American and Puerto Rican children as fundamentally foreign was bad enough. But these same teachers also talked about these children "as if they were lepers." Were such professionals suited "to teach any child," black or white? Except for the Negro Teachers Association and the radical Teachers Union, *all* the other teachers' groups, allied in the new Joint Committee of Teachers Organizations, "declared that the integration recommendations, 'if carried out to the letter, will produce new hostilities, conflicts, resentments and separations of peoples.'" [26] In December 1956, a month after the board of education backed off from integrating Brooklyn's JHS 258, the High School Teachers Association held a press conference to protest the proposed "rotation of experienced teachers to difficult schools." Although not formally opposing integration, and even nominally supporting it, the association placed blame for segregation on city housing policy and housing patterns and suggested that transferring teachers would not improve the poorer schools. "Since sympathetic, satisfied teachers are needed in these schools, the transferring of experienced teachers to difficult schools will not solve their problem. It will only create more dissatisfied high school teachers and create new problems for the entire division." How to provide "satisfied" and "experienced" teachers was not explained. Integration was an answer to "their," that is, the minority community's "problem." [27]

The New York City Board of Education itself was ambivalent about implementing the recommendations of its own Commission on Integration. In late November 1956, the rising tension between Kenneth Clark and superintendent of schools Jansen erupted in a public forum on public school integration, held in Philadelphia. Clark repeated his charge that "seventy per cent of the children attending public elementary and junior high schools in New York City do not have an opportunity to come in contact with children of a different color." The *New York Post* reported that, "at this point, Jansen jumped up from a chair at the back of the speakers' platform and exclaimed: 'that's completely false.'" Clark, refusing to back down, cited figures from the Public Education Association's report to substantiate his charge. As the *Post* reported it, "showing great irritation, Jansen reddened as he argued 'it would be hard to find a school in New York City where one can't find three or four children of another color.'" After Kenneth Clark's speech, Jansen continued the argument, "following him to an adjoining room and asked Clark to repeat what he had said." When Clark responded that perhaps Jansen had misunderstood him, Jansen said that "that makes the figures worse" and "stalked out" of the room.[28]

Days later, in December, even before the teachers began to oppose school transfers openly and just as white Brooklyn parents threatened violence, the board decided to delay reassignment of experienced teachers to minority schools as well as rezoning school districts to stimulate integration. The chairman of the Intergroup Committee, Hubert Delany, who had succeeded Clark in that post when he stepped aside to serve on the board of education's Commission on Integration, told the board, in response, that "these are the first reports to test the willingness of New York City to abide by its firm moral obligation to observe the clear dictate of the Supreme Court ruling that separate can never be equal."[29]

The New York Citizens' Committee for Children, composed of many of Northside's founders, board members, and supporters, among them Trude Lash, Marion Ascoli, Viola Bernard, Shad Polier, and Exie Welsch, announced its own support for the commission's recommendations. "That a Commission on Integration should be necessary in this northern City is tragic, indeed." Even so, on 17 January, the board of education once again postponed action on implementation, prompting Delany to warn that "delay can be as effective as negative action in preventing the implementation of these recommendations."[30]

The Intergroup Committee itself was now beginning to encounter opposition from some of its organizational members. Just as its chair, Delany, was writing to board president Silver, the president of the New York Teacher's Guild, one of those members, wrote to Delany that they, like many other teachers' groups, were opposed to the entire commission report. They urged the committee to drop its support for teacher rotation so that the guild could support the committee's general goals without internal opposition in its own ranks. They suggested the committee propose a program of "voluntary" transfers, instead of mandatory rotation. The New York Teacher's Guild was "deeply concerned that the policy of integration be pursued . . . nevertheless with realism and without needlessly antagonizing those that will have to effectuate it, namely, the professional staff."[31] How integration was to be achieved without antagonizing those who had opposed it was not made clear.

The ebullient optimism of the first post-*Brown* years quickly began to dissipate as civil rights leaders and educators ran up against the entrenched opposition to change throughout the country. Kenneth Clark continued to believe that segregation would ultimately be defeated, but he began to voice concern about lack of commitment from local and national white leadership. He singled out for special criticism "professional educators and their national organizations," "church organizations," "Southern labor unions," and "Northern white liberals." Educators "have been conspicuous by their silence, ambiguity, or equivocation on this issue." With the exception of the Roman Catholic Church, religious faiths and denominations had not gone beyond their initial praise for the *Brown* decision "to bring about a single desegregated public school in a given community." Clark saw Northern liberals, for their part, as "confused, ambiguous, and often blocked by [their] own guilt." He recognized that the African American needed allies but could not, as he told the Annual Dinner of the Unitarian Service Committee, in Boston,

> accept offers of help or friendship which are conditioned by arbitrary limitations on how much of his rights he should demand. . . . Nor can he now permit his white liberal friends to bargain or intercede for piecemeal rights or determine the pace of his liberation. . . . He desires no more than any other citizen of a state or the nation receives by lawful right. He will not willingly accept any less. He will not be coerced or intimidated to do so by the bigots; nor can he be cajoled or bribed by his liberal white friends.[32]

By the end of the summer of 1957, Kenneth Clark had gone beyond general criticism of white leadership to a more open reproach of local leaders. School superintendent William Jansen, for one, was dragging his feet, "deliberately confusing, delaying, distorting, and sidetracking reports of our

Commission," "no more likely to implement our reports than he was two years ago. . . . We do not intend to stand by and permit ourselves to be used as cat's paws for the Superintendent. . . . When we meet with [board president] Silver we are going to demand action. . . . The people of the City will not tolerate this sabotage." Two and a half weeks later, the minority population of the city formed a five hundred–person picket line around City Hall. A delegation of twenty-one went to Mayor Wagner's offices to demand that he "desegregate our schools or we will use our votes to defeat you in the November election." The *Amsterdam News* reported what happened when Ella Baker, later a key organizer for the Southern Christian Leadership Conference, confronted the mayor: "Standing while the Mayor twitched nervously, spokesman Baker said: 'We parents want to know first hand from you just what is, or is not going to be done for our children.'" The parents insisted that the mayor preside over a conference that would include Negro and Puerto Rican parents, Kenneth Clark, and representatives of the board of education.[33]

By the opening of the school year in September, Jansen and the board of education had elected to yield to the growing pressure from teachers' groups and white parents, not to the pressure from minority groups. Jansen issued a twenty-nine-page "Report on Integration," boasting of great progress toward rectifying inequality in the schools, as recommended in the commission report. To draft a statement of response, the Intergroup Committee appointed Marion Ascoli and June Shagaloff, of the NAACP Legal Defense and Education Fund; that statement called the superintendent's report a "vague, defensive" apology that was "not responsive to the recommendation of the Commission." The Intergroup Committee was particularly upset that Jansen had so quickly backed away from both the rezoning of school districts to achieve racial balance in these schools and the principle of assigning experienced teachers to schools in primarily African-American communities. Jansen's report had put integration "third in the usual list of zoning criteria: changed from a 'cardinal principle' to an 'important consideration.'" Kenneth Clark reported that eighteen months after his sub-commission on curriculum and standards had issued its report, "no progress has been made in improvement."[34] A year later, in August 1958, Jansen, then seventy, retired and Dr. John Theobold, formerly Mayor Wagner's Deputy Mayor, was appointed to succeed him.

That year, the "long simmering Harlem school controversy" over de facto segregation burst onto the pages of local newspapers when Bernice and Stanley Skipworth, and four other Harlem parents, refused to send their children to JHS 136 at 135th Street and Edgecomb Avenue and JHS 139 because the schools were segregated, underfunded, and therefore of inferior quality. The nation's attention was riveted on Little Rock, Arkansas, where state and local authorities had refused to allow nine children to attend Central High School until President Dwight D. Eisenhower was forced to call upon the National Guard to protect them. New York's own school authorities refused to allow black children in segregated elementary schools to move to predominantly white schools in other areas of the city. A comparison with Little Rock was never far from Kenneth and Mamie Clark's personal consciousness, for they had taken it upon themselves to provide a home and schooling in Hastings-on-Hudson to one of the "Little Rock Nine," Minnie Jean Brown, who had been expelled in the middle of the school year for throwing some chili onto a white child's head.[35]

When the five sets of Harlem parents kept their children home, the board of education's response was swift and punitive: it brought legal charges of neglect against the parents, accusing them of denying their children an education. The case went before Judge Justine Wise Polier of the Domestic Relations Court, former Northside board member. Polier held extensive hearings (including testimony by Kenneth Clark) that exposed the inequities in funding, staffing, and resources for the schools of the city. Her decision, echoing the arguments of the Court in its 1954 *Brown* decision, was to dismiss the charges. She held that the children, in what was commonly known as the Skipworth Case, were receiving "inferior educational opportunities . . . by reason of racial discrimination."[36]

The board contemplated an appeal of Polier's decision, as community organizations, among them a newly formed Harlem Neighborhood Association (HANA), united to press the board to abandon a position they considered racist. HANA warned the board that "to prosecute an appeal of the Polier decision solely on the grounds of the legal issues that may be involved, will, inevitably, increase the gap separating the Board of Education from our community." HANA summarized the history of distrust that had existed between the Harlem community and the board of education:

> Since the great decision of the Supreme Court of the United States in 1954, the nation has been confronted with a dominant moral issue in the desegregation of the public schools attended by our children—both North and South. In New York City, the Board of Education's Commission on Integration established the fact that de facto segregation in the

public school system was accompanied by inferior educational opportunities for children in attendance at such schools. Since the Commission's report in 1956, the Board of Education's actions on the Commission's recommendations have not made any appreciable change in the situation. This has called forth widespread criticism from parents, churches and civic groups in our community and in the city at large, because of the slow rate of implementation and the piece-meal approach used in the elimination of segregation and inferior educational facilities.[37]

The board's decision not to appeal was reached in late December 1958 during a newspaper strike of the major dailies, but word spread through other channels and reaction throughout the city was strong and direct. The *Amsterdam News*, the *Brooklyn Daily*, the *New York Age*, and other African-American newspapers hailed the decision as acknowledging that de facto segregation was every bit as pernicious as de jure segregation itself.[38]

For Kenneth Clark, the Skipworth case was "a major development in the struggle of Negroes in northern communities to obtain equal and non-segregated education." Until this time, the members of the New York City Board of Education, like most northern liberals, rarely acknowledged the impact on children of de facto segregation in northern urban communities. In court, the board of education no longer contested the fact that segregation existed but did deny the claims of African-American parents that de facto segregation was as destructive and harmful as was southern de jure segregation. Kenneth Clark was convinced that Judge Polier's decision acknowledging the inferiority of segregated schools in New York could provide an opening to attack invidious northern de facto segregation just as the U.S. Supreme Court's decision of 1954 had provided the basis for challenging de jure segregation in the South.[39]

White Boycott and Flight

As the new school year opened in September 1959, a group of Harlem parents demanded transfer of their children from segregated Harlem schools to prosperous and predominantly white schools in Riverdale in the Bronx, one of the wealthiest areas of the city. They argued that the board had already transferred to Riverdale a group of "predominantly white" children from an overcrowded school in Inwood, an Irish-American enclave at Manhattan's northern tip, and that their own children should receive the same opportunity. The board may have maintained that race was not a factor in their decision to relieve overcrowding by busing the children, but the parents in Harlem believed otherwise.

The white community of Queens now began to organize a boycott of local schools, parents protesting the busing of a group of black and Hispanic children from schools in Brooklyn's Bedford-Stuyvesant area to their own predominantly white schools. The board explained that it had begun to transfer these children from Bedford-Stuyvesant, and also a few other black and Hispanic children from East Harlem, to predominantly white schools in Queens and Yorkville to "relieve overcrowding." It continued to refuse to transfer students out of central Harlem to achieve integration since, they said, overcrowding was not an issue there as it was in Brooklyn and East Harlem. To black parents in Harlem, the decisions of the board smacked of subterfuge.

In the late 1950s and early 1960s, thousands of white children left the school system, entering a proliferating number of private and parochial schools. The inadequacy of the schools of Harlem and the racism implicit in a segregated school system increased the problems minority children faced, straining the resources of the few agencies that continued to serve the growing black population.[40] Between 1955 and 1963, the board of education's resistance to integration combined with a rapidly expanding population of African-American children to create a more and more segregated school system. The number of elementary schools with overwhelmingly African-American and Puerto Rican students almost tripled, from 42 to 118, and junior high schools of overwhelmingly minority enrollment rose from 9 to 29. The troubling observation of Kenneth Clark in the mid-1950s that the gap between white and minority students' average achievement scores on standardized tests increased with grade level was as true in 1963 as it had been in 1954. If anything, the gap had widened. In 1955, eighth-grade students in predominantly African-American schools had been two and a half years behind their white counterparts, by 1962 they were three and a half grades behind. Of the 1276 junior high school students who graduated from schools in Harlem in 1959, only 398 went on to receive high school diplomas, of these, only 43 were academic diplomas. In 1963, "approximately 67,000 children in the junior high schools were more that two years behind in reading, and . . . 10,000 children in seventh grade could not even read third-grade books." Rather than helping children make up these deficits, the schools appeared to exacerbate the problem. The longer children stayed in the school system, the further behind they fell. "In reading comprehension from 13 percent to

39 percent of pupils in third grade are below grade level. . . . By sixth grade, from 60 percent to 93 percent score below grade level." [41]

By 1963, there was no concrete progress on the two controversial proposals on rezoning and teacher transfers the Commission on Integration had proposed in 1955 to achieve school integration. Indeed, matters were worse: "A substantial number of new schools have been built in segregated areas in direct conflict with the recommendations of the Commission on Integration," while the use of substitutes and inexperienced teachers in minority schools was still the model rather than the exception. The board of education said that there had been substantial progress in location of new facilities in order to integrate the school system, but a 1964 State Education Department report concluded that "Puerto Rican, Negro and other students in public schools in New York City suffer extensive and serious ethnic segregation" and that "this segregation increased between 1958 and 1963." [42]

Harlem's youth were even more segregated in school by the early 1960s than they had been in the mid-1950s. The flight of white children to the city's private and parochial school systems and to the suburbs had heightened the frustration of black parents committed to integration. A 1961 study by the United Parents Association, an independent group concerned about the growing segregation of New York's schools, found that "the proportion in these schools has increased in recent years, so that (as of 1960) nearly a third of New York City's children are in other than public schools. Although many parochial schools and some private schools admit Negro children, the overwhelming balance of these school populations is white, thus reducing the proportion of white children in the public schools of the city." [43]

Community activists argued that integration could be achieved only if Harlem's schools became first-rate educational institutions that could draw black and white students alike. Although it might be possible to move children from Harlem's schools to predominantly white schools, it was clear that white parents would never allow their children to be shifted to inferior schools in a black community. On the other hand, an elite school like the High School of Music and Art had been attracting whites for decades despite its location on the edge of Harlem at 135th Street and Convent Avenue. But it was deeply distressing to Harlem parents that, even in this relatively affluent period, the city administration was unwilling to invest the resources necessary to transform the other schools in Harlem and other black communities into superior educational institutions.

The inaction of the city's educational and political establishment was no doubt in part a consequence of the inertia that afflicts bureaucracies generally. But forces other than inertia had led to the abandonment of Harlem's schools. Many educators, administrators, and politicians saw little yield from a massive investment in black children. Some, indeed, assumed that African-American children could not learn regardless of the educational investment. Some openly argued that African-American children were afflicted by cultural, psychological, and even genetic, deficits that impeded their capacity to learn. As a result of such attitudes among administrators and teachers, Northside's Bea Levison recalled, "in the public schools there was a [widely held belief] that these kids aren't going to learn anyway and what's the point" of investing in their education. Elaine Gaspard, a Harlem community activist who joined Northside's board in 1969 after becoming involved in her local school board, remembers the terrible price Harlem's children paid for the casual racism of teachers and administrators. "I was at one conference and . . . a principal said, 'well, they really can't learn but they're so cute! I could play with them all day.' I'm not even going to go into my reaction to that statement. All I know is that it reinforced my determination to become more involved and see if we could not make some changes about the opinion or decision that our children could learn, given the right opportunity."[44] Such attitudes among teachers and administrators affected every aspect of the children's experience in Harlem's schools, including assessments, testing, and evaluation of their emotional and intellectual capabilities.[45]

In New York, race became merged with a growing public concern about a rise in juvenile delinquency, when, in 1957, several newspapers sensationalized an incident in a Brooklyn public school in which a minority youth was accused of throwing lye in the face of a white student. What became known as the "Kessler lye-throwing case" led to a grand-jury investigation of crime in and around school buildings. Enormous press attention followed the suicide of a distraught junior high school principal who "jumped to his death from the roof of his apartment house a few hours before a scheduled appearance in front of the jury." Newspaper accounts of the apparently widespread fears of teachers and administrators in some of the city's schools led to the grand-jury recommendation "that a uniformed police officer cover the corridors, stairways and playgrounds of the City's Public Schools in order to prevent violence and depravity which have become so commonplace in recent years." Teachers interviewed by the press "spoke of being afraid to go to work, and described classroom teaching as chiefly an exercise in discipline." The board of education responded to the publicity by suspending nine hundred pupils (and another seven hundred soon thereafter) who were "looked upon as threats to the schools."[46]

What followed is not difficult to understand, given the tumult over education and integration then overtaking the city. By 1959, two-thirds of Manhattan's school children and one-third of the city's public school children were African American or Puerto Rican. The Public Education Association noted that race and delinquency "merged in the public minds." The newspapers were filled with lurid stories of widespread delinquency and youth gangs. Schools in minority neighborhoods or with large minority populations became "the 'difficult' and 'dangerous' schools of the newspaper headlines. . . . To an alarmed public the school system seemed to be beset with delinquents (presumed to be black and Puerto Rican) and staffed—or rather, understaffed—by cowed teachers unable to teach because of the incapacity of their students to learn." As the association pointed out, "the generalized fears of the community found a ready focus in the school system." [47] Nearly all city and state political leaders adopted the prevailing view that something extraordinary had to be done to isolate and identify delinquents. On 12 February 1958, New York's Mayor Wagner and Governor Averill Harriman issued a joint announcement that $500,000 would be made available for establishing four more temporary schools for delinquent students (schools for such students were assigned PS numbers in the six hundreds). The next month, three "700" schools opened for offenders considered the most troublesome and incorrigible. The city's board of education requested an appropriation to provide six new "600" schools.[48]

Rather than invest resources in improving ghetto schools in order to undermine white resistance to integration, the board of education embarked on a plan that further isolated minority children, and reinforced the white community's general opinion that all minority children were "troubled," ergo, in need of segregation from the mainstream. As Harrison E. Salisbury reported in the *New York Times*, the board planned to open twenty-five institutions for the delinquent child, overwhelmingly in minority neighborhoods. For many in the black community there was little doubt who would be the primary "beneficiaries" of the 600 school program: it was feared that these institutions would primarily take African-American and Puerto Rican children, who were seen as having the most acute behavioral problems. There was a clear understanding that these institutions were not expected to address the needs of children but were one step removed from the reformatory. When Mrs. Eleanor Roosevelt spoke to a Harlem audience in 1958 with a critique of this special school program, the *New York Times* reported, "she held that 'difficult' children needed more and better paid teachers, guidance and psychiatric help rather than 'special' schools." [49] The 600 schools were a reaction to a broad societal perception that juvenile delinquency was out of control and also a special reaction to the perception that delinquency was a problem of African-American and Hispanic youth, who needed long-term segregation from other, less "troubled" youth. This marked a change from the late 1940s and early 1950s, when delinquency was seen as a problem associated with ethnic white youth.

In the early 1960s, Harlem political leaders were engaged in parallel struggles to improve the quality of life for its residents: to fight poverty and delinquency and to integrate the city's public schools and improve schools in Harlem. Both struggles saw the problems in Harlem as a consequence of the neglect by the white power structures, and both recognized that society's neglect rested on racist assumptions about the African-American community and its children. Northside's own historical commitments to integration and education had led it to become deeply involved in trying to undermine such racist assumptions that black children and youth were incapable of learning and that black families did not value education. And, surely, the school boycotts, demonstrations, and picketing of the board of education, which had continued almost unabated since 1958, had demonstrated concern with education.

Justine Wise Polier, in a speech before Intergroup Committee on New York City's Schools in March 1960, reflected on the meaning for the city of the acceptance of and collusion in the maintenance of de facto segregation. "We have also come to be far more aware of how superficial and inadequate are the relationships between white and non-white citizens." She worried that "walls are rising in this community between rich and poor, between skilled and unskilled, between white and non-white." With African Americans more likely to work in low-paying jobs and live in substandard housing, it was "doubly imperative" to ensure that they enjoyed a "good and unsegregated education. . . . The schools cannot be expected to correct all the injustices and hardships of urban life in America, but they can be expected to do whatever lies within their power to give each child a sense of his personal worth, and to give him every reason to want to learn." [50]

Kenneth Clark summed up the dilemmas facing those committed to integration in the mid and late 1960s:

What do you do in a situation in which you have the laws on your side, where whites smile and say to you that they are your friends, but where your white "friends" move to the suburbs leaving you confronted with segregation and inferior education in the schools, ghetto housing, and a quiet and tacit discrimination in jobs? How can you demonstrate a philosophy of love in response to this? What is the appropriate form of protest? One can "sit-in" in the Board of Education building, and not a single child will come back from the suburbs or from the private or parochial schools. One can link arms with the Mayor of Boston and march on the Commons, but it will not affect the housing conditions of Negroes in Roxbury.[51]

Reading Programs as a Form of Therapy

Northside's struggle against the segregation of Harlem's schools was based not only on the schools' failure to educate, but also on the impact of segregation on the students' self-esteem and self-respect, the argument the Court had accepted in *Brown*. The educational system, in effect, condemned children to lives of poverty, delinquency, and emotional turmoil. At Northside, the results of this abandonment and destruction were all too apparent. As Mamie Clark and Jeanne Karp noted, eighth graders who came to the center were two to four years behind in school; Northside's remedial staff were alarmed that administrators and teachers barely noted if children were falling behind in their academic subjects. Indeed, administrators were telling parents from first grade on that their children were progressing "satisfactorily." "Not until the child was in sixth grade did [parents] learn that [their child] could not meet the 5.0 reading level required for admission to J.H.S.," Jeanne Karp, Northside's remedial department head, said. "The fact that the schools did not consider the problem serious until the 6th grade reflects the lowered expectations [of teachers and administrators]."[52] The New York United Federation of Teachers and board of education representatives increasingly argued that the children could not learn because they came from homes where education was not prized. Harlem's parents—if not the children themselves—were said to be at fault, not the school system itself.

Northside's original goal was to overcome the racism and denial of services to Harlem by helping children who needed psychological counseling. But, almost immediately, in 1946, it had supplemented counseling with remedial educational services. Northside's staff believed that "if the kid couldn't read, he was going to have trouble in school."[53] Unlike other child guidance centers, which defined themselves principally in terms of counseling, Northside early on saw educational services as integral to the psychological health and social adjustments of their clients: "Treatment in therapy could become more effective were these children helped to overcome the frustration and humiliation they encountered in the classroom everyday because they could not read."[54] Northside's first remedial reading services were within its psychology department. But, in 1952, when Jeanne Karp came to Northside from the public schools, Mamie Clark asked her to head a remedial department.

In Jeanne Karp's first year of teaching in an elementary school in the Bronx, she had a class of thirty-six black and white first graders in a classroom devoid of art materials, puzzles, or creative play materials. The children, mostly under six, were required to sit in chairs in formal rows. The protocol of the school system was so rigid that she was not allowed to begin reading instruction until a student passed the sixth birthday. Despite the fact she had been trained at the educational clinic of the City College of New York—one of only a handful of such training programs in the City at that time—and was prepared to develop a curriculum suited to each child's particular needs, "in order to teach phonics to those children who needed it, I had to lock my door and not let the principal see me." During the previous summer, "black families had moved into a project that fed into our elementary school," and, as a result, "this school, which had previously been all white, now had a handful of black children in each class." "The teachers were so antagonistic to these black children," Karp said. "They talked very openly about them in very denigrating terms as inferior and, most shocking, even used the term 'garbage' in referring to some of these children." Her experience taught her "how rigid the Board of Ed could be, how poorly trained teachers were for work in teaching reading and finally the kind of racism, subtle and not so subtle, that existed among the teachers in the public schools and how this impacted on children."[55] Whereupon Karp had written to Northside and thus began a relationship that was to last thirty-nine years.

Bea Levison also felt a special affinity for Northside in part because her husband, Stanley, worked as a civil rights attorney and was a close friend and advisor to Martin Luther King Jr.: "The whole background of interest in the civil rights movement, my husband's work, made [Northside] even that much more attractive to me because . . . I felt that I was . . . participating in what was one of the most decisive and critical areas in the country at this point: the needs of the underprivileged children who were not getting what they needed in school or at home and Northside seemed to offer all of this."[56]

Northside presented "an incredible contrast to my public school experience," Jeanne Karp recalls. "First of all, whereas in public school the staff consisted of all white teachers in their fifties or older, Northside had a young dynamic staff, very diverse in background, and all committed to helping children." Through staff meetings, informal conversations in the hallways, and in conferences organized by Stella Chess and Mamie Clark, the staff developed a way of working together "so different from the isolation that took place in the teaching situation I was previously in." "In contrast to the public school situation I experienced where the children were indelibly labelled as inferior or emotionally disturbed and were treated as such throughout their school experience at Northside we shared a belief that each child had potential and that it was up to us to bring about improvement in the most effective manner." [57]

At Northside, Karp found children with a wide range of social, emotional, and educational problems. Her first students were all boys, aged ten to twelve, "sad, troubled children." The "children were not only unhappy at home, but were experiencing failure at school" and "saw themselves as stupid." Many of them were four to five years behind grade level.[58] They came to Northside without any of the "basic things . . . they should have gotten from school and were capable of learning," as Bea Levison recalls. Jeanne Karp saw Northside as providing "a special experience" for such children because it afforded "an opportunity to work with an adult who cares for them, listens to them, and helps them learn." [59] Through remedial therapy, Northside sought to give each child insight into individual difficulties: to stimulate a desire to learn, and to restore the child's self-confidence. The program was "very unusual in a clinic setting" because it depended on a one-on-one approach "equivalent to the private tutoring middle class families provided for their children at high fees." [60] It was also consistent with Northside's clinical orientation, offering a form of psychologically based therapy.

The Clarks and the remedial staff agreed that, for every child they were able to help, a hundred more were falling farther behind. Together they sought to confront the cynical view of many teachers and administrators alike that nothing could be done to help African-American children, developing programs to demonstrate that children's performance in school could be improved with a modest investment of educators' time and effort. From 1955 to 1964, Northside provided intensive remedial reading tutoring daily for one month each summer. The results were dramatic. The children made average gains of eight months in oral reading skills, the equivalent of almost a full school year's improvement. It was clear that even with a brief period of daily remedial education the children could make significant improvements in reading. Such results confirmed Mamie Clark's and Jeanne Karp's conviction that children could learn to read if taught properly.[61] "Long before it was fashionable," Kenneth Clark recalled a decade later, "a remedial reading program was developed which gradually expanded without medical domination and . . . even without clinical psychologists' domination. . . . This to me is one of the most important things that Northside has contributed to expanding the concept of mental health and therapy in its thirty years: namely, to give youngsters certain kinds of skills which the public schools have denied them and to give them those skills within the context of respecting their humanity and helping them to accept themselves as human beings worthy of respect and love."[62]

Northside also initiated an experiment outside the center at JHS 43 at 129th Street and Amsterdam Avenue, working with the schools' teaching staff. Borrowing from the example of Northside's staff culture, the plan sought to help participating students and teachers feel part of a special enterprise by providing smaller classes, remediation, extra counseling, and greater parental involvement in the school and in the educational process itself. It, too, achieved dramatic results: "six times as many students went to college (25 percent) than had earlier (4 percent). The dropout rate fell one-half, from 50 percent to 25 percent. Eighty-one percent were judged to have greater intellectual capacity than their earlier I.Q. and achievement scores would have predicted. . . . The 'miracle' seemed due primarily to an implementation of the belief that such children can learn."[63]

The success of the JHS 43 experiment depended fundamentally on a commitment of resources and money. Yet, when it was expanded in 1959 to eighteen other schools in what was called the Higher Horizons program, the amount of money allocated per student by the board of education was drastically reduced. The original program spent above $250 per pupil: Higher Horizons spent $40. When students failed to benefit from the Higher Horizons program, assumptions regarding the inability of African-American children to learn, already rampant in the white population and among professionals, resurfaced, fueling resistance to future systematic efforts to invest tax dollars in black children.

The experience with these early attempts to boost educational achievement led Northside to initiate broader efforts. In 1962, Northside applied to the Field Foundation and to the New York Foundation for funds to allow the center to expand its intensive daily remedial program to children in the public schools who were not Northside clients. The grants were used to work with average or above-average students from neighboring elementary and junior high schools in Harlem who were two to four years behind in reading.[64] Again, student achievement improved dramatically with the one-to-one daily tutoring and attention the Northside staff provided. But, once again, when students "left the program, they stopped making progress."[65]

The contrast between Northside's successes with individual students and the continuing deterioration of test scores among the vast majority of children in Harlem's public schools led Karp and others at Northside to propose a dramatic break with past practice within the public school system. Karp recalls a central question: "If children could make the kind of progress they were making in our reading program, why weren't they making progress in school with all the time they spent there?" It was evident to Karp, with her almost twenty years' experience teaching children to read, that these children could be educated and also that most of their families heartily supported efforts to help them. However, remedial efforts alone could not adequately address the reality that 85 percent of Harlem's youngsters were continuing to fall behind their white peers in public schools south of Harlem on the East Side and West Side of Central Park. Warning the board of education that "time was running out," Karp rejected "part-time after-school, or weekend remedial programs" as too little and much too late. She felt it was necessary to address the inadequacy of the school system as one would address any natural disaster—by mobilizing all of the city's resources to save and aid those in desperate need.[66]

In 1965, Karp called for a Reading Mobilization Year, recommending replacement of the normal public school curriculum for an entire year with an intensive remedial reading program in which reading would be the essential tool taught, no matter what subject the students were taking. The emphasis would be on reading, on learning to read and understanding. Despite inclusion of the recommendation in Kenneth Clark's *Dark Ghetto* and despite year after year of agitation by Karp, by the Clarks, and by the center's board for city adoption of this emergency plan, their calls fell on deaf ears at the board of education.

The frustration of African-American parents with the unwillingness of the New York City Board of Education to invest in Harlem's children crested in early 1964 when nearly half of the city's school population "stayed home during a one-day boycott protesting *de facto* segregated schools." *Time* magazine called this action "the biggest civil rights demonstration in U.S. history";

the board of education dismissed it as "a fizzle." James B. Donovan, then the board's president, told the press that the board would not respond to the demand for integration or for busing. "This is not a board of integration," Donovan remarked, "or a board of transportation."[67]

Northside was not directly involved in the school boycott. The staff felt pulled between its professional commitment to work with the schools and its outrage at the pervasive racism and low expectations that marked the professional culture both at the central board of education and in the neighborhood schools. Norman Wyloge, then in Northside's social work department and later to become a therapist, tells of one child who brought a comic book to school; his classmates made off with it, a trivial incident that nonetheless escalated. The teacher had "retrieved and destroyed [the comic book] ignoring the protests of [the student] that it was his book." When the student "asked for the pieces of the book back" because, as Wyloge said, he was "an extremely deprived child," the teacher "called him 'crazy'" in front of the whole class, hitting him with her pointer. In retaliation, the boy called her a "bitch" and, as a result, "was put on a five-day suspension." Wyloge went to the school to talk to the teacher, who, again in front of the entire class, said in a loud voice that the student was "crazy." It was apparent that the student was anything but. The boy told Wyloge the teacher "just doesn't care!!" In a letter Mamie Clark alerted the superintendent of the district to "a situation in P.S. #179, Manhattan which is destructive for one of our children and which we believe to be destructive for many more children in your school."[68]

Treating the 150 to 200 children who came to the center each year could not be meaningful, Northside believed, without the center joining a much larger effort to help the thousands of other Harlem children languishing in public school classrooms everyday. Northside "redoubled its search for new ways to apply its professional skills toward the betterment of the functioning of the community as a whole." In 1965, it developed a "model program" to show that "an attitude of mutual respect and emotional responsiveness between the teacher and the student is of primary importance in the motivational process towards learning." It would also address the "emotional factors operating in the teacher-student confrontation." "Northside's central focus," noted a report on the program, "is, and always has been, the development of the healthy emotional and intellectual resources of the children." It would provide guidance, support, and therapy to teachers in small groups, in the belief that negative attitudes toward the children could be overcome and, in turn, lead to a better learning environment. At Northside as well as within the larger Harlem community, emphasis shifted away from the pathology of an individual child and began to emphasize the ways in which race and racism affected teachers' ability to teach.[69]

The model program was initiated in 1965 as a result of a request for help from Seymour Gang, himself white, the principal of PS 192, an elementary school on the edge of central Harlem adjacent to the City College campus. With Gang's help, Northside developed psychiatric and psychological seminars for the school's teachers, provided direct educational services for the children, and initiated parent discussion groups. Donald Watt, a psychiatrist on leave from the Community Psychiatry Division of Columbia University's School of Public Health, headed the psychiatric training sessions for the teachers; Edna Meyers, head of Northside's psychology department, organized a "how-to-think" program for the children; and Olivia Edwards, of Northside's social work department, developed a parent group. The overall goal was to develop "a Mental Health Program for the Enhancement of the Educational Process in the Public Schools" and to develop ways of using professional personnel "more efficiently."[70]

But, almost immediately, differences arose over the goals and direction of the PS 192 program. Gang and Watt envisioned a community psychiatry program more than an educational or community development activity. They wanted to improve the relationship between students and teachers by sensitizing teachers to the "emotional interaction occurring between them and individual students." Northside staff considered this too narrow a definition of community psychiatry. Olivia Edwards complained to Mamie Clark about the "serious implications for the future . . . as psychiatrists move more and more into community psychiatry." She worried that "all we have done in community work will be absorbed or forgotten."[71] Edna Meyers, Kenneth Clark, and even the center's chief psychiatrist, Paul Benedict, who had succeeded Albert Bryt in 1960, all agreed with Edwards that the traditional child guidance faith in psychiatry could not alone address the real issues of the nature of the schools; professional resistance to change; poverty and its impact on parents and children; and the pervasive powerlessness of children and parents. Lack of attention to these issues would undermine whatever benefits could be achieved by psychological counseling.[72]

"A Strategy of Despair": The Development of Community Control

As Harlem's residents faced the unwillingness of the city's political structure to address seriously the de facto segregation and poor services of the city's minority neighborhoods, they began to see integration, as a means of redressing the inequalities of the public school system, as virtually impossible to attain. One dramatic event that galvanized the Harlem community undermined the older faith in integration as social policy. This was the controversy over the opening of a new Harlem junior high school, Intermediate School 201.

IS 201, one of the first middle schools to be built in Harlem in decades, became the focus of intense controversy as soon as it became apparent that it was almost certain to be an all-black and Hispanic school. For years, the Clarks and others—not to exclude the U.S. Supreme Court—had argued that only by integrating the public schools could high quality education be attained, a rejection of the "separate but equal" theory of the 1896 decision, *Plessy* v. *Ferguson*. Indeed, initially, the board of education had maintained that IS 201 would be integrated by attracting to it white students from the Bronx and Queens, pointing to the school's prospective location on 127th Street at Madison, easily accessible to the Triborough Bridge. Board president Donovan said that IS 201's "superior" facilities would naturally attract white students. But despite such assurances, by 1966, as the *New York Times* reported, many in Harlem had "lost confidence in the . . . board," believing that its promises were merely a ploy to get the school open, again as a segregated institution.[73] The board, a Harlem community newspaper maintained, "had no intention of fulfilling its moral and legal mandate to integrate I.S. 201." Coming at the same time that "Black Power" advocates were attracting media attention nationwide and were forcing a public debate on the limitations of integration as a means to full equality, IS 201 became a flashpoint for simmering angers and frustrations. Built as a boxlike fortress without any windows, the school was a symbol of and testament to the board of education's disdain for the community and its people. A call for "community control" over this soon-to-be all-minority, poor children's school began. A Harlem parents' group, The Harlem Parents Committee, asserted that "if the school MUST be *segregated*, then [the] community MUST have a *decisive* voice in determining the school's *program, Staff,* and *evaluation.*"[74] Initially, the only request from community activists had been for the right of a community board to select the principal, a request rejected by the board of education, leading to broader community demands to select teachers and control budgets.

Until 1966, the struggle ranged the city's board of education against a variety of African-American community groups. Kenneth Clark introduced a plan he hoped would reconcile the forces in the board with community activists in Harlem: "that the Board of Education invite two or more universities in the New York City area to conduct the educational program in IS 201 and its present feeder schools." The "universities should consult with and involve the parents and appropriate community representatives in setting up [a community advisory] board which would develop and operate the educational programs of these schools." This board would consist of nine members, four from the university community, four from the "parent-community," and one "selected jointly by these eight."[75] The appeal of the plan was its ensuring the community a degree of autonomy while assuaging fears of the city's political leadership that community boards would become an independent power base. Respected academics would sit alongside parents and community residents, presumably guaranteeing a degree of moderation, sophistication, as well as knowledge and accountability for decisions on personnel and budgetary matters. Even the board, intent on avoiding a prolonged and potentially explosive boycott, went along with the plan as did the IS 201 parents, local civil rights organizations as divergent as the Student Non-Violent Coordinating Committee (SNCC), the NAACP, and the Congress of Racial Equality (CORE), as well as Mayor John Lindsay and the *New York Times*. But almost immediately, the New York United Federation of Teachers, under Albert Shanker, saw in this plan a threat to its ability to protect its members from partisan community decisions. The federation quickly sought to quash this proposal; as a consequence, the board of education opposed it.

In the following months, as sit-ins and boycotts brought the community control debate to the front page of newspapers, Mayor John Lindsay came to see the issue as possible leverage for more funds from the state treasury for the city's board of education.[76] If the administration of the city's schools were broken up into numerous local districts, the mayor's office believed, more state money to the city would need to be allocated. In late April 1967, Lindsay established an Advisory Panel on Decentralization of New York City Schools, with McGeorge Bundy, recently retired as President Lyndon Johnson's National Security Advisor and now head of the Ford Foundation, as chair. Simultaneously, the Ford Foundation provided planning funds for three experimental programs in community control: IS 201 district in Harlem, a Two Bridges project on Manhattan's lower east side, and the Ocean Hill–Brownsville district in Brooklyn.

The dissipation of school activists' confidence in integration as the best means of addressing the obvious inequalities in the public schools in the years between 1964 and the fall of 1968 is, in retrospect, remarkable. Diane Ravitch wrote in 1974 that in 1964, the City-Wide Committee for Integrated Schools, under Reverend Milton Galamison [a Brooklyn activist minister], wanted to see the school system destroyed because of its unwillingness to break the neighborhood school pattern. Little more than two years later, Galamison wanted to see it destroyed in order to achieve total local control. By the end of 1966, many of those who had most passionately advocated integration and overriding of local parent organizations had been converted to the cause of community control of the schools, even though it meant abandonment of school integration.[77]

Yet, far from being a callous abandonment of a principled goal by African-American community leaders, the change was, in fact, an implicit acknowledgment of the larger society's failure to even try integration. Kenneth Clark, perhaps the nation's most prominent proponent of integration in public education, reflecting on the resistance to integration that had led him, too, to call for community control, said at the time, "Most of those in the minority communities who are now fighting for community control have been consistent fighters for integration. . . . Their support for decentralization is not, therefore, to be seen in terms of a desire for separatism or a rejection of integration, but . . . it is a strategy of despair determined by the broken promises of the white community." Clark recalled that over the years white families had abandoned the city's public schools and even the city itself in order to avoid true integration. Public officials had used their political power and authority to maintain segregation through gerrymandering of district lines and the location of new schools "in segregated neighborhoods." While he himself refused to abandon the long-range goal of integration, he supported "the demand for community control" as "primarily a desperate attempt [by African-American parents] to protect their children in the schools they are required to attend."[78]

By the fall of 1967, the Ford Foundation's experimental Ocean Hill–Brownsville district, under district superintendent Rhody McCoy, appeared ready to put its program of community control into action. But, a constellation of events presaged a tremendous upheaval a year later throughout the city. At the opening of the school year, a two-week strike was called by the New York United Federation of Teachers over wages and a host of other traditional grievances. In the entire city, only the three demonstration districts stayed open, thus exacerbating the existing tensions and distrust between the teachers and the community boards in minority communities. In the spring of 1968 following this strike, and just after the assassination of the Reverend Martin Luther King Jr. and the subsequent rioting in many U.S. cities, superintendent McCoy tested the district's autonomy by seeking to reassign nineteen teachers whom the local board had identified as ineffective and disruptive, ordering them to report instead to the central board of education headquarters at 110 Livingston Street in downtown Brooklyn, not to the Ocean Hill–Brownsville schools. In the process, McCoy gained the personal enmity of Shanker, president of the teachers' federation, and of most of the teachers in the federation. By the end of the academic year in 1968 it was clear that the United Federation of Teachers had targeted community control and the related demonstration projects as a threat to its power and position within the city's educational and political hierarchy.[79]

The struggle over the school system stripped away many of the layers of rhetoric and moral righteousness in the city, especially within the liberal white community that had allied itself with the civil rights movement, if more in the South than in the North (Albert Shanker was among many white New Yorkers who marched in Selma, Alabama, the previous year). In the strike, the primarily Jewish United Federation of Teachers had come up against much of the African-American political, intellectual, and religious leadership. Although the southern civil rights movement had allowed these groups to work together, the struggle for integration closer to home, as in the campaign for community control in New York, tore this coalition apart. Because of Kenneth Clark's own long involvement in the desegregation effort of the 1950s and 1960s, he understood perhaps better than anyone the centrality of education in the broader struggle for equality and political power. In the midst of the school decentralization struggle in 1968, Clark's Metropolitan Applied Research Corporation (MARC), its headquarters near the affluent heart of the East Side at 75th Street between Madison and Park Avenues, organized a conference to discuss the future of Northside. Kenneth Clark asked each of the participants at the Delmonico Hotel meeting to address the central issue that had emerged from the school strike: "How do neglected, rejected, dehumanized people protect themselves in this crucial area called education, which controls the destiny of their children?" He maintained that "it is a fact that whoever controls the educational system controls the destiny of the people." Rather than interpreting the southern and northern integration movements as simply a moral or religious crusade, Clark wanted it made clear that the desegregation struggle was really about "the need to increase the quality of education, and to make it possible . . . for oppressed people to throw off the yoke of oppression."[80]

"Well, you know what happened to [the civil rights] struggle. Seeking to throw off the yoke of oppression through that path was severely defeated, not only by bigots, but by liberals," Kenneth Clark noted. This resulted in "seeking another path of trying to throw off the yoke, mainly through control . . . accepting the fact that when other people control those schools they were criminal in their destruction of children." He argued that community control was simply an attempt by parents to "assume the responsibility for controlling these schools, so that we can increase the quality of education for these children." Reflecting the pragmatism that, along with idealism, marked much of his analysis over the years, Clark held that "if there is any hope of changing [educational opportunities], it will have to be changed by the instruments of power." Such struggles were not likely to be fought politely in traditional academic, legislative, or institutional arenas. Rather "people who do not have the usual instruments of power available to them, and who are chronically frustrated in trying to make certain institutions be responsive to their needs . . . [do not have available to them] techniques which are comfortable to people such as those of us in this room."[81]

It was clear that "if you're going to change [the school system] you're not going to change it by pious requests. You're not going to change it by reports; you're not going to change it by clinical diagnosis." Clark challenged the audience of psychiatrists, social workers, local politicians, and Northside staff to formulate new models for the role and place of a community mental health center in the highly charged political environment of Harlem. "How can an agency of specialists really contribute systematically to the realistic problems of people whose interests are generally ignored, people who are generally subjected to flagrant or subtle forms of contempt and dehumanization."[82]

In 1968, Northside and the Metropolitan Applied Research Center became deeply involved in the movement to empower parents through the community control and decentralization struggles. In June, Kenneth Clark and Hylan Lewis, professor of sociology at Brooklyn College and vice president of MARC, realized after a meeting with the Ocean Hill–Brownsville governing board that "indigenous parents and community representatives needed an organization to protect their rights just as teachers and supervisors have organizations to protect their interests in the system." During the summer, Kenneth Clark and his MARC staff decided to promote a Union of Concerned Parents to empower "people now ignored and otherwise abused because they are unable to mobilize the requisite forces to reach their goals." To Clark, the group would represent "a systematic and carefully considered approach to achieving a mass-based mechanism that will allow parents and youths in deprived communities to define and articulate their educational interests and to get results."[83] After the start of the school strike in September, the Union of Concerned Parents placed ads in the New York Times and the Amsterdam News in support of the Ocean Hill–Brownsville community board. The advertisement was signed by many of Harlem's leaders, including authors Leroi Jones and James Baldwin, architect Max Bond, psychiatrist June Jackson Christmas (later to become head of New York City's Department of Mental Health), James Dumpson (then welfare commissioner), Seymour Gang (principal of PS 192), Charles Rangel, singer Nina Simone, Percy Sutton (Manhattan's borough president), and Livingston Wingate, (Adam Clayton Powell's protégé and Clark's successor at Harlem Youth Opportunities, Inc. [HARYOU], the antipoverty program he headed in the early 1960s, see chapter 6). It argued that "the primary issue is—and always was—providing for minority group children. . . . It has been fashionable for the educational bureaucracy to complain that ghetto parents were 'apathetic' about the education of their children. This alleged apathy was given as an excuse for the failure to teach these children. Now that these parents are aroused with a concern for the education of their children, the educational establishment now threatens to defeat them."[84]

Northside was central to the Union of Concerned Parents' early organizing efforts. Mamie Clark became the original secretary-treasurer, convening its first meetings and leading its early membership drives. Northside's address and offices became the union's headquarters. Working on the principle that community control and decentralization would be "a kind of empty form unless we rapidly develop people at many levels who can respectively play the roles that are called for in local school boards," the Union of Concerned Parents sought to become a "political apparatus" aimed at lobbying and planning activities to empower parents in low-income areas throughout the city: "We . . . have this arm at Northside, and what we're talking about is ` developing it all over the city, and when we have it all in shape it will be something that will be known throughout the city as a union equally as powerful as the United Federation of Teachers, a union that we are calling the Union of Concerned Parents." This was the Clarks' hope.[85]

The parents' union never achieved that broadest objective of a countervailing grassroots organization to the teachers' federation. It was, almost immediately, plagued by practical problems brought on by its initial successes. Shortly after publication of the advertisement in the Times and Amsterdam

News, the Northside offices were swamped with letters, contributions, and inquiries that virtually immobilized the secretarial help loaned to the operation by Northside and MARC. These newspaper advertisements generated tremendous interest but nearly bankrupt the poorly funded organization. A January 1969 mass meeting that attracted hundreds to the New York Theological Seminary downtown ended without a clear statement of organizational direction, goals, or program.[86]

Although the Union of Concerned Parents was unable to establish chapters throughout the city, Olivia Edwards, Elaine Gaspard, and Mary Hester, a parent at Northside, and Northside staff established "one of the first and most active chapters." Between February and May 1969, Northside's Chapter Two was the most active local group. Those involved with Northside's chapter were deeply impressed by Mamie Clark's early position that empowerment was central to Northside's own mission.[87] At a meeting in January 1969, Isadore Zwerling, a psychiatrist at the Bronx State Hospital and a long-time ally of the Clarks, observed, "Aside from the issue of its [UCP's] effectiveness politically, as a purely clinical device, if I were serving the area Mamie's clinic serves, I would want to foster a union of concerned parents as a mental health device for beginning to make people act in a way which will help to control their own destiny." Such activity "goes beyond the more formal diagnostic work-up and therapeutic effort." He hoped that the clinic would "serve . . . as a kind of seed for crystallizing out community impulses." In the light of the earlier efforts of Northside's board to limit the center's work to psychiatry, this comment was particularly relevant. Leonard Duhl, a professor of education at the University of California at Berkeley, even suggested that Northside should abandon all labels that tended to box it into traditional categories. "I'm not sure that Northside should [be] a mental health center. I think what we're talking about is a comprehensive human service center . . . [that] operate[s] on many levels. There are times you operate on the individual level, but the individual level should only give you clues to how you should operate on a much broader level, which is the level of power—political power."[88]

The IQ Controversy and Northside's "Think" Program

As Northside reformulated its mission to address broader needs of the Harlem community, it encountered a formidable challenge from what some must have considered the most unlikely place—the academic world. In 1968, a movement of intellectuals and academics brought into the open a lingering racism and hostility in the context of seemingly unbiased, scientific, and apolitical evaluation of the relative intelligence of African Americans and whites. Historically, psychological tests, specifically the Wechsler Intelligence Scale for Children (WISC), had been used to establish what were generally assumed to be "fixed" measurements of intelligence. In the years of World War II, in part as a reaction to the racial theories undergirding Nazi eugenics policies, many psychologists—some of them refugees from Germany—had challenged not only the notion of fixed intelligence but also the professional presumption that a verbal test could measure such a complex and poorly understood concept as intelligence. IQ was not, they said, an identifiable, measurable, immutable, or genetic characteristic of the individual, let alone of any group, such as Jews or Negroes. Further, culture, class, and environment explained observed differences between races, as they could explain individual differences within races (if, indeed, "race" itself was a defensible category scientifically at all).

By the late-1960s, however, in the wake of the social turmoil and disaffection that accompanied the late civil rights movement, a few psychologists and educators had begun to argue that the lack of measurable economic progress by African Americans during the 1960s could be explained by genetic factors. One of the prime pieces of evidence cited in this academic war by authors such as Arthur Jensen, professor of education, at the University of California at Berkeley, and Richard Hernnstein, professor of psychology at Harvard, was that average test scores of African-American youth were lower than whites. This focus on IQ testing was part of a much wider, scholarly attack against some of the more progressive aspects of the 1960s War on Poverty and the Great Society programs. Head Start, the Office of Economic Opportunity, funding for minority college scholarships, affirmative action programs of various sorts, had been rooted in the assumption that differences between African-American and white achievement in the country was attributable, in large part, to social, environmental, and historical oppression. By the late 1960s, however, certain academics maintained that African Americans, far from being at a disadvantage, had received too many special privileges. This white backlash seized on evidence offered and theories attributed to perceived differences in IQ between groups as "objective" proof of the fallacy of the environmental argument. Social programs could not, they argued, compensate for what they regarded as essentially innate and genetic inferiority.

Unbeknownst to scholars and the public alike, this new attack on environmental explanations for differences in "intelligence" was supported by a small wealthy foundation in New York that had, since 1937, backed research focused on genetic differences. In the 1950s and 1960s, the founder of this Pioneer Fund, Wyclyffe P. Draper, heir to a Massachusetts textile machinery fortune, funded groups that sought to establish a link between genetics, race, and intelligence. Board members included James O. Eastland, a pro-segregationist U.S. Senator from Mississippi; Henry E. Garrett, the professor of psychology who had been Mamie Clark's advisor at Columbia, and who testified for the defendants in the pre-*Brown* civil rights cases, and who the *New York Times* identified in 1977 as "an educator known for his belief in the genetic inferiority of blacks"; and Representative Francis E. Walter, chair of the House Committee on Un-American Activities. The Fund's impact had been relatively limited, no doubt because of the strong intellectual resistance to the eugenics movement earlier in the century, associated in its ideological theories with the subsequent horrors that accompanied the rise of German fascism. But the Pioneer Fund's impact was boosted in the late 1960s and in the 1970s when the beneficiaries of its largesse, among them Arthur Jensen; William Shockley, a Stanford University professor of physics, who had recently won the Noble Prize; and certain others began to find a more receptive public and academic audience.[89]

The appearance of Jensen's article on "How Much Can We Boost IQ and Scholarly Achievement?" in a *Harvard Educational Review* issue of 1969 seemed to give the cloak of legitimacy to his views on the inherent inferiority of African Americans. It was given further credence by a "scientific" statistical reanalysis of data gathered by other psychologists and educators. Kenneth Clark was greatly concerned about the potential impact on educators, administrators, policymakers, and the broader public, many of whom lacked the training or familiarity with such statistical claims to evaluate Jensen's work. Kenneth Clark, then president of the Metropolitan Applied Research Center, decided to "convene a small meeting of authorities to discuss the scientific and policy implications of the resurgence of this point of view," especially focusing on the view that compensatory programs like Head Start were failing and that investment in education for minority youth was wasted money. "Jensen's position has been consistent with the reduction of compensatory programs in education, a slowdown in school desegregation and an increase in white attitudes of superiority. In addition," Clark wrote, "teachers who apply Jensen's recommendations will abandon their efforts to impart the necessary symbolic skills and will stress only rote learning for minority groups pupils."[90]

Clark pointed out that Jensen's theories were consistent with past theories based on assumptions of racial inferiority, his "statistical apparatus notwithstanding." "Because the concept of race itself is so elusive for certain distinct physical characteristics," he maintained that "genetic differences identifiable by race have so far proved impossible to determine." Even if one could determine racial differences, African Americans themselves could be identified not as "a biological or 'racial' entity" but as "a socially defined group with common characteristics generated by social and institutional exclusiveness [which] has existed for too brief a time to develop any meaningful genetic character by inbreeding."[91]

The reemergence of the hereditarian argument was especially painful to the Northside staff, a number of whom had engaged in a long struggle to abolish use of IQ (or other) testing to label certain children as retarded and to relegate them on that basis to inferior education in the Harlem public schools. One of its very first struggles in the 1940s with the Harlem schools was to challenge the New York City Board of Education's reliance on IQ tests to diagnose children as retarded. In that struggle, the skills of the Clarks as psychologists had a central role and a real public policy implication. The psychology department at Northside did interpret results of WISC IQ tests, which it administered to its child clients as a means of evaluating their strengths and weaknesses. The public schools, however, used the low test scores rather as evidence that children were unable to learn. Edna Meyers, the head of Northside's psychology department, used IQ tests as a tool of treatment and to assess prior school placements: "Because of the importance of challenging the results of group IQ tests which in the inner city community provided a high population for the CRMD classes and no population at all for the AGC [Academically Gifted Children] classes, Northside [gave] each child referred to it an individual IQ test." Over the course of eighteen years, Meyers estimated that Northside tested more than two thousand children. "The conclusion all our psychologists arrived at during this period was: 1. many of the children's responses, scored as wrong according to the manual, were the result of forethought, foreknowledge and experience, and that therefore should have been given credit." Unlike many in the discipline of psychology who considered IQ as immutable, Northside started with the assumption that the IQ test could be used as a guide for a specialized and individualized educational program that could, in most cases, lead to improvement in IQ scores. "Have we the temerity," Meyers asked, "to transform the concept of the intelligence test into a teaching procedure?"[92] Far from immutable, IQ improved with education.

Meyers, one of the few whites on the staff who had lived in Harlem, had been born on East 97th Street, later moving to "a better neighborhood" on 127th Street between Madison and Park Avenue, a neighborhood that was almost entirely Irish. There, she had felt the pain of discrimination through her experience as a Jew in a then overwhelmingly Catholic community— "they made my life very miserable calling me a 'kike.'" When African Americans moved into the area after the start of World War I, the Irish "moved out very quickly," and "by the time we left 127th Street we were the last white family in the apartment house, and it had all become black and they were our friends." When she came to Northside in the late 1940s, she was not being "introduced to a strange society. I belonged there. I felt Harlem was my country, too."[93]

Meyers's approach is reflected in a paper she prepared for an American Psychological Association conference in 1974:

> Our communities need community psychologists whose skills transcend academic training, whose insights begin where the manuals leave off, and who are possessed of the unbudgable conviction that we are dealing with an intelligent population and that our job is not to test, nor to investigate, but also to teach and to learn how to teach.
>
> We have to radicalize our approach to testing, not by eliminating an individualized IQ battery entirely . . . but by limiting ourselves from the strictures placed on us by manuals or academicians. We owe this not to ourselves or our professional stance, but more importantly to the community who for all these years have suffered from our limitations and our rigidities.[94]

Meyers cited the works of Alexander Luria, a respected Soviet psychologist and neurophysiologist, who had written and lectured extensively that the IQ test should not be used to measure "fixed intelligence" but rather as a diagnostic tool to evaluate areas of strength and weakness. Using concepts developed by Lev Vigotsky in *Thought and Language,* in Piaget's theories of child development, Meyers constructed what became known at the center as the "Do Your Own Think" program. Preceded by five years of formal and informal trials, the program began in earnest in 1968 and continued for over a decade. It sought to develop analytic skills and abstract thought processes, "providing the disadvantaged child with a type of free-wheeling, 'brain-storming' intellectual stimulation that departs significantly from typical compensatory educational programs." It went beyond tutorial services to empower parents and paraprofessionals, who, in turn, would be "trained in the use of, and the development of, non-curricula, fun-and-games materials, designed to foster concrete acquaintance with abstract cognitive processes as a means of affecting positively the self-esteem and behavior" of children. Verbal games, cartoons, and puzzles developed intellectual curiosity about language and ideas as well as analytic skills and abstract reasoning.[95]

The Think program was born of the same observation that had inspired the philosophy of Northside, when the staff "noticed that the children being tested were brighter than their scores indicated [and] that their comprehension of ideas were far in advance of their skill with phonics." From Meyers's perspective, "their lively brains were hungry for a playful exchange of ideas [and] that, removed from school subjects, . . . children *enjoyed* thinking, *enjoyed* learning [and] had creative ideas." She concluded that the children Northside saw "*could* think, but nobody seemed really interested enough in finding out how well, or how much better they could do." [96]

Meyers, almost single-handedly, encouraged groups of parents, teachers, and staff to make use of materials she had developed. After most sessions they prepared written evaluations of what worked and what didn't. Typical of the responses of mothers was: "I can't stop now. . . . He wants to know more now that he knows he has a brain. He even talks more and asks more questions." [97]

Edna Meyers's "Do Your Own Think" program had been tested and perfected within the center on select groups of clients, but by the early 1970s it expanded and moved into schools and community organizations throughout the area around Northside. Meyers organized Think programs at five schools, including one program for Spanish-speaking parents in East Harlem.[98]

The remedial reading department under Jeanne Karp also had to deal with the resurgence of racially based assumptions about children's abilities. The reality was that, as a small center in Harlem, Northside could not counter the power the city's board of education had historically refused to Harlem residents. Hence, Karp and Northside decided on a two-pronged approach for Northside: on the one hand, continue to work with community groups outside of the formal institutions of the school system; on the other hand, bypass the board of education and work directly with teachers. Turning Jensen's argument on its head, Karp called for more involvement with Harlem's school children rather than less. The problem was not that there were too many programs and that they had failed, but that there were virtually no programs and those that did exist were inadequately funded. "With the reading scores of the children in our school districts the lowest in the city—it is our belief that only a broad range program, such as teacher-education can improve this situation." [99]

Undergirding what came to be known as "Clinic-in-the-Classroom" was an innovative program designed to bring the skills of Northside's reading specialists directly to the classroom teacher. Northside had come to the conclusion that one of the "fundamental reasons for the education gap" was "the inadequate pre-service and in-service training of teachers and the lack of availability in schools of specialists in the areas of reading and learning disabilities." Clinic-in-the-Classroom, Karp wrote, provided observations, demonstration lessons, assistance with classroom management problems, diagnosis of special learning problems with children, individual plans for children in classroom settings, teacher training, and assistance with special problems that children presented. Initiated in 1971, with a five-year grant from the New York Community Trust Fund, this program rewarded teachers for participating with in-service college credit for improving techniques in "reading instruction, the diagnosis of learning disabilities, and the planning of curriculum for children." After two years, fifty teachers in four public schools had taken part. [100]

From the beginning, Northside had been drawn into larger struggles around the place of education as a tool of repression and control. Indeed, it had been born as a response to the prevailing labeling of black children as stupid and had sought to undermine such ideas both through its remedial program and its wider concern with institutional change in the school system itself. The Clarks and Northside could not educate the children of Harlem without educating the white community whose power and preconceptions had shaped and dominated public and educational policy over the generations.

5. "The Child, the Family, and the City"

The Family as a Source of Dysfunction or Health

The Negro Family report published by the Office of Planning and Development of the U.S. Department of Labor in March 1965—"The Moynihan Report," as it came to be known—was released in November after months of private discussion and leaks in the popular press. It detailed the very real suffering of black Americans in urban centers; it ascribed the causes essentially to what Daniel P. Moynihan described as the "disintegration" of the black family in the experience of slavery. Much of the report was factual, providing data about unemployment, discrimination, and social statistics but incorporated unstated value judgments that were still being hotly debated in 1968, when the Northside Center and Children's Hospital teamed up for a seminar entitled "The Child, the Family, and the City." Moynihan pointed out, for example, that the high unemployment rate for African-American men "persisted at catastrophic levels since the first statistics were gathered in 1930" and that "one third of nonwhite children live in *broken* homes" (our emphasis), whereas only 10 percent of white children did.[1] As it happened, similar data had appeared in the 1964 Report of HARYOU ("Youth in the Ghetto: A Study of the Consequences of Powerlessness and a Blueprint for Change"), under Kenneth Clark's sponsorship.

In its own interpretation of these data, however, the Moynihan Report found the roots of urban decay, educational failure, and juvenile crime in the "matriarchal structure" of the black family and the absence of a male role model and wage-earner. Moynihan, previously a professor at Harvard and then an Assistant Secretary in the Department of Health, Education and Welfare, like a number of other liberal scholars had been writing on the "tangle of pathology" that marked the "Negro family" and suggested that the origin of this sickness was in the destruction of a strong family unit during slavery.[2] Because it pointed to the high "illegitimacy rate" of African-American women, especially among those in low-income groups, the report was interpreted by many black intellectuals and white political activists as a condemnation of the black family, rather than as a call for better educational or economic opportunities.[3] In the context of the rioting of 1965 in Newark,

Detroit, Los Angeles, and other northern cities and the white community's growing lack of sympathy—even antipathy—toward the goals and methods of the northern civil rights struggles, the Moynihan Report came to focus the nation's attention on what was wrong in the African-American community itself rather than on the sickness of racism.

The storm of protest that arose centered on what Harvard psychologist William Ryan found the underlying goal, that is, to "blame the victims" for their own suffering. Ryan, in an extensive article in the *Nation*, encapsulated what would emerge as a major critique of the report:

> The explanations [for black-white inequality] almost always focus on sup-posed defects of the Negro victim as if those—and not the racist struc-ture of American society—were the cause of all woes that Negroes suf-fer. The Moynihan Report, following this line of thinking, singles out the "unstable Negro family" as the cause of Negro inequality. But the statis-tics, as has been suggested, reflect current effects of contemporaneous discrimination. They are results, not causes. . . .
>
> If we are to believe the new ideologues, we must conclude that seg-regation and discrimination are not the terrible villains we thought they were. Rather, we are told the Negro's condition is due to his "pathology," his values, the way he lives, the kind of family he leads. The major qualification—the bow to egalitarianism—is that these conditions are said to grow out of the Negro's history of being enslaved and op-pressed—generations ago.
>
> It is all an ingenious way of "copping a plea" as the murderer pleads guilt of manslaughter to avoid a conviction that might lead to his being electrocuted, liberal America today is pleading guilty to the savagery and oppression against the Negro that happened one hundred years ago, in order to escape trial for the crimes of today.[4]

Although Kenneth Clark had initially not objected to Moynihan's Re-port—in *Newsweek* he endorsed it—he came to believe that it and other such commentaries were providing "public officials with rationalizations for re-gressive policies of malignant neglect," (a reference to "benign neglect") and thus had become "not only accessories to the perpetuation of injustices, . . . [but] indistinguishable from the active agents of injustice." He was greatly troubled that social scientists were abandoning their challenging of the sta-tus quo and subtly assuming a more regressive role. Referring to them in *Pathos of Power* in 1974 as a "new breed of social science mercenaries," he held "that they have supplanted the optimism, the drive for social change of the social scientists of the Allport era with their use of social science as a weapon for the maintenance of things-as-they-are." In contrast to some of the early social scientists who had sought to empower the poor, the new academics "align themselves with those with power and against the aspirations of the powerless victims of flagrant and subtle inequities."[5]

Kenneth Clark was particularly concerned because he himself had introduced the expression the "pathology of the ghetto" in the HARYOU document, published in 1964 and also in his book, *Dark Ghetto: Dilemmas of Social Power* (published the same year as the Moynihan Report), in which he had described the despair and hopelessness that had led to Harlem's high rates of drug abuse, delinquency, teen-age pregnancy, and truancy. But, his view of the origins of this social pathology lay in the destruction wrought by powerlessness, by the society's racism, and by economic and social dislocation. Kenneth Clark saw problems in the black family as a symptom of the American dilemma of racism.[6] In *Pathos of Power*, he wrote of his particular outrage with Moynihan and Harvard professors, who, he charged, had become "dependent upon the politicians for small consultant favors or public exposure" and, hence, "in spite of their scientific pretensions, are no more dependable in the quest for social justice than are other citizens." In their quest for "power, fame, and political influence" they had become, in actuality and in effect, "politicians, using scientific jargon, methodology, and computers in an attempt to disguise their essentially political role — a disguise facilitated by identification with a prestigious academic institution."[7] Referring to Moynihan's important role in both the Johnson and Nixon administrations, Clark characterized the subtle and not-so-subtle impact on academic thought of scholars from elite universities who doubled as policy advisors. He called this recent confusion of political and academic roles part of the "Moynihan Era," which "might be characterized as an era in which certain social scientists, . . . [who] will be resident liberals, social scientists whose main responsibility will be to explain or apologize for the actions of those who wield political and economic power."[8]

The Moynihan Report had had a significant impact on policy makers and intellectuals; they were interpreting Moynihan's analysis as meaning that white society could have only a limited impact on what were historically entrenched and self-generating pathologies within black families themselves. Moynihan's argument resonated especially strongly with psychologists and psychiatrists whose professional task it was to seek out and try to remedy pathologies of individuals and of family dynamics. For Freudian psychoanalysts, and for the family and group therapists, the family was the source of individual neurosis; treatment entailed a dissection and introspective examination of the social and sexual relationships between children, mothers, fathers, and siblings. Northside, in rejecting David Levy's and Albert Bryt's concept and the efforts to reformulate Northside as principally a psychiatric treatment program, had rejected major tenets of this psychoanalytic model, such as the assumption of individual pathology as rooted in familial relationships. While acknowledging that many dysfunctional relationships exist, the center had always seen in its families one of the few sources of strength and protection in an otherwise hostile and racist city. The family was, or could be, in the words of historian Christopher Lasch, a "haven in a heartless world."[9]

Although Northside was moving to reject the more restrictive tenets of psychoanalysis, it had not, by the early 1960s, found a viable and wholly coherent alternative therapeutic model. In 1960, Mamie Clark knew that the center could not "remain a traditional clinic"; it had to "move in a new direction."[10] The question was, what new direction would that be and what would its theoretical basis be? The staff had met demands of clients whose lives were in danger of crumbling under the weight of pressing social problems, with attendant consequences of very personal traumas. Victor Carter and Olivia Edwards, two of the center's most respected social workers, both African-American, noted that "many clinics would not accept the type of cases [that Northside did] as they would be considered untreatable."[11] Schools had to be dealt with, foster-care agencies placated, social-welfare service bureaucrats assuaged. Mamie Clark suggested that Northside's "children don't fit the APA's [American Psychiatric Association's] diagnostic and statistical manual of mental disorders."[12] But there were no comparable alternative agencies since other social-service groups had all but abandoned Harlem's children.[13] Over the course of the next few years, Northside would develop a therapeutic model that built on its original insight that sought in the family itself resources of hope and health.

The process of reformulation began simply enough in the latter months of 1964 and early 1965 when Mamie Clark, in meetings with Northside's staff, said that it was necessary both to avoid "pat interpretations" of a client's behavior and also to "adapt clinic procedure" to new realities. Poverty mandated the development of new theoretical conceptualizations and programmatic initiatives: therapists needed to examine how their own training, as well as their class and racial assumptions, might interfere with the therapeutic process. On the most basic level, she said, psychiatrists would interpret missed appointments as a form of client "resistance or lack of motivation." Such a view took no account of the reality of many poor clients' lives. Northside's staff had to learn to "provide carfare, case aides, babysitters in the clinic, a bus or car to pick up children" before assuming that personal intrapsychic issues were responsible for client behavior.[14]

Other "self-evident" traditional interpretations were equally inadequate in serving an impoverished clientele. Group therapy, for instance, was directed toward enabling children to "act out" when, in fact, it might be more helpful to use the group experience as a means of providing limits for some children. Also, for therapists to give children toys or food was traditionally viewed as interfering with treatment, yet, among children who had little, the simple act of giving allowed case workers to establish relationships more easily. Carfare, books, vitamins, toys, birthday gifts, and even food were natural expressions of caring that had an important and meaningful place in treatment. So, too, the use of psychological tests had to be rethought as indicators of clients' abilities or problems. In sum, the entire lexicon of terms and ideas on which the APA diagnostic categories rested had to be reexamined.[15]

Cultural Deprivation as a Rationale for Neglect

While poverty challenged traditional psychiatric treatment, race was even more confounding. Mamie Clark noted that the terms "underprivileged" and "deprived" had become code words in the educational and mental health literature for describing urban African-American and Puerto Rican youngsters who were "hard to reach." Racism had shaped the psychiatric and social-welfare literature about minority children; in addition to the general stereotypes of minorities as "lazy, dull, diseased, promiscuous," invidious analyses romanticized the "underprivileged child [as] more independent—[a] door key [latchkey] child can function on his own." The result of this was not only a merging of stereotypes, but also the construction of an "acceptable block against helping" that relieved professionals of any responsibility to develop "a fresh approach to [the] problem." Even worse, Clark feared that the new awareness of racism could lead, paradoxically, to acceptance of low school performance as normal. Just as genetic arguments had isolated and harmed black children in earlier decades, so theories of "cultural deprivation" could be just as crippling: she noted that some liberal educators were already legitimating low expectations for minority youth among teachers by claiming that the "deprived child suffers culture shock at entrance into school." [16]

Mamie Clark's critique of the terms "underprivileged" and "deprived" as applied to young children mirrored a broader critique of the "culture of poverty" argument as it affected minority and poor communities. In the late 1950s and 1960s, *The Children of Sanchez* and *La Vida* by Oscar Lewis, the anthropologist, popularized the view that poverty was something more than "economic deprivation . . . or the absence of something. . . . [It was a] way of life . . . passed down from generation to generation along family lines." [17] Although Lewis himself hoped to use his analysis as a mechanism for change, conservative analysts used it to bolster views of the intractability of poverty and as a justification for eliminating antipoverty programs. In response, liberal and radical analysts developed a wide-ranging critique of the "culture of poverty" argument that questioned its theoretical premise that culture is virtually inherited, and is the essential source of poverty. Rather than focus on the poor themselves, these critics maintained, analysts should look at the role of elites in denying opportunity to move out of poverty, and, as Michael Katz has written, focus on "economic justice and political mobilization." [18]

In March 1965, Mamie Clark called the staff together to distill the results of a series of meetings with staff that had focused on how they could "define our approach to treatment at Northside" and avoid the traps of the cultural deprivation analysis as it applied to children. Paul Benedict, Northside's director of clinical services and chief psychiatrist, summarized the ongoing formal discussions and informal debates: "There seemed to be major differences in approach, and even differences as to whether there should be differences." At the core of the disagreements were differing interpretations as to the true nature of their clients' problems, in general, and the importance of Northside's social analysis on individual treatment, in particular. What *was* the proper relationship between clinical one-on-one services, remedial services, and family services? What weight *should* be given in individual therapy to the socioeconomic condition of clients? Northside's social workers, psychiatrists, and other professionals showed a "marked disagreement as to whether one does (or should) modify his approach [to therapy] in dealing with socio-economically disadvantaged clients." There was a "range of opinion . . . from 'significantly' to 'little if any.'" [19] The staff believed that Northside could best serve the Harlem community as a center in which social services augmented—rather than fundamentally changed—how therapy was done.[20] Its concern that a reliance on traditional psychotherapy alone was inappropriate for Northside's children was reinforced by early conclusions from the center's ongoing study on the effectiveness of psychiatric intervention in reversing behavioral problems in early grade school-age children and their younger siblings. In the early 1960s, Northside had begun what it called the Problem Prevention in Primary Grades project, whose purpose was to identify children in danger of developing emotional or behavior problems, and, through group therapy and intensive follow-up with teachers and parents, to prevent the onset of behavioral or antisocial activities. Problem Prevention had a dual purpose: to provide general services to children and parents, and to sensitize the school system to the special needs of these families.

Funded by a grant from the National Institute of Mental Health, during the period when psychiatry was the primary influence among therapists at Northside, the Problem Prevention program sought to demonstrate the potential value of psychiatric intervention in young children,[21] but by 1965, when the preliminary results of the study were being tabulated and evaluated, psychiatry had lost much of its attraction for the staff. Nor did the preliminary results improve psychiatry's status. Although parents did seem to appreciate the group therapy sessions and the individual counseling, statistical analysis indicated that children's and their siblings' behavior did not significantly improve for the experimental group over the control group. Teachers reported no improvements in classroom behavior among those receiving therapy, and, in some cases, observed that behavior had, in fact, deteriorated. Barbara Rubinstein, one of the evaluators, summarized the ambiguous results: "Teachers and observers report few differences in school behavior between the Experimental and Control groups. There is some indication that therapy may facilitate an increase in positive behavior, but differences here, too, are small."[22]

Although the discussions at Northside reflected the center's own history, they also grew out of a much broader discussion in the professional literature on the effectiveness of psychotherapy and in challenges from some African-American mental-health workers about the legitimacy of psychotherapy for black clients, in particular.[23] Was psychoanalysis effective for a population whose basic problems were racism and poverty? Was individual psychotherapy more or less effective than family and other forms of intervention? Paul Benedict noted that clinicians at the center represented differing schools of psychotherapy, "ranging from fairly orthodox Freudian to entirely eclectic, problem-oriented." The field itself had "no really valid way of evaluating our therapists. . . . It seems quite clear that any evaluating of a therapist's effectiveness . . . must be high[ly] subjective." The most important factor was the patient's personality and "social and cultural factors." Benedict concluded that "it hardly behooves any of us to make dogmatic pronouncements" on the effectiveness or ineffectiveness of any particular approach. At Northside, as in the field of psychotherapy, in general, no one was really sure what constituted professional boundaries. "Lively disagreement . . . [existed] about the degree to which a given profession (psychiatry, psychology, social work) does (or should) contribute a unique or distinctive approach to treatment (or casework)." [24]

Psychiatric Treatment, Education, or Advocacy

In early 1965, Northside's board decided to examine how to integrate the new ideas about therapy the Clarks and the staff had been exploring with Northside's broad mission to serve the community. The board created a special Committee on Future Program and Policy, headed by Richard Cloward, a Columbia University professor of social work and one of the original organizers of Mobilization for Youth, which had just experienced a bitter and devastating attack from opponents of community action. The committee met for more than six months, discussing in nearly a dozen meetings Northside's future direction [25] and conveying in the waning months of 1965 its report to the board.

The report laid out a number of models for Northside's future, ranging from the narrowest of psychiatric counseling functions through a complete revamping of the institution into a community action program. One alternative differed little from the program of traditional child guidance centers and envisaged little if any innovation; it assumed that psychiatric disturbance was fundamentally a problem of the individual to be addressed essentially in the same way as any physical complaint: by seeking the source of the child's problems within the individual and seeking to cure the individual's pathology. The goal of this plan for the agency would be to treat "a maximum number of individuals presenting clinically defined problems." A second model focused on remedial education and proposed an expanded cadre of professional teachers who would supplant psychotherapists as the basic staff of the center. The rationale for this approach was that "educational deficiencies constitute the most disabling single handicap of Harlem children . . . [and] since this handicap tends to feed directly into a lowered self-image and thus initiates or aggravates emotional difficulties, any lessening of the handicap should serve to improve emotional status." A third model emphasized the importance of the "professional advocate," an individual trained to represent clients and to aid Northside's clients in their negotiation of the social-welfare maze and educational bureaucracy. The rationale for this approach was that "no service to low-income people can be meaningful that fails to come to grips with their powerlessness in dealing with the governmental welfare system." Advocacy, in this model, demanded a "readiness to become an adversary, to pit oneself against a system with whatever means at hand, whether skills in persuasion, manipulation, or straight-forward pressure (including court action)." This model was based on the conviction that the principal problems of clients of Northside were the result of "external forces," especially those of government itself in denying clients benefits or prerogatives. Its program implications were that the psychiatric and psychological staff would be reduced in favor of lawyers and social welfare workers.[26]

The fourth model, the most radical of all, and the one that Cloward himself found most promising for Northside, as the subsequent discussions made clear, demanded a critical self-evaluation of the staffing and ideological foundations of the center and of the board. This model, a "public policy and social action" approach, sought to "effect changes in policies and procedures which will in turn significantly reduce or eliminate educational, economic, social, and emotional deprivation now suffered by many families." It would transform Northside, in effect, into an anti-poverty agency rather than a mental health clinic or social service center serving children.[27]

The discussions taking place in Northside's board room were occurring in the midst of one of the most tumultuous periods in U.S. history. The 1950s civil rights movement in the South had raised expectations for fundamental change throughout America, and Harlem itself had experienced major demonstrations, civil disobedience, and in the previous few months even violent disturbances. Northside, as part of the Harlem community, could hardly ignore the ferment and turmoil around it, especially since its own families and neighbors were beginning to make wholly new demands on the organization. As Mamie Clark told the board at its first meeting to discuss the committee's models, "if the agency doesn't move with the times, the parents (whom the agency serves) will be far ahead" of us. She explained to a board, the majority of whom were white and lived and worked far from Harlem, that parents had come to the agency that year "very angry." Parents had let Clark know that "they were tired of talking and they wanted to feel they were accomplishing something." She warned that "the parents want action and question how far Northside Center as an agency is going to go with them." The parents "want more for their children and want Northside to help secure it for them." [28]

The meeting was tense. Some board members, among them James Dumpson—recently appointed New York City's first African-American Commissioner of Welfare—supported Mamie Clark's conviction that Northside had little choice but to adopt a more activist stance as advocate for parents so long deprived of the most basic social services. Dumpson told the board that "he is now persuaded that no agency, no matter how it defines its functions, can leave out . . . [advocacy]." [29]

For the more cautious board members, Mamie Clark's and Dumpson's description of the mood in Harlem was alarming and the mood at the meeting was tense. But Cloward argued that "advocacy [for clients] is nothing new"; it had been practiced by settlement house reformers since at least the turn of the century. People in the community were faced with "the pressing problems of . . . being evicted, children who are being suspended from schools, etc.," and it was appropriate for Northside to act on their behalf. Cloward pushed the more radical approach to advocacy, one consistent with his thinking and writing generally, urging Northside to use its "experience with its clients to help effect social changes." Board members who agreed with Cloward's intent were nonetheless troubled by the implications of turning Northside into an agency dedicated to advocacy and organizing. Without a firm professional base, Northside might emerge from the struggles of the period with no genuine identity and with little political or social or financial support. [30] Some of the staff worried lest Northside be perceived as an "outsider" in the very community, now newly aroused, of which it was a part. Victor Carter believed that most board members, with the best intentions, were by and large unaware of the real struggles Harlem's residents endured every day. With the exception of individuals like Dumpson, who had "lived in the community," as Carter said later, "most of the other people and this includes some of the Blacks who come from privileged backgrounds [didn't] really know. . . . They read about it but they really [didn't] know." [31]

Staff members like Carter who were privy to the discussions at the board reacted negatively to the model of public-policy and social-action, that Cloward favored. Despite the conflicts of the late 1950s and early 1960s over the role of psychoanalysis, direct professional service to children remained the core of Northside. Blanche Pugh, who had joined as a secretary but by the 1960s was a critical link between Northside and the community, said, in retrospect, that "staff was not of the community" and was therefore uninvolved in their daily struggles to survive. "As well known as Northside was in its earlier days, it was still a very closed kind of thing." [32] Most of the staff, trained in university social work and psychology departments, were focused on helping individual clients within the walls of the institution. Working with theoretical models that all-but-ignored extra-personal factors, some clinicians tended to see community outreach as beyond their own expertise. [33] Staff representatives like Benedict and Carter were concerned about the ability of a professionally dominated clinic and a middle-class board to become effective organizers and spokespeople for a clientele that was overwhelmingly composed of poor people. Given the specialization of most professionals and their individual-treatment emphasis, the advocacy role would be difficult to define and harder to implement. Professionals in the mid-1960s had been "educated" to try to protect the interests of their clients, and for them, the call to challenge the system and push the limits of reform might seem—and indeed might actually be—counter to individual clients' interests. They had been trained to negotiate the system, not overturn it. Challenges were the province of lawyers, organizers, and potential activists, not of psychologists and social workers.

Although most of the staff were unaware of the specifics of the debates raging in the board room, a few who were aware formed a committee and drafted their own "Model of the Future" for board consideration. As persons in daily contact with clients—both children and parents—this staff group said that Northside must respond to the increasing demands of the Harlem community because "our current experience with parent groups indicates a far more militant mood among the parents." But, the staff group argued, Northside should build on its own demonstrated strengths. It called for an *accretion* of services, not an abandonment of therapy, remediation, and attention to individual clients. The primary change it put forward was to build on the new multiservice approach in which family treatment took precedence over child-centered therapy. It called for identifying children's "talents and superior capacities"; "involving fathers in new and creative ways"; developing a preschool modeled on Head Start; expanding "techniques of teaching the children how to think"; providing legal-aid services for families, and expanding "community and family life education, involving club groups of parents of children not in treatment." Through community involvement of this sort, Northside could aid in channeling the "energies" of the Harlem community into "a healthier life for their children and all children." [34]

The staff model, as it was called, rested on a set of assumptions that reflected prevailing professional opinion. Some staff members said Northside should act as a "surrogate parent" for its clients and, thereby, "help families in all those ways in which middle class families help their children. The goal of help should be to instill healthy middle class values and to achieve middle class ways of functioning in the families." It asserted that the "surrogate parent role which Northside should assume should begin at as early an age of the children as possible. The work of the Center would be most effective if it could begin at the pre-school level." [35]

The measured staff response to the board committee report masked the anger and frustration certain staff members felt about the underlying motives of some on the board in proposing a dramatic change in direction. One clinician who had been privy to the committee deliberations was outraged by what he perceived as an attack on direct services to children; despite the high-sounding radical rhetoric, some board members would abandon clinical treatment for financial, not ideological, reasons. "In general, the committee seems to want to *constrict* [Northside] rather than to *expand* it." This clinician attributed this to a "preconscious" desire to make Northside more "efficient," hence less costly; thus meeting "the needs of the operators of the system rather than its clients (victims) (patients)." More fundamentally, however, he was concerned that constricting of services would represent "a kind of prejudice against our clinical population." As this clinician described it,

A Board member explained to shocked friends that it was "all right" to serve on the NC board, even though the clinic is not psychoanalytical, that "these people don't need psychoanalysis," that their needs are really only related to poverty, housing, food, education, etc. that "of course" there are some "really disturbed" children, but it turns out that these are *psychotic* and need hospitalization, etc. Actually, what might superficially sound like a sophisticated analysis of the relationship between mental health problems and the socioeconomic milieu, tends to become simply another example of one group of people deciding what another group "needs." In practice, it means that simpler and cheaper methods will "do." . . . In general, again, I sense a kind of magical or adolescent aura about the whole operation, as if a kind of game were being played. [36]

This clinician reflected some of the staff's frustration with a board he considered out of touch with the real work of the center— which was to serve children.

At the next board meeting, Cloward opposed the staff model, calling it the least attractive of the various alternatives, except perhaps for the straight clinical-service model. He explained that he was not "suggesting that Harlem does not need mental health service, but it is not seen as a priority need." Cloward's difference with the staff was on "a fundamental sense of priority." [37]

Cloward's rejection of the staff model came not from Northside's specific experience but from his more general critique of the role of the social work and psychiatric professions in the emerging antipoverty programs. He was convinced that these professions' new-found infatuation with psychotherapy was leading them to "disengage from the poor." The professions had undergone a metamorphosis since the turn of the century when social service agencies had accepted the charitable precept that "help should be given where the problems are greatest and the capacity to overcome them least." In the post-war era, a new ideology of "egalitarianism" had defined the social service constituency more broadly as the poor and middle class alike. While this shift was rationalized in the social service literature as "democratic," he believed that it allowed institutions to organize their services around the needs of ethnic whites and to abandon African Americans: "The shift away from the poor has been concomitant . . . with the migration to urban centers of extraordinary numbers of economically distressed rural Negroes." [38]

Social work defined its prewar mission as alleviating the hardships as well as the social conditions that produced poverty for large portions of the population. In the postwar "affluent society," however, social-work professionals, Cloward believed, had come to view poverty as caused by individual pathology. The concrete needs of the poor for direct advocacy and service were abandoned as the field moved to "psychologize" problems. This, in turn, he held, alienated social-service workers from their clients. Whatever value clinical services had would be lost as the poor concluded that social-service workers were irrelevant to their everyday needs.[39] "As a consequence, disengagement occurs— disengagement by workers because they probably do not feel that clients can make effective use of service, and disengagement by clients because they probably do not feel that available services have a significant bearing on the resolution of their problems." [40] Cloward held that, "in an earlier era, the field revealed its middle-class biases in its tendency to discriminate between the morally worthy and unworthy poor" but "now exhibits these biases in its tendency to discriminate between the psychologically 'accessible' and 'inaccessible' poor." In sum, "The field has substituted middle-class, mental-hygiene bases of evaluation for the traditional middle class moral bases." [41]

Clara Rabinowitz, who had begun working at Northside in 1946 as a volunteer, shared Cloward's analysis of the changing profession of social work. Although private agencies promoted themselves as addressing the needs of the poor, in fact, she said, the social-work field, since the 1940s, "has dealt more or less with an elite population compared to those represented by the 34 millions [living in poverty]. . . . As recently as 1955, in reviewing the literature, I found only one article . . . on treatment of the underprivileged." [42]

A Psychosocial "Model for the Future"

Northside could not abandon its therapeutic core, the staff model had said, but nor could it ignore the new social onslaught directed at African Americans and blaming the black family and the community itself for its own suffering. Kenneth Clark thought that "it would be a serious mistake to de-emphasize the clinical service as it would be difficult to interpret this withdrawal to the community." Reminding the board that Harlem had experienced abandonment by the downtown voluntary social service agencies, he remarked that "this community is constantly suffering because of the withdrawal of service." For Northside to repeat this pattern would be another bitter pill residents of Harlem would neither want nor accept. "Northside should offer itself as a model of excellence," he maintained. "One thing that the Harlem community suffers from is that it rarely has an institution which can be pointed to as a model of excellence." Too often, agencies that served Harlem did so in a way that reinforced rather than undermined prevailing racism. "Whatever this agency decides to be it should be the best of that. Northside is contributing to the lives of people who have had very little." [43]

James Dumpson agreed with Kenneth Clark. Northside had developed expertise and skills that could help children—and therefore, Harlem—confront racism and powerlessness. Dumpson did not want "to see the withdrawal of the staff training and experience that had come in twenty years"; a new Northside should "build on," not deny, its historic mission. Still, he agreed that advocacy was important and urged that the staff proposal "be enlarged so as to provide a staff person who could perform an advocacy role for the families as no agency could be effective that did not fulfill this role." [44]

For Cloward, the issue was not merely one of reorganizing the existing structure or adding new professionally defined programs, or a single new staff person, but, rather, development of a new ideology and political commitment to radical change. He argued that his approach was in keeping with the best of Northside's traditions of providing essential service to the community. Seeking to quell what he sensed as the board's growing uneasiness at his proposals, Cloward held that in this time of turmoil and change, advocacy was a natural and needed extension of its mission: "Changing the agency in many ways would not be abandoning tradition." [45]

The board grew wary of the implications of the most radical of the alternatives. The public policy and social action model depended upon Northside's ability to mobilize grass roots support, which, in turn, depended upon the board's legitimacy as a voice of the community and interpreter. Yet, after the mid-1960s, it was all the more clear that a predominantly white and middle-class board could hardly set social policy or presume to represent Harlem's interests. Board president Howard Sloan voiced the belief that "the whole board structure would have to be reconstituted if" the social action approach were adopted. The staff, too, would have to be "replaced," since lawyers, organizers, and community activists, not social workers, psychologists, and psychiatrists, would be required to implement the proposal. The result would have to be the "resignation of the Board and the releasing of the staff" in order to build "a whole new Northside." [46] No one on the board other than Cloward was willing to contemplate such a drastic course.

The Clarks, Sloan, and Cloward now met as a sub-committee to develop a proposal for Northside's future that would integrate clinical functions with new approaches to providing help to Harlem's residents. They came up with a proposal that significantly redefined the assumptions upon which the center was founded. They began by reasserting the "psychosocial" axioms that had long-defined Northside's clinical program, pointing out that "the presenting problems of the children are symptomatic of the overwhelming pressures of ghetto existence and family disorganization." But they noted that Northside's mandate for years had gone beyond treatment alone: "Northside Center, as an agency, fulfills a function in the community which is broader than clinical; it involves community education, community action and advocacy." However, the *core* of Northside's program had continued to be its clinical work. It now proposed to "abandon the concept of a core function" altogether for clinical work or any other and embark on a "massive saturational" approach. Northside would seek to become a multi-service center, "the closest analogy of which is an umbrella." Reflecting the rhetoric of the War Against Poverty, the program called for modelling itself as "an individualized anti-poverty program. . . . Under this concept the core is determined flexibly by the needs of the families referred." [47]

On 7 February 1966, Mamie Clark asked all professionals to reorganize their schedules so they could attend a special staff meeting.[48] At the meeting, the staff received the new document, "A Model for the Future," which sought to put into a historical perspective the recent debate that had roiled the board and the staff and to reconcile the diverse professional and political concerns at the heart of the contention. It offered thirteen assumptions about the nature of Northside's clients' problems and the crisis of the larger Harlem community. It balanced older clinical assumptions about the lack of self-esteem, (on which the Clarks' own early work had rested), and its importance in the pathology of children and parents served by the center, with a broader social analysis of the "ghetto" environment as unresponsive to individual therapy. With the new demands on the center by parents and community activists, and in view of the disintegrating infrastructure of the community, Northside would seek to become an even more proactive and outward-directed institution. Mamie Clark sought to reassure the clinicians that Northside was not abandoning, but enlarging, its traditional commitment to the individual client; she reminded them that the needs of their patients were "broader than clinical," involving "community education, community action and advocacy."

Mamie Clark reminded the staff that the old pre-1960 model of "one-to-one psychiatric treatment" had for some time been replaced at Northside by a program that, while still having a core of psychiatric treatment, had layered on top of it "casework for parents, remedial reading for children, physical examinations, close cooperation with school and other agencies, some advocacy function and some social action function, some mass community education approach, etc." What was new was a decision to "abandon the concept of a core function in favor of a massive saturational concept." She laid out the vision of providing an "umbrella" of services, and Northside as evolving into "an individualized anti-poverty program," a "multi-service center for child development," not a mental health clinic: "We assert that effective help for emotionally disturbed children can not be given in terms of dominance of one-to-one psychiatric treatment but must involve clear, definite, and realistic ways of meeting the total needs of deprived children and their families. In effect we are asserting and planning for a functional [equivalent] to community psychiatry. We are refusing to deal with the child in terms of isolated segments." On the programmatic level, the center's model for mental and social health was "to achieve healthy middle class functioning in the families." Clark identified the "goal of help [as being] to instill healthy middle class values" in families threatened by very real social and economic problems. To be effective, Northside had to play a much stronger role in the lives of the families that they were going to touch. The concept of surrogate that had been important in the staff model was retained: "Northside Center will serve as a surrogate or supplementary parent to the children and as concerned neighbors to their families." Observing that families were disintegrating as fathers were forced out of the home by unemployment and by a welfare system that undermined family cohesion, the document saw Northside as an agent that could "integrate fathers into the families and enhance the role of the father." [49] As recalled by Lisa Paisley-Cleveland, a Northside social worker whose parents came from Jamaica, West Indies, and who earned her bachelor's degree at Howard University and her Master's in Social Work from New York University, Northside focused on "the family's strengths." "I've worked in other mental health facilities and I can tell you that the focus has to do more on pathology and correcting the pathology, rather than understanding the strengths of the family and building on those strengths." [50]

To achieve these goals, the center would revamp its procedures and program. Instead of its earlier focus on the child, "a family treatment approach will take precedence." Organizational changes would reflect this coordinated approach; in the past, different members of the staff had been assigned to work with the child, the parents, and siblings—psychiatrists saw the child; social workers would see family members and negotiate on behalf of the child with public agencies; psychologists would do the testing, and remedial staff would work with the public schools. Henceforth, "a worker will be assigned an entire family to work on its needs." [51] Formal boundaries between professionals would be broken down so the staff could work together in the best interests of a family.

Norman Wyloge remembers that when he came to Northside in 1965 as a social worker, the treatment structure reflected traditional distinctions between psychiatrists and social workers. "The social worker did very little child treatment. In fact in those days the social worker never even saw a child. They just saw the parents." The child would come in, be tested by the psychologist and then interviewed by the psychiatrist while the social worker saw the family for the "psycho-social." [52] Still, in the culture of Northside, "because we all respected each other and worked together so well, it didn't seem fractured." An "appreciation of other people," "respect for the [client] with whom you were working" and the general "feeling that you had something to offer" lessened potentially contentious situations. [53]

As Paisley-Cleveland recalls, under the new system the case would be assigned to one of the clinicians—psychologist, social worker, or psychiatrist, which was "quite unusual at the time."[54] The new model called for an integrated treatment of both family and child. A "coordinator" was assigned to each child based on specific professional skill, but with responsibility for multifaceted demands that often went beyond their professional training. A psychiatrist, for example, treating a child whose behavior recommended medication, might be responsible for contacting the school to arrange special services and for counseling family members. Social workers assigned cases based on their skills in family therapy and system negotiation would sometimes find themselves having to learn techniques of play therapy. Wholly new would be direct advocacy through the development of a legal department to provide services to family members. "For some families, the legal efforts may take precedence over all other approaches."[55]

The new program necessarily required a reorganization of the internal hierarchy. The position of clinical director, which had had coequal status with that of the executive director for the period 1959-1960, was eliminated. Now, "each department will have equivalent status and prestige with every other department." A chief psychiatrist, chief social worker, chief psychologist, chief educational therapist, chief of community and family life education, and a chief of research would coordinate their efforts and thus "preclude the isolation of departments." In a sense, this new structure marked the culmination of the center's evolution from a medical model with psychiatry in ascendancy in the 1950s, to the emergence of a social-service center organized around the needs of the families Northside served. The struggles of the mid-1960s sought to reassert the less formal, less hierarchical culture that had prevailed in Northside's earliest years, to recapture, but in a new way, the early family culture of Northside.[56]

In the early years, Clara Rabinowitz had already questioned the division of labor and status that gave precedence to medical staff and divided professionals in other clinics: "There is no basis in history, science or philosophy for the view that environmentally-created mental illness is necessarily or should be solely the province of the medical profession."[57] Victor Carter says that, before the mid-1960s, in the larger professional world, it was "heresy that social workers and psychologists could work with children just as effectively as psychiatrists."[58] Carter remembers being bothered by the rigid distinctions that marked professional relationships and activities in the 1950s and early 1960s. During the late 1950s, seeing remedial-reading specialist Bea Levison's sensitive attention to a child's poor self-esteem during a tutoring session, he had pondered the often arbitrary distinctions among the professions. He had seen Jeanne Karp at work with a child on remedial reading. "The intensity of the relationship was clear"; he could "see her breathing education into him." Such experiences convinced him that not to understand Levison's and Karp's work as "therapy" was a limited perspective, destructive to the children. Karp and Levison were providing "emotional vitamins" as essential to the mental health of the child as it was to his or her educational achievement.[59]

With social workers, psychiatrists, and educators alike at Northside now dealing directly with families, educational institutions, and community agencies, at every level the staff were drawn into unfamiliar territory. Some professionals appreciated the expanded role that they were given. Norman Wyloge, for example, found that he was drawn to advocate for children in the public schools and welfare offices: "I think that was probably my early role: to help them see that they did have power to make some changes. I think that was the important piece. Most of the parents came in and felt absolutely powerless as though there was nothing they could do to make any change and what I helped them to see was that as a parent they did have power." But then, "I always saw Northside as an advocate, as an ombudsman representing the families and the community, helping them negotiate the system. I think that was the most important thing, teaching people how to negotiate a very difficult system and helping them to understand that they had a right to certain things that were available in the community that most parents did not know of."[60]

It took some of the other professionals awhile to adjust to their new and unfamiliar roles.[61] Psychiatrists resisted the movement of social workers and, later, psychologists into their territory, and also resisted taking on traditional social-work roles themselves. "There was resistance all over," Wyloge says, because "a psychiatrist might have to do some more community work and some more outreach, which they had not been doing before. . . . If the child was having a problem in school, [if] there was a housing problem, since [the psychiatrists] were assigned the family, they too had to make outside calls now." No longer could they simply call up the case worker and say "You do it."[62] The case work department, comprised primarily of social workers, many trained in psychotherapy, also felt the strains acutely. Carter noted the reemergence of the "perennial problem of the casework-psychiatrist controversy," exacerbated because "case workers [had] been asked to assume responsibility on cases for services traditionally handled by other professionals."[63]

Edna Meyers, chief of the psychology department, was troubled because her own staff, mostly part-timers who came into the center a few hours a week to do testing, was not being fully integrated into the new approach. Now, excepting the chief psychologist, her department was "the only one where professional staff members have *no* ongoing relationship with any of the clients." With only a part-time staff, she feared that "a tendency develops for the psychologist to become both logistically as well as psychologically alienated from the ongoing work of the Center." With professional isolation, the staff was "deterred . . . from deepening and broadening its skills beyond that of testing." Why did not the psychology department have as much right and as important a role in the new Northside program as any other group of professionals? After all, the psychologists hired to do the testing also had experience as teachers, researchers, and therapists in training programs. "Why not at Northside?" Isolation had "not served to heighten morale." [64]

In 1969, Meyers proposed to "introduce changes which will . . . integrate" the psychology department "more creatively into the Center's projected program," first, by adding a full-time African-American psychologist

who . . . professes a real desire not only to work at Northside but to remain and work in the community which Northside serves. . . . Special programs [in group dynamics] can make Northside a more relevant and meaningful center to the community. . . . Every professional should be able to lead groups, conduct group meetings, organize group programs, whether it be in reading or in parent counselling or in community action. Were this type of skill highly developed in our professional staff, there would be less hesitation on the part of personnel to engage in community activity, I think.

. . . In the educational field we will have to address ourselves to the question of devoting a major part of remedial time paradoxically not to remediation, but to prevention. This requires counselling groups of parents, groups of children, groups of teachers, and particularly working with pre-school children and their parents on developing an innovative model for establishing reading readiness and motivation at an early age. Here again staff would have to be enlisted on an interdisciplinary basis— psychologist, social worker, remedial therapist, para professional, volunteer students as part of an educational team. Such a program can have broad implications in the community, providing programs like Head Start groups with new techniques and new materials, and a new outlook. [65]

At a 1976 conference celebrating Northside's thirtieth anniversary, the Clarks brought together the center's board and staff with scholars and city officials to review its program and mission. Norman Wyloge spoke of how

Northside's unique culture had transformed his own sense of his role. While the rest of the professional world was battling over how to distinguish disciplines from one other, Northside had allowed for the merging of professional identities and therapeutic approaches. "It has long been realized that the traditional psychoanalytic approach is not the best way to treat the multi-problem family." Northside had demonstrated that "no longer can the clinician sit in the privacy of his office, treat his patient and expect to see positive results." In short, "at Northside . . . we believe that the multi-nature [of] the child's problem basically affects all of his mental health. We feel that a treatment agency is charged with the total needs of the child rather than the singular need of the psychotherapeutic session." [66]

Empowerment of Mothers and the Social as Political

Although the center had always been committed to working with parents of children, in the mid-1960s Northside worked specifically with mothers around activities and programs that sought to provide them a sense of the power they could exercise over their environment and lives. In the late 1960s, as many middle-class women focused on an intellectual rationale and "consciousness" for "women's liberation," a parallel, largely unrecognized movement was stirring among minority women of all classes. Among poets, playwrights, and intellectuals the double jeopardy of African-American women was explored with great bitterness. While the women at Northside were not part of either movement, by their very central place in African-American society as mothers and as objects of national debates over medical programs, welfare reform, birth control, and abortion programs, they often drove social policy. In the late 1960s, the women at Northside would seek ways of redressing their own powerlessness.

Just as Northside's staff had built its esprit de corps around a sense of family among the clinic staff, so too, did the therapeutic process depend on integrating into this family the clients as well. Beginning in early 1967, a group of mothers of Northside's children began to gather at the center for what was initially supposed to be a discussion of mutual problems on the governance of Harlem's public schools and on the misuse of standardized testing. The Northside staff had carefully planned an agenda with specific issues and problems, but, almost from the start, the staff's agenda was hardly ever addressed. And yet, parents and staff alike believed that something very important was happening. Joel Frader, a Northside staff member who attended the sessions, remarked to Mamie Clark, "it seems impossible, at least at this point, to define the purpose of the group." Yet, he thought it important that the women in the group "be allowed to develop confidence with and trust in each other." He believed that "trips, frequent meetings and activities such as piano recitals . . . will allow the women to find out what each can contribute." The mothers were "quite anxious to accomplish *something*, yet they [were] insecure about their roles." If Northside's staff could continue to work closely with them, the women would "learn the necessities and procedures of responsible leadership and organization." The meetings convinced Frader that the mothers were "the most intelligent, articulate and conscientious parents from the Northside community," and he emphasized how important it was "that these women develop [their] resources." [67]

It was clear from the start that this "mothers' group" was not going to fit into any neat category in the clinical program. It was not at all clear, however—at least not at first—what relationship this group would have to mental-health services. But Mamie Clark and Victor Carter's casework staff recognized that the women would determine their own direction and purpose. The mothers' group was, in fact, engaged in a political process as significant for poor African-American women as the women's liberation movement was for middle-class whites. The center could help not by giving direction but by empowering them to take control. Paisley-Cleveland remembers that the mothers' groups served multiple purposes.

> We actually took mothers to the theater, took them shopping downtown, had people come and show them how to put on their makeup, had luncheons, just did a number of things that were enjoyable to take them out of their homes and to just open up their minds that there is a big world out there and they certainly don't have to sit at home, feel depressed, feel hopeless. . . . They came as "single mothers" who didn't really venture outside their homes [but by the end, they were] "graduates" because many of them . . . found full-time jobs. [68]

In the summer of 1967, the mothers' group planned a weekend trip to Pennsylvania Dutch country, their primary purpose "to have fun." [69] But having fun turned out not an easy thing to do for they had neither the funds, the time, nor social support for certain kinds of leisure activities. One of Victor Carter's social workers, Roz Granger, approached him with the idea, as

Carter said later: "'Victor, I think I'd like to take some of the mothers on a bus outing.'" "'How we going to do it?'" According to Carter, Granger added, "well, these mothers work hard and they need a chance to get away from the children. No children, just the mothers." "'Roz, well that's a great idea but you know, where do we get the money?'" Carter responded. "She talked to the mothers. They saved their quarters. I forget how much they each had to pay, six dollars or five dollars, and then she called perfume companies and what not to get little gifts and favors and she got them, fashionable Fifth Avenue stores, the whole bit. The mothers met and had a super Sunday—left the kids at home with fathers, aunts, whatever, and had a great time." [70]

A year later, another mother came to Carter, "a very proper lady from Jamaica." "'Mr. Carter, do you think we could have a bus outing this year?'" Carter had forgotten all about the previous year's outing: "Here's my mind on all these other cases and doctors and psychiatrists and she's talking about a bus outing. So then I caught myself and . . . we got together another bus outing." It has become clear to everyone how important this seemingly ordinary event was to the mothers themselves. It was also clear to the mothers that more was accomplished than a simple act of "having fun." Mrs. Charlotte Williams, one of the mothers, remarked that "the idea of a group of mothers going away together informally! It made me feel like a person, not just a mother." [71]

The mothers pushed Carter and Northside to build on the success of this "social" affair. Could they continue to meet? Carter hesitated, until he realized that it was as important for Northside as for the women. Not only would Northside be serving its goal of community service, but it would be developing leadership skills, serving a broader goal of fostering indigenous independent action. "I realized that . . . the ladies up in Westchester had been to Bennington and Vassar and [were] always active in various community and civic organizations. . . . They know how to speak, they know how to organize." They had learned or acquired skills that were often denied poorer, African-American women and families. They and their families, in consequence, had gained distinct advantages for "their children . . . grew up knowing their mothers, fathers were involved in important things. . . . why can't we in a miniature way have that?" [72]

Carter and Blanche Pugh spurred the women to assume control of meetings, to organize community activities and sponsor workshops, concerts, and fairs. Before long, Carter and Pugh could barely believe the sense of authority and power the women had gained. "And now they are leading things in the Tenant's Association, in their churches. . . . It is one of the most gratifying things." By the late-1960s, the "mothers' group" had been fully incorporated into the Northside "family," and had been renamed the Parents Council of Northside Center. Their wide variety of activities went well beyond the early purely social functions. They raised money for children to go to summer camp; they organized theater benefits and educational programs; they sponsored concerts for and by Northside and Harlem children to "show case community talent and expand cultural experiences to children and parents in central and east Harlem." They became involved in local Democratic party events, sponsored senior citizen's lunches, and invited guest speakers to talk to parents at monthly workshops about everything from consumer protection to art and culture.[73] The Parents Council became Northside's eyes and ears in the community.

Perhaps the signal program that evolved from the Parents Council was the local Nutrition Fair, an annual event after Northside moved to Schomburg Plaza in 1974. Not only did the "preparation for the Nutrition Fair and the Fair itself [serve] to heighten awareness of the critical nutritional needs in our families," but it integrated nutrition education as a new service under Northside's umbrella. Northside "hired a nurse whose responsibilities are, in part, to develop a nutrition education program for these premises." Under the leadership of Bertha James, Parents Council chair, the organizing effort generated "immeasurable goodwill" in the community; twenty-six organizations participated in the fair, the Metropolitan Museum of Art among them. But the fair's importance went beyond public relations to become "a significant milestone in the development of the Northside Center program." The agency staff "has long recognized that a narrow clinical approach to our families is ineffective. We have long been aware that the concept of mental health must be interpreted in its broadest sense."[74]

By the late 1960s the "core" of the Northside program was still mental-health services, particularly psychotherapy and testing for children referred from a variety of social services and schools. But it had expanded to provide professional services not only to families as units but also to teachers and institutions throughout Harlem. By the early 1970s, Northside had undergone a profound transformation in its program both within and outside its own walls. Relationships with the professional communities in social services and education were augmented by closer ties to neighborhood and activist groups. It was clear to Carter that "benefits have already accrued in terms of the clinic's image as a dynamic and concerned agency" and, along with this outward reach, came problems and benefits that possibly even Mamie and Kenneth Clark, as well as the Northside board and staff, had not anticipated. Originally conceived as a service to the parents, Carter found that the Parents Council was a valued resource for Northside itself. The council served to teach "us a great deal about working with community groups." [75]

The outreach to the community forced a rethinking of traditional definitions of clients and professionals. Northside certainly continued to provide counseling, an educational program, social services, and psychotherapy, but the involvement of parents led to more wide-ranging programs that were, nonetheless, a logical culmination of the process and not a departure from the original conception of Northside that had begun more than a decade before. In the late 1950s, Northside had rejected traditional psychoanalysis and psychiatric treatment as its core professional base; now it returned to build its program even more broadly on the strengths rather than on the pathologies of its clients. By the middle years of the tumultuous 1960s, Northside had expanded to become the "umbrella of services" it set as its goal. By the late 1960s, Northside built upon its new program to strengthen not only its clients, but also the schools and the communities in which they lived. In the 1970s, as the parents organization developed an identity and strength of its own, the center was led once again to reexamine its own assumptions and to accept the challenges they presented openly. Carter, who had been instrumental in all of the outreach programs, in 1972 called the new relationship with community groups a "'blurring' of lines between clients and staff" that could emerge as either a "strength or weakness." [76] In 1970 and 1971, a divisive experience with unionization was to demonstrate his insight.

The Union Challenge to the Northside Family

Jeanne Karp, reflecting on Northside in the period between 1965 and 1974, remembers an institution "exploding in all directions," with new ideas, new programs, and a new mission. [77] The number of clients and the size of Northside's budget also exploded, as table 1 demonstrates.

In the 1950s, sometimes subtly and sometimes overtly, the culture of Northside that Mamie Clark had cultivated was threatened by a challenge to the Clarks' vision and control from within the board room as white philanthropy sought control. In the late 1960s and early 1970s, a new challenge

Table 1. Growth of the Center

Year	Number of Children Treated	Budget
1947	156	$34,932
1957	375	166,914
1967	497	375,096
1974	1,274	914,146

Source: "More Help for Those Who Need It Most—A Statement about Northside Center for Child Development Prepared for a Few Select Friends of the Center," January 1975, NCCD.

came from within the staff and from outside the institution as well. With its larger budget, new programs, and a larger staff, Northside had a difficult time sustaining the sense of family that had carried it through tumultuous changes over its first quarter century. The informal relationships and decision-making processes that worked so well in the past were based upon an appreciation among the staff of the Clarks as the embodiment of Northside. While older staff saw Mamie as having created a "magical place, . . . a warm place, kind of like a family atmosphere," some younger, newer staff members found this quality "irritating—that this lady was always so much in control."[78] Then, as the center expanded and as new staff joined, what had been begun as an enterprise with shared assumptions and values faced another challenge as the labor movement attempted to provide Northside's staff with an alternative form of authority and control.

In 1970, Lisa Paisley-Cleveland says, about a dozen staff members "marched into Mamie's office," breaking up a meeting that the executive director was holding with a group of visitors. Led by an organizer from Local 1199, the hospital workers union, staff members confronted Clark: "During the course of the interaction . . . somebody used the word 'hell' and Mamie became infuriated and said 'You not only showed me such gross disrespect but you also cursed' and she went off." Paisley-Cleveland herself was stunned by the exchange, and "just wanted to click my heels and disappear." "Mamie was just enraged that [her staff could act] in such poor taste. . . . We heard afterwards that she was in shock, she was mortified by what happened." Mamie Clark, Paisley-Cleveland believes, thought "she did very well by her staff and there was really no reason even to have a union and then for the union to gain so much authority with us that we would have done something like that, I think it really devastated her further, how could her staff turn on her in that way. So that was one of my low points here at Northside." [79]

Shortly thereafter, the crisis moved into the board room as the board learned that a majority of the staff "desired to be represented by" the union. Local 1199, originally a union of pharmacists throughout the city, had, in the late 1950s, begun a concerted organizing drive among low-paid, largely Hispanic and black workers in the city's various voluntary hospitals. Throughout the 1960s, the union had forged strong links with the civil rights movement and other liberal and progressive organizations in New York and elsewhere. In fact, the leadership of Leon Davis and Moe Foner, who were white, had made a particular point of linking the union to the broader movements for equality, peace, and civil rights, forging a close relationship with Reverend Martin Luther King Jr. Presenting itself as a radical defender of the rights of minority workers, the union had organized the mostly poor, African-American and Hispanic workers in the largest and most powerful hospitals in the city. By the late 1960s, it sought to expand its membership and scope by moving beyond unskilled workers and paraprofessionals to hospitals and nonprofit social-service agencies, to organize social workers, nurses, and other professional staff. Because Northside's staff and administration shared so many of the social and political ideals of Local 1199, the union assumed its organizing efforts at Northside would not meet much resistance.

The board's chief negotiator, Herbert Prashker, reported at its October 1970 meeting that "Local 1199 had presented Northside with evidence that the majority of staff members desired to be represented by that Union for purposes of collective bargaining under the State labor laws." Prashker agreed with the union that the bargaining unit would consist of thirty-five employees, including all social workers, remedial therapists, research workers, clerical workers, and psychologists. Excluded would be administrators and supervisors, confidential secretaries, persons holding M.D.s, part-time paraprofessionals, and part-time workers averaging fewer than eight hours work per week. The initial election resulted in "approximately 20 staff members [of the 35 who] voted to be represented by Local 1199." [80]

Local 1199 had recently won a big wage increase at voluntary hospitals, and the Northside board was greatly concerned that Northside would be asked to match that contract. "The dimensions of the union's proposed demands are best indicated by Northside's salary scale of $9000 for a beginning caseworker (new base had been determined at $9750) as compared to Local 1199's settlement for voluntary hospitals beginning at $10,938—the same as they are requesting of Northside." Prashker feared that, if the board could not meet these financial demands, the union might strike; he told the board that his labor committee needed guidance on the "agency's ability to take a strike and the Union's ability to conduct it." He warned that "this Union has proven to be strong, effective and tough and will call a strike against the agency."[81]

In November 1970, three long and intense negotiating meetings occurred between Northside and Local 1199. At first, it appeared Prashker's efforts to reach an accord might avert serious discord between the staff and administration. In December, he reported to the board that the estimated cost of wage increases in the union contract could be $23,000 in first year and $39,000 in the second year, a 16 percent payroll increase in the first year and 23 percent in the second; still, Prashker felt confident that the city, through its mental health contract with Northside, would ultimately bear much of the relatively high cost of the raises. The city had covered many of the increased costs that had accrued to the voluntary hospitals since the early 1960s as a result of the union's victories. However, Medicaid and Medicare rates for hospital patients had risen to reflect the new costs associated with unionization; by 1970 the city and the state were adjusting their rates for public patients following a union victory. Prashker reported that "in relation to absorbing additional costs the New York City Department of Mental Hygiene and Retardation Services has been sounded out but there has not been any attempt made to secure a definite commitment." However, Brooklyn Psychiatric Center, which had recently settled with 1199, was pressing the city's Department of Mental Health and Retardation Services for higher reimbursement rates and it seemed likely that the department would accept the additional responsibility for the added costs.[82]

Many on Northside's board believed that the only roadblock to an accord with the union was financial, but it quickly became apparent that the principal problem was not financial but the potential threat of a union shop demanded by the union contract: all current and future members of the bargaining unit had to be members of the union as a condition of their employment. Kenneth Clark saw the union as a clear challenge. To him, it was "one of the most crucial issues to come before the board in the 25 years [because] the question of Northside [was] at stake." Personally, he opposed the union shop because it threatened to undercut staff relationships and the harmony that had previously been the basis of the entire culture of the organization. Mamie and Kenneth Clark were proud of Northside's family-like, nonhierarchical atmosphere, with decisions reached through discussion and debate, not vote, or strike or threat.[83] Just as a decade earlier the Clarks had fought Marion Ascoli (losing her personal and financial backing) because of her support of an autocratic attempt to take over the clinical services of their center, so now, from the Clarks' perspective, the union posed a similar threat to their informal, flexible structure. Kenneth Clark told the board that "professionals on the staff have said that they would resign rather than be required to pay dues under any circumstances." He felt so strongly about this issue that he said that he, himself, would resign and "would influence Dr. M. Clark to do likewise." In addition to the immediate issues, Kenneth Clark had a long history of distrust of the labor movement that had originated with the discrimination his mother had experienced while working as a shop steward at the hands of the ILGWU. He later recalled, "I was very pleased years later when the NAACP exposed discriminatory pattern in New York's garment industry and attacked the racial practices of the ILGWU."[84]

Kenneth Clark was concerned that the board, primarily composed of liberal philanthropists, might not understand the complexity of Northside's struggles to survive or how fragile the center was. "With the exception of a few persons, no one cares" about a small center in Harlem, he said, and this made Northside "very easy to destroy and this Union was very wise in selecting this agency." "If this Board votes a union shop, it should go the entire way and vote to turn the agency over to the Union giving them responsibility for raising funds and determining criteria for standards." The board must resist the union shop if the historic and unique integrity of the center were to be preserved. "This is a non-negotiable item for Northside." Many on the board "did not believe . . . that the union would have control, [and] doubted very much that there would be much change in Northside's operations." Still, it decided to postpone a final decision pending a special board meeting three days later.[85]

Alexander Thomas, the eminent psychiatrist on the Northside board, and then head of Bellevue's department of psychiatry, offered the clearest and most detailed analysis of this conflict that threatened to tear the board apart. In a private letter to Kenneth Clark, Thomas acknowledged Clark's "principled position in this issue" but urged him to consider that this was not a question "of sticking to principle or abandoning it but which of the conflicting principles are the best guides out of this difficult situation." He held that "most unions are reactionary . . . not only on the racial issue but on other vital questions as well," yet, he argued, "unions are becoming important mass organizations of black workers" and some unions may come to play a positive role in the city and the country.[86]

The conflict at Northside over unionism and Clark's hostility to 1199's push for a union shop occurred just after the city had been riven by a major conflict between the African-American community and the New York chapter of the United Federation of Teachers, when, in 1968, community leaders of the "decentralization" movement in Harlem and the Ocean Hill–Brownsville sections of Brooklyn had sought to induce the city's public schools to become more responsive to the needs of African-American children by gaining control of the hiring and firing of teachers in their community schools. In response to this threat to its power, the teachers' federation had struck the city's schools, leaving hundreds of thousands of children without education. The strike had, in effect, pitted Jewish teachers and African-American community leaders and parents against each other. Thomas worried that if the Clarks opposed 1199 at Northside, Shanker's United Federation of Teachers would "seize on your fight as proof . . . that your criticism of the teachers union was not because of the decentralization issue, but because you were anti-union." On a very practical level, Thomas said he feared that the Clarks' broader agenda to find a way to force the city to educate African-American children would be undermined. "Any open fight by you against the union shop could compromise your position in relation to the miserable racist group in the teachers union." Thomas urged Clark to accept the union shop as an "accepted fact of life in many professional agencies"; he had not seen, in his own experience in the city's hospital system, any evidence that a union would seek to "assume any responsibility for the professional program of the agency."[87]

At a special meeting of the Northside board in December, the deep divisions were not resolved, and, after much discussion, the board split, voting eight to six to give Prashker authority to negotiate a contract but not to agree to a union shop. The union issue not only set the union leadership against the board and staff members against staff members, it split the board itself. The December meeting narrowly led the board to refuse to negotiate on the union shop issue; at the January board meeting, union representatives and staff members argued that "the union shop is important to the Union because it strengthens it; because other employees who receive same benefits should bear responsibility of dues; because without it management may erode the Union by hiring anti-union staff." After a long meeting in executive session, the board reversed itself and voted to "reconsider the issue of the union shop."[88]

The close votes of the board and the internal friction on the staff on the matter threatened to destroy Northside. As in 1960, when a predominantly upper-class white board tried to impose its vision on a center begun and run by African-American professionals, so the challenge from 1199 pitted ostensible allies against each other. In many respects, Northside and Local 1199, like the white liberal board, were products of the same civil rights movement, both committed to improving the lot of African Americans in the city. But the Clarks were particularly upset that 1199 had chosen to focus its efforts on one of the few institutions in the city with significant participation of African Americans on its board and staff and among its clients. As a small but successful integrated facility, it was particularly vulnerable.

James Dumpson, elected Northside board's president in 1966, was particularly pained by this conflict. In other circumstances, as head of the Human Resources Administration of the City of New York, he had supported 1199's successful organizing efforts in the voluntary hospitals. Dumpson told the board that "Local 1199 could not understand why the union shop was a problem as this was traditional with unions." He tried to explain to 1199 "the unique nature of Northside which could prevent some [generally pro-union board members] from voting for a union shop" when "in another setting they might vote for it."[89] Dumpson was torn by his support, in principle, for 1199 and unionization, by his understanding of the role of race, and by his personal loyalty to the Clarks and to Northside.

The agonizing tension of the executive session on 4 February 1971 was heightened by Mamie Clark's response. She had previously remained on the sidelines of the board debate, but now she read a personal statement of opposition to the union shop, her major fear that "a union shop would give almost total control of the agency, including professional control, to the union leadership, most of whom are not professionals." The result would be to "make the role of supervisors and the director subordinate to that of the union leadership. This is totally unacceptable professionally." Whereas "a union shop may be . . . relevant or essential to large agencies where professional judgements are not crucial to the evaluation of performance of employees," Northside could not be that kind of agency. Northside had to deal with the myriad problems of an impoverished community; crucial was its flexibility in adjusting to constantly changing community needs. Northside had gone through a turbulent period of adjustment to break down the rigid professional boundaries that interfered with its ability to serve the community; Clark now feared that the union effort would impose a new set of restrictive boundaries and regulations. "The nature of Northside and the particular demands of its families require its staff to function as a smoothly working team. The rigid requirements of a union shop," she argued, "are inconsistent with [Northside's] needs and special qualities." [90]

Herbert Prashker, a labor lawyer, advised the board on a pragmatic approach. The union issue was threatening to destroy Northside and he believed that only "the question of survival [w]as crucial." He thought the more serious threat 1199 posed was not the issue of its control over the professional program but a strike that "could put the agency out of business . . . over the union shop issue." He feared that "an ugly situation" would develop "if a union shop is not accepted." He reminded the board that initially it had not taken "action to keep the union out as it appeared that most employees wanted it; there was no campaign to vote against it, therefore there was a victory for the union." Now, he argued, it was impossible to change course. He pointed out that "a number of agencies . . . have union shops and manage to continue to function." And while there were always predictions of disaster when a union comes in, "the predictions did not largely turn out to be accurate; business went on as usual." [91]

Kenneth Clark responded that many members of the board did not understand the difference between Northside, a small mental-health clinic in a poor community, and large hospitals that were more responsive to their professional staffs and trustees than to poor people. When the union first approached Northside, Clark said he had told its chief negotiator (Prashker) that "the union was making a mistake if the issues formulated for a hospital were transferred to this kind of agency. This is not a large hospital where there is clear exploitation of minorities and the poor." He felt that the union did not seem to care if Northside's vital services to the Harlem community were destroyed. Rather, he believed, the union was solely interested in expanding its power into the new field of mental health. "This is a small agency which could be put out of business tomorrow; and the parents and children would suffer. There is no overt sickness here. The union may destroy one of the best agencies in the area." [92]

The meeting went on late into the night with James Dumpson, Elaine Gaspard (a mother and a community activist involved in school integration fights, housing battles, and urban renewal in Harlem), Walter Eberstadt (an investment banker and treasurer of the board), and others, desperately seeking a compromise that would allow the board to remain united. Eberstadt suggested trying a union shop for two years, a suggestion Dumpson rejected as impractical. "A lot has been said about the survival of Northside and trying a union shop. But survival without freedom is not surviving." The reality, however, was that there was little room for compromise. When Prashker moved that the "negotiating committee be authorized to sign a union contract which includes a union shop and provides instructions for them to make every possible effort to exempt all current employees who oppose a union shop," the board vote reflected its continued deep divisions. Seven members voted to accept Prashker's motion, and seven opposed, with one abstention.[93]

The issue of race, which had played an important but unstated role in 1960, had once again played a critical role during this struggle. Lorna Goodman, a board member who voted in favor of the union, describes the impasse:

> There came a time when some members of the staff decided they wanted a union, and the board was a very integrated board. About half the members on the board were black, about half the members on the board were white, and I remember it was the first issue on which the board split, right down the middle, on racial lines. I think Mamie and Ken had watched unions for many years; had watched them be very, very discriminatory against blacks. In their mind this was confirmed when the union sent a representative to Northside, a black man named White . . . accompanied by a short white man who did all the talking. It was very apparent that the black union representative was a token and a figurehead. Kenneth and Mamie saw that at once, and the other black people on the board saw that at once. I won't say that the white people on the board didn't see that, but I think the white people on the board, being largely kind of left, Democratic liberals (and not union members; the board members were not the working class), who cherished a concept of the nobility of labor unions; and led by Herb Prashker, a labor lawyer who kept lecturing us about the inevitability of there being a union at Northside, favored the union. So, this was a very serious issue, a very serious problem.[94]

At a follow-up meeting on 22 February, a board member inquired whether Northside was in danger of losing the Clarks if they voted for a union shop. Dumpson reminded them that "Dr. K. Clark had already stated that he would resign and would use his influence on Dr. M. Clark to do likewise. Therefore, Northside is faced with as a consequence, the loss of Dr. K. Clark and the eventual loss of Dr. M. Clark." The board had no viable options: on the one hand, rejection of the union shop meant unknown staff frictions and an almost certain strike, with a possible consequence that Northside could be closed down; on the other hand, acceptance would guarantee departure of Northside's founders, who were responsible for its existence and survival, its meaning, and its inspiration, which would in turn lead to the departure of many staff and board members, and an inevitable end to Northside. Dumpson said a strike seemed to be the lesser danger of the two.[95]

Alexander Thomas confessed that, though "impressed with Mr. Prashker's arguments" and believing a union shop "preferable," he recognized that it "may be the end of Northside without the Doctors Clark and certain members of the Board. As you know this may be a personal basis on which to make a decision but if one wants Northside to continue, it requires the Board and the Doctors Clark to continue. In his case a vote influenced in this way is legitimate, as he knew how much they have sacrificed. If this is the case and there is no union shop, he thought there was a special responsibility to see that nonunion members are not exploited." Dumpson had the same dilemma; as the minutes put it, he was in "conflict because of his commitment to unionism and because Northside is seen by him as being unique"; "in another setting the question of a union shop would be supported by him." But, he thought it a mistake to see Northside as "an industrial complex" like the hospitals with which 1199 was accustomed to dealing. "It is the only voluntary agency of its kind in the area serving black and Puerto Rican children who have a specific need that a union cannot address itself to." He feared that "damage can be done to the families Northside serves unless there is freedom of choice. It is necessary to have the most flexibility in selection of both professional and nonprofessional staff." Prashker, the principal board advocate of the union shop, said Northside "would lose either way." In the end, the board voted 15 to 3 to reject a union shop. Kenneth Clark urged board and staff to prepare to meet "the needs of the [client] families" in the event of a union strike. "Plans must be made to continue operations of this agency in face of the most extreme negative approaches, including violence."[96] Two days later, the union "broke off negotiations, stating there was no point in further discussion."[97]

In the next two months, however, Northside managed to achieve a modus vivendi with the union. Prashker told the board in April that an agreement had been reached that "anyone now employed by Northside who has not joined the union and does not wish to join at this time will not be covered by the contract and consequently will not be subject to the union shop. All new employees will be required to become members of the union shop." Prashker, Kenneth Clark, Mrs. Peggy Davis, and the other members of the negotiating team had won this concession for present staff. They even managed to limit the initial year's cost of the settlement for staff increases to $8000; the second year's cost, for a 10 percent raise, would be $25,000. The board voted to accept unanimously the compromise agreement. Kenneth Clark concluded the discussion by acknowledging the contributions of Prashker and Davis: "Dr. K. Clark stated that he had attended many of the negotiation meetings and had many discussions with Mr. Prashker and Mrs. Davis. He watched them go through this difficult, abrasive, intolerable, and insulting procedure to which they responded with patience, wisdom and humor. Without having observed, it is not possible to appreciate the extraordinary contribution that they made. . . . to the survival of Northside." Mamie Clark told the board that "in the beginning Northside was faced with a possible split at Board and staff levels which would have been destructive to the agency as well as the clients, [but] "the Center came through the negotiations with a stable staff, board and clientele." [98]

To Victor Carter, writing just after the crisis was resolved, "the year 1970-71 was the worst in the history of the Casework Department at Northside Center"; morale "reached ground-zero and three caseworkers resigned while a fourth was dismissed." Although "in spite of all the turbulence, clients were served with a degree of 'adequacy,'" Carter deemed the period "a 'lost' year as far as any growth or development was concerned." Lucienne Numa, head of the therapy department, considered even the following year as "one of stagnation"; "the members felt quite isolated in the climate of hostility that prevailed in the Center during the union negotiations." Her department's services suffered and, "as far as the staff morale [and] the spirit of cooperation between the different departments . . . this was a year of disaster." She urged that a manual on clinic procedures and employees' duties be made available to staff, many of whom said they were "confused about their responsibilities." She called for a clearer sense of order, organization, and hierarchy to abolish what she saw as deep internal divisions within Northside, divisions exacerbated by the struggle over the union. [99]

The union struggle at the center should not have been unanticipated in view of union expansion into new and previously untouched areas of the social-service industry. Yet, it had a special meaning within Northside. Until the 1960s, Northside had been successful because it embodied the personal vision and goals of two individuals, Mamie and Kenneth Clark. The culture of the institution had been built around the view that Northside was a family agency and that the staff and clients were part of a common community. The typically adversarial relationship of union to management was antithetical to its style and its sense of its mission.

The first major challenge to this view of Northside had come from the board earlier in the struggle to give psychiatry the central place and to give the philanthropic board that favored this precedence effective control of Northside. Had this struggle been lost by the Clarks, they would undoubtedly have closed its doors and reorganized elsewhere, rather than sacrifice their sense of their responsibility to the children of Harlem. To them, those efforts to undermine their authority had had serious implications for black professionals working with predominantly white boards and predominantly white funding sources. In the process, Northside had changed, no longer trusting support of its mission to the benevolence of private philanthropists, and turning instead to the city and state governments and to the African-American community for more balanced support. This new diversity of funding and more racial diversity on the board had freed the Clarks and Northside to expand into new areas of service and provided a more stable base.

The union struggle was the second serious challenge to the family culture at Northside, a quite different intervention that sought control by outside forces, forces represented on staff as well as on the board. During the 1960s, Northside had developed a set of new community initiatives, reinforced its long-standing commitment to the reform of the public-school system, and undertaken community organizing through its involvement with the Union of Concerned Parents. It was not surprising, therefore, that outside groups saw it as a legitimate territory for incursion. Also, the center's own program had become more diffused, with new departments, new personalities, and a larger staff that did not necessarily view Northside through the historical lens of the civil rights movement. Empowerment had different styles and different substance to a staff that lived through the turmoil of the mid- to late 1960s; to some, no doubt, loyalty to the vision of integration itself, and even to the Clarks themselves, had lost some of its earlier allure. The union, in this context, proffered an alternative form of authority and power that promised both to protect the financial interests of staff and also to ease the personal, and to some, arbitrary, control by the administration.

Although the union struggle was resolved in a way the union, the staff, the board, and the Clarks eventually could live with, the Northside culture had inevitably changed, and in a direction unlikely to be reversed. Idealism was now less important as a glue that kept the center intact. The personal authority of Mamie Clark, as Northside's founder and executive director and principal spirit, did remain a powerful force, holding the center together and providing vision and direction during the next decade of economic crisis and conservative national politics. Nevertheless, the family model was losing its appeal among younger staff members, less aware of Northside's history and culture but attracted to Northside more for professional and personal reasons. The family model, embodied in Northside's African-American professional leadership had, at least for the time being, won, more or less, over outside forces, but it could not survive, at least not in the same way, forever, and certainly not as that leadership aged.

1. Miriam Clark, Kenneth B. Clark's mother. (Courtesy Library of Congress, Prints and Photographs Division, KBC MSS)

2. Kate Florence Phipps and Dr. Harold Phipps, Mamie Clark's parents, Hot Springs, Arkansas, in front of Dr. Phipps's office. (Courtesy Library of Congress, Prints and Photographs Division, KBC MSS)

3. Portrait, Kenneth B. Clark, ca. 1935. (Courtesy Library of Congress, Prints and Photographs Division, KBC MSS)

4. Judge Hubert Delany, Dr. Kenneth B. Clark, announcer, Dr. Dan Dodson, and Dr. Albert Deutsch during radio interview, "How Can We Work for Interracial Understanding?", WNYC, 16 April 1946. (Courtesy Library of Congress, Prints and Photographs Division, KBC MSS)

5. Kenneth B. Clark observing child with black and white dolls. (Courtesy Library of Congress, Prints and Photographs Division, KBC MSS; photograph by Gordon Parks; courtesy of Gordon Parks)

6. Mamie Phipps Clark at her desk at the Northside Center. (Courtesy NCCD)

7. Psychologist and client at Northside. (Courtesy Library of Congress, Prints and Photographs Division, KBC MSS)

8. Kenneth Clark in class at City College. (Courtesy Library of Congress, Prints and Photographs Division, KBC MSS)

9. NAACP lawyers and expert witnesses on the steps of the Court House in Rich-
mond, Virginia, in February 1952. In front are Spottswood Robinson III and Oliver
Hill, the NAACP's principal lawyers; Kenneth B. Clark is standing between them.
(Courtesy Library of Congress, Prints and Photographs Division, KBC MSS)

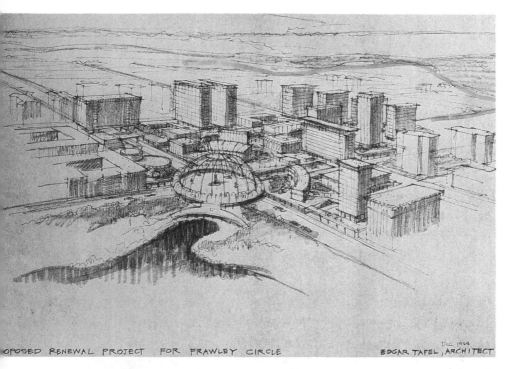

OPOSED RENEWAL PROJECT FOR FRAWLEY CIRCLE   DEC. 1964
EDGAR TAFEL, ARCHITECT

10. Original plan for the Milbank–Frawley Circle project at the corner of Central Park at 110th Street and Fifth Avenue, December 1964, Edgar Tafel, architect. (Courtesy NCCD)

11. Kenneth B. Clark, ca. 1965. (Library of Congress, Prints and Photographs Division, KBC MSS; photograph by Raimondo Borea, courtesy of Phyllis Borea)

12. Sam Walton (*left*), an organizer of the We Care program, with Dr. Lucienne Numa (*center*), visiting with neighborhood residents, ca. 1972. (Courtesy NCCD)

13. Schomburg Towers as viewed from Central Park, 1974. Located at 110th Street and Fifth Avenue, the twin towers housed six hundred units. The extensive renovation of the neighborhood envisioned in the original plan was never achieved. Note the public housing units to the left of the towers. (Courtesy NCCD)

14. Assembly of children and staff at Northside's third-floor gym at the Schomburg Plaza. (Courtesy NCCD)

15. Mamie and Kenneth Clark. (Library of Congress, Prints and Photographs Division, KBC MSS; photograph by Ken Heyman, courtesy of the photographer)

6. Juvenile Delinquency and the Politics of Community Action

An Integrated Center or a "Negro Clinic"

In 1963, Kenneth Clark reflected on the meaning Northside had for Harlem and its children. When Northside was organized in 1946, life in "Harlem was pretty desperate," but in the intervening seventeen years, little progress had been made in the community as a whole. "I would like to believe that the existence of Northside Center did, in fact, make a difference in the lives of the majority of youngsters in this community, but I cannot tell you that for a very simple reason. I don't believe it would be true." Although Northside had improved "the lives of the majority of kids with whom it [had] come in contact," it would take one Northside "every ten blocks" to have a serious impact. If Northside were going to change the dynamic of race and power in New York and Harlem and if it were going to establish an environment "consistent with human dignity," it had to reach beyond its walls, beyond the clinical interventions with individual children. Northside had to "change or influence . . . society and community conditions which affect the lives of youth."[1]

When, in 1946, Northside had begun, the Clarks had proposed a relatively limited set of goals: Northside was to be a consultation and guidance center providing psychological testing services and therapy for patients and their families. But very quickly its mission had expanded as parents came into conflict with the New York City Board of Education, during the 1950s, and as Kenneth Clark himself became deeply embroiled in national and local controversies over education, poverty, and social policy around race. Northside had continued to broaden its own mission, bringing it into conflict with those members of its own board who wanted to impose a more medical model of treatment of illness rather than a social-psychology model of social transformation.

The Clarks and the Northside community came to believe that significant change would not happen without multiple forms of empowerment. Thus, the Northside staff had developed new forms of intervention with clients aimed at providing a greater sense of control over their individual fates. The Clarks and the staff increasingly pressed also for a more direct involvement with community groups that sought to challenge the bastions of power outside of the clinic setting. Of special, long-standing importance to the Clarks, as chapter 4 makes clear, was the need to shape a new educational system responsive to the needs of Harlem's children. They came to believe that a truly responsive educational system depended on the empowerment of African Americans long locked out of the political power structure. Judge Robert Carter, who joined the board in 1965, reflected, in retrospect, that "the whole basis of Northside [was] that you had to look at ghettoization, the impact of discrimination and racial subjugation on these kids and . . . give [the children and their parents] some strength so that they [could] really try to meet these issues and not be defeated by them." [2]

In the 1950s and early 1960s, nearly every index of Harlem's quality of life declined as the city's economy shifted from manufacturing and unskilled service jobs, where new migrants to the city had traditionally found work, to white collar and professional services, largely reserved for those with formal education. In 1950, workers in Harlem earned approximately 86 percent of the median wage in the city as a whole. By 1960, they earned only 75 percent of the city's median. In 1960, fully 49 percent of Harlem's housing units were deteriorating or dilapidated, compared with only 15 percent in the city as a whole.[3] In 1960, 90 percent of Harlem's housing units were more than thirty years old and nearly half were built before the turn of the century.[4] Despite the optimism engendered in 1954 by *Brown* v. *Board of Education*, New York City schools were becoming more segregated, not less. By 1964, of the twenty elementary schools in central Harlem, all but one were at least 99 percent black and Puerto Rican, sixteen more than 90 percent black. The four junior high schools, taken as a whole, were 99.4 percent black and Puerto Rican and 0.6 percent white and Asian.[5]

The rhetoric of Kennedy's New Frontier and Johnson's Great Society had promised significant change, but real change was illusory in Harlem. Few outside of Harlem were willing to commit the resources necessary to reverse Harlem's downward drift into despair. Northside itself was not immune to the forces making Harlem poorer and more isolated. Whereas in the late 1940s and 1950s it attracted about one-fifth of its clients from the white communities surrounding central Harlem and from the private New Lincoln School, housed in the same building—in 1957, for example, the center's clientele was 54 percent African American, 26 percent Puerto Rican and 20 percent white[6]—by 1961, Mamie Clark told the board that "the number of Negro children had always been at a high level" but that "the proportion of white children had been decreasing." The area around Northside had experienced a dramatic increase in the Hispanic population; soon, she said, "the Center will almost be serving totally Negro and Puerto Rican children." She offered the board two alternatives: redefine Northside's catchment area to attract more white clients or consider serving "only Negro or Puerto Rican children."[7]

The Northside board was convinced that by resolving to maintain an integrated clinic, a core goal from Northside's first days and at the heart of the Clarks' own philosophy, and by establishing guidelines that would commit the center to serving African-American, Hispanic, and white youth, Northside could sustain its original character even in the face of the growing segregation and isolation of the minority community. A newly resurgent Black Muslim movement in Harlem, as elsewhere, was voicing a growing discontent with integration as a primary objective, but its voice was still relatively weak. In 1961, the principal pressure the board felt was demographic, not ideological. In 1960 and 1961, a board Committee to Consider Inter-Cultural Aspects of Northside met to devise recommendations "to preserve diverse ethnic composition." Such diversity could, it concluded, be maintained only if none of the three major ethnic groups in the patient population—black, Puerto Rican, and white—fell below 15 percent of the population served by the center.[8] By late 1963, it was becoming apparent that affirmation of the principle of integration was not enough.[9] From the first, Northside had positioned itself to be available to both blacks and whites; its original location at 155th Street and its relocation to 110th Street were deliberate attempts to be on the border between the black, Puerto Rican, and white communities. By 1963, however, the number of white children served fell below the 15 percent goal the board had set just two years earlier. Paul Benedict, Northside's clinical director, said the next year that the center, which had "long played a pioneering role in the mental health field in its adoption of an integrated approach, as regards clients as well as staff," now had to face "a most serious and basic problem . . . whether to continue in its efforts to create and maintain such a status" or to accept that Northside "is a 'Negro Clinic.'"[10]

Northside could maintain an integrated staff because it could attract committed professionals and social-service workers without regard to race; and it could maintain an integrated board because it could attract leaders of the city's liberal white and black communities. But it could not, as a magnet only, ensure a continued integrated client base. It now took the step of suggesting to the broader voluntary social-service community that agencies exchange clients with Northside: the center would take a certain number of referrals of white children and, in return, send a number of African Americans to them. Since Northside had a predominantly black and Hispanic population and the other agencies a predominantly white population, an exchange would integrate both systems.

Once again, however, as it had in Kenneth Clark's efforts to integrate the New York City schools, Northside came up against the stubborn reality that New York City's voluntary social-service system did not share its goal of integration. Not one white child guidance clinic was willing to send white children to a center that served primarily black children. In the early 1960s, a time of enormous hope and apparent goodwill, even such a progressive private school as New Lincoln was now sending white middle-class children who needed counseling or therapy to clinics and services downtown rather than right upstairs to Northside.[11] This left Northside in a paradoxical position, either cut down on services to the Harlem community in order to ensure that 15 percent of its clients would be white or become a center solely for minority children.

At about this time, Richard Cloward, the Columbia University professor of social work who had joined the Northside board in 1963, had completed a study, "Administration of Services to Children and Youth in New York City," confirming Northside's experience that the downtown agencies were abandoning black children. His report showed that New York City spent $1.6 billion on services to children and youth but had no impact on "the major social problems affecting children and youth—poverty, racial discrimination and unemployment."[12] The Northside board concurred with Cloward's critique that one of the reasons for this situation was that the "Harlem community . . . lacks any type of strong federation that works in its behalf" and that Northside was virtually alone in addressing the needs of "Negro and Puerto Rican children."[13] The traditional voluntary social-service agencies run by the various religious groups had made bad matters worse by discriminatory practices. In the early and mid-1960s, as integration as a social goal for the city and social-service world receded, Northside was forced to accept the fact that integration might remain an unfulfilled dream.

Between 1956 and the mid-1960s, the optimism of the mid-1950s that the white community could recognize the evils of segregation and remove traditional barriers to African Americans' full participation in American life had eroded. No longer could the Harlem community depend upon the ambivalent and halting actions of even the most enlightened northern white liberals. Harlem had to turn inward, to its own resources and institutions, to develop new ways to combat the ingrained racism and resistance to change that had left Harlem's children in segregated schools, poor housing, and economic crisis. The problems of Harlem were understood to have their roots in segregation, the conditions of housing, the lack of job opportunities, the transformation of the city's economic base from manufacturing to services, the deterioration of the school system, and drugs, among many other things.

Northside, along with others in Harlem, now began to explore more intensively the efficacy of "community action," the attempt to empower local populations through political organizing and community mobilization aimed at altering these relationships. At the same time, throughout the nation, social-service agencies and political activists were debating the strategies and tactics necessary to force fundamental political reforms. Some in the African-American intellectual community pushed for greater "self-reliance" and self-determination. Others, angered at the larger political community for denying blacks a "place at the table," argued for greater militancy and confrontation. The few older community institutions that had withstood the exodus of social services from Harlem were forced to confront troubling questions about their own purpose and direction. Nationalists, such as the Black Muslims and followers of Malcolm X, along with a host of organizations from CORE to Jesse Gray's rent strike committees in New York, were pressing for grassroots participation in existing programs and control of the new antipoverty agencies which began to emerge in the mid-1960s. How should established institutions respond to Black Nationalists' demands for black control? Northside and other established organizations in Harlem, especially those associated with professionals and the African-American and white middle class, had to develop a response or be swept aside. Since most of the remaining social services were staffed by white professionals, how should these institutions address the community's growing distrust of professionals and of the middle class in general? Should middle class–led organizations simply relinquish control on demand to grassroots community residents? How does an organization follow the lead of the community when the community itself is in turmoil and does not speak with a clear voice?

The President's Committee on Juvenile Delinquency and the Competition for Funding

The origins of the War on Poverty and community action programs of the mid-1960s can be traced back to the 1960 election of John F. Kennedy as president and the 1961 appointment of Robert Kennedy as attorney general. The coming of the "New Frontier" marked heightened federal attention to domestic issues. In May 1961, Attorney General Robert Kennedy organized the President's Committee on Juvenile Delinquency,[14] which in effect, assumed, by default, primary responsibility in the Kennedy administration for issues affecting northern black urban communities.

Just as concern about the unemployed had generated the social programs of the New Deal a generation before, so the growing attention to the problem of youth and juvenile delinquency during the 1950s—a common concern in postwar periods—helped stimulate the programs of the early 1960s to restructure northern cities. Social scientists had long been asking questions about the relationship between youth, social class, and crime. At the turn of the century, settlement house workers, and other reformers had linked occurrence of crime to poverty. But in the 1940s, many academics began to emphasize psychological explanations for delinquency, a reversal of the older views that rejected concepts of inherent behavior and personality.[15]

By the postwar period, public policy–makers were asking such questions as these: Should the society seek revenge or reform? Were there too many prisons or too few? Should youthful offenders be treated with mercy because of their youth or punished because of their transgressions? Politicians who called for harsher penalties for juvenile delinquents one day might, on the next, advocate allocation of resources to reclaim their souls and bodies.[16]

Among professionals, several alternative models for action were propounded, and, for the next decade, advocates debated the effectiveness and morality of each. Psychiatrists emphasized personality, social-welfare advocates environmental issues, penologists new correctional philosophies, educators better school guidance services. Yet, most professionals during the war agreed that the family itself had to be a prime focus of study: "The family is either the strongest barrier against delinquency or a potent cause."[17]

Before the outbreak of the war, the initiative for reform came primarily from those associated with the criminal-justice system, especially those concerned with corrections. In late 1940, for example, a distinguished group of lawyers, judges, and corrections officials responded to a call from the American Law Institute to study and analyze the need for a Youth Correction Authority dedicated to "a more scientific and humane procedure in the handling of delinquent youth." They worked on a model act that aimed "to protect society more effectively by substituting for retributive punishment, methods for training and treatment directed toward the correction and rehabilitation of young people found guilty of violation of the law."[18] Members of New York's welfare and philanthropic communities began a dialogue on approaches to delinquency, penologists and the social welfare community recognizing that each must reevaluate its own traditions and assumptions to confront what was perceived to be an emerging crisis. Even camp leaders and supervisors of youth hostels joined in the legislative and professional efforts to redefine juvenile delinquency.

What had begun as an effort to develop new means of rehabilitation soon focused on prevention and alternatives to prison. It was widely accepted that adult prisons and traditional reformatories were not addressing the underlying causes of delinquency and not even rehabilitating those who were sent there. Children were being sent to these institutions as juvenile offenders and coming out as adult criminals. But how could the system be reformed? John D. Rockefeller III, along with other philanthropists and leaders in New York's social-welfare movement, created the New York State Committee on the Youth Correction Authority Plan to support alternative forms to incarceration of youth. New treatment facilities had to be created that would replace the traditional mass-treatment reformatory. Individual diagnosis of offenders' psychological problems rather than sentencing would determine the kind of institution to which the child would be committed, perhaps a mental hospital, maximum or medium security prison, forestry or road camp, farm, training school, hostel, or foster home. Although unsuccessful, this reform effort presaged the growing emphasis on mental-health and educational services that would lead Rockefeller and other philanthropists to support noninstitutional, community-based programs such as the Clarks' at Northside.[19]

The confusing and cacophonous tenor of the moment is perhaps best captured in the popular musical of the mid-1950s, *West Side Story*, a play of love—and of two juvenile gangs—in New York City. The members of one gang, the Jets, sing their confusion in their depictions of "Officer Krupke," the police force, social workers, psychologists, judges, and psychiatrists, all of whom provide competing and contradictory interpretations of the "delinquents'" problem. The boys insist that these professionals don't really understand them and that "Deep down inside there is good!"

In 1960, Lloyd Ohlin and Richard Cloward (of the Northside board after 1962), two urban sociologists from Columbia University, in their book *Delin-*

quency and Opportunity, pointed to the structural and economic factors of youth crime. Lack of economic opportunity, they wrote, was the major cause of criminal behavior among the nation's youth. Delinquency, white and black, was indeed a rational response to limited horizons, and the anti-social behavior of black youth was a consequence of limited opportunities. The book had an extensive impact as "the most up-to-date interpretation of delinquency."[20] The Ford Foundation and federal agencies adopted its analysis as a rationale for a number of activities in which, by 1960, they were already engaged. For example, in the late 1950s, Ford supported a coalition of social-service agencies on New York's Lower East Side organizing Mobilization for Youth, among the first community agencies seeking to address delinquency by encouraging the "maximum feasible participation" of residents in efforts to reshape the communities.

Ohlin and Cloward's principal contribution linked juvenile delinquency to issues of poverty and social class; their book acknowledged but did not center on the desperate conditions of America's burgeoning racial ghettoes or on the role racism played in shaping the behavior of black youth. From 1945 on, however, the Clarks and Northside had been struggling to define this issue. Community disorganization, economic disadvantages, and poor housing created conditions for delinquent behavior for all children, but antisocial activities were also "reactions to racial frustrations, deprivations, discrimination, and segregation." While most social scientists viewed delinquency as generic to poverty, the Clarks observed that delinquency had reached epidemic proportions in the African-American community, representing two and a half times the expected number of arrests. In contrast to the experience of the white ethnic communities, where, in the analysis of Ohlin and Cloward, delinquency created the opportunity for advancement, among black youth, delinquency was particularly destructive. "The larger society not only punishes [African-American] individuals, but," Kenneth Clark noted in the *Journal of Negro Education* in 1959, "also often interprets their aggressive and anti-social behavior as a justification for the existing patterns of prejudice, discrimination, segregation, rejection, and humiliation."[21]

The President's Committee on Juvenile Delinquency issued policy guidelines for funding proposals for "demonstration projects for the prevention and control of juvenile delinquency" that emphasized that "the sources of delinquent behavior lie in the individual *and* in his social situation." In urban slums, "the sections of our cities frequently populated by Negroes and other low-income minority groups," it said, "even the healthiest personalities can be overwhelmed by delinquency patterns which are environmentally supported." Principal federal and local efforts should therefore be aimed "primarily at changes in social arrangements affecting target area's youth rather than changes in the personality of the individual delinquent." In this approach were the seeds of the broader War on Poverty during Lyndon Johnson's presidency. In sharp contrast to the earlier delinquency programs that sought to address the problems of youths already in trouble with the law or society, this new federal initiative sought to support programs "whose potential target is *all* youth in these most vulnerable areas of our cities" through "the *prevention* of those conditions which are seen as causal to delinquency." [22] In the policy and academic arenas, social ramifications of poverty had replaced individual pathology as the paradigm for explaining delinquency.

During this period, some of the older white "downtown" social agencies that had withdrawn from Harlem during the 1950s now worked on plans to reenter Harlem. The city and the National Institute of Mental Health were providing grants to combat juvenile delinquency, and the agencies realized that Harlem seemed a likely area. In June 1961, the Jewish Board of Guardians proposed to the city a "Pilot Project of Mental Health Services in Support of Street Club Work." It envisioned a joint endeavor with the Community Mental Health Board and the New York City Youth Board to send social workers to Harlem to work with youth gangs, providing "diagnostic and treatment service to disturbed street club members." [23]

The African-American and white groups that remained in Harlem had organized in 1958 as the Harlem Neighborhoods Association to confront delinquency and poverty. Originally staffed through funds provided by the Community Service Society, the association was, in many ways, a traditional, middle-class organization that represented some of Harlem's oldest and most established institutions. It drew its members from among merchants, professionals, and church leaders, but unlike neighborhood associations elsewhere, HANA, as an integrated organization in a black community, had to confront the inequality and the special circumstances of racism. HANA had grown out of the abandonment of Harlem by the "downtown" voluntary services agencies. In the 1940s and mid-1950s, its predecessor, the Central Harlem Council for Community Planning, was the regional representative of the New York City Welfare and Health Council. In 1956, the parent council was reorganized as the Community Council of Greater New York. When it decided to drop regional affiliates, it became financially and administratively impractical for the Central Harlem Council to continue.

Therefore, in 1958, the Community Service Society helped the Central Harlem Council reorganize independently of the downtown agencies; the society loaned a staff member to the council and provided office space and clerical assistance at its East 125th Street headquarters. At the same time, the Central Harlem Council decided to broaden its traditional base in the white social-service world by including community groups from Harlem "to develop a multi-purpose 'grass roots' organization." [24] Northside thus joined the distinguished board of directors representing a wide cross section of Harlem's and the city's black middle-class and some sympathetic whites to found the Harlem Neighborhoods Association. Among HANA's founding members were representatives of the New York City Board of Education, the Bowery Savings Bank, the Urban League, the Children's Court, Harlem Hospital, the YWCA, the New York Hospital Council, the Children's Aid Society, the Community Service Society, and major churches.

Because of the new and the growing interest of Kennedy administration officials in juvenile delinquency and poverty in the black community, HANA began to organize the Harlem community to protect Harlem's interests and to attract to the community resources now becoming available through the city and, later, from the federal government. In 1960, after Northside revamped and reorganized its board following the Ascoli-Bryt crisis, the Clarks began to work even more closely with HANA; Kenneth Clark joined its board of directors and Mamie Clark its mental-health committee. The Northside board lent rooms to HANA for committee meetings, and Mamie Clark later chaired the organization's personnel committee.

Having been abandoned by the downtown agencies, the Clarks and their allies had struggled to develop services and programs for many years virtually alone. Now, with outside money on the horizon, Kenneth Clark and HANA members were outraged to discover the way these outside funds were being spent. Clark had learned that the Jewish Board of Guardians was about to receive federal and city funds to send social workers into Harlem to work with gangs. To Harlem's leaders, the possibility that the city and the National Institute of Mental Health might now provide money to the Jewish Board of Guardians without even consulting Harlem's few established agencies was galling enough. But that they would provide these funds without even considering the desperate plight of the Harlem agencies themselves was rankling. To Clark, the Jewish Board of Guardians' effort to reassert a position in Harlem after all these years of neglect smacked of "social work colonialism." He was "furious." As he described the episode in retrospect,

"Here is an agency [Northside] in the community that's struggling, and the decision-makers downtown decide that an out-of-community agency should be given money to come into the community and do something with the Harlem youth." [25]

A host of Harlem organizations, HANA among them, joined Kenneth Clark in opposition to the plan. After a tense meeting with representatives of the Jewish Board of Guardians, HANA's mental health committee (on which Mamie Clark now sat), together with representatives of the Community Mental Health Board, the New York City Youth Board, the Morningside Clinic, and Northside, voted to "condemn" the program. "Community agencies," they protested, "had not been involved in the planning," and "relationship[s] with community agencies [were] vital if treatment were to be planned for the children found in need of it." [26] Kenneth Clark challenged the traditional relations between voluntary agencies and their clients.

> I wanted youth in Harlem to have as many services as we could get. But it seemed to me that it was damned important to begin the issue now of what really does that community need? You know. To me, it was not colonialism anymore. It was no longer the Lady Bountiful, white is right, whites know better, and blacks should be grateful to their benefactors, no matter what the conditions are. And I used such words as condescension. You know. Well, this was a revolt. I mean, the natives were clearly restless, you see, and I was the most restless of the natives. [27]

In the summer of 1961, a series of meetings on the matter were held at Northside and, from those meetings, the Clarks and representatives of HANA and other community social-service agencies produced a statement, "A Program for Harlem's Youth." By October, HANA representatives were meeting with Mayor Robert F. Wagner to present a six-point program to address the issues of mental health and juvenile delinquency. At its heart was a plan to establish a Harlem Youth Services Council to develop a "community strategy for youth services" through "a cooperative planning process of public and voluntary agencies and citizen groups." HANA proposed "neighborhood teams of the schools, churches and social agencies to coordinate the professionals working with youth at the neighborhood level." [28]

Through these contacts with the city and downtown agencies, HANA and the Clarks learned that the President's Committee on Juvenile Delinquency was about to make significant commitments of money through Mobilization for Youth on the Lower East Side. Kenneth Clark's response was,

"Hell, sure, the Lower East Side has a delinquency problem, but so does Harlem."[29] He called upon Mayor Wagner and won a commitment to support a Harlem-based anti-delinquency program through HANA. Kenneth Clark reported to the Northside board on the meeting with the mayor, recommending that Northside involve itself in planning and supporting a larger, community-wide effort for Harlem's youth. Such community activity was central, he said, to Northside's mission of outreach and community involvement: "Social agencies have been leaving the Harlem community in spite of the fact that this area is in most desperate need of services, particularly for youth. HANA is on the threshold of being helped by the federal government to bring systematic basic services to young people of the Harlem area. . . . HANA will contribute to the work of Northside and other community agencies."[30]

The board unanimously "RESOLVED that Northside Center for Child Development accept responsibility in the planning and executing of this Harlem Neighborhoods Association's program and offer its whole-hearted support of its goals."[31] Over the course of 1962, Kenneth Clark and members of Northside's board began to develop a "new and independent structure" for a "comprehensive youth services program in the Central Harlem community." Clark wrote the planning grant; it was funded by the President's Committee on Juvenile Delinquency at the end of 1962.[32] The $230,000 established Harlem Youth Opportunities, Inc., known as HARYOU, to become one of the principal federally funded programs in the coming War on Poverty.[33] HARYOU gave new hope that Harlem was on the verge of a new renaissance and in control of its own destiny. Northside's involvement in HARYOU convinced the board and the staff that the center itself, now firmly established as a major institution serving the Harlem community and its children, should involve itself to a degree never before considered necessary or possible.

Rather than start with answers, HARYOU began with questions.[34] The first tack was a comprehensive survey to determine what facilities were available for youth, how they were being utilized, and what new programs were needed.[35] At the meeting of the Citizens' Advisory Council of the President's Committee on Juvenile Delinquency, Kenneth Clark announced that "HARYOU is not an agency, not an action program, not a demonstration. It is only planning—thinking, looking, researching to understand the problems of youth in Harlem and to develop a solid, comprehensive program providing opportunities for the maximum adjustment of Harlem youth."[36]

Almost from the beginning, HARYOU was mired in controversy, in part because it was one of the few Harlem institutions that had substantial financial support from outside public agencies. Barely two months after HARYOU's formation, James Hicks, the editor of the *Amsterdam News*, issued a scathing attack on HARYOU and on Kenneth Clark. He parodied HARYOU's and Clark's research approach through a hypothetical interview with an "expert" who convinces the powers that be to give hundreds of thousands of dollars to study Harlem's problems: "'I don't have all the answers, gentlemen,' he says. 'But I think I'm on the right track toward a solution of the problem. With about $250,000 I could pull together a research team of eminent social workers, psychologists, psychiatrists, anthropologists—the whole bit—and these men will come up with the answer for you in eighteen months.'" Hicks wrote, "the average social worker in Harlem is like a professional pimp."[37]

After Hicks attacked HARYOU, "More than 75 representatives of social agencies," as the *New York Courier* reported, "along with a group of youths directly involved in the projects moved to rally full community support of the projects." The possible loss of federal monies set off shock waves in Harlem. The implications of a successful grant application had not been lost on a myriad of agencies, professionals, block captains, and other community groups that might benefit from a substantial infusion of federal money. With congressional conservatives already criticizing the federal government's tentative and small-scale involvement in alleviating poverty, Harlem's community leaders charged that Hicks's attack was wrong and irresponsible. "It would be a tragedy if your column was used as an excuse to keep Federal and other funds for our youth out of Harlem," said a letter signed by representatives of more than thirty agencies.[38] In response to Hicks's attack on the HARYOU agenda for siphoning resources from Harlem, his publisher took the unusual step of inserting into the *Amsterdam News* his own front-page editorial lauding the infusion of federal and city money into the Harlem community.[39]

In the meantime, however, under Kenneth Clark's direction HARYOU continued to develop a planning document, citing the enormous discrepancies in social services, educational opportunities, employment opportunities, housing, recreational facilities, and other services directly affecting Harlem's youth and the social consequences in mortality and educational deficiencies. Northside had been deeply involved in every aspect of HARYOU from its inception, and later on, it would bear the brunt of attacks on Kenneth Clark and on others from Northside who helped sustain HARYOU in its early years. Most of the planning meetings for the original federal grant had been held at Northside. Kenneth Clark was chairman of HARYOU's board, and Mamie Clark served as a HARYOU consultant; other Northside board members, J. Raymond Jones and Jim Dumpson, had been deeply involved in organizing HARYOU. Northside had also conducted a series of in-depth interviews for HARYOU. Mamie Clark was chair and Victor Carter one of four other members of a HARYOU committee that assessed the "nature and quality of existing services for youth in the Harlem community," identifying existing services for adoption, day-care, employment and vocational guidance, family services and financial assistance, hospitals, mental-health programs, recreation, group work programs, settlements, neighborhood centers, and vocation services.[40]

Northside's own history had deeply influenced HARYOU. Drawing on the still-fresh experience of psychiatry and Northside, Mamie Clark sought to reorient the HARYOU staff's conception of the way mental-health services for children could be integrated into the HARYOU program. She argued that "the orthodox and traditional approach to psychiatric treatment is not an effective way of helping families from deprived and depressed areas." The problem was that, except for Northside, the other existing agencies were still wedded to methods that took place within clinic settings and between individual patients and a professional therapist. She called for an approach she and Olivia Edwards had been developing at Northside that de-emphasized traditional professionals and created a new category of what she called "mental hygienists." She saw mental hygienists as persons without traditional credentials who could "fan out into the community" and work with individuals, groups, and professionals in their ordinary settings. They could be, for example, nurses, teachers, or ministers, social workers or psychologists. Rather than focusing on the pathology of the individual, "the emphasis is on what are *healthy* ways of handling children and the prevention of emotional problems."[41] So Kenneth Clark would "report to the clinic regularly on what was going on with his work," and both Clarks would invite speakers to keep the staff and board abreast of the latest HARYOU developments.[42]

Community Empowerment

A retreat at the Harlem YWCA on 135th Street in January 1964 was set up to define a role for HANA in implementing HARYOU's "Blueprint for Change." HANA's integrated board of directors and its white executive director, Milton Yale, were facing new problems, as middle-class leaders, in seeking to develop programs and policies for the working class and poor of Harlem. The Reverend Eugene Callender, a member of HANA's board, admitted that HANA didn't "really represent sufficiently the grass-roots elements," and he asked the retreat to consider how to respond to the demands by "militants" in Harlem who were calling for the resignation of "the agency people or the so-called leadership people." Should the community people "become the dominant force" on HANA's board, Callender asked.[43]

Racial and class cleavages were shaping the politics of Harlem in ways unheard of only a few years earlier. The mere suggestion that the present HANA board had no place in Harlem caused an uproar. Initially, many at the meeting reacted to Callender's rhetorical questioning of their legitimacy with hurt. One white clergyman who lived and served in Harlem was distraught that his motivations were suspect; an agency head expressed anger that charlatans and politicians were using the community's frustration for their own political purposes.[44] But as the afternoon wore on, the participants at the retreat slowly began to understand what the attacks and militant calls for empowerment really meant. Harriet Pickens, chairman of HANA, told the meeting:

> Everybody else plans what are Harlem's problems and what Harlem needs and gives it to them. Now if we have an aware citizenry who know what they're talking about and how to function, you would know what power means.
>
> If you've ever gone down to the Board of Estimate and seen those mothers from Queens come down there and get the school they want, where they want it, and what's in it that they want. When the Harlem schools come up, there are a couple of agencies, social agencies—there is no power there—there are no votes. The Board of Estimate just looks at it and goes about doing just what they want.
>
> This is what I mean by power. These are aware citizens who are organized and speak. And they speak as one voice and say this is what we want and this is what we need.[45]

Milton Yale, HANA's executive director, agreed that it was necessary to "help the community to mobilize its strength . . . so that it can become part of the power structure to influence social policy, the economy, etc." A new strategy was needed in order to effect such a fundamental change: "community action . . . a process in which people take on responsibility and the changes in the community [which] are accompanied by changes in the people themselves."[46] Perhaps it was not possible for HANA to be a community action organization as long as it was led by a white male from outside

the community. Was the middle-class faith in the importance of stable, financially sound institutions now alienating working-class residents whose primary interests were in organizing around concrete political, economic, and
social goals such as better housing, jobs, and services. Perhaps older reformers were too concerned about the continuity of organizations and not atten-
tive enough to immediate needs, such as Harlem's recent successes with the
rent strike movement and the school boycott movement. As with Saul Alinsky in Chicago and the organizers then developing the Mobilization for
Youth strategy on the Lower East Side, Yale believed that what was important was that people organize and define issues for themselves.[47]

An agreement emerged on the importance of "community action" as a
strategy, but the term lacked precision. For Yale, it meant mass struggle without regard to institutional structure. For Mamie Clark, institutional structure
was essential in the context of community action: who could possibly consider forsaking decades of struggle to build organizations in Harlem? The
lack of a long-term historical perspective could easily lead to tragedy if the
few stable organizations in Harlem were allowed to disintegrate. Clark argued that structure was all that Harlem had at that point; only a few organizations existed, and an embattled middle class led them. How could a community achieve self-determination without a leadership that could formulate
a program? Social action demanded organization and organizations needed
people willing to develop and carry out an agenda. "You have got to have
some structure to permit the people to then be self-determined," she stated.[48]

Mamie Clark's analysis of the weaknesses of Yale's position on community organizing reflected both hers and Kenneth Clark's broader analysis of
Saul Alinsky's growing popularity among antipoverty activists in the 1960s.
"It is ironic that the Alinsky community action programs," Kenneth Clark
and Jeannette Hopkins (a MARC vice president and a senior editor at Harper
& Row) wrote in 1970 in *A Relevant War against Poverty*, "regard[ed] as daring
and radical by many, actually expect and demand the most from the poor, in
effect plac[ing] the further burden of their own salvation upon them." They
asked "whether the poor should be held responsible for their own condition,
or be asked to assume the major responsibility for reversing that condition."
To focus on the process of involvement by the poor, they argued,

> obscured the primary goal: to alter the conditions of the poor and to
> abolish poverty. The anti-poverty program has tended to confuse the
> means with the end. It is, in effect, asking the victims of long-standing so-
> cial injustice to change injustice on their own, in effect asking the sick
> person to get himself well. . . . The most insidious defeat comes with the

best intentions through the placing of the burden of transformation of society on the victims, who by virtue of the very nature of their problem, are unequipped to engage more sophisticated adversaries.[49]

Much of the rhetoric of community action had its origins in the attempt by the Democratic party to shore up its own base among the increasingly fragmented working-class populations of the city's ethnic neighborhoods. With the decline of Tammany Hall, the New York City Democratic Party in the late 1950s began to plan ways to hold onto local power. In the late 1950s, the concept of the neighborhood association and community organization developed to replace the link between local communities and City Hall once provided by Tammany. City administrators in the Wagner administration had actively supported organizations like the Lower East Side Neighborhood Association (LENA) and HANA because they believed the benefits of supporting community groups far outweighed the risks of diffusing political power. The Democratic Party wanted to bolster the support of the traditionally democratic constituency for state and federal elections. There was little awareness of the forces that could be unleashed in communities long starved for resources and little awareness that the monies provided to primarily middle-class leaders of these community organizations would result in a "march on City Hall."

Yet, by the mid-1960s, the disillusionment with traditional political machinery among an increasingly frustrated black and Puerto Rican working class was leading to confrontations with the very governmental agencies that were funding antipoverty programs. A vigorous debate ensued among community organizers about testing the limits. In the Lower East Side's Mobilization for Youth, as well as HANA, activists tried to figure out how far they could go in mobilizing the community before the governmental agencies would withdraw funding and even try to destroy them. At the HANA retreat, Yale presented a view—common at the time—that community groups could be isolated and paralyzed if they worried about the consequences of confrontation. No organization that accepted antipoverty funds could hope to have any impact on poor communities unless it was willing to be disruptive and confrontational. Real change, Yale said, "cannot be accomplished with anything less than total war." Dr. Elizabeth Davis, a black psychiatrist at Harlem Hospital and former Northside board member, married to Ray Trussel, a professor of public health at Columbia who had recently authored an important report on hospital care in New York, disagreed; she saw Yale's approach as naive and potentially destructive. No funding agency would allow HANA, for example, to create "a real opponent to the goals of the white power structure." Those advocating a confrontational approach were "in for a great disillusionment." Charles Rangel, a rising political star in Harlem, suggested a third approach, arguing that the white power structure's own rhetoric could be employed to empower community organizations. "I do believe that while it will be a power struggle, they [the city's administrators] will appreciate it because it would create a higher type of citizen action in New York." When Davis expressed incredulity at his suggestion that the "'white power structure' want[ed] to develop better citizens," Rangel replied, "I defy them to honestly and candidly admit that they don't want this type of thing. . . . Whether they deal with HANA or not they're going to have to deal with somebody in Harlem," and it was to their advantage to know who that somebody was. Echoing Clark's earlier observation, he said "you can't bargain with anyone unless you have an organization structure. This is what we're asking HARYOU to allow HANA to do—to create the atmosphere so that people can assume the responsibility and ultimately bargain with the so-called dominant white power structure."[50]

HARYOU's final report, *Youth in the Ghetto*, issued in 1964, was shaped and much of it written by Kenneth Clark, whose *Dark Ghetto* of 1965 grew out of it. Given Clark's theories on social power, it is no accident that the HARYOU report was subtitled *A Study of the Consequences of Powerlessness*, for it was born out of his growing frustration with traditional dependence for dealing with problems of poverty in the black "ghettos" of America on the benevolence of the private philanthropy and governmental bureaucracies. His hope for an integrated assault on social pathology was undermined by years of disappointment, and Clark was now convinced that Harlem would have to turn inward, to its own resources and political base to effect meaningful change. Only by drawing on its own strengths as an African-American community with the potential for real political power could Harlem seriously address the rapidly accelerating problems associated with poverty, social dislocation, drugs, crime, inadequate housing, and disastrous schools.[51] Not that he believed this approach would actually work. Without massive infusion of funds and an end to Harlem's isolation, in the long run no meaningful systemic change could occur. But he saw no way forward except to attempt to meet immediate needs with available resources—to try, as he often said, not to sacrifice another generation of children.

Ironically, HARYOU, and specifically, Kenneth Clark, now became the target of a massive and well-coordinated campaign from within the community (or so it appeared) that sought to undermine them as an independent force. With the government's commitment of resources in view, Adam Clayton Powell Jr., then chairman of the House Education and Welfare Committee, had set up ACT, Associated Community Teams, as a competitive community agency to HARYOU. It, too, was funded by the President's Committee on Juvenile Delinquency. While the HANA board was debating the meaning and limits of community action, Powell was mobilizing federal and local official support to dislodge Kenneth Clark and take over HARYOU. He employed the rhetoric of coordination, activism, and community empowerment to try to take advantage of federal suggestions that HARYOU and ACT ought to join forces, not compete. In June, he began a concerted attack on Clark and, in the process, targeted Northside itself as a political tool of both the Clarks; he also targeted his own political opponents, such as James Dumpson, who were members of the HARYOU board. Powell sought to portray the Clarks as profiteers benefiting from public monies that might otherwise go to more worthy antipoverty programs—such as his own. He charged that Kenneth and Mamie Clark were "making a tremendous sum of money" from their activities in HARYOU, in HANA, and in Northside, with Northside taking "between $10 and $12 million of the $110 million allocated to the antipoverty program." [52]

Kenneth Clark said privately at the time, and repeated in his oral history, that Powell offered him an opportunity to share the spoils of federal largess and was offended when Clark turned him down.[53] Northside's board president, Howard Sloan, issued a press release that pointed out the total budget of Northside was only $240,000 a year and that "the antipoverty budget is already drawn up and no funds are ear-marked for the Northside Center for Child Development." [54] A few weeks later, on 7 July 1964, the newly merged HARYOU-ACT board failed to elect Kenneth Clark as one of its officers and, three weeks later on 29 July, Clark resigned from the organization he had founded. The impact of this resignation from HARYOU brought to the fore HARYOU's political importance; it was perhaps the largest source of federal antipoverty money in the nation, and Powell had felt he had a right to direct its use. As Kenneth Clark pointed out, the experience at HARYOU proved that Powell had "this community all locked up." Clark saw HARYOU as "the last chance available for thousands of young people in Harlem" and Powell's political maneuvering as endangering that chance.[55] For liberals, white and black, the message was particularly troubling, since Clark represented the scholarly and professional communities. "Dr. Kenneth Clark was recently crushed by practical politicians when he tried to steer the local anti-poverty program on an independent professional course," said the *Nation*. Woody Klein, the reporter from the *New York World-Telegram*, who had broken the story of the HARYOU-ACT split in the *Nation* piece, described "the mild-mannered, 50-year-old City College of New York psychology professor [who had] . . . stepped out of his role as scholar when he publicly accused Powell of trying to make HARYOU a 'political pork barrel.'"[56]

If one door closed, another opened. Clark now began to write what became his most noted book, *Dark Ghetto: Dilemmas of Social Power*, which discussed, among other things, the nature of Powell's power. He turned over his royalties to Northside and laid plans to reenter the fight over Harlem from another direction. With funding from the Ford Foundation, the Carnegie Corporation, and other sources, he organized the integrated MARC Corporation, from which new base he was to work with national civil rights leaders, provide significant leadership in the school decentralization struggle, undertake major research into racial segregation, accept a request from the school board of Washington, D.C. (and propose reform of that system), help organize black elected officials nationally, found the Joint Center for Political Studies in Washington, D.C., and so on.

In the midst of the struggle over HARYOU and over the meaning of community empowerment and action had come the bitter fruit of the "Harlem riot" of July 1964. Over the course of several days, store windows were smashed and angry residents of Harlem and Brooklyn's Bedford-Stuyvesant clashed with police. Two people were killed, dozens injured, and there was tremendous property damage. Although the Harlem disorders seem relatively tame compared to the soon-to-come uprisings in Watts, Detroit, Newark, and other African-American communities, at the time they were startling and terrifying to a city accustomed to seeing itself as a mecca of liberalism and racial enlightenment. City administrators and public officials portrayed these disorders as the product of outside agitators. Paul Screvane, then Acting Mayor, saw "Reds" behind the rioting, also "Fringe groups," "pick-pockets, thieves and burglars," and "youngsters with nothing better to do."[57] Screvane focused his outrage especially on the militant Lower East Side antipoverty program, Mobilization for Youth, accusing it of issuing an inflammatory leaflet charging the police with the murder of a young black man. Over the course of the summer, the *Daily News* and other New York tabloids trumpeted that MFY had a cadre of communists intent on inflaming racial and class passions in the city. Accusations of communist infiltration of antipoverty programs, almost commonplace by now, crippled MFY and drove radicals out of it and certain other government funded community action groups.

The confluence of internal battles in HARYOU and the outside attack on MFY combined to undermine the faith of the Harlem community in the once so promising federal antipoverty program. When, in August 1964, President Johnson, with much fanfare and media attention, had launched his War on Poverty, many in Harlem reacted at first with cynicism and anger. From Kenneth Clark's perspective, such cynicism was legitimate. In a study sponsored by the Stern Family Fund, he analyzed the conditions under which antipoverty programs failed or succeeded, including the tactics of participation by the poor on governing boards and in confrontation with white power. In *A Relevant War against Poverty*, Kenneth Clark and Jeannette Hopkins concluded that federally funded antipoverty programs foundered on the inability and unwillingness of the powerful in the society to "share even a modicum of real power with those who have been powerless." The "poor and the powerless are perceived and treated as if they are objects to be manipulated, taunted, played with, and punished by those with power." The poor "are required to be grateful for the verbalizations and crumbs of power and are rejected as incorrigibly inferior, childlike, or barbaric if they rebel against and otherwise disturb the convenience of their more powerful benefactor." Despite the rhetoric of meaningful empowerment, "antipoverty programs . . . were doomed to failure because they reflected a total lack of commitment to eliminate poverty, to share power with the powerless." At root, the antipoverty programs were based on racist assumptions and paternalistic traditions that saw the objects of charity as "inferior human beings" and "did not want to, and would not, operate in terms of the rationale and goals of the potential equality of all human beings. They did not seek to accept and strengthen the humanity of the deprived through compassion, empathy, and a serious sharing of power."[58] Screvane's attack on New York's antipoverty programs after the Harlem riots, for one, could be seen in this light.

Community Outreach: Power as Therapy

The Northside Center, as a professionally dominated institution with a middle- and upper-class board, black and white, drawn primarily from outside of Harlem, was now struggling with a newly urgent question. How does an organization created and maintained by professionals and wealthy benefactors maintain relevance in a poor community, much of whose political leadership seeks self-determination and political empowerment? Northside's answer was to reorganize both the program and its board and to strengthen its roots in Harlem. It needed to recruit "community members . . . whose contributions are primarily in terms of reflecting the basic community currents and concerns." [59]

As Mamie Clark observed, "within the past ten years, the community pressures and demands on the Northside Center have increased significantly and have been made more insistent by the impact of the civil rights movement and most recently by the repercussions of the 'war on poverty.'" As a result, Northside developed a more intensive emphasis on community involvement and advocacy, in part a natural outgrowth of its experience with their clients and their needs, in part a response to their "current experience with parent groups [that evidenced] a far more militant mood." [60] Northside was evolving a therapeutic program in which empowerment was a critical element in treatment. Now, Mamie Clark focused more on developing political as well as personal strength for Harlem's children and residents, and she began to cultivate links to groups Northside had never before approached.

Mamie Clark pondered the evolution of Northside. It had, at first, "responded to the urgent need for direct service" even while it "recognized its limitations in terms of helping the vast number of families in Harlem who are in need." Then, it built a program "of mental health education for large groups of persons, other than those in service on the premises," but Northside had had to break down the resistance in Harlem to the very idea of "seeking psychiatric help." This early phase of Northside's "community *education* approach . . . was highly intellectual [for] at that time children in service at Northside Center were seen by the community at large and rejected or punished as 'crazy.'" Then the staff at Northside began to provide consultation services to "public school personnel, ministers' groups, nurses' groups and nursery schools' staffs." [61]

As "parents became more restive and militant, it became apparent that new approaches to the community were required." As Mamie Clark noted in 1968, "as I look at the Northside Center for Child Development program from an historical perspective, it is apparent that this agency, serving the Harlem and East Harlem areas, has itself been strongly influenced by the dynamic and changing forces in the ghetto." Northside needed to find ways of "channelling . . . energies into active and realistic ways for parents to help themselves, their children and their community to a healthier life." Earlier attempts at community outreach focused on ways individual families could aid themselves, while now "discussions [were] geared to planned action," with parents' groups, which included "far more 'indigenous' members." In 1968, it supported parents' efforts at organized protest against crowded conditions and poor staffing in a local elementary school: "Last year one group worked successfully to organize a 'constructive' protest against conditions in a neighborhood school rather than 'protest for protest sake.'" [62]

Many aspects of Northside's program would have to be developed and changed if the center were to become a vehicle for true empowerment in the community. Northside's board itself would have to reflect that change. At its inception two decades before, Northside's board had been composed primarily of white liberal philanthropists plus black professionals and, in the 1960s, a larger number of African-American political leaders and professionals, among them J. Raymond Jones, known as the "Harlem Fox," and Robert Carter, who had been Thurgood Marshall's principal assistant in the *Brown* case. Mamie Clark now brought onto the board a long-time grassroots activist in the Harlem community, Elaine Gaspard, a mother who had been deeply involved in school integration fights, housing battles, and urban renewal in Harlem. She described Gaspard as "very dedicated, very sincere," as one who had "worked very hard programmatically, financially to secure the welfare of this community." [63]

Gaspard promptly demonstrated the dynamics of a broader class-mix on Northside's board, finding herself "at odds" with some members who, she felt, "really didn't [have a] complete understanding of the needs [of Harlem]. I guess in some ways I was a rebel on the Board." [64] In August, the Los Angeles neighborhood of Watts had exploded as did a number of African-American communities throughout urban America, leading to the creation of the historic National Advisory Commission on Civil Disorders by Lyndon Johnson. Also known as the Kerner Commission, it warned that the "nation is moving toward two societies, one black, one white, separate and unequal." [65] In September 1965, Olivia Edwards, Northside's director of community education programs, had brought together a few of Northside's staff and Harlem residents to consider how Northside could respond to the growing anger and frustration of the Harlem community. As a representative of one of the most important social-service agencies in Harlem, she found herself in the midst of a political cauldron as public officers and community activists responded to the growing frustration and unrest in black communities.

Until the mid-1960s, much of the impetus for reform in northern African-American communities had come from established organizations like Northside, largely controlled by middle-class, generally middle-aged boards, a few of them integrated. But, by the mid-1960s, younger, more militant activists were claiming to speak for the disenfranchised and the poor. Unlike older social-service and civil rights organizations, they rejected the older middle-class and white leadership, arguing that the African-American poor had to speak—and organize—for themselves. A new class- and race-conscious political militancy emerged in Harlem, as groups like the Black Panthers, the Black Muslims, and SNCC, among others, began to vie for the loyalty of young activists. Northside had to reconcile the new demands with its long-standing ties to the established social-service agencies and community groups, and to the white power system itself.

Olivia Edwards called together at Northside's offices thirteen former clients who lived in the Central Park North area near Northside. She explained that Northside sought a broader role in addressing "family and community problems." Speaker after speaker at the small meeting conveyed a "sense of hopelessness and frustration," but to Edwards this itself provided an opportunity for Northside. "They have not yet found anyone to whom they can turn for help and direction," Edwards confided to Mamie Clark afterward, targeting this as "where Northside can play an important role." It became apparent that an enormous gulf existed between the Northside professionals and the community residents, however. But at the next meeting, and again ten days later, twenty-three residents, most unknown to the Northside staff, engaged Edwards in heated arguments, demanding to know just "how far Northside is prepared to go, participate, cooperate [in] . . . actions that were illegal." It was, after all, a time of rent strikes, school boycotts, and sit-ins on bridges and at traffic intersections, some legal and some extralegal. They wanted to know if Edwards was trying to form a group independent of Northside and outside of its control? Or was this an attempt by Northside's professional staff and elite board to control them and militants in the community?[66] Edwards was caught unaware. Without more guidance from the Northside board, she could not, of course, commit Northside to activities, certainly not to illegal ones. Her demeanor, hesitation, and uncertainty fueled more suspicion and distrust. What appeared to the Northside staff at the meeting as their genuine attempt to reach out to the community seemed to certain community militants as another example of middle-class resistance to change. The next day, Edwards told Mamie Clark that "there appeared to be growing hostility and doubt as to Northside's intentions, within the group." [67]

While Northside was grappling with the practical problem of how to empower a community under attack from within and without and torn apart by released anger, Kenneth Clark was formulating his analysis of the nature of power relationships in the larger city and nation as a whole, that would lead, in 1974, to his *Pathos of Power*. In the mid-1960s, Clark was defining "social power" as "the force or energy required to bring about, to sustain, or to prevent social, political, or economic change." To him, social power, like electricity, was a neutral force that could be used positively or negatively. Beginning with the assumption that established politicians and white groups had little interest in upsetting the status quo, he sought to understand the place of Harlem in this power equation. Harlem was first and foremost a ghetto, Clark observed, and as such was a creation and manifestation of the white system's intent on maintaining existing power relations by isolating and confining troublesome blacks. Harlem and other segregated communities were evidence and proof of the powerlessness of their African-American residents, whether or not at times they were able to appear to transcend the boundaries, as in the Harlem Renaissance of the arts in the 1920s. "The confinement of powerless individuals to restrictive ghettos in the North can be seen as an example of power by control." [68] He studied the approaches necessary to confront the oppression of African Americans in the American South and in the North. In the South, the civil rights movement had been able to mobilize hundreds of thousands of middle- and working-class blacks in an alliance with northern and southern liberal whites and an eager generation of young people, white and black, to tear down the citadels of segregation. In the North, without the clearer, more vulnerable, more dramatic targets of de jure segregation, such unity had been elusive, if not impossible. [69] What new strategies could work in the North? The antipoverty programs were a revealing and discouraging test.

Kenneth Clark's 1971 presidential address to the American Psychological Association would review the theoretical basis for Northside's expansionist definition of therapy, developed during the 1960s. He looked at the schism that had developed between professionals there with psychiatrists tending to maintain a strong commitment to Freudian and other traditional forms of psychoanalysis and those who were seeking theoretical legitimacy for community empowerment as part of the therapeutic process. He argued that "Freudian theory does not appear to offer a theoretical basis for a psychology concerned [with] social change or a psychotechnology other than one-to-one psychoanalytic therapy." Indeed, it inhibited "the quest for a more enlightened social policy" because "morally and rationally determined social change could not proceed from the premise that man is a totally or primarily nonrational organism whose most powerful drives are instinctive and animalistic." With the Northside Center's staff searching for a way to reconcile individual therapy with efforts to change the negatives in the individual's environment, he, as had Mamie Clark, warned against uses of environmental theory, as in theories of "cultural deprivation," that he saw as a newer, more subtle process of blaming the victims for their maladjustment. Kenneth Clark turned to other interpersonal theorists, specifically, to Alfred Adler who, he felt, showed a "concern with man's social interaction." Adler placed a greater "emphasis on the human struggle for self-esteem," concerns "much more compatible with my main research and action." In contrast to Freud who, in Clark's view, saw humans as essentially powerless to alter and shape their social environment, Adler demanded greater personal and social control over one's fate. The ability to "bring about, to sustain, or to prevent social, political or economic change" had to be at the heart of any successful psychological theory. "The core Adlerian idea which persists in its influence on my thinking concerns the nature of psychological power in understanding human beings and human society." Clark held that "Bertrand Russell's assertion that 'the fundamental concept in social science is Power, in the same sense in which Energy is a fundamental concept in physics' reinforced the influence of Adlerian theory in my thinking."[70]

The American Psychological Association paper stirred up a hornet's nest of protest in the profession and in the press, ostensibly because of its prescription of medical, specifically drug, intervention in preventing extreme behavior among top political leadership. Commentators all but ignored Kenneth Clark's theoretical arguments on power and powerlessness in psychotherapy.

At the conference organized by MARC at the Delmonico Hotel in New York in 1969 to consider Northside's future program, Isadore Zwerling, a psychiatrist from Bronx State Hospital, addressed what he called "this question of powerlessness" as "a real turning point in the current period in psychiatry." Zwerling noted the correlation between community action and "the growing awareness of the artificiality of the current diagnostic categories which are divorced from the social reality in which people live." In response to a comment by Dr. Elizabeth Davis, who thought it impossible for clinicians to avoid political activities, Zwerling remarked that, if Northside's clinicians addressed themselves to "powerlessness," which he saw as "a mental health problem of the patients [they] serve," the clinicians themselves would "in no time" find themselves "involved in . . . political activities." [71]

By the end of the 1960s, some black psychologists would argue that the very "pathologies" that Kenneth Clark, Northside, and HARYOU identified were, in fact, strengths, necessary positive adaptations to a hostile, racist world. In their most extreme form, these arguments strongly attacked the very idea of therapy. Preston Wilcox, for example, a black educational consultant long active in the East Harlem Council for Community Planning, in an essay in a 1973 collection, *Racism and Mental Health*, said, "my message has been that people have a right to suffer mental health problems; that for black people many of these problems emanate from the condition of white institutional racism; that many of these problems will disappear the moment that Blacks begin to define themselves; that the treatment of Blacks must be officially assigned to Blacks or the consumers themselves." [72] In this context, the Clarks and Northside were mediators between the dominant professional and political world and the emerging tendencies among some in the African-American professional and political communities to see virtues in what the Clarks would view as "segregation."

Mamie Clark was concerned that Northside, by providing services for its clients and adopting an advocacy role, "might even be perpetuating the condition of powerlessness on the part of our clients, and this is something that stumped me, because I hadn't thought about it before." As she had said at the 1969 conference, "I think you [Zwerling] implied that by even [having] an area of diagnostic categories here [we] are really perpetuating a sense of powerlessness." "The implication of what we're saying here today can stem a little farther . . . it really implies that our treatment of choice—whether it's family therapy or individual therapy or whatever—involves helping families to determine their own needs—which is pushing therapy, I think a little towards political activity, and involving political activity within the treatment program and plan itself." [73]

Kenneth Clark, in a summary of the intellectual and programmatic changes that had transformed Northside's program over the previous decade, cautioned the broader mental-health community of the dangers professionals faced if they did not reform their own attitudes, beliefs, and assumptions: "We can no longer afford our past rationalizations, our past defenses, for that matter, even our past prejudices." Psychiatrists, social workers, psychologists, and other mental-health workers had to

> break down the distinctions between mental health as a personal problem . . . and mental health as a problem of social stability. This to me is probably the most significant thing that has happened in recent years [in the field]. . . . we can no longer afford the luxury of looking at mental health problems in terms of the adjustment of a particular individual. . . . [Rather,] we must now see the problem of our cities, the problem of equality in nature, the moral substance of our society, and the problem of individual adjustment as one or—at worst—interrelated. . . . The goal of mental health, therefore, can no longer be one in which we help individuals to adjust to their environment no matter what the quality of their environment.

Empowerment of the client, through personal growth or political action, had to be central to any serious therapeutic process: "The individual has to be helped to attain the strength to mobilize his own energies and resources to bring about the changes in the environment which are consistent with human dignity." [74]

Earlier, in the summer of 1968, with a $10,000 grant from the Greater New York Fund, Northside had established an intensive summer tutorial program for twenty-six children from Northside's waiting list and another fifty children from local schools. Unique to the program was its utilization of local high school students as tutors for children reading between one and three years below grade level. The politics of Harlem in 1968, following Martin Luther King Jr.'s assassination at Eastertime, had stirred many community activists and many young people to abandon and distrust what they saw as accomodationist approaches. Interested in teaching reading, writing, and arithmetic, the high school and college tutors in the Northside program were determined also to provide the children with a new radical culture, politics, and even a new language. Jeanne Karp, reflecting later on the tensions that developed over that hot summer as the students struggled with their own personal reasons for participating in Northside's program, says, "the tutors were much concerned with issues such as whether to teach the children Swahili or whether to condone the idea of a separate black state." In the end, although they rejected both the practicality of teaching a new language in one summer and also the politics of black separatism, some tutors came away from the experience wishing that Northside would play a much more active role in the political movements and protests of the time.[75]

Two who participated as tutors evaluated the program as it was winding down in the fall of 1968. They were, they said, "extremely proud of what happened at Northside this summer," but troubled by certain community reactions to Northside. They reported hearing conversations that reflected a general ignorance of Northside's purpose and relevance. "Either they did not know its function or of its existence and did not care to, or they reacted negatively to its function, indeed to its existence." This was disturbing to the student tutors because "we felt that Northside could effectively deal with those complexities [of the society] and had the potential to be a meaningful force in clarifying or altering them." Despite Northside's extraordinary clinic program and its attempt to reach out to Harlem, the tutors worried that "Northside does not thoroughly relate to the rapidly changing contemporary problems which the Harlem residents face because Northside does not treat those problems in a contemporary way." The tutors diagnosed Northside's problem and prescribed a remedy:

> What is needed is to attack the problems of that community offensively rather than attempting to react to them. Northside must take stands on relevant issues (i.e., Welfare, housing, job discrimination, ghetto schools) by participating with those groups *as an institution* and thereby establishing communication links with the community, putting itself on the line as an institution in order to graphically show that they are *for* the community—that they are a part of the processes and resources of the community. . . . It is said over and over again that times have changed.[76]

The school decentralization struggle of 1968 and the Union of Concerned Parents were important in establishing Northside's legitimacy among many parents and children. Still, as Victor Carter recalls, considerable tension confronted Northside during these years. Sometimes, when Carter reached out to skeptical militants, he had to tell them that many of Northside's leadership and staff, including himself and Kenneth Clark, had been raised in Harlem and educated in its public schools.[77]

Sam Walton, then a young activist and now a social worker with the New York City department of human services, recalls the exciting social and political environment in which Northside's staff was working. An African American, Walton had grown up in central Harlem near 137th Street and 8th Avenue. "On 125th Street and 7th Avenue all these militant guys would be on

the corner," he recalls. They would stand "on a ladder with a black national-
ist flag . . . speaking to us and telling us we should do things for the community." The themes of many of the speeches revolved around "Black Power"
and self-help. National and local orators such as Adam Clayton Powell Jr.,
Malcolm X, and Porkchop Davis, a local activist, would arouse the crowds:
"Every week," Walton says, "I would go to that corner religiously and listen
to them, and they just gave me that direction, that sense of pride." As a
young teenager, Walton had been stirred by the Freedom Riders and the civil
rights movement, in general, and by the Harlem Education Project, a group
of black and white students from City College and New York University who
organized tutoring and summer-camp programs for children in Harlem.
"We were intrigued with this interracial group in the middle of Harlem," he
remembers. "We began to look into some of the militant groups, and we
were doing a lot of listening to the street corner philosophers. Whatever
group we went to and whatever person we listened to, we got something out
of it. We never bought the whole message completely."[78] The part of the
message that Walton, skeptical or not, and his friend Sam Gaynor did take
away from the ongoing dialogue in Harlem in the early 1960s was the conclusion that African-American youth must assume new responsibilities for
bringing about change in the Harlem community. In contrast to much of the
revolutionary rhetoric of the moment, the overall message that got through
was that small, highly personal changes were as important as national antipoverty initiatives.

"One day a mother came to me and said, 'Sam, you know my son never
had a birthday party before and he's ten years old and would you be interested in having a party for him.'" Thus began We Care, formed by the two
Sams and four other young people in September 1968. It was the middle of
the UFT teachers' strike, and, shortly afterwards, the group of six met Ella
Baker, a founder of SNCC and by then a legend in the civil rights community. "In the midst of all her organizing, she found time for a small outfit like
ourselves," Sam Walton recalled. "She put on paper for us the guiding concept of We Care." In many ways, of course, We Care was not so different
from the traditional church and civic programs for children throughout poor
neighborhoods. We Care members took children to museums, the United
Nations, special exhibits. It set up a speakers program on African-American
history and culture because the youth "realized that no one seemed to be
caring for the children who were neglected and exposed to neighborhood
vices (drugs, crime, poverty, etc.)." But they framed these activities differently, seeing them as part of a political, as well as cultural, activity that would

benefit the children and the young staff members alike. Joyce Cleveland, one of the group, described We Care as "a group of youngsters between the ages of 17 and 25 dedicated to combat social evils in the Central Harlem Community through meaningful community involvement." We Care was also distinguished by its view that "a significant part of the youngsters' problems" stemmed from "negative attitudes. . . . We Care tries to make them understand what conditions made them feel the way they do. They make the kids see how the system operates against them—not only because they are Black, but because they are poor." Walton recalled that the inspiration for We Care was the principle laid out in Kenneth Clark's *Dark Ghetto*: you can send a message from the bottom up. Young people needed to make demands on the larger community.[79]

Ella Baker had provided the group with a coherent set of principles and ideals; Emma Bowen, another Harlem community activist, provided ongoing encouragement. We Care was in serious financial trouble; their planned after-school and summertime activities all required money. "In the very early days of We Care, we were often in the struggle for survival. We were like a sick person who needs help. At that time Emma gave us oxygen," Sam Walton said in 1976. Bowen suggested that Northside, as one of the few stable child-care agencies in Harlem, "could help us to get our program better organized . . . and Emma arranged to bring the Northside group to us" to discuss a possible collaboration. Mamie Clark assigned Blanche Pugh and Victor Carter to meet with We Care to see if such a alliance would fit with Northside's efforts to establish new relationships with community organizations. Their first meetings were fraught with misgivings and distrust. From We Care's perspective, Northside seemed an extraordinarily wealthy and established institution with over a half-million dollar budget and a professional staff with access to political and economic power in the white community "downtown." "We were cautioned by some of the street corner philosophers not to go to Northside. They said that Northside was full of magicians and that they had plenty of tricks." Sam Walton was told that Northside represented the "establishment" and that all it wanted to do was "to expand its empire." Besides, Northside would not respect them.[80]

Victor Carter recalls their first encounter at Northside's professional quarters:

> One day [Walton] came into my office. I'll never forget it. He's about six feet tall and other Sam was about that and . . . they brought this little wiry cat, slim dark-skinned fellow, what you call a "bad cat." . . . He just looked

hostile. So we were talking and they [had] a lot of questions about North-side. I said "Well, now look. I know you have a lot of questions but my advice is you check something out before you start coming to a conclu-sion." I said "Now I don't know what you think of me." I said "You come in here and you see me. I got this desk and Dr. Mamie Clark's down there and she's the boss and I'm wearing this suit and this tie and you're going to think I'm the biggest square thing you've ever seen." I said "But you don't know that yet." And I said, "That cat out on the corner with his dashiki and his full, you know, he—you may think he's right and he may be the shucking and jiving type." So I said, "If you're smart, you check me out. You check him out. Now if you check me out and find I'm the big phony you think I am, then fine. You try to kick my butt. But you don't know that yet. So if you drop me or drop Mamie Clark or anybody before you do it, that's just dumb." [81]

It is an understatement to say that "at first both sides were a little suspi-cious of each other," especially in light of Northside's response to We Care's first request for funds. We Care tested Carter by asking for "$50 to go on a trip." Carter said Northside couldn't provide the money. "We never really could understand," Walton related, "how could you have all of this money and we can't get $50." Carter explained the intricacies of budgets and monies that were committed to specific projects, but "it was kind of difficult to un-derstand because as we went back to the street corner philosophers, they said, 'Well, these are nothing but musicians. They're just instruments for the government. . . . They're just professional people just trying to get over.'" [82]

Carter and Pugh continued to work with the "two Sams" and Joyce Cleveland, slowly building trust. "Victor's style put me at ease," Walton re-called. "They helped us plan our first summer program [in 1969], ... We were able to hire 50 youth leaders whom we trained in our workshops. . . . That summer was a real breakthrough for us. In the past, Sam and I had been involved in drop out situations. Now we had a success in that we completed everything we had planned." Although Northside and Mamie Clark did not directly fund We Care in its first years, it did lead the group to other funding sources and tried to train Walton and Gaynor in grantsmanship skills. Slowly, "Northside became our conduit agency. It helped us to get a grant of $10,000 from the Greater New York Fund. . . . [but] Northside . . . did not interfere with our plans. Northside gave us advice but did not force it upon us." [83]

We Care saw tangible benefits of the collaboration, but the rewards were just as important to Northside itself. By 1971, Carter and Pugh had adopted We Care into the Northside family, as they earlier had the mothers' group, seeing it as a concrete connection to the Harlem community. In 1972, the two Sams, through the Manpower Development program, became a part of the paid Northside staff, on salary and with benefits. Carter called this a "giant and unprecedented step" for Northside, one that raised "some challenging and still unresolved problems"; he had originally seen the We Care youth as "clients" in the sense that they were coming to Northside for help. Now, the relationships were changing and these youth were increasingly seen as "colleagues," a transformation that required a new, more egalitarian relationship with the center's staff, who reported to Mamie Clark that the relationship "must be clarified since it is ambiguous and could be a source of difficulty" at some future time.[84]

In 1970-71, We Care became active in a communications program to train high school students in "the theory and techniques of the mass media," developing contacts with CBS and Time-Life, in establishing youth programs with the 137th Street Block Association; it also placed a number of summer interns at Kenneth Clark's MARC. Together, "these projects . . . brought into play the total resources of the agency, including the direct involvement of the Executive and Medical Directors." The most concrete outcome of the relationship to CBS and Time-Life was a film written, directed, and produced by Walton and Gaynor entitled *Sam, Sam in Harlem*. In many ways, the film itself was about empowerment, beginning with a scene showing African dances performed to the beat of a drummer on a hot summer's day on a Harlem street. An elderly, one-legged performer on crutches entertains the crowd; significantly, at the end of the film, he has thrown away his crutches while continuing to perform on one leg. Dealing with issues of poverty, powerlessness, and drugs, *Sam, Sam* is infused with a sense of hope and the possibility of change and renewal. Produced with funds provided by WCBS and WABC television, it was broadcast by New York's Channel 7 in 1974.[85]

Sam Walton approached Dr. Lucienne Numa, Northside's chief of therapy, to suggest that the two of them go into "the community [to] deal with some of the people that need professional help," so that "we can reach them together as a team," and Numa agreed. Every Tuesday between 5:30 and 7:30 P.M. the two took to the streets of Harlem. "We would run into people that I knew at random and we would talk to them . . . and they would talk easily because they knew me and I told them this was Dr. So-and-So. It was very informal, right on the street corner or sometimes in the local bar." This outreach located people who might never have made their way to Northside services and treatment. But, there was a larger purpose: "She was teaching, by her being in the community face-to-face and giving us some point of views about some of the conditions. . . . And it was fascinating because people just shared themselves right there." [86]

Mamie Clark wrote in a review of the center's history in 1976, "one of the problems that has plagued social agencies over the years has been the fact that large segments of our communities, perhaps those most in need, do not make of our services. We have long realized that our services as presently organized and delivered rule out, by their very nature, those who are not able to mobilize themselves, due to lack of understanding, fear or what have you, to use the standard office or home visit approach." [87] We Care was in constant contact with Harlem residents "far out of reach of [the] agency," as Walton said, and therefore, "many such residents have been brought into the agency services." [88] Northside recognized that We Care was "that bridge for them [because] we were reaching that segment of the community." [89]

Walton believed that "the community was saying they want to . . . feel [Northside's] presence in more ways than a clinic with just one child. Activists in Harlem kept "asking for more," demanding that Northside become "involved in housing or . . . rent strikes or . . . other issues." A more traditional center might have simply said that these were not mental-health issues. Over the years, We Care became an important addendum to Northside's clinical program. The two Sams published a newspaper by and for young people called *City Scene* between 1973 and 1978.[90] At other levels, Northside was also extending its network. Olivia Edwards had organized a Community Service Council for Northside and put out a newsletter, *Inside Northside*, in 1966, just as Mamie Clark was introducing her concept of Northside as an "umbrella" organization. The council had sponsored workshops on housing and welfare procedures and on children's behavior and learning problems, helped to mediate parent and teacher conflicts, and provided advocacy for parents and others. Members also worked in the community to involve parents in school meetings and associations.[91] Yet, almost immediately, as the council sought a more egalitarian and less professional image, its character began to change. The newsletter altered its name to become *Inside and Outside Northside*, responding to the need to reach beyond Northside's walls. Few centers elsewhere had ever attempted this balancing of traditional professional services for children and community involvement.

By 1970, Olivia Edwards was organizing a community and group projects department and setting up a new Northside position of a community organizer. Edwards proposed to address "both the psychological set of the people and the environmental defects in the community," and a radicalizing function for psychotherapy itself: "We feel that once aroused and alerted to the possibility of doing something together about their mutual problems, the healthy aggressive drive which is present in people will emerge so that they themselves will take over responsibility for finding ways of improving their condition. We expect also that a chain reaction will be set in motion whereby those people encouraged to assume leadership will seek out others to bring knowledge and hope to them." [92]

The new department, staffed by Edwards and four workers, provided information about community groups seeking to change conditions and itself sponsored two such groups. One of these, the Group Leadership Program, an outgrowth of the Union of Concerned Parents, was set up with impetus from Northside and MARC to respond to the teachers' strike of 1968, organized meetings for community residents on how to deal with issues of housing, health care, urban renewal, political power, and the general impact of powerlessness on the community's self-esteem. The second group, Love, Service and Devotion (LSD), developed an educational and treatment program for narcotics addicts and their families.

Northside's most far-ranging outreach program of the late 1960s and early 1970s was its Walk-on-in Service Center. Between 1969 and 1972, the number of yearly visits to the Walk-on-in Service jumped from a hundred to more than eleven hundred. It attracted people with a host of problems, most seemingly only tenuously related to traditional mental health, principally, housing issues, complaints about Harlem and East Harlem's educational system, the inadequacy of day care, consumer fraud issues, and other legal problems; marital difficulties, business matters, and narcotics addiction. Edwards believed the Walk-on-in Center's role was not one of "simply . . . telling the client where to go. The community consultant took on an important advocacy role here in linkage between client and one or more agencies." [93]

Class and Race in Neglected El Barrio

Northside's move to 110th Street, just to the west of "El Barrio," had brought in a new group of clients with a different language and its own culture. In the two years between 1953 and 1955, the percentage of total client caseload that came from across Fifth Avenue, or Spanish Harlem, nearly doubled, from 11 percent to 20 percent. By 1974, one in four of its population was Spanish-speaking.[94] There would be an even more dramatic rise in Hispanic children at Northside in the next two decades; by 1990, they were about half of Northside's patient population. The number of Spanish-speaking staff had increased; and productive relationships had been established with PS 155 and PS 165, both bilingual schools in East Harlem.[95] In 1952, Northside began to try to accommodate this growing number of Puerto Rican clients. It hired bilingual staff to bridge the cultural gap[96] and in 1953 established a Spanish-speaking clinic team of two psychiatrists, a psychologist, and a psychiatric caseworker.

"A psychiatrist of Puerto Rican background worked with our Puerto Rican youngsters and particularly those who did not speak English well," as Kenneth Clark remarked later. By the end of that psychiatrist's first year at Northside, his entire caseload was Puerto Rican. Yet when the administration evaluated the progress of these children, it discovered they "had not made much improvement," nor did they the following year. "We had to look into this," Clark said, "and finally we found the clue. Dr. Y was an upper class Puerto Rican. He had come from a high status family in Puerto Rico and somehow or other his empathy, attitude toward the working class Puerto Ricans, left something to be desired. We learned from seeing this, many things." What the clinic learned confirmed what the Clarks had been maintaining since the mid-1940s: that the child's or the staff's ethnicity or race alone was not the crucial factor in determining success in therapy. What was most crucial was quality of the professionals, especially whether they were willing to try to overcome their own social, class, and racial biases. "At Northside we have been banking on the possibility that exposure to children of different backgrounds would, in time, affect the professional skill and competence of work. I have not ever heard before in my knowledge of social agencies, any social agency that had decided to look at the problem of sensitivity, insight and understanding of inter-group relations, and how such understanding could be made to improve professional[s]." Kenneth Clark concluded that "effective work with our children at Northside is not always the [product of] training or even experience."[97]

Northside had had a long and solid relationship to institutions and individuals in the African-American community, but it did not develop as strong ties to the neighboring Hispanic community of East Harlem until the early 1970s. It was then planning another move, to the east side of Fifth Avenue and 110th Street, historically the informal demarcation between African-American and Hispanic Harlem. Josefa Quintana, an Hispanic staff member active in Victor Carter's case work department, led the new effort to establish relationships with Puerto Rican and other Hispanic groups in East Harlem. "Spanish Harlem has many small groups, but not any of them is strong enough to influence the entire community," Quintana maintained. "This lack of organization reflects the lack of services that the community needs [and people] must go out of their area for services . . . [they need but do] not have the strength to demand." She believed that, with "patience and constant work," Northside could "play an important role with this neglected group." Northside would benefit from the involvement in Hispanic East Harlem; should Northside be perceived as tied solely to the African-American political community to its west, it could face "a very serious problem." It was important to allay any fear that Northside was part of an eastward push by African Americans but also to avoid the numerous pitfalls of racial politics among Puerto Ricans themselves. She suggested establishing a new storefront center in East Harlem and initiating a series of workshops to train Northside staff itself for the new work. Soon Northside had set up an annex on upper Park Avenue.[98] But, by early 1974, staff morale was low—the annex was isolated from the main center; the building lacked heat and hot water, and was inaccessible to public transportation. The impact on the staff was "a disaster. . . . Our morale [was] reaching the lowest stage."[99]

The center was again placed between a broader society that was abandoning Harlem and the demands for action from white and black activists that the Clarks saw as acts of despair rather than as creative uses of power. Neither of the Clarks found doctrine of any sort—social science or political—congenial; and neither gave primary loyalty to any political ideology. Liberal in style and goals, even radical and daring, they nonetheless found liberal and radical theories and practice confusing, and they sought allies wherever they could find them without regard to race or station or ideology. They were as likely to be friends with a Rockefeller or a McGeorge Bundy as with Malcolm X or a liberal or radical activist, perhaps even more likely. They saw the taint of racism in many sites of power that others did not see and the absence of it where others would have expected it.

7. Urban Renewal and Development and the Promise of Power

Plans for a Gateway to a New, Integrated Harlem

On New Year's Eve 1964, Kenneth and Mamie Clark lunched with a small group of architects, realtors, and friends to discuss a project important both to the stability and progress of Northside and Harlem as a whole. The proposal was to rebuild the area from East 107th and 112th Streets between Fifth and Lexington Avenues. The Clarks believed the southeast corner of Harlem at Central Park, known as Frawley Circle, could become the foundation for the transformation of the entire community. Frawley Circle was less than a block away from Northside's home in the New Lincoln School and at the nexus of African-American Harlem to the west and north, Spanish Harlem to the east, and white upper Fifth Avenue to the south. It could become a symbol of the integrated, multiethnic, multi-class community the Clarks had envisioned for many years. "The scheme would turn the area, now a pocket of decay, into a development for whites and Negroes in a kind of middle ground blending Harlem with downtown Manhattan," announced a feature story in the *World-Telegram and Sun*.[1]

The group sought to "develop a cultural, commercial, educational, entertainment . . . gateway at the northeast corner of Central Park," envisioned with a wide variety of institutions, programs, and industries in a model community. Plans included an auditorium, a theater, private and public schools, a college, a library, a department store, medical facilities, state, city, and federal office spaces, a community center, as well as upper- and middle-income apartments and town houses. The project was ambitious and visionary, and all participants agreed to contact local and national leaders to begin to gather the necessary political and economic support for this "Gateway to Harlem."[2]

Two weeks later, Northside hosted a larger follow-up meeting. Mamie Clark was voted temporary chairman of the Committee for Central Park North. Economists, planners, architects, and community members discussed a preliminary set of bird's-eye–view drawings by Edgar Tafel, the group's architect. In them, from a perspective high above Central Park, a promenade surrounded a magnificent fountain at the northeast corner of the Park.

Modern high-rise apartment buildings were interspersed with lower row houses; public buildings and open spaces lay to the east and north. Fifth Avenue and 110th Street passed below the fountain through underpasses into and from East and Central Harlem. The area between Fifth and Park Avenues from 108th to 112th Street would be completely rebuilt with the exception of two public housing units and PS 108.[3]

In 1965, just as the Clarks were organizing the group to rebuild Frawley Circle, Constance Baker Motley, the African-American Manhattan borough president, told a group of Harlem political leaders that Harlem's residents, like others elsewhere, "want communities where [they] live by choice not by compulsion." She outlined a revitalization of Harlem and East Harlem in which the "residential, recreational, cultural and economic potential of the area" would be developed.[4] But, in the late 1950s and early 1960s, urban renewal had aimed to improve the housing stock of a variety of neighborhoods, in Manhattan, of the Upper West Side, bordering on Harlem, where massive rebuilding began at Lincoln Center and continued uptown along Columbus and Amsterdam Avenues, among the community's most depressed streets. For Harlem's leaders, this effort in the mostly white West Side was in stark contrast to the virtual abandonment of Harlem by the city's leadership.

The West Side rebuilding had concentrated on new cultural centers like Lincoln Center and new and rebuilt housing. But for the city's African-American community, urban renewal historically meant disruption, dislocation, and destruction of the few institutions that served their communities. David Dinkins, then chairman of the HANA Housing Committee—and twenty-two years later elected the first African-American mayor of New York—said that the role in urban development of institutions in creating the climate of a neighborhood that can attract and hold middle-class residents "strangely appears to escape legislators and urban planners when they think about the *Central Harlems* of our great cities," Dinkins continued. In Central Harlem, he said, renewal had "meant the uprooting of families, the destruction of neighborhoods, the exodus of the middle-class and the disruption of the limited business and commercial patterns . . . a varied and complex urban unit is transformed into a rigid, single-purpose low-income housing area. The cleansing of the area is so thorough as to create a sterile community that is barren and lacking in supportive and social resources."[5]

The Central Park North Committee, of which Mamie Clark became chair, was to be an "advocate for the people of Harlem and East Harlem to bring basic social and enrichment services to the Frawley Circle–Milbank area" and it was to "bring into the area a variety of people and services of all income levels."[6] In an early meeting of the committee, Kenneth Clark had objected that urban-renewal projects "designed for the people of a ghetto community exclusively reemphasize the ghetto." The challenge now was to "design a project which will attempt the difficult job of opening up the ghetto. . . . Central Park North should be a place where people come from all over the city." The committee was committed to the view that an "ugly, run down, neglected and dilapidated" area could "with systematic and imaginative planning . . . become an attractive, racially integrated community that would facilitate eventual renewal and a two-way opening up of the larger Harlem area." The Central Park North Committee organized a cultural subcommittee to develop a cultural component to the plan that would "be the best (no second Lincoln Center)."[7] But, despite support from a wide variety of political, philanthropic, business, and academic leaders, in its first year, the committee meetings with members of Mayor Robert Wagner's city administration were "generally discouraging." Its only concrete accomplishment was a change in the name of West 110th Street to Central Park North, an event widely publicized in the city's newspapers as a sign of the city's efforts to revitalize the area. To Mamie Clark it was a "symbolic thing" that could redefine the community much as "Central Park South" had defined the lower end of the park. Even then, Kenneth Clark suspected that the city may have seen the name change not as a beginning but as an end in itself. He told the *Times* that "frankly, the name change of itself is not going to do a damn thing."[8]

In January 1966, President Johnson announced a Demonstration Cities program aimed at "eradicating" the nation's slums and, in a special message to Congress, decried the nation's apparent abandonment of its cities and its poor. The creation of suburbs throughout the nation had left those behind abandoned in squalor and degradation. "If we stand passively by . . . the center of each city becomes a hive of deprivation, crime and helplessness," he warned. "If we become two people—the suburban affluent and the urban poor, each filled with mistrust and fear one for the other—if this is our desire and policy as a people, then we shall effectively cripple each generation to come." Johnson proposed a program to "offer qualifying cities of all sizes the promise of a new life for their people . . . make massive additions to the supply of low and moderate-cost housing, . . . combine physical reconstruction and rehabilitation with effective social programs." A "demonstration should be of sufficient magnitude both in its physical and social dimensions so to arrest blight and decay in entire neighborhoods . . . and bring about a change in the total environment in the area affected." The president called on Congress to appropriate a national budget of $400 million a year for six years. But Herbert Evans, chairman of the New York City Housing and Redevelopment Board, noted that it "did not look as if it would result in a 'massive infusion' of federal money to New York."[9]

The heady rhetoric of federal and local politicians spurred the Central Park North Committee to begin serious discussions with City University of New York and with a wide variety of cultural institutions in an effort to attract them to the area. In November 1966, Mayor John Lindsay announced that the "Frawley Circle–Milbank area was one of three depressed areas in the city designated for immediate renewal under a new Federal model cities financial aid program." The City Planning Commission had found the new "Milbank-Frawley" district to be in worse shape than other neighborhoods in Harlem. Of its 1,054 residential buildings, 1,044 had housing violations and 50 percent were "dilapidated or structurally substandard." In a widely reported news release that purported to herald a enormous infusion of money and effort into Harlem, the mayor pledged "a massive attack on the blight in these areas . . . [that] would not bog down in the usual red tape delays of two or three years." Simultaneously, the city spurred the development of a Milbank-Frawley Renewal Council to involve residents "in the planning and development of four to six hundred units of vest-pocket public housing."[10]

Mamie Clark and the Central Park North Committee had originally defined the community as the few blocks around Frawley Circle, but the city administration was now designating the new planning district more broadly. Lindsay's area of 190 acres stretched from 125th Street to the north, Park Avenue to the east, 107th Street and Central Park North to the south, and Lenox Avenue to the west. As a consequence of the enlargement, political and racial conflicts between African Americans in the northwest section of the district and Puerto Rican constituents to the southeast were set into motion. The Central Park North Committee had begun planning for four thousand people, almost equally divided between Puerto Rican and African-American, but the city's plan encompassed forty-five thousand people, two-thirds African-American and one-third Puerto Rican.

Northside's board recognized the limitations and potential conflicts of any successful effort to rebuild and revitalize the community. To Mamie Clark and the board members, urban renewal meant breaking down the definition of Harlem as a poor, predominantly African-American and Puerto Rican community and introducing institutions and services that would attract an African-American and a white middle class. This, in turn, would mean altering the political power relationships of Harlem.[11]

The Clarks and Jim Dumpson were suspicious of the intent or motivation behind the city's designation of a far larger Milbank-Frawley. Mayor Lindsay and his housing and urban development commissioner, Jason Nathan, had committed the city to a policy of "opening the ghetto gateway" and delivering meaningful power to community groups. But, as political actors actively involved in neither local African-American or Puerto Rican politics, had the city administration assumed that all of the poor in the district had similar interests, agendas, and goals? Or was the city deliberately fostering trouble? A "citizen's" housing council had been organized within the district with little attention to ethnic and social rivalries within and between the East Harlem and Harlem communities. Was the city naive, or was it unconcerned about fundamental alterations in the class and social relationships within Harlem or in the larger city? Kenneth Clark was convinced that the city's politicians did recognize the plan's profound challenge to existing political relationships and under the guise of democracy and support for community involvement in decision-making, that the administration was, in reality, ensuring the "maintenance of the ghetto."[12] What happened later did not cause him to revise his gloomy prediction.

Power Relations and the City's Resistance to Change

The next few years confirmed the Clarks' and Northside's board's worst fears. The "immense" amount of money both the federal and city governments had promised never materialized. Nor did the city eliminate the "red tape," as Lindsay had promised. By 1968, four years after the first committee to build a Gateway to Harlem was formed, not only had the city failed to create a new community, but it also failed to build any new housing at all: "Two years after Mayor Lindsay's solemn public announcement, not a single site has been designated; not a single dilapidated tenement has been torn down; not a single example of ugliness has been displaced by beauty; not a single social welfare or cultural program has been initiated or specifically planned for the Central Park North area. *As a matter of fact, the proposed 'Gateway to Harlem' is more ugly, deteriorated and neglected than ever."*[13] The Model Cities program raised expectations but provided only limited resources to communities in need; combined with the city's insensitivity to the political—at least—realities, it would ensure that constituencies would be forced to compete for scarce resources. The newly created Milbank-Frawley Housing Council became mired in internal conflicts about its philosophy, purpose, and control. Real and imagined differences between the African-American and Puerto Rican communities reinforced protestations by city officials trying to shift responsibility for inaction from the city back to the community.

In September 1968, Mamie Clark wrote to the city's head of housing and development administration that the city's inaction had convinced the Central Park North Committee that "our efforts to persuade you that development of the Gateway to Harlem would give people of this community hope and would be a most appropriate beginning of further renewal in Harlem have failed." Time after time, members of the committee met with Jason Nathan and other city representatives, only to receive "promises which were always affably ignored." The final straw came on 19 September with cancellation of a scheduled meeting between Nathan and Eugene Callender. Clark wrote Nathan to advise that members of the committee "no longer have any faith or hope that the City of New York means to assign any priority to the development of the Frawley Circle–Central Park North area." The committee had no recourse but "to seek other avenues of approach to a constructive solution of this problem."[14]

Governor Nelson Rockefeller, who was nurturing presidential ambitions at the time, had proposed some months earlier, in February 1968, the establishment of a state agency, an Urban Development Corporation able to bypass local and regional roadblocks to develop poor communities. Unlike the federal program the city had planned to rely on, which depended upon disbursement of block grants to localities, the UDC would have extraordinarily broad powers, virtually combining in one office the power to condemn property, plan new projects, provide planning grants and seed money, designate community advisory committees, and arrange mortgages. One observer noted that "the corporation was authorized to move into any community in the state, take whatever property it wants or needs by condemnation, raze any structures on the site and replace them with homes, factories, schools, or office buildings, as it sees fit—limited only by a legislative directive to follow a partnership approach."[15] The proposal to establish the UDC had been overwhelmingly rejected by the legislature a year earlier, but the assassination of Martin Luther King Jr. in April 1968 turned around several key legislators, and the bill passed on the day of King's funeral.[16]

The following months were among the most traumatic in U.S. political and social history. Following the assassination, many of the nation's cities erupted in fire and in violence. In June, Robert F. Kennedy, who had just won the California presidential primary and was seen by many as the last and best hope for extending the liberal social and racial agenda, was assassinated. Alabama Governor George Wallace was courting white voters, North and South, with blatant racist appeals in his campaign for the democratic nomination. In August, a brutal "police riot" against anti-Vietnam war protesters marred the Democratic National Convention in Chicago.

In this context of horror and crisis, the liberal commitment to revitalize the cities and secure racial justice crumbled. Mamie Phipps Clark, in a letter to Edward Logue, head of the newly created Urban Development Corporation, written on the same day in September as her angry letter to the city administrator, wrote: "We have been completely frustrated by the indecision and inaction [of the city] administration. Two years ago Mayor Lindsay announced that the development of the Milbank Frawley Circle area would begin within months. In these two years the area has continued to deteriorate and has become more ugly and unclean at a terrifyingly rapid rate."[17] Although she had had many meetings first with Mayor Wagner and then with Mayor John Lindsay, "every six months we'd have to go back, because nothing would happen. We'd leave, and nothing would happen."[18] Mamie Clark appealed to Logue to meet with the Central Park North Committee to discuss the "next steps in a serious pursuit of the goal of developing this symbolically important area of Harlem."[19]

Northside's board had recognized that the Urban Development Corporation "was ready to move and assume responsibility for planning and developing in the area" and that such a realignment with the state would benefit the community and Northside alike. To accomplish at least part of their original goal, Mamie Clark, Jim Dumpson, Kenneth Clark, and others on the Northside board decided to construct their own plans, work with the UDC, and distance themselves from the political turmoil of the city's larger urban renewal effort. Rather than plan for rebuilding of the entire Frawley Circle area from 107th through 112th Streets, they would opt simply for "pursuing the construction and financing of a building."[20] Northside would direct its energies to "Site 23" of the Milbank-Frawley Planning District, bounded by 110th Street on the south, 111th Street on the north, Fifth Avenue on the west, and Madison Avenue on the east.[21] By the end of November, Northside joined with La Hermosa Christian Church, the Omega Psi Phi Fraternity, and the United Mission Christian Society to form the 110th Street Plaza Housing Development Corporation, with Mamie Clark as chair and the UDC as the developer.[22]

By aligning with the state's UDC, the group gained some important new advantages, first and foremost, the enormous political advantage of its "unlimited power [to] build, finance, sell or lease" property.[23] Also, the UDC provided "planning monies and arrange[d] for long term financing." The UDC agreed that the 110th Street Plaza Housing Development Corporation be designated as the Community Advisory Committee, officially recognized as spokespersons.[24]

A home for Northside itself would be included in the site. It needed to move in any case. By the late 1960s, Northside's new programs and activities had overflowed from their space in the New Lincoln School. The condition of the space had deteriorated as New Lincoln, contemplating its own growth, resisted investing scarce funds in the now aging structure. "[Our] present headquarters are on one floor in a 54-year old obsolescent building where the Center has a total of 5,000 square feet of space," Mamie Clark had written in a fundraising letter to the board. "[The] rooms are small and ill-suited for many of the regular Center activities. It is often necessary for individuals and groups needing separate work places to share cramped quarters."[25] Furthermore, the surrounding neighborhood had continued to erode with increased drug sale and use, higher unemployment, more deteriorated housing, and an uninspired educational system.

By February 1970, the initial sponsors, the UDC, and the Milbank-Frawley Housing Council had agreed on what would be included in Site 23: permanent homes for Northside and the Cadet Academy of the New York City Mission Society; space for a day-care center for seventy-five children; commercial space capable of housing either several small shops or a supermarket and a parking garage; and, the centerpiece, two towers with apartments for six hundred families of low and moderate incomes. Ideally, the residents would be drawn in equal proportions from the African-American, Puerto Rican, and white communities, fulfilling at least part of the Clarks' and Northside's original vision of an integrated community that could serve as a gateway to an economically and socially integrated Harlem.[26] The plan would allow those in the area to remain, while also opening up new housing units for newcomers. Northside board member Elaine Gaspard became involved in the planning of the forty-block Milbank-Frawley renewal area because, as she said later, this "is my community, this is where I was born, this is where I was raised and this is where I want to remain." [27]

Plaza Arturo Schomburg

East Harlem was among the city's first primarily immigrant communities dating back to the middle and late nineteenth century, when Irish and Eastern European Jews and then Italians established communities in the area stretching from the East River westward to Fifth Avenue. Between 1910 and 1940, the Italian community came to dominate the political life of the area (in 1934 Vito Marcantonio, a radical independent Republican was elected to Congress representing the district). For the first half of the century, the neighborhood was an amalgam of competing ethnic and racial groups connected to the larger city by the elevated rail lines of the Third Avenue El.

The community had always been poor, with a housing stock aging and ill-maintained, much of it constructed shortly after the Civil War. Even the "newer" stock dated back to the turn of the century, built primarily for factory workers in tanneries, breweries, foundries, and other peripheral industries along the East River north of 86th Street. By the outbreak of World War II, the institutions and hospitals on the community's southern and western edge lined up on Fifth Avenue between 97th Street and 106th Street comprised the only substantial construction in the East Harlem area: Mt. Sinai and Flower Fifth-Avenue Hospitals, New York Medical College, the Museum of the City of New York, the Hecksher Foundation for Children and its adjoining Society for the Prevention of Cruelty to Children, and the New York Academy of Medicine.

Despite the housing stock's and schools' drab, crowded, and run-down character, East Harlem had developed a vibrant political and economic life. Small businesses flourished along Third Avenue, 116th Street, and 125th Street: Italian bakeries, Jewish kosher butchers, Irish bars, and most recently, Puerto Rican bodegas. Then, after World War II, a boost in Puerto Rican migration changed the demographic makeup. Moving from the western edge on Madison and Fifth Avenues toward the river, the newcomers sought housing, often competing with a growing African-American population itself expanding eastward out of Central Harlem. A massive urban-renewal effort of the time built substantial new housing for thousands of new residents and provided new schools and playgrounds for the area's children, but the design

and scale of the massive, high-rise public projects disrupted the street life of
East Harlem. Entire streets of shops, peddlers' carts, ethnic groceries, and
bodegas disappeared. In all, three thousand small stores were displaced.
Some attempt was made to attract middle-class whites to some of the projects but, on the whole, the barren towers of high-rise, lower-class public
housing solidified into impenetrable ghettos. East Harlem had always been a
community of poor residents, but, by the late 1950s, urban-renewal efforts
had turned it into a closed community, a poor and minority ghetto. Ninety-
sixth Street east of Park Avenue separated an affluent Upper East Side from a
poverty-stricken East Harlem. A physical barrier of large institutions and
housing projects from the East River to the older line of institutions along
Fifth Avenue reinforced the division between rich and poor: beginning with
Metropolitan Hospital between First and Third Avenues and continuing with
the Lexington Houses between Third and Park Avenues, and the Carver
Houses, a public project along Madison from 99th to 106th Street.[28]

In 1961, Alfredo Alfano, a resident of East Harlem, reflected on the
tremendous impact that urban renewal efforts had had on his community:
"Housing developments of the past twenty years . . . intended to remedy a
slum situation, caused untold hardship to countless displaced families and
small businessmen, drain[ing] the community of unseen and unappreciated
values." He told of one old woman in the neighborhood who said that she
had "'a clean apartment—but I must walk a mile for a loaf of bread.'" He
agreed that the housing projects were "well-intentioned and apparently forward looking," but they had led to the "now deplored 'bull-dozing' tactics."[29]

To some in East Harlem, the Clarks' new proposal raised fears of a repe-
tition of the mistakes of the past. Two more high-rises, filled with a new
group of newcomers, might once again threaten havoc with the lives of
those already in the area. In any case, the Clarks' negotiation of the sensitive political issues began to unravel. A long struggle ensued between the
Milbank-Frawley Housing Council and another group that claimed to represent the Puerto Rican community, the United Residents of Milbank–Frawley
Circle–East Harlem Association, which charged that the council had been
captured by African-American politicians and interest groups. As early as
1967, Puerto Rican spokespersons had been arguing that they had "been excluded from receiving [their] share of the Demonstration Cities fund [and
that] 90% of these funds have benefitted the Negro community," and that
Puerto Ricans had to be "protected from the devilish notion of some people
in government that the bulldozer approach and people's removal is the first

step for effective urban renewal and community redevelopment programs."
The new residents association now proclaimed that "until the responsible
leadership of the Central Harlem area kicks out the present vultures . . . the
Demonstration Cities program will not have a meaningful effect in the East-
Central Harlem area." [30] The *New York Times* reported that the city administration had been caught unawares by the fight. The *Times* quoted unnamed
city officials that "basically a fight over money" and "racial hatred" within
Harlem had created the uproar. "City officials are now acknowledging that
'community participation' in government programs is a far more difficult
concept to implement than they believed several years ago." [31] The *Times* did
not note that the small amount of planning money from the Lindsay administration and the federal government to a community of mammoth needs almost guaranteed internecine warfare among competing groups.

The Young Lords Party, an organization of primarily Puerto Rican activists who modeled themselves on the Black Panthers, along with the residents' association were the most vocal opponents of the relocation of the
117 residents of Site 23. Even Northside's planned move a mere block to the
east was seen as an intrusion into the Puerto Rican community by Central
Harlem interests, though the center served East as well as Central Harlem.
The Lords' own offices were in a tenement building on the very spot that
was to house Northside. [32] In June, Felipe Luciano, chairman of the Young
Lords Party, at a meeting of the 110th Street Plaza Corporation, raised the issue of community control and participation in the planning process. Although the UDC had designated the 110th Street Plaza Housing Development Corporation, with representatives of Northside, La Hermosa Church,
and the Christian Mission Society as the "community" group for the renewal
project, a designation approved by the Milbank-Frawley Housing Council,
the council itself was perceived by these Puerto Rican activists as a front for
the African-American community. [33] To Mamie Clark, the meeting "represented a 'sit-in'" by the Young Lords; after it she was told that Luciano and
another Young Lord claimed to be acting as representatives of the Christian
Mission Society. She was outraged at the society's apparent surrender to an
attempt at intimidation. [34]

In April, the Young Lords distributed a leaflet titled "Borinqueños: Defend Your Home and Stores." They suspected that the alliance between the
110th Street Housing Corporation and the state's UDC was part of a larger effort to displace Puerto Rican residents and provide new housing for the expanding African-American community. [35] A plan was afoot, they said, by "the

Federal Government" to "tear down buildings on 111th and 112th Street between Fifth and Madison to put up what they call moderate to middle income housing (for people who make $4,000 to 10,000 dollars)." The leaflet attacked specifically, La Hermosa Church, Northside, and other sponsors of the 110th Street Housing Corporation, for sponsoring an "anti-poor, anti-Puerto Rican plan." Urban renewal was nothing more than "spic removal," and the new housing was "too expensive for the poor to afford." They demanded community participation in the planning of the project; a guarantee of housing in the immediate area; a right for displaced businesses and tenants to move into the new housing at prices they could afford; new facilities, such as "schools, day care centers, health centers, recreational centers," to be constructed along with the new houses' and reversion of ownership of the new buildings to the tenants.[36]

Northside had been careful to include La Hermosa Church and the Christian Mission Society in the original planning for Site 23 on purpose to avoid just such a racial polarization. Mamie Clark herself had met with the Young Lords and mobilized important Puerto Rican activists and leaders in the community in an effort to defuse a crisis.[37] In mid-April, the 110th Street Housing Corporation now issued a "Fact Sheet" to correct the misinformation and fears. It said the 110th Street Plaza was a joint effort of the African-American and Puerto Rican communities and that the towers were being designed by an Hispanic architect, David Castro-Blanco. It guaranteed that the families to be displaced would be given first priority for new apartments: "83 of the families are eligible for low rentals with subsidy and this is well below the numbers of such units which will be available."[38]

But, despite these promises, the reality was that the city itself controlled that part of the process of relocation. One UDC official, explaining the "critical relocation problems" that had held up construction, projected "a deficit of 500,000 dwelling units for low and moderate income families" in New York City that year. From Mamie Clark's perspective, the slow moving "City of New York machinery" was undercutting both construction and community relations.[39]

Relations between the Young Lords and other organizations in the neighborhood had long been tense. They had "sat in" and disrupted churches, social-service agencies, city offices, and hospitals in an attempt to draw attention to the problems of the East Harlem community. Even Northside had had a contentious relationship with the Lords. "During the militancy period, [the Lords] were the most aggravation to us, because they would come into the agency making all kinds of demands from us which we couldn't meet." Mamie Clark said the Young Lords were "always threatening us with something if we didn't meet these demands, which were highly unrealistic and unreasonable," demands for money and services.[40] Victor Carter also remembers that the Young Lords were "tearing the place up," but he found them personably approachable. In one incident when a rumor about a sit-in in the Northside offices at New Lincoln reached the staff, Northside found itself in a dilemma. "Now the Young Lords . . . didn't like us. They knew us but they don't like us. They're going to come in and just take over . . . and sit in your office. . . . We were a bit uncomfortable because it's [unclear] how to handle this. You don't want to get mean and hateful and call the police . . . [but] you can't let them take over." Because Carter and Olivia Edwards had established relationships throughout the community, and, specifically, because they helped a Young Lords member with a personal problem involving a city social-service agency, Carter was able to mediate between Northside and the Young Lords.

> I said, "Now look. I appreciate you guys want to help the community and that's very honorable. But now Northside's part of the community, too. Now we may not look like it to you, but we are." And I say "If you think we're screwing up . . . don't jump all over us. Why don't you help us? If you can help us see the light, you come and you show us where we're off the track and see what we can put together." . . . It worked. They didn't come and tear us up and we continued to work with them. But the point is . . . I just happened to have known Ruben and got Ruben to help. . . . I'm sure many of the other staff members could tell you many other instances. But it was that kind of alertness and sensitivity to the community and . . . I really meant it when I told that young man I wanted him to help us because he could help us.[41]

But sometimes these tensions could not be defused so readily. Blanche Pugh recalls meetings with "residents of East Harlem . . . where there was even violent pushing with Olivia Edwards."[42]

By the end of January 1971, Mamie Clark, reported to Harold Dolly, the head of the Milbank-Frawley Housing Council, that the scheduled beginning of construction, 1 February 1971, was "no longer realistic." Residents were still on the site.[43] By fall 1971, with thirty-eight families still there, construction plans had to be altered to avoid undermining the remaining tenements. The foundation of the first tower was laid but construction delayed on the second.[44] The Milbank-Frawley Housing Council, recognizing that its credibility and legitimacy as the planning body and as representative of Milbank-Frawley residents was threatened by its support for the 110th Street Housing

Corporation, now reversed its position and filed a legal challenge to stop re-location.[45] The suit was unsuccessful in stopping construction or tenant relo-cation, but Cora Walker, its attorney, credits the state supreme court suit with a requirement that the agencies be "compelled to find housing for the tenants."[46]

Mamie Clark's persistence and the support of individuals from the com-munity finally overcame all efforts at delay or cessation, although the scale of rebuilding of Frawley Circle was severely constricted. Still, the basic idea of the gateway to Central Harlem and a multiethnic residence remained. The Plaza, the only remaining part of the original plan, would seek to attract stable institutions to this northeast corner of Central Park. There would be space for Northside, a day-care center, a therapeutic day school, commercial properties, including a large supermarket, and parking for two hundred cars.[47] Mamie Clark's plan for six hundred apartments in the two towers and an eleven-story building on Madison Avenue would reserve 10 percent of the smaller apartments for low-income, elderly residents and another 20 percent of the larger units for low-income families. The rest of the units, more than four hundred, were reserved for families of moderate incomes.[48] As the site was being prepared in 1971, and as inflation was beginning to spiral out of control, the estimated cost for the project was $19 million.[49]

The architects had designed the site so that the commercial and insti-tutional components of the complex would be on Madison Avenue and the prime residential locations on Fifth Avenue overlooking Central Park. Northside's entrance and its address would be on Madison Avenue facing East Harlem, thus physically cut off from Central Harlem, which had always been its base. As Mamie Clark protested to the architects at a meeting in July of 1970, "the area of influence of the Northside Center lay more towards Central Harlem . . . than towards East Harlem." "The location of the Center within the east building on Madison Avenue would be detrimental to its pro-fessional associations and its funding." Was there a way of providing "a Fifth Avenue entrance" for the center to allow direct access to clients to the west, from Central Harlem? The architects suggested one entrance to Northside from the plaza area facing west and another on Madison Avenue and 110th Street, maximizing access both from the African-American and the Hispanic neighborhoods, and also of providing for Northside a Fifth Avenue address (at 1301), no small matter for funding sources, since the address would have overtones of prestige.[50]

Although the vision of what Milbank-Frawley might be had to be severely contracted, the two towers did represent a hope that the project could serve as a multiethnic, multi-class and multiracial gateway to Harlem. But, in the coming months, as construction began and as applications for apartments were gathered, the gulf that separated African Americans and whites and Hispanics was once again apparent. At the April 1972 meeting of the Housing Corporation, a prolonged discussion ensued on whether the tower's name "should reflect [the] Spanish and/or Black constituency" and on how to minimize any symbolic slight to the Hispanic community if English won over Spanish in the official title. Mamie Clark, emerging from struggles with the Young Lords over the relocation, was especially sensitive to Hispanic suspicions of the African-American leadership of the planning effort, and one of her top priorities was to find a name for the towers that would signal its place in both the African-American and the Puerto Rican communities. The name the corporation decided on was Plaza Arturo Schomburg, named for a black Puerto Rican who had been a noted bibliophile and collector of literature on African, African-Caribbean, and African-American history and culture, and whose collection had become the basis for the Schomburg Library of the New York Public Library in Central Harlem. It was a perfect choice, a "name that both Black and Spanish residents [could] identify with."[51]

Other issues were less easily resolved. Of signal importance in a community that lacked high-paying jobs and decent housing would be hiring of minority workers on the construction site and allocating apartments fairly. The effectively white construction trades unions had long resisted attempts to break down their discriminatory hiring practices against minority workers, and in Brooklyn and Harlem, hospital and office construction sites had been disrupted by protest groups such as Fightback. Minority contractors had organized to gain access to lucrative state and city construction projects, from which they felt unlawfully excluded. An African-American-headed coalition of architects, urban planners, and construction firms, had developed the "Harlem Plan," to "ensure that minority sub-contractors will have a real opportunity to participate in governmentally assisted housing programs."[52] Although the plan had gained some contracts for minority businesses, it had not resolved the contentious issue of employment of minority workers on Site 23.

In February 1972, the *Amsterdam News* published an attack on the UDC for failing to hire African-American workers: despite the "array of Harlem construction projects," black workers and contractors were few and far between. It pointed to the sites at 110th Street and Fifth Avenue, the Lionel Hampton Houses, and the state office building on 125th Street and criticized the plaza project for granting a $1.8 million contract to a white electrical contractor, quoting a UDC official as saying that "the problems of the minority worker and the minority contractor are directly related." Black-owned businesses, generally small, had "found it difficult to get bonded" and thus were excluded from consideration under UDC regulations. Under Mamie Clark's prodding, the 110th Street Plaza Association contacted Fightback and contracted with the Douglass Urban Corporation, a minority employment agency, to ensure the hiring of African Americans. Two months after the *Amsterdam News* article, a survey found 154 black, 143 white, but no Puerto Rican workers on the site. Whereupon the Douglass Urban Corporation was ordered to increase both Hispanic and African-American employment.[53]

Work on the site progressed despite all the obstacles, and on 17 May 1973, the nineteenth anniversary of the historic Supreme Court desegregation decision in *Brown*, the cornerstone was laid for the first of the two towers. In attendance were numerous luminaries and five children of the late Arthur Schomburg. More than five hundred Harlem and East Harlem residents and business people stood in the cleared site as borough president Percy Sutton introduced Mayor Lindsay, Edward Logue (the head of UDC), and other city and state dignitaries. Mamie Clark, in a recounting of Schomburg's life, told the assemblage: "As we participate in these ceremonies, we once again renew the ties which unite our Black and Puerto Rican communities in a bond of mutual self-help and brotherhood as so exemplified in the life of the late Arthur A. Schomburg."[54] But, as late as September, the Clarks' goal of equal representation of Puerto Ricans, African Americans, and whites in Schomburg Plaza housing had still to become a reality. Faced with overwhelming needs for decent and affordable housing, community activists were resisting the plan to earmark one-third of the apartments at Schomburg for whites. One leaflet, addressed to "Spanish residents of El Barrio," demanded an "equal share of occupancy in the new Schomburg development" and charged "discrimination against former Spanish residents of the area in the tenants selection process," and said Spanish residents of El Barrio must receive primary consideration for apartments in Schomburg Plaza to "relieve their present terrible housing conditions."[55]

In a significant analysis in the New York *Times* of 20 November 1973, "Hopes and Fears on Rise with New Harlem Skyline," Charlayne Hunter wrote that "there are those in Harlem who view the new skyline as positive evidence of a renaissance" for the community. The new offices and apartments would permit "the participation of black people as owners and operators and managers, with a stake for the first time in planning the destiny of their community." However, "others in Harlem . . . view the new skyline rising north from 110th St from river to river with suspicion," fearing that "Harlem is being revitalized only for middle-class blacks and whites." In the controversy over the Schomburg towers, former residents "argue that they were not allowed to participate in the decision affecting the site and that they have been displaced and forced into either worse housing or compelled to leave the city." She quoted Cora Walker, attorney for the Housing Council, who had sought to stop the relocation of tenants displaced by the Schomburg building, as having an "overriding concern that Harlem not become another area where urban renewal comes to mean black and Puerto Rican removal." [56]

In December 1972, a concerted advertising and publicity campaign by the 110th Street Corporation began to address the Hispanic community. Spanish-speaking organizations were contacted, Spanish-language promotional materials were written, and Spanish-speaking staff members were hired to answer the phones and welcome potential applicants for housing. As construction "move[d] to completion there [was] growing interest on the part of the neighborhood in who [would] live in the apartments." By September 1973, more than six thousand application forms for six hundred available apartments had been distributed, and selection criteria began to evolve, with efforts to maintain a balance among African-American, Hispanic, and white applicants. People displaced from the site had priority, then others from the project area, then persons displaced by urban renewal in the rest of the city.[57] But the reality was that the goal of an integrated housing development could not be met. The Committee on Tenant Profile of the Corporation reported in September that "applications to date are mostly all black and Puerto Rican." It summoned all members of the board of the housing corporation to "try to help" recruit whites. They developed a profile of the first 179 families who applied that met criteria for Schomburg apartments; of these 85 were African- American, 85 Hispanic, and only nine were white. The occupations of these applicants spanned the spectrum of working-class and white-collar jobs: six professionals and five laborers and the vast majority (83 percent) hospital, civil service, or office workers.[58]

These findings spurred a renewed effort to attract white and also Asian applicants. A new advertising budget of nearly $50,000 was approved,[59] and from January through December 1974 ads were "run in various newspapers, meetings [were] held with representatives from Flower Fifth Avenue and other institutions." Even though apartments had begun to be rented to African-Americans and Puerto Ricans, the corporation decided to retain one-third "for other ethnic groups . . . in order to achieve an integrated community." By early 1974, four thousand applications had been received, and "a very extensive advertising campaign was launched." [60] Brochures, posters, and special events sought to "achieve our projected integration levels at Arthur Schomburg Plaza." The intensity of the campaign reflected the belief of the management and the corporation, and, of course, the Clarks, that "integration is a must if the development and community are to be stabilized." Ads appeared in a number of foreign language papers, including The *China Tribune, Aufbau, Il Progresso,* and the *Jewish Daily Forward.* Yet, it was apparent by September 1974 that few whites would apply. George M. Brooker, secretary-treasurer of Webb, Brooks, and Brooker, Inc., the real estate broker and managing agent for the project, reported that personal recruitment efforts at businesses and institutions notwithstanding, and "in spite of herculean effort and follow-up, our white applicants applied in very small numbers, and now we are processing even fewer who seem prepared to go all the way." True integration of Schomburg was impossible without a much broader effort within the white as well as the African-American community.[61]

Indeed, integration at the Schomburg could be attained only through a similar "effort in all developments" throughout the city—only then "we'll see more racially balanced and stable communities." Brooker urged that "a like effort . . . be made to bring about Black and Hispanic integration in all white areas." [62] The next day at a meeting of the board of the 110th Street Plaza Housing Corporation, Mamie Clark reported that, with only thirty white families submitting pre-applications, "it now appears unrealistic to expect the level of integration originally sought." She proposed a change of strategy, suggesting a special effort "to select quality tenants who, by their care, concern and devotion to the project, will attract more white applicants." By November, Clark and the board concluded that the housing mix would be African-American and Hispanic middle- and working-class and a mere token number of white families. "A more realistic policy," Mamie Clark reported, was a racial composition of "49% Black, 49% Spanish, and 2% White." [63]

Despite all the setbacks, the Christmas season of 1974 marked an enormous victory for Kenneth and Mamie Clark, for Northside Center, and for the board and community supporters of the 110th Street Plaza Housing Development Corporation. On 17 December, the new mayor, Abraham Beame, and a host of other dignitaries joined community residents in dedicating Schomburg Plaza and welcoming its first twenty-seven family tenants. The towers, the mayor declared, represented "the beginning of a renaissance for Harlem." Edward Logue, for UDC, was less sanguine, recounting the enormous struggle it took to get these few apartments built. There had been ten applications from Hispanic and African-American citizens for every apartment. "We can see the dimensions of the job when we realize that close to 50% of the 216,000 Harlem-area apartments are old-law walk-up tenements of the type whose construction was outlawed in 1901." [64] Mamie Clark also reflected on the struggle to build. "This is a very happy day for all of us who can now see a long dream come true. Close to ten years ago a number of us envisioned this site being developed into an impressive 'Gateway to Harlem'—a large step toward breaking through the dark walls of a Harlem ghetto. Today this beautiful Schomburg Plaza complex realizes that goal. We still have a long way to go here in Harlem but a significant beginning has been made." [65]

Charlayne Hunter began her story in the *New York Times* by recalling the "ten often controversial years" it took to build the "symbolic pillars of the Gateway to Harlem." "As a chilling wind swept across the spacious central plaza," one of the first tenants, Joseph Mattos, told of the long wait and the wonderful reward that the towers represented: "I got an application four years ago, before they even started pouring concrete. . . . But after moving two-three times, and living in run-down buildings with no heat or hot water half the time, we began to have doubts. But the rental agent kept telling us, 'You're going to move in here.'" He desperately "wanted to have Thanksgiving here. And we moved in on November 25th," he proudly reported. "It's beautiful, it's peaceful and quiet." [66]

The enormous struggle to build Schomburg grew out of Northside's evolving philosophy and purpose during the 1960s and 1970s, including a determination to guarantee the future of the families that came to Northside through the rebuilding of the community itself. Northside now had a considerably expanded space, three floors of more than 30,000 square feet, dwarfing its old quarters in the New Lincoln school down the block. As it turned out, it had also taken on new responsibilities for an expanded program—most significantly the new therapeutic day school that had been scheduled from the beginning for the new complex—for youngsters "too disturbed to attend public school . . . [and an] Aftercare Program for those returning from residential treatment." Dora Johnson, a white southerner who had six months before joined the center staff specifically to head the day school, remembers that Mamie Clark, "a woman of great vision," encouraged her to critique every aspect of the physical plant with the children in mind. At a time before educators had focused on the importance of environmental design, Northside's rooms were color coded so that children with visual impairments and those unable to read could learn their way around quickly; rooms were large, bright, and airy, and even the doorknobs and room numbers were lower to the ground so as to be accessible to the children. As in the old Northside, art and sculpture adorned the walls and hallways. In the words of one its most senior staff members, Teodora Abramovich, Northside "was indeed an oasis in East Harlem." [67]

Mamie Clark's commitment to build a multiethnic community had affected Northside's program as well. As she and the Northside board became deeply affected by the politics of building in New York City, they inevitably assumed a considerable measure of responsibility for the survival of their community. Northside was the only stable and long-term tenant in the new community. Mamie Clark continued in her post as chair of the 110th Street Corporation. But none of the other new institutions that had been envisioned in the plan of 1964, such as a college, a nursing school, a library, or a theater, which the Clarks deemed so important to a vibrant multiracial, multi-class community, had become a reality.

White Control through Outside Funding: A Psychology of Siege

Northside had, in the process, increased its reliance on grants received through the city's department of mental health and mental retardation, the state department of mental health, and the federal government. In the mid-1970s, not long before the dedication of the Schomburg Plaza, New York City experienced the worst fiscal crisis since the Great Depression. The fiscal bottom fell out from under Northside itself, when, in the early months of 1974, Mamie Clark learned of several impending budget cuts. In the course of a few months, after Northside's move into Schomburg, New York City's department of mental health and retardation services reduced its appropriations to Northside drastically, and the state department of mental health virtually eliminated its funding for the new therapeutic day school, to which Northside had committed itself; and the federal government recast Medicaid funding (which covered the fees of most of Northside's patients) so that virtually only psychiatric services were to be reimbursed. Northside would have to restrict its program and rethink the broader social mission it had developed over the past decade.[68] Ironically, having freed itself, after a tremendous struggle, from the campaign of the 1950s and 1960s to impose a psychiatric-psychoanalytic model on Northside, once again white-dominated power relationships might impose from the outside—this time with the state, not philanthropy, as the instrument—a narrowing of program and a professional dominance.

By March 1974, it was all too obvious. "I am sad to tell you," Mamie Clark wrote in a memo to the staff, "that the financial situation of the agency is so critical that we will not be able to meet our 3/8/74 payroll." She attached a letter from the city showing that their "funds have been delayed for a long period of time." She hoped the city would give Northside funds by the following pay period, but the staff should be aware of the severity of the growing financial crisis. Less than a month later, she was forced to warn the staff again, this time that Northside might "not be able to meet the 4/5/74 payroll on time. . . . I am sorry to send this memorandum, but under the circumstances we have no choice in the matter."[69]

From 1974 and through the spring of 1975, Northside, as also the rest of the city, watched the near collapse of the government's financial structure. In the brief period of a year, New York City ended some of its hallmark programs: it closed four of the twenty-one hospitals in its unique municipal hospital system; the City University ended its 125-year-old policy of free tuition to high school graduates; and throughout the city programs were cut, staff fired, and city funding of public as well as of private agencies plummeted, decimating their budgets. In the public schools, always inadequately funded, classrooms became even more crowded and teachers were pressed into roles for which they were unprepared. As for Northside's constituency, Jeanne Karp observed the devastating impact on the lives of Harlem's children. "The extent to which the New York fiscal crisis has affected the quality of education in our public schools" could be measured by the complete elimination of guidance counselors and assistant principals, reduction of teacher preparation periods from five to two, and larger classes.[70] "These cuts hurt the children," she said, "but they also made teachers feel demoralized, overworked, and angered."[71]

The fiscal crisis could hardly have hit at a worse moment for Northside itself. The state mental hospital system was releasing more children back into the community, and the social and economic crises of African-American and Hispanic families had been greatly exacerbated by the failing economy. Heroin use was reaching epidemic proportions; the foster-care system, traditionally unwilling to address the needs of African-American children, was the target of an extensive lawsuit brought by the New York Civil Liberties Union, charging discrimination and abandonment of African-American children; and low-income housing and redevelopment had all but ceased. Large swaths of the South Bronx had been abandoned by absentee landlords, creating, in turn, greater pressure on the already decaying housing stock of Harlem. Abramovich, the psychiatrist who had been at Northside almost from its founding, saw the impact of it all on the mental health of Northside's children: "The children who are referred to Northside Center are hyperactive, neurotic, schizophrenic, with behavioral problems, with elective mutism, with learning disabilities." She noted that "each year we see sicker children and sicker parents." "We do have mothers who are concerned about their children despite their preoccupations" but it was immensely difficult to act on that concern. "For example, mothers who have to spend eight hours to pick up their checks at the Welfare Office. How can we ask them to be patient and kind to their children, when they are exhausted and frustrated?"[72] Karp confirmed Abramovich's sense that the children now at Northside reflected new and even more troubling problems than in Northside's earlier years. She noted that "the population seen by the reading department is changing. We now see," she observed, "a younger group of children, with more severe reading problems than we had in the past." Simply put, "the majority of children in our current program, and on our waiting list, come to us as total non-readers."[73]

By spring 1975, the signs for Northside of impending disaster were unmistakable. New York City's department of mental health and mental retardation services informed the center that it should prepare two budgets, "one to include normal increases and the other to reflect increases up to the annualized amount for 1974-75." The Northside board recognized that "if the agency [had] to take this latter it will necessitate severe cuts." Two months later, Mamie Clark "was informed [by the city] that Northside's total budget cut was 27%." Among the first elements of Northside's outreach program to feel the impact were those departments in Northside that did not directly provide services to children, specifically, the Walk-on-in Center that had been set up in a storefront on Park Avenue as part of the outreach to the Hispanic community but that was now at Schomburg, and in "research and consultation." In addition, she recommended "reducing staff where service is very minimal or not yet established." The Aftercare program, established for children otherwise destined for a state mental hospital, would be cut because it "had not yet gotten off the ground as staff for it was only hired in January." [74] Next to feel the impact of the fiscal crisis were outreach programs deemed nonessential to Northside's survival, even though they were at the cutting edge of its community service expansion. "Budget cuts, lay-offs and low teacher morale" had made Northside's Clinic-in-the-Classroom "even more urgently needed than before," [75] but lack of new programmatic support following termination of the five-year start-up grant from the New York Community Trust now doomed it. "Before the city's fiscal crisis, the Clinic-in-the-Classroom program received high priority in the proposed budget plans of the New York City Department of Mental Health and Retardation and was to become a permanent part of Northside's clinical program. Unfortunately the city's fiscal crisis intervened and in the past year, services under this project were completely curtailed due to lack of funding." [76]

In a 6 June 1975 memo to the staff the day after Mamie Clark received word from the city of the cuts in Northside's allocation, she expressed her gloom about the impact of the 27 percent cutbacks on the staff: "I am very sad to send this memorandum to you. We have known for some time that our agency could not escape the reductions in services that New York City is experiencing. We now know the extent of the damage to our children and their families. . . . The implications of such a reduction are some unavoidable and drastic staff lay-offs." [77] By the end of 1975, the city informed Northside that it would have to absorb yet another—this time 18 percent—cut. Barbara Jones, Mamie Clark's secretary, said that the center "had to cut back in every category: psychiatrists, psychologists, social workers, remedial, clerical, across the board." By early 1976, Northside once again missed a payroll, and Mamie Clark told the board that "our financial situation is far worse than it has ever been." [78]

Despite all the evidence of disaster, the center's staff had assumed that all this was a temporary crisis. Indeed, unlike the wrenching debate over unionism that had pitted administration, staff, and board against one other in 1971, this crisis, caused by outside forces and without internal board or staff dissension, appears to have brought them together. A collective psychology of siege set in. The center had just moved to a new home, reorganized its program, and absorbed new faces and personalities in an expanded staff. Department heads reported to the administration and board that spirits and morale seemed high. Jeanne Karp reported in July that "the school year 1974-75 was an excellent year for the Reading Department" despite "the current fiscal cutback [which] has . . . hampered our work." The department had lost a full-time educational specialist and eighteen hours per week of remedial time, the Clinic-in-the-Classroom program was tabled due to lack of funds, and "until these remedial hours are restored, and our new programs funded, our services to the community will be seriously curtailed." And yet, the move to Schomburg, with its "spacious, attractive setting for the Reading Center," provided a "calm and conducive" learning environment. "The Library added an important new dimension to the total educational program, giving children exposure to exciting books, films, and story hours." The seventy children seen weekly by the remedial department demonstrated improved test scores, but "improvement of test scores alone cannot convey the excitement the children, parents and remedial staff experience in seeing the children achieve higher goals." [79] In the short term, the remedial department reorganized services and expanded certain aspects of its program. In 1975-76, despite the "severe budget restrictions, and a reduction in professional remedial time of over 20%," Karp reported that "the Reading Department had served more children than ever before, both in the Clinic and in the community." An expanded volunteer program and a newly developed relationship with City College's School of Education had helped "take up slack and allow for expansion." [80] The Clinic-in-the-Classroom, organized before the fiscal crisis occurred, took on new meaning as the public schools of Harlem and elsewhere in the city experienced the city's fiscal crisis, cutting staff dramatically. [81]

Although the sense of common purpose at Northside, combined with the improved working conditions at Schomburg, appears to have lifted morale in the short term, over the longer term, the crisis, along with earlier changes in federal social policy, undercut some of Northside's transformations of the previous decade. Northside's shift to a family model of treatment and its role as an "umbrella" social-service agency was undermined when, in the early 1970s, the War on Poverty and its funding ended, and the Nixon administration dismantled the Office of Economic Opportunity. "Law and order" had become buzz words for racism; punishment once again replaced prevention as goals of national social policy; the fight against poverty and urban decay was, essentially, abandoned. Northside, along with scores of other agencies that sought to address a multitude of social problems associated with poverty, found federal and local governments employing financial constraints as a means of undermining programmatic change.

The best documented case of how antipoverty programs were derailed only years after they got into motion is that of the neighborhood health centers, developed to provide health-related services to the nation's poor through a series of clinics in under-served communities. The neighborhood centers had become a battleground between liberal advocates of Office of Economic Opportunity programs and the Nixon policy of destroying the programs spawned by the war against poverty. In 1966, these centers had began to broaden their scope by including numerous allied professionals and community workers, as well as medical personnel. By 1970, centers were not only offering well-baby care, but distributing food and, in rural regions of the South where intestinal water-borne diseases were ravaging poor communities, they were even drilling wells to provide pure water. With the OEO dismantled, funding for such centers shifted from block grants controlled by area administrators to Medicaid funding for medical care alone as defined by patient visits to medical personnel. In retrospect, it is even more clear that, although business and fiscal arguments were employed to justify these broad political and social goals, the real objectives of the new federal regulations were to destroy programs and agencies of the 1960s, now controlled by administrators with civil service status often drawn from the liberal wing of the Democratic Party. Poor peoples' programs were attacked for being "inefficient" or poorly managed, and controls were insisted on as a stimulus for organizational and administrative reforms.

Resisting Pressure

As voluntary contributions proved insufficient for supporting Northside's broadened goals, Medicaid became one of the few dependable sources of income, but Medicaid only reimbursed for medical treatment of individual patients, not for services aimed at strengthening families by nonmedical personnel. Once again, the successful earlier efforts of Northside to resist an exclusively medical model, with its assumptions that child misbehavior or deviancy was a result of disease—especially mental disease—was threatened. This had subtle, and not so subtle, effects on the administration and on the focus of Northside as clinic visits and individual counseling and therapeutic services emerged as the most reliable and largest source of income. Board member and psychiatrist Alexander Thomas, drawing on his knowledge of the impact of Medicaid funding on out-patient mental-health services in general, placed Northside's dilemma in a broader perspective. "Methods of third-party payment for mental health services" traditionally underfinanced innovative out-patient programs. But, the most recent fiscal crisis had meant that "*all* mental health institutions—public or voluntary—are faced with . . .

pressure to . . . cut . . . community services, rehabilitation services, special community projects and out-patient treatment services." [82] Northside's new medical director, Antonio Parras, almost immediately felt the impact of the shift in funding. In 1975, even before the worst of the fiscal cuts, he worried that the direction of Northside was shifting toward increasingly medicalized goals. "Aren't we focussing our therapy too much on the child and diminish[ing] the importance of the mother, parents and family? Even if we do agree on the importance of helping the family, do we really practice it?" [83]

Northside, faced by the demands of a reimbursement system that demanded accountability measured in units of service, and hours of "treatment" of "patients," (measures still in effect nationwide as of the mid-1990s) now began to put in new management systems that threatened provision of innovative and flexible services. "Each worker has the responsibility to provide psycho-therapeutic services to children and their families in the caseload assigned to him or her," explained the assistant director of the casework department. "It has been a heavy burden for the staff because they also have to meet the goal of productivity demanded by funding sources. . . . The level of productivity [has become] an unquestionable issue." In 1977, "the Department began the practice of writing an annual evaluation on each workers' performance to be part of the personnel record of the worker." [84]

Victor Carter, who had lived through every aspect of Northside's tumultuous history, saw "in the current climate [a] regression to a more distinctly medical model." The intellectual assault on the social origins of individual pathology were part of a broader attack on the principles of equality and justice. Northside, it seemed to him, had continued a struggle others were abandoning. "It seems particularly important that Northside Center does not lose its birthright and tradition of attunement to the community." In the early 1970s, new federal and state regulations were seeking to encourage centers to serve as many clients as possible and to justify government payments based on identifiable medical procedures; Carter saw this as limiting in Northside's context. At the same time, increasing federal and state fiscal instability, with consequent reductions in available funds, threatened agencies like Northside. "Efficiency" and "accountability" were, of course, legitimate goals "long overdue and really not too difficult to achieve." Yet, there was "a great danger that unless we keep our birthright in mind, we might find ourselves efficient and well recorded but sterile." [85]

By 1978, caseworkers were "struggling with the pressure engendered by the 'new' productivity guidelines and recording requirements." The new pressures to provide a narrowly circumscribed set of reimbursable services could in the long run undermine Northside's quality and range of service. Victor Carter came to believe that "appropriate consideration" was not given "to the tremendous needs of our clients." With no more funding for "activities outside of the 'therapeutic session,'" the center was failing to address issues "not only important in the daily lives of children and families but which are growth producing and enhancing in their own right."[86] Carter felt that the pressures created by the new fiscal environment had more subtle and profound effects on Northside's mission. "In the area of our clinic activity, which is the heart of our service, we are concerned, but a sense of direction is lacking," he said. Although the center now might be functioning more "efficiently" in documenting case loads and seeing more patients, "the excitement of elaborating broader goals, the stimulation of the exploration of ideas and the thrust towards the creation of new modalities or defining new directions is absent." The new emphasis on "maximizing" the use of staff was stifling the creativity and experimentation that had always characterized Northside's program, its research, cultural, and intellectual life. "Without a feeling of exploration and quest we are in danger of becoming increasingly rigid and of figuratively dying on the vine."[87]

New forms and new guidelines for receiving funds seemed to arrive at the agency every week with psychiatrists, social workers, secretaries, and administrators constantly squeezed by the differing agendas of the various government bureaucracies, all of which were trying to cut back. Northside was being forced to cut its cloth to fit the pattern of a traditional psychiatric clinic in order to guarantee funding, at the same time trying to work around the constraints to save as much as possible of its broader mission of helping children and their families cope with the exigencies of poverty and racism. Northside's ability in the mid-1970s to survive owed much to the vision and sense of mission that imbued its founders and older staff members. Kenneth and Mamie Clark, Victor Carter, Jeanne Karp, Bea Levison, Edna Meyers, and Barbara Jones all had been at Northside for more than two decades and all had lived through Northside's crises of the 1950s and all the transformations of the 1960s.

James Dumpson, board president from 1966 through 1974, noted at the time that "New York City and Nation [were] in the throes of an economic convulsion," which national leaders "referred to as a recession." But "in the Black community we are most accurate in stating that we are experiencing an economic depression with all the attendant social consequences." Just when a vision of social reform was most needed political leaders were abandoning their obligations to their people. The 1970s, he argued, were marked by an absence of national policy towards mental illness and he wondered "how valid it [was] to pursue [an examination of] changing concepts of mental health . . . without identifying currently the absence of a comprehensive, rational, integrated, *national* policy." [88]

Like the crisis within Northside over psychiatry in the late 1950s, the new fiscal crisis, along with alternations of national reimbursement and social policies, compelled Northside to reevaluate its capacity to provide innovative and community-oriented approaches to mental-health services. If earlier confrontations were intensely personal, in the 1970s crises, impersonal forces seemed to be at work. Perhaps because of the seemingly irrefutable logic of financial contraction, Northside had to turn in on itself to look at its very reason for being. A particularly apt opportunity for this introspection, its thirtieth anniversary celebration, came ironically, in 1976, at this very time.

The centerpiece of the celebrations was a conference on children that brought together Northside's board, staff, and city officials. Alexander Thomas of the Northside board, a professor of psychiatry at New York University Medical Center and director of psychiatry at Bellevue, gave one of the most eloquent and insightful presentations, outlining the deepening intellectual dilemma posed by the fiscal crisis and the increasingly regressive social thought of the 1970s. In a brief review of the competing concepts and rationales for the "problem" of the African-American child, he pointed out the limited and even reactionary implications of views that, on the surface, might appear sympathetic to the needs of poor people. One was that the problems of African-American children were psychological problems to be addressed in the same way as those of middle-class whites. Another, the more prevalent and insidious idea, he believed, was that "the terrible effects that social, economic, cultural factors such as racism and poverty have on children . . . must inevitably [make them] permanently and severely crippled emotionally by the time they are four to six years old." The first ignored the emotional consequences of environmental deprivation; the second used it in a way that stood on its head earlier social-science environmental theory by making environment, in effect, unchangeable, or its effects irremediable.

He identified two variants of this latter view, both of which alleviated the responsibility of professionals to address inequity and injustice and which provided an intellectual rationale for abandoning these children. On the one hand, some argued that "it may not be the fault of the Black or

Puerto Rican family and child that they are so handicapped and crippled [that] the emotional as well as cognitive damage cannot be cured." On the other hand, some recent investigators, if with the best of intentions, assessed "the effect of malnutrition in early childhood, on the intellectual, perceptual, and cognitive development of children," building a case for improving early childhood and infant nutritional programs for future generations, but unable to free themselves from "the implication that the damage that's done from this early malnutrition is permanent." Thomas pointed out that Kenneth Clark and he, along with others at Northside, had countered these claims "because, philosophically, it just seemed in error." This intellectual jousting had, in turn, led Northside to develop the "umbrella of services" approach and to avoid the subtly fatalistic if superficially sympathetic analyses of the problems that poor families faced. "Northside has avoided both these extremes and has at all times taken the position in its work with children and their families that the treatment, as Mamie has indicated, has to be within the context of the larger social environment." [89]

Norman Wyloge, a member of the case work department who had recently gained psychoanalytic training, reinforced Thomas's statements, exploring the way Northside's unique culture had transformed his understanding of his own professional role. Rather than abandoning his social-work orientation after attaining a new identity as a psychoanalyst, he had sought to redefine and enlarge the role of therapist. "It has long been realized that the traditional psychoanalytic approach is not the best way to treat the multi-problem family." [90] Northside had shown him that "no longer can the clinician sit in the privacy of his office, treat his patient and expect to see positive results. . . . At Northside . . . we believe that the multi-nature [of] the child's problem basically affects all of his mental health. We feel that a treatment agency is charged with the total needs of the child rather than the singular need of the psychotherapeutic session." [91] Despite the trauma of financial constraints and federal policies, Northside could not abandon its historical commitments to the broader needs of a poverty-stricken community. Victor Carter, veteran of Northside's entire exciting history, was deeply concerned that the intellectual assault on the social basis of individual pathology could be part of a broader attack on the principles of equality and justice. [92]

Despite the massive cuts and the elimination of specific programs, Northside had found ways to maintain its commitment to broaden its program beyond the provision of clinical services. Through the Parents Council, volunteers, and We Care, it participated in and provided a home for community activities. The importance of community involvement and of the social basis of pathology were understood as essential for Northside's long-term survival and mission. Only by expanding the experiences and exposure of children to the rich environment of New York's cultural life could issues of mental health and cultural deficits be effectively addressed.

In 1978, the center's staff was shaken by the almost simultaneous announcements that Mamie Clark and Victor Carter were both planning to leave Northside. Carter's retirement, which took place in December, ten months before Mamie Clark's, produced a profoundly depressing atmosphere because everyone knew they had a friend in Victor. His door was always open, and they knew they could talk about any problem with him.[93] At the time, the case work department noted that "the department operated this year under great stress due to . . . the loss of Victor Carter."[94]

And Mamie Clark embodied the center. In a very real way, it was her views, her philosophy, and her soul that held the center together. Many of the staff worried that Northside could never be the same without her. Dora Johnson considered her own retirement when she heard of Mamie's plan to leave. "I thought about it. . . . my heart said, 'you've had the best of everything, Dora, and you really wanted to work with this wonderful woman . . . and with these wonderful children. You really don't want to work without her.'" Johnson captured the importance of Mamie Clark to Northside: "When an unusual and unique person pursues a dream and realizes that dream and directs that dream, people are drawn not only to the idea of the dream, but to the uniqueness of the person themselves. I think this is what Dr. Mamie was like. . . . I think a lot of the axis of Northside, including today's school, really revolved on her ingenuity, her dream, and her sophisticated ability to balance the situation."[95]

In December 1978, Victor's staff threw a party at Jule's, an East Side restaurant. In October 1979, the board and staff joined Mamie Clark at the Top of the Sixes in the heart of midtown Manhattan for skits and poetry, hugs and farewells.[96]

A real depression set in at Northside after Victor Carter and Mamie Clark left. Despite the fact that Mamie always said that she would retire at age 65, no one at the center believed it would really happen, and certainly not at 62. As the staff and board contemplated Northside without her, there was foreboding. Bea Levison remembers the sense of disbelief and of loss that accompanied the two retirements. "It was as if a whole era had passed and that we were in a different world; one that we didn't especially like."[97] In 1983, Mamie Clark died of cancer at the age of sixty-five.

In the fifteen years after Mamie Clark left, Northside had four executive directors, all of whom saw, in different ways, Northside's history and traditional mission as an essential guide to its future. The center went through changes, some tumultuous, as old issues and new personalities tried to redirect an institution whose traditions had been set by history and personality. Its clients became more impoverished as federal antipoverty moneys dried up, their problems became more acute as drugs, crack, and AIDS destroyed families and communities, and their fear was heightened as violence became endemic.

In 1985, Kate Harris, Mamie and Kenneth Clark's daughter, a graduate of Oberlin College and of Smith College's School of Social Work, became Northside's executive director and served for five years. In her last annual report (1989) she wrote, "We at Northside have witnessed a combination of community embattlement and resilience that is truly remarkable." Social programs, public support, and private philanthropic support for Harlem had continued to erode.

> The seemingly uncontrollable spread of the drug crack has precipitated a dramatic increase in violent, anti-social acts. We now see far more children who are grossly neglected and physically and/or sexually abused by parents who are substance abusers. Hand in hand with crack addiction is the equally uncontrollable spread of AIDS. It is no exaggeration to say that these two epidemics threaten to eradicate an entire generation of inner-city children. At the same time we continue to cope with the age-old problems of inner city poverty – substandard and crowded housing, inadequate education, and health care and high unemployment.

Still, despite the enormity of the old and new crises, "the children and parents who seek Northside's services show an inspiring resilience. And they in turn inspire us."

Northside had changed dramatically in the five decades of its existence. It had transformed itself from a small "consultation and testing center" in cramped ground floor offices of the Dunbar Apartments on 155th Street, at Harlem's northern edge, to a multi-floor, multipurpose mental-health, educational, and social-service program in the Schomburg Towers, at 110th Street, which Kenneth and Mamie Clark had been instrumental in building where the white elegant Upper East Side met black and Spanish Harlem. Yet,

Kate Harris believed the principles and the issues that had informed North-side over the course of her parents' leadership had remained consistent and steady. Despite the civil rights movement, the War on Poverty, and the Black Power movements of the 1950s, 1960s, and 1970s, the deleterious impact of white racism on African-American children continued. "Forty years later," she pointed out, African-American children were "still shunning the black doll" her parents had made famous in the social-science brief of the 1954 Supreme Court decision declaring segregated schools unconstitutional. "That is why our goal remains the same as it was when Northside first opened its doors in 1946: to improve children's self-esteem in order to minimize the pernicious impact of racism and discrimination."

Northside, through the clinic directed by Pamela Straker, continued to provide psychotherapy sessions for children, groups, and families, as well as referral and testing. Its reading and educational services continued with after school tutoring, remedial reading, and the Do Your Own Think program. It had added new programs, for example, an IBM-sponsored computer-assisted reading program. Simultaneously, the early childhood center, directed by Rose Ann Harris, shifted its focus from grade school children to preschool and primary grade children with emotional problems, learning disabilities, or mild neurological impairment.

New programs at Northside were seeking to address the health and social conditions of Harlem. In the early 1980s, for example, well before other social-service agencies acted, Northside organized a bereavement service to help children who had lost a loved one to violence or drugs; in 1985, it set up Project Safe, a special program aimed at stemming child sexual abuse and a clinical treatment program for children living with parents, siblings, and foster caretakers who were suffering with AIDS.

In 1994, Northside's board appointed Thelma Dye—who brought a decade of experience at Northside as its chief psychologist, director of clinical services, and director of research and training—as its newest head. In December, a reception was held to honor Dye at the Museum of the City of New York, seven blocks south of Northside. A month earlier, the country had voted for a republican Congress whose members promised a "Contract for America" of stringent cuts in social spending, "smaller" government, fewer social services for children, the resurrection of orphanages, meaner times for the poor, and better times for the rich. Judge Robert Carter of the Federal District Court, veteran of the *Brown* cases of the 1950s, and a member of Northside's board for more than thirty years, reminded the audience that this was not the first time politicians and other powerful elites had abandoned the nation's poor and tried "to deny the centrality of race and racism in American life." Dye spoke of the continuing work of Northside and its special relationship to its past. "As Northside approaches its 50th year anniversary," it was important to remember that it was Mamie and Kenneth Clark's "desire to fight the negative effects of racism on children and families [that] have helped to ensure that thousands of children and families not only know that they can achieve, but they also know how to fight for themselves. . . . The key for us at Northside is helping to ensure that children and families know that they are worthwhile human beings and are not victims of their past, but in control of their present, so that they can be masters of their future." [98]

Kenneth Clark, frail at age eighty, spoke of the tough times Northside had gone through in its continuing challenges in a city and a nation often unresponsive and uncaring. He reminded the audience of African-American, white, and Latino staff, board members, and supporters that Northside had been founded to combat "subtle or blatant racism." It was a struggle that had not ended.

The history of the Northside Center has been framed by withdrawal of services in the early 1940s and the abandonment of minority youth in the years following the War on Poverty. In the 1940s and 1950s, despite an expanding economy and a strong liberal presence in New York City, Northside virtually stood alone in the city as a defender of principles of integration and equality of opportunity for African-American children. But, by the 1990s, many of the most cherished principles of the center's core have been strained: integration of the city, quality education for *all* children, better social services, and housing for black children are no longer priorities in New York City's public agenda and have virtually vanished from the rhetoric and policies of even the most liberal political and community leaders. Over its first half-century, Northside had responded to crises both within the clinic setting through its various individual therapeutic programs and also outside the center, in the political and social world. In the 1980s and 1990s, it confronted a new set of emergencies, in many respects the consequence of the city's and nation's failure to address the profound inequality of its segregated communities: a sharp increase in violence, drug abuse, AIDS, and the consequent disruption of family and neighborhood life.

Mamie Phipps Clark, who headed Northside from its founding in 1946 to her retirement in 1979, had inspired and shaped the clinical program and the center. Kenneth B. Clark, Northside's cofounder and research director from 1946 through 1966, and a board member from 1966 until the present, had advanced Northside's broader social agenda through his wide variety of activities in New York's contentious political arena. Northside was, in a sense, a laboratory in which the two Clarks' ideas and values were put into practice and tested. As James Dumpson, a long-time Northside board member, former board president, and close friend of the Clarks, pointed out, Northside was a microcosm of the world the Clarks wanted: a world of social equality, humanity, integration, and caring for all children and their families, without regard to race and circumstance. It was a place where black children, in particular, could learn to value their own worth and abilities and believe that they could shape their own future. Kenneth Clark said at the time, "we don't want psychiatry to be a panacea or substitute for social justice; what we conceived of when we started Northside was helping children to develop the kind of strength and belief in themselves, and the kind of personality stability which are necessary for them to contribute to making a better society." Northside's core agenda was "a more just society" for Harlem's children.[99]

To outside observers, it may have appeared that Kenneth and Mamie Clark operated in separate spheres—she inside and he outside Northside. Yet, as the Clarks and anyone who knew them well observed, they were essentially partners who depended on each other's insights, strengths, and values. They provided a source of empowerment for the children served and for their parents, and for the community of which Northside was part. But the full range and depths of their work has not always been apparent. Kenneth Clark said that Northside operated on many levels. It could only meet a tiny fraction of Harlem's needs, but it could serve as the catalyst for other organizations and activities with a broader impact on the quality of life of the children of Harlem. "Northside's job," he said, "would be impossible if there weren't also other groups working for better housing, better economic opportunities for human beings and against certain social injustices."[100] Only by recognizing this can Northside's involvement in the school desegregation efforts of the 1950s, community action programs in the 1960s, the battles over community control of schools, and urban renewal in the late 1960s and early 1970s be understood.

In many ways, the crisis today is as bad, if not worse, than fifty years ago. Poorer African-Americans in the cities of the North are socially and racially as segregated today as in the 1940s and 1950s. The form of these crises is different, but their effect on the children is the same or even more grave—lives destroyed, futures and hopes cynically taken away. In numerous symbolic and very real ways, African-American children are made to bear the brunt of social policies that see children and their parents as the cause of the nation's social and even economic problems.

Whether the debate is in Congress, in academia, or in barrooms, it is stunning to reflect on how minority children have emerged once again as its focus. Whether we discuss welfare "reform," unwed teenage mothers and their "inappropriateness" for welfare, Medicaid funding of abortion, school lunches, support for public education, or public hospitals, the subtext of race is always there. It is ironic that the dependent child becomes the symbol around which America discusses issues of race. In a society that cannot look honestly at its past, and cannot openly address the role that racism has played in that past, children become a surrogate for what is really being spoken of. But the use of children in this way at best smacks of paternalism and, at worst, racism, all too familiar to those who know the history of the United States.

Paralleling the continuity of the effect of racism on "children apart" has been a terrible continuity of racism in the white-led intellectual and public policy worlds and, perhaps especially, in the world of social science and education theory. In the 1960s and 1970s, in the midst of the heated resistance to school integration and Head Start, Richard Herrnstein, William Shockley, and Arthur Jensen sparked a revival of eugenic and genetic arguments based on unsupported assumptions of the inherent intellectual inferiority of African Americans. In 1969, Kenneth Clark organized a task force at his recently established Metropolitan Applied Research Corporation to marshal a broad social-science refutation of these authors' assertions. In the mid-1990s, the academic and professional communities were once again forced to confront and address an issue that Kenneth and Mamie Clark and the staff at Northside spent their lives battling, as intellectuals once again debate the proposition that observed differences in intelligence test results between blacks and whites are rooted in inheritance and genetics and, hence, in effect, immutable. It is a sad and tragic testament to the persistence of racism in the social sciences, and to the absence of historical consciousness, that social scientists and editorial writers commenting on Charles Murray and Richard Herrnstein's *Bell Curve*, for example, are only passingly aware of past intellectual rebuttals of such argument. In the current climate of reaction and retrenchment, it seems almost as though the early battles that Otto Klineberg and a generation of social scientists engaged in over eugenics, or the arguments developed by Kenneth Clark, Viola Bernard, or others in the "social science brief" of *Brown*, or the intellectual debates of late 1960s and 1970s following Jensen's article and Herrnstein's first appearance, had never occurred. The reappearance of such arguments, and America's cultural inability to go beyond race as the defining historical divide, shows, as with the defense of liberty, that the battle is never wholly won.

Essay on Sources

The breadth of Northside's various involvements in education, psychiatry, social welfare, urban renewal, and community action led us into a vast number of archives, personal collections, and oral histories. Among the most useful materials were at Northside itself. Stored in various file cabinets and closets were documents relating to its internal history and its founding, as well as to its ongoing work with children. But, in addition, the center had in its possession materials on the founding and organization of HARYOU in the period from 1960 to 1964 and the Harlem Neighborhoods Association (HANA) from 1957 to 1964. These were invaluable in recreating the political and social environment of Harlem during the early 1960s and, we believe, supplement and offer perspective on the papers of Milton Yale, the executive director of HANA, that are deposited at the Social Welfare History Archives at the University of Minnesota. Another useful set of materials were the pamphlets, letters, memoranda, and reports relating to the building of the Schomburg Plaza housing units. Of particular interest are those documents relating to the Young Lords and the community organizing efforts, both in support of and opposed to the Plaza's completion.

Among Northside's records that address the center's internal history were organizational memoranda, including minutes of board of directors' meetings, unpublished scientific and technical reports, correspondence between members of the staff, city agencies, social-service, and philanthropic groups, and Mamie Clark's personal files. The records, stored in cabinets, boxes, storage rooms, and desks, were not complete (since the center had neither the staff nor the space to maintain a formal archive), but they were voluminous and valuable. When we saw them, these records were completely unprocessed; we have collected them, and along with the records of HANA and HARYOU, they will be deposited at the New York Public Library, where they will be indexed and made accessible to scholars. The one set of records we were not allowed to use related to patient treatment and family histories. Although these records might have added a dimension to our story, the center's commitment to the privacy of its clients ultimately and rightfully prevailed.

The materials at Northside led us to other archives and personal collections. The papers of Mamie Phipps Clark are in the manuscript division of the New York Public Library at 42nd Street, a small collection consisting primarily of published documents relating to Northside such as annual reports and brochures. One very important transcription of a conference organized by the Metropolitan Applied Research Center (the MARC Corporation) which specifically addressed "The Future of Northside" proved to be quite valuable.

We were extremely fortunate to gain access to the papers of Dr. Viola Bernard. At the time, these papers were being processed and part of this enormous collection had already been moved to the Columbia University School of Medicine's Hammond Library at 168th Street and Broadway. The bulk of the papers, numbering literally scores of boxes, is still in the possession of Dr. Bernard at her residence on Fifth Avenue and are being indexed and cataloged by Kathleen Kelley and Viola Bernard in preparation for transfer to Columbia. Dr. Bernard was gracious enough to give us access to these papers and to spend many hours with us discussing various aspects of child mental health and the politics of child welfare in New York City. Her collection was essential for our understanding the history of mental-health services and philanthropy, the origins of the Northside Center, and the complex place of race in the psychiatric and political negotiations of the 1930s, 1940s, and 1950s. For anyone interested in child welfare; race and foster care; mental-health policy in postwar New York City and the origins Columbia's Psychiatric Institute; psychiatry and racism; the politics of adoption; philanthropic interest in psychiatry; the activities of the American Jewish Congress; and many other ancillary topics, Bernard's papers are invaluable.

The Columbia University Rare Books and Manuscripts Division has the records of the Community Service Society as well as a smattering of records of its predecessors, the Association for the Improvement of the Conditions of the Poor and the Charity Organization Society. These records contained materials on the activities of its Harlem office in the 1940s and 1950s and on Jane Judge, the office's head. Similarly, the Oral History Research Office of Columbia University provided us with access to their wonderful collection of oral histories, of which, of course, Kenneth Clark's and Mamie Clark's oral histories are of primary importance. But through the office's participation in this project, they have now collected more than sixty other oral histories of Northside's board members, staff, and clients.

Another source that proved important were the papers of Richard

Cloward. Richard Cloward was kind enough to give us bound photocopies of virtually every New York City newspaper article that pertained to the political crisis of Mobilization for Youth in the early 1960s. While the focus on MFY was not directly related to Northside, they were invaluable in providing us a sense of the tremendous political cauldron into which Northside was thrust when it became involved in community action programs. Also, these volumes were critical for understanding the political contention that would engulf Kenneth Clark and Northside during the early years of HARYOU.

Frances Fox Piven was similarly helpful, allowing us to interview her and to use her extensive files of material. She provided us with a variety of documents detailing the early federal antipoverty programs. Among her papers are transcriptions of interviews she conducted in the early 1960s with a variety of officials and activists involved in antipoverty programs. Since our work with them, her papers have been deposited at the Smith College Archives, where they are being indexed and cataloged.

In Washington, we were fortunate to gain access to Kenneth B. Clark's papers deposited at the Library of Congress Manuscript Division. These material were voluminous, spanning several hundred feet of shelf space. At the time we first visited them, they were uncataloged and not indexed. We sifted through hundreds of boxes and, with the generous help of the staff, were able to examine a vast amount of material. These papers cover virtually every aspect of Dr. Clark's life. Among the papers is an extensive correspondence with Mamie Phipps from the late 1930s when he had moved to New York to attend Columbia and she was still in Washington, at Howard University. Also, among the papers are many boxes of material relating to Dr. Clark's years at City College; his activities in various attempts at school desegregation both in New York and elsewhere; the establishment and activities of MARC; an extensive clipping file of newspaper articles relating to all aspects of race and racism in the United States from scores of newspapers across the nation; various speeches, drafts, and redrafts of his numerous papers and books; official and personal correspondence; and personal memorabilia. Included are some of the original data upon which Mamie and Kenneth Clark based their famous "doll studies" of the 1940s. Virtually every issue of importance in race relations from the 1930s through the 1980s is covered in these papers, among them education, *Brown* v. *Board of Education*, community control, "Black Power" and nationalism, the War on Poverty, segregation in housing and public facilities, the 1968 Ocean Hill–Brownsville controversies, and the school strike of 1968–69.

Also, in Washington, we spent a considerable amount of time at the National Archives, where we were fortunate to gain access to recently declassified materials on federal investigations of HARYOU, Mobilization for Youth, and other federal antipoverty agencies. We sorted through the records of the National Institutes of Mental Health, the Children's Bureau, and the President's Committee on Juvenile Delinquency, this latter a collection fascinating for the insights on the origins of the War on Poverty, particularly the concern of its early founders in the postwar concern over the crises of youth and juvenile delinquency.

Early on in the project we learned that HANA's executive director, Milton Yale, had deposited his papers at the University of Minnesota's Social Welfare History Archives. We found there a wealth of material on Mobilization for Youth, settlement houses in New York and East Harlem, and, specifically, the papers of the Henry Street Settlement. The Minnesota archives are probably the nation's most extensive collection of materials on voluntary social-service agencies.

Another important source of material relating directly to Northside's funding is the Rockefeller Family Archives in Tarrytown, New York. As one of the early supporters of Northside, the Rockefeller Brothers Fund periodically evaluated the center, and we found these evaluations extremely useful. This massive archive contains materials relating to the institutional history of Northside, as well as to the history of social services, mental health, and activities surrounding juvenile delinquency in the city, state, and nation. Because of the Rockefellers' various and varied activities in the broader world of politics, social welfare reform, health, and children, this collection was valuable for us.

We made numerous trips to Cambridge, Massachusetts, to visit the papers of Justine Wise Polier, the early Northside Board member and longtime justice on the Domestic Relations Court in New York City. Her papers, at the Schlesinger Library at Radcliffe College, are invaluable for scholars interested in race relations and child welfare from the 1930s through the 1970s. We were fortunate to be among the first scholars to see these papers in their unprocessed state. Like the Kenneth B. Clark manuscripts, the Polier manuscripts are voluminous and relate virtually to every aspect of juvenile justice, civil liberties for children, New York City politics, foster care and adoption, psychiatry, and psychological services. They are literally a treasure-trove that deserves the notice of scholars. We sincerely hope that some younger scholars will pay close attention to Polier's life and use these archives extensively.

Polier, who came from a prominent New York family, long involved in the city's social welfare, political and Jewish communities, was the daughter of Stephen Wise, the noted Reform rabbi, and of Louise Wise, the founder of the Louise Wise Services, one of the few children's services that openly and fervently integrated its services before the 1960s. Her husband, Shad Polier, was Northside's lawyer for many years; he was a leader in the American Jewish Congress, and a leading civil libertarian who, among many other activities, was willing to oppose many in the New York Jewish community by representing Abel and Anne Meeropol in their quest to adopt Michael and Robert, the orphaned sons of Julius and Ethel Rosenberg. The papers of both Stephen Wise and Shad Polier, located at the Jewish Historical Society at Brandeis University in Waltham, Massachusetts, have interesting materials relating to Justine Wise's early years as well as about Northside's activities.

Many of Northside's original board and professional advisory committee had become involved with the New York Citizens' Committee for Children, the child advocacy organization, whose archives were graciously opened to us. They were valuable in evaluating the ways the philanthropic world established priorities and organized its activities. The files of the committee, as one of the leading advocacy groups for children, are virtually a chronicle of the children's advocacy struggles in the second half of the twentieth century.

One of the most interesting set of documents that expose the role of race in New York's foster-care system is housed in the basement of the New York Civil Liberties Union and the American Civil Liberties Union offices in New York City. For more than twenty years, the NYCLU and the ACLU documented discrimination in foster placements and were useful in shaping our perspective on the continuing importance of race and racism in the lives of New York's minority youth. These records are vast and deserve to be carefully cataloged and maintained.

As we were beginning this project, the La Guardia Archives at La Guardia Community College in Queens, fortuitously received the papers of New York's Mayor Robert F. Wagner and were beginning to catalog them. We were fortunate to be allowed access to this large collection and found a number of files related directly to Northside and the interests of city hall in its various activities in housing and neighborhood organizing.

The New York City Municipal Archives and the Municipal Library were both useful during the writing of this book. Of special interest were the mayoral records of Vincent Impelliteri and William O'Dwyer, valuable in tracing the history of New York's concern over juvenile delinquency in various neighborhoods of the city in the immediate postwar years. The city's severe financial constraints, which during the past few years led to reduced staffing and periods of closure, limited our ability to utilize these records fully.

Many of the sources we uncovered were neither cataloged nor organized, and therefore, our references in the chapter notes that follow are sometimes incomplete. For example, the papers of Kenneth B. Clark were still being shipped to the Library of Congress when we first visited and were in cartons stored in a narrow, dimly lit room in the basement of the Adams building. Each carton was brought to us in the reading room, where we rifled through each one. Similarly, the papers of Justine Wise Polier at the Schlesinger library were uncataloged when we arrived and, while the library staff was wonderfully accommodating and the working conditions pleasant, these papers, too, had not been ordered. So, too, the papers of the Northside Center have not yet been delivered to the New York Public Library, nor have all Viola Bernard's papers been sent to Columbia, and the Citizens' Committee papers are not yet cataloged either. The documents of the New York Civil Liberties Union on discrimination in the foster care system, in the basement of their building in midtown Manhattan, are stored in file cabinets.

While the fact that we were among the first to view many of these materials made the research endeavor all the more exciting, it has made our footnoting difficult. In the notes, complete references are provided for documents that reside in a permanent archive and which, at the time we visited them, were boxed and indexed; only partial documentation is provided, necessarily, for those primary documents, like the Kenneth B. Clark Manuscripts at the Library of Congress, that were not cataloged at the time of our research.

Notes

Abbreviations

Bernard Papers	Viola Bernard, private papers, New York
HANA	Harlem Neighborhoods Association
KBC	Kenneth Bancroft Clark
KBC MSS	Kenneth Bancroft Clark Manuscripts, Library of Congress, Manuscript Division, Washington, D.C.
MARC	Metropolitan Applied Research Center
Minutes, NCCD	Minutes, Board of Directors, Northside Center for Child Development, New York
MPC	Mamie Phipps Clark
MPC MSS	Mamie Clark Manuscripts, Manuscript Division, New York Public Library, New York
MSPCC	Manhattan Shelter for the Prevention of Cruelty to Children
NCCD	Northside Center for Child Development
NCCD MSS	Northside Center for Child Development Manuscripts, New York
O'Dwyer Papers	Mayor O'Dwyer Papers, Municipal Archives, New York.
OHC	Oral History Research Center of Columbia University, New York
Polier MSS	Justine Wise Polier Manuscripts, Schlesinger Library, Radcliffe College, Cambridge, Mass.
RFA	Rockefeller Family Archives, Tarrytown, N.Y.

1. The Abandonment of Harlem's Children

1. "11 Boys Are Jailed in S.P.C.C. Outbreak," *New York Times*, 8 October 1943, 21.

2. "The 'Black Book' of Children's Punishment," *PM*, 23 January 1944, 12.

3. "Food," [Summary of Children's and Staff Testimony], carton 2, folder Investigation of MSPCC (1943), 2 and 3, Polier MSS.

4. New York State Department of Social Welfare, "Summary of Report of Inspection of the Manhattan Shelter maintained by the New York Society for the Prevention of Cruelty to Children," June to September 1942, carton 2, folder MSPCC 1937–1942, Polier MSS.

5. "The 'Black Book,'" 12.

6. Ibid.

7. "Minutes of the Meeting of Sub-Committee on Crime and Delinquency of the City-Wide Citizens' Committee on Harlem," 23 October 1943, box Racism, Bernard Papers.

8. Albert Deutsch, "Isolationist Role of SPCC Helped Lead It into Decline," *PM*, 5 October 1943, 11.

9. Nathan Irvin Huggins, *Harlem Renaissance* (New York, 1971), 4.

10. James Weldon Johnson, "Harlem: The Culture Capital," Alain Locke, ed. *The New Negro* (New York, 1974; originally published 1925), 301–2.

11. Ann Douglas, *Terrible Honesty, Mongrel Manhattan in the 1920s* (New York, 1995), 90.

12. Robert Fogelson and Richard E. Rubinstein, eds., *The Complete Report of Mayor La Guardia's Commission on the Harlem Riot of March 19, 1935* (New York, 1969); hereafter cited as [Frazier], *Harlem Riot*. Anthony M. Platt, in *E. Franklin Frazier Reconsidered* (New Brunswick, N.J., 1991), 246, fn.10, explains that this report was authored by E. Franklin Frazier when he was research director of the Mayor's Commission on Conditions in Harlem that had been appointed to investigate the causes of the riot in 1935. "The Commission's final report was never released to the public by La Guardia. One version was published in full in the New York *Amsterdam News*, July 18, 1936. This version was reprinted, with a few errors and without proper credit to Frazier, by Robert Fogelson and Richard E. Rubinstein."

13. [Frazier], *Harlem Riot*, 63.

14. See Cheryl Lynn Greenberg, *"Or Does It Explode?" Black Harlem in the Great Depression* (New York, 1991), 3–6, for a description of the riot.

15. Platt, *Frazier*, 106.

16. [Frazier], *Harlem Riot*, 92.

17. Ibid., 92, 95–97.

18. "Report of the Sub-Committee on Health and Hospitals of the City-Wide Citizens' Committee on Harlem," May 1942, box Racism, Bernard Papers.

19. [Frazier], *Harlem Riot*, 97–98. See Vanessa Gamble, *Making a Place for Ourselves* (New York, 1995) for a discussion of the race struggles at Harlem Hospital in the 1920s and early 1930s.

20. [Frazier], *Harlem Riot*, 79–80, 81–82.

21. Ibid., 84.

22. Mrs. Yorke Allen to John D. Rockefeller III, 23 October 1944, carton 2, folder Racial Discrimination, 1938–1949, Polier MSS.

23. "The Story of the City-Wide Citizens' Committee on Harlem" (typescript), 23 May 1943, box Racism, folder City-Wide Committee on Harlem: Sub-Committee on Crime and Delinquency, Bernard Papers.

24. "Statement of New York State Committee on the Youth Correction Authority Plan," in Austin McCormick to John D. Rockefeller III, 10 March 1944, RFA, record group 2, Welfare Interests—General, box 13. See also "Has the American Home Failed?" *Town Meeting* [broadcast by Stations of the Blue Network], 2 December 1943,

record group 102 (Records of the Children's Bureau), Central File, 1941–44, file 7-1-2-3, folder War in Relation to Juvenile Delinquency, National Archives, Washington, D.C.; "Survey Shows 3000% Wartime Rise in Delinquency," *PM*, 6 August 1944, 6.

25. "Domestic Relations Court, City of New York, Children's Division." O'Dwyer Papers, subject file Juvenile Delinquency, 1946, box 78.

26. "Story of the City-Wide Citizens' Committee on Harlem," 7, Bernard Papers.

27. City-Wide Citizens' Committee on Harlem, "Suggested Summary of Highlights of Crime and Delinquency Committee's Report" [typescript], [1942], box Racism, Bernard Papers.

28. City-Wide Citizens' Committee on Harlem, "Tentative Report of the Sub-Committee on Crime and Delinquency," in Paul Blanchard, Chairman to Committee Member, 8 June 1942, box 36, folder 443, Polier MSS.

29. "Story of the City-Wide Citizens' Committee on Harlem," Bernard Papers.

30. Bernard to Walter White, NAACP, 15 April 1942, box Racism, Bernard Papers. Also in Polier MSS, box 41, folder 497.

31. City-Wide Citizens' Committee on Harlem, "Tentative Report of the Sub-Committee on Crime and Delinquency," Polier MSS; see also "Race Bias Seen Key to Harlem Crime," *New York Times*, 2 August 1942, box Racism, Bernard Papers.

32. City-Wide Citizens' Committee on Harlem, "Suggested Summary of Highlights of Crime and Delinquency Committee's Report," Bernard Papers.

33. City-Wide Citizens' Committee on Harlem, "Tentative Report of the Sub-Committee on Crime and Delinquency," in Paul Blanchard, Chairman, to Committee Member, Polier MSS.

34. "Report of the Study Committee of the Children's Services Committee of the Riverdale Children's Association, May, 1946," RFA, record group 2, series Welfare Interests, sub-series General, box 39, folder Riverdale Children's Association.

35. City-Wide Citizens' Committee on Harlem, "Suggested Summary of Highlights of Crime and Delinquency Committee's Report," Bernard Papers.

36. "Project Memorandum, Winthrop Rockefeller, Riverdale Children's Association," 23 December 1947, RFA, record group 2, series Welfare Interests, sub-series General, box 39, folder Riverdale Children's Association.

37. "Inmates of Five Welfare Institutions To Be Removed because of Commissioner Hodson's Race Bias Charges," *New York Times*, 30 October 1942, 21; see also "Commissioner Hodson Scores Child Care Institutions' Race Bias," *New York Times*, 10 December 1942, 19.

38. "Minutes of the Meeting of Sub-Committee on Crime and Delinquency of the City-Wide Citizens' Committee on Harlem," 27 May 1945, box Racism, Bernard Papers.

39. Ibid.

40. Agnes Fowler, Superintendent of Hopewell Society of Brooklyn to Mrs. Lillian Brown, Manhattan Children's Court, 28 September 1945, carton 2, "Racial Discrimination, 1938–1949," Polier MSS.

41. Polier to Timothy Pfeiffer, 19 October 1945, carton 2, "Racial Discrimination, 1938–1949," Polier MSS.

42. Agnes Fowler to Mrs. Lillian Brown, 28 September 1945, carton 2, "Racial Discrimination, 1938–1949," Polier MSS.

43. "Minutes of the Meeting of Sub-Committee on Crime and Delinquency of the City-Wide Citizens' Committee on Harlem," 27 May 1945, Bernard Papers.

44. "Report of the Study Committee of the Children's Services Committee of the Riverdale Children's Association, May, 1946," RFA.

45. City-Wide Citizens' Committee on Harlem, "Tentative Report of the Sub-Committee on Crime and Delinquency," Polier MSS.

46. "Second Annual Report of Executive Director to Board of Trustees, The Youth House, April 3, 1945 to March 31, 1946," 1 July 1946, subject files Juvenile Delinquency, 1946, box 78, O'Dwyer Papers.

47. Harriet L. Goldberg, *Child Offenders: A Study in Diagnosis and Treatment* (New York, 1948), 200. Goldberg was a former Assistant Corporation Counsel assigned to the Children's Court of New York City; at the time she wrote the book, she was a justice in the Domestic Relations Court of Toledo, Ohio.

48. Mayor's Committee on Juvenile Delinquency, "Report on Truancy in New York City Schools," 5 June 1944, box 77, subject file Juvenile Delinquency, 1944–45, O'Dwyer Papers.

49. Polier to Fiorello H. La Guardia, 27 July 1940, box 33, folder 411, Polier MSS.

50. Articles of Incorporation, May 1941, box 33, folder 411, Polier MSS.

51. Newspaper article, "Harlem to Obtain Guidance Clinic," 9 October 1940, box 33, folder 411, Polier MSS.

52. "Minutes, First Meeting of the Joint Advisory Committee of the Special Child Guidance Service Unit in Harlem," 15 November 1940, box 33, folder 411, Polier MSS.; Exhibit F shows receipts of organization was from three $5,000 contributions from Marion Ascoli, Adele Levy, and Marshall Field.

53. Max Winsor, M.D., "Report to the Joint Advisory Committee of the Special Child Guidance Service Unit in Harlem," June 1942, [prepared 1941], box 33, folder 411, Polier MSS.

54. City-Wide Citizens' Committee on Harlem, Report of Subcommittee, "Psychiatric Recommendation as Related to Negro Children," 26 March 1942, box Racism, Bernard Papers, prepared by Drs. Zachry, Winsor, and Bernard (Sub-Committee on Crime and Delinquency). "A psychiatric clinic in the out patient department of Harlem Hospital is badly needed, and the psychiatric clinic of the Children's Court should be expanded." City-Wide Citizens' Committee on Harlem, "Suggested Summary of Highlights of Crime and Delinquency Committee's Report," [1942], [typescript], Bernard Papers.

55. "Negro Youth," *Survey Mid-monthly*, March 1942, box Racism, Bernard Papers.

56. City-Wide Citizens' Committee on Harlem, "Tentative Report of the Sub-Committee on Crime and Delinquency," Polier MSS.

57. Justine Wise Polier et al., "Report on the Harlem Project, September 1943-June 1945," [Mimeo], December 1947, box 35, folder 438, Polier MSS.

58. "Harlem Project Urges New Plan in Dealing with Problem Pupils," *New York Herald-Tribune*, 23 March 1948, 23.

59. Joseph F. McGuire, Hubert T. Delany, and Justine Wise Polier, "Report on the Critical Situation Facing the Children's Court of the City of New York in Regard to the Placement of Neglected and Delinquent Children for Temporary and Long-Term Care," 28 December 1945, in Polier to William O'Dwyer, 11 January 1946, subject files Juvenile Delinquency, 1946, box 78, O'Dwyer Papers.

60. Channing H. Tobias, "Crime and Prevention—A Harlem Point of View," Press Release, 23 November 1946, subject file Juvenile Delinquency, 1946, box 78, O'Dwyer Papers.

61. "Report on the Critical Situation Facing the Children's Court," O'Dwyer Papers.

62. "Report of the Child Welfare Commission—Union for Democratic Action," under the chairmanship of Polier, quoted in "Summary Analysis of Program and Activities of Northside Testing and Consultation Center Prospectus and Budget for 1947," KBC MSS.

63. See Ralph G. Martin, "Doctor's Dream in Harlem," *The New Republic*, 3 June 1946, 798–800; "Psychiatry in Harlem," *Time*, 1 December 1947, 50, 52; "Frederic Wertham," *Current Biography*, 1949, 634–35; Ralph Ellison, "Harlem Is Nowhere," *Shadow and Act* (New York, 1964, 1995), 294–302; Jack Greenberg, *Crusaders in the Courts* (New York, 1994), 135–39. In the late 1940s and early 1950s, Wertham would emerge as a major critic of comic-book violence. He would publish widely on the relationship between violence in comic books and the rise of juvenile delinquency.

2. The Northside Center for Child Development

1. Minutes, NCCD, 8 April 1946.

2. KBC, tape-recorded interview by Ed Edwin, 4 February 1976, OHC.

3. MPC, tape-recorded interview by Ed Edwin, 25 May 1976, OHC.

4. Minutes, NCCD, 8 April 1946.

5. MPC, interview; KBC, interview; Welfare Council of New York City, "Report on Northside Center for Child Development," March 1948, series 3, box 83, folder "Northside, 1948–1969," Rockefeller Brothers Fund MSS, RFA; Dr. Miriam Weston, tape-recorded interview by Jonathan S. Lee, 8 December 1990, OHC; *Washington Post* reported that the center "opened in a $35-a-month basement room," "Northside Center Aids Anxious Children," *Washington Post*, 24 November 1948, H2.

6. "The Center's Beginnings," [1947–48], KBC MSS.

7. "Northside Testing and Consulting Center," letter to community professionals, 25 February 1946, [invitation to opening on 28 February and 1 March 1946 from 10 A.M. to 6 P.M.], KBC MSS.

8. "Summary Analysis of Program and Activities of Northside Testing and Consultation Center Prospectus and Budget for 1947," KBC MSS.

9. Ibid.

10. "Northside Testing and Consulting Center," letter, 25 February 1946.

11. Stella Chess, untitled, 16 February 1951, box Northside Center for Child Development, Bernard Papers.

12. Stella Chess, tape-recorded interview by Jonathan Lee, 3 November 1990, OHC.

13. "Northside Testing and Consulting Center." The original staff included the following. *Consulting staff*: Pediatricians: Samuel F. Jenkins, M.D., Cecil Marquez, M.D., Thomas W. Patrick Jr., M.D.; Psychiatrists: Ruth Foster, M.D., Jane Pearce, M.D., Carl Sulzberger, M.D.; Psychologists: Kenneth B. Clark, Max Hertzman, Ph.D.; Psychiatric Social Workers: Victor E. Carter, M.A., Olivia Edwards, M.A., Edward P. Norris, M.A. *Members of sponsoring committee*: Jane Bolin, Dr. John R. Clark (Ex-pres., Lincoln School, Teachers College), Albert Deutsch, Edward Lewis (Exec. Dir., Greater New York Urban League), Thurgood Marshall, Mrs. Helen Meade (Dir., Little Brown School House), Dr. Ernest Osborne (Teachers College), Dr. Lawrence D. Reddick (Curator, Schomburg Collection). Soon after, Edward Dalton joined the social work unit, Stella Chess joined the psychiatrists, and Claire Charen, M.A., joined psychologists. See "To Meet a Community Need: Northside Testing and Consultation Center," brochure, KBC MSS.

14. "Harlem Opens New Center for Child Guidance," *New York Herald-Tribune*, 3 March 1946, KBC MSS.

15. "Problem Kids," *Ebony* 2 (July 1947), 20–25.

16. Ibid.

17. KBC, interview.

18. "Summary Analysis of Program and Activities of Northside."

19. MARC, transcription, Northside Conference, 10 January 1969, Afternoon Session, New York, Delmonico Hotel, 2, MPC MSS.

20. "Summary Analysis of Program and Activities of Northside."

21. MARC, Northside Conference, 2.

22. Arthur B. Clark to KBC, 25 January 1938, KBC MSS.

23. KBC, interview.

24. KBC, interview; see also KBC, "Racial Progress and Retreat: A Personal Memoir," in Herbert Hill and James E. Jones Jr., eds., *Race in America, The Struggle for Equality* (Madison, Wisc., 1993), 7.

25. KBC, interview.

26. Ibid.

27. Ibid.

28. MPC, interview.

29. "Mamie Phipps Clark" in Agnes N. O' Connell and Nancy Felipe Russo, eds., *Models of Achievement: Reflections of Eminent Women in Psychology* (New York, 1983), 268.

30. KBC, interview.

31. H. H. Phipps [Physician and Manager, Pythian Hotel and Baths in Hot Springs] to KBC, 19 July 1937, KBC MSS.

32. H. H. Phipps to Mamie Phipps, 19 November 1937, KBC MSS.

33. See, for example, Mamie Phipps to KBC, 4 August 1938, KBC MSS.

34. Mamie Phipps to KBC, 12 February 1938, KBC MSS.

35. Mamie Phipps to KBC, 24 March 1938, KBC MSS.

36. KBC, interview.

37. Quoted in Murray Friedman, *What Went Wrong? The Creation and Collapse of the Black-Jewish Alliance* (New York, 1995), 68.

38. "Clark" in O'Connell and Russo, *Models*, 268.

39. Mamie Phipps to KBC, 4 August 1938, KBC MSS.

40. "Clark" in O'Connell and Russo, *Models*, 269.

41. Mamie Phipps to KBC, 25 April 1939, KBC MSS. See also Mamie Phipps to KBC, 29 April 1939, KBC MSS.

42. "Clark" in O'Connell and Russo, *Models*, 269.

43. KBC, quoted in "Staff Development Program," [Riverdale Children's Association], 24 November 1961, group 1, KBC MSS.

44. KBC, interview.

45. Ibid.

46. KBC, quoted in "Staff Development Program."

47. Ibid.

48. Otto Klineberg to KBC, 15 July 1954; KBC [statement on behalf of Otto Klineberg], 22 July 1954; Otto Klineberg to KBC, 20 September 1954; KBC to Otto Klineberg, 28 September 1954. For a detailed discussion of the relationship between UNESCO and the U.S. government, see William Preston, *Hope and Folly: The United States and UNESCO, 1945–1985* (Minneapolis, 1989).

49. "Clark" in O'Connell and Russo, *Models*, 270.

50. KBC, interview.

51. "Clark Named Instructor at N.Y. College," *Chicago Defender*, 31 May 1941, 6.

52. "Clark Named as Instructor," *Amsterdam Star-News*, [ca. Oct. or Sept. 1942], KBC MSS.

53. "CCNY Sets Democracy in Action, Adds Negro to Regular Faculty," *People's Voice*, October 1942, KBC MSS.

54. MPC, interview.

55. KBC, interview.

56. KBC, untitled oral history, [ca. 1960], courtesy of Jeannette Hopkins.

57. KBC, interview.

58. KBC, untitled oral history.

59. KBC, interview; KBC, untitled oral history.

60. "Clark" in O'Connell and Russo, *Models*, 270.

61. MPC, interview.

62. KBC, interview.

63. "Clark" in O'Connell and Russo, *Models*, 271.

64. MPC, interview.

65. KBC, interview.

66. MPC, interview.

67. M. Moran Weston, tape-recorded interview with Jonathan Lee, 8 February 1991, OHC.

68. "Summary Analysis of Program and Activities of Northside."

69. M. Moran Weston, interview.

70. Viola Bernard, tape-recorded interview with authors, 13 May 1993, New York.

71. Executive Committee Meeting, Citizens' Committee on Children of NYC, Inc., 22 April 1947, folder, "Finance Committee," Citizens' Committee on Children Archives, New York.

72. "Summary, Operations of Association: Northside Center for Child Development," [ca. December 1947], NCCD MSS.

73. Viola Bernard, tape-recorded interview with Jonathan Lee, 14 December 1990, OHC. Others remembered the coming of the new board differently. Clara Rabinowitz recalled that some of the staff saw them as "a coterie of upper class Jewish women. . . . We didn't want them, we were enjoying the situation and thought them to be interlopers." Jeanne Karp, Olga Taylor, Clara Rabinowitz, and Stella Chess, interview with authors, 21 October 1993, New York.

74. NCCD, "Annual Report," 1960, NCCD MSS.

75. "Northside Center: 20 Devoted Years," *Amsterdam News*, 7 May 1966, KBC MSS.

76. NCCD, "Annual Report," 1960.

77. Bernard, interview, 14 December 1990.

78. "Summary, Operations of Association."

79. Bernard, interview, 14 December 1990.

80. "Summary Analysis of Program and Activities of Northside."

81. Karp, Taylor, Rabinowitz, and Chess, interview.

82. "Summary Analysis of Program and Activities of Northside."

83. Rockefeller Brothers Fund, Inc., NCCD, Project Memorandum, July 1948, series 3, box 83, folder Northside, 1948–69, Rockefeller Brothers Fund MSS, RFA.

84. Miriam Weston, interview.

85. Doris Goss to Mr. Packard, 1 March 1949, "Memorandum, Northside Center for Child Development": Progress Report Northside Center for Child Development, Inc. Submitted by the 1949 Fund Raising Committee of the Board of Directors, August 1949, series 3, box 83, folder Northside, 1948–69, Rockefeller Brothers Fund MSS, RFA.

86. William O'Connor, tape-recorded interview with Lisa Miller, 3 June 1992, OHC.

87. Stella Chess, interview.

88. Minutes, NCCD, 10 November 1960.

3. Philanthropy and Psychiatry, an Exercise in White Power

1. Gertrude Samuels, "Where Troubled Children Are Reborn," *New York Times Magazine*, 13 June 1954, KBC MSS. This scene is largely drawn from Samuels's article. However, this is also a composite sketch based upon an interview on 21 October 1993, with Stella Chess, Olga Taylor, Jeanne Karp, and Clara Rabinowitz, staff members who helped us reconstruct a typical day at the center in the mid-1950s.

2. Karp, Taylor, Rabinowitz, and Chess, interview.

3. Bea Levison, tape-recorded interview with Jonathan Lee, 20 October 1990, OHC; Joanne Stern, tape-recorded interview with Jonathan Lee, 16 July 1990, OHC; Miriam Weston, interview.

4. Catherine Lombard, tape-recorded interview with Lisa Miller, 7 June 1993, OHC.

5. Levison, interview; Miriam Weston, interview.

6. Chess, interview; Karp, tape-recorded interview with Celia Alvarez and Jonathan Lee, 24 July 1990, OHC.

7. Karp, interview.

8. Mildred Stevens and Dr. Rutherford Stevens, tape-recorded interview with Jonathan Lee, 11 January 1991, OHC.

9. Karp, interview.

10. MPC, interview.

11. Miriam Weston, interview; Edna Meyers, tape-recorded interview with Jonathan Lee, 14 January 1991, OHC.

12. Victor Carter, tape-recorded interview with Jonathan Lee, 11 December 1990, OHC.

13. Karp, interview.

14. Chess, interview; Carter, interview; Norman Wyloge, tape-recorded interview with Jonathan Lee, 12 December 1990, OHC.

15. Carter, interview.

16. Teodora Abramovich, tape-recorded interview with Jonathan Lee, 18 January 1991, OHC.

17. Abramovich, interview.

18. Miriam Weston, interview.

19. MPC, "Evaluation of the Effectiveness of an Interracial Child Guidance Clinic: Intercultural Factors," 8, [typescript], NCCD, March 1957, NCCD MSS.

20. Bernard, interview, 13 May 1993.

21. Bernard, interview, 14 December 1990.

22. Bernard, interview with authors, 9 March 1994, New York.

23. Bernard, interview, 13 May 1993.

24. Bernard, interview, 14 December 1990.

25. Ibid.

26. Joanne Stern and Howard Sloan, tape-recorded interview with authors, 2 February 1995, New York.

27. Bernard to Wolf Schwabacher, City-Wide Citizens' Committee on Harlem, 29 March 1945, box Racism, Bernard Papers.

28. Bernard, interview, 14 December 1990.

29. Miriam Weston, interview.

30. Karp, Chess, Rabinowitz, and Taylor, interview.

31. Stern, interview.

32. Stern and Sloan, interview.

33. Bernard, interview, 13 May 1993.

34. Carter, telephone interview with authors, 7 February 1995, New York.

35. Bernard, interview, 13 May 1993.

36. KBC, interview with authors, 26 June 1992, Hastings-on-Hudson, N.Y.

37. "Introduction," Margo Horn, *Before It's Too Late: The Child Guidance Movement in the United States, 1922–1945* (Philadelphia, 1989).

38. Ibid., 185-86.

39. Herschel Alt, "Introduction," *Primary Behavior Disorder in Children . . . Two Case Studies* (New York, 1945), 2; Frederika Neumann, "Evolution of an Integrated Child Guidance Program," ibid., 6.

40. Richard Cloward and Erwin Epstein, "Private Social Welfare's Disengagement from the Poor: The Case of Family Adjustment Agencies," in George A. Brager and Francis P. Purcell, *Community Action Against Poverty: Readings from the Mobilization Experience* (New Haven, 1967), 40–63.

41. David Rosner, "Health Care and the Truly Needy: Nineteenth Century Origins of the Concept," *Milbank Quarterly* (fall 1982), 85–105.

42. "Preface," Frank Reissman, Jerome Cohen, and Arthur Pearl, eds., *Mental Health of the Poor* (New York, 1964), vii–viii.

43. B. E. Jones, O. B. Lightfoot, D. Palmer, R. G. Wilkerson, and D. H. Williams, "Problems of Black Psychiatric Residents in White Training Institutes," *American Journal of Psychiatry* 127 (1970), 298–303, quoted in Alexander Thomas and Samuel Sillen, *Racism and Psychiatry* (New York, 1972), 136. There were, however, psychiatrists such as Joel Kovel, Alexander Thomas, Stella Chess, and Ben Pasamanick in the 1950s and 1960s who sought to awaken the field and challenge implicit and explicit racism.

44. KBC, interview.

45. Appendix to Appellant's Briefs, "The Effects of Segregation and the Consequences of Desegregation: A Social Science Statement," in appendix 3, KBC, *Prejudice and Your Child*, 2d ed. (Boston, 1963), 168; NCCD Minutes, Professional Advisory Committee Meeting, 2 February 1951, box NCCD, Bernard Papers.

46. KBC and Viola Bernard, "Personal Adjustment of Minority Group Children—A Program for the Future," [1951], Bernard Papers.

47. Stella Chess, Kenneth Clark, and Alexander Thomas, "Edward," in "Importance of Cultural Evaluation in Psychiatric Diagnosis and Treatment," *Psychiatric Quarterly* (January 1953), 7–9.

48. Ibid., 9–11. They admonished the profession not to succumb to a "racist approach to variation in human behavior."

49. "Summary Analysis of Program and Activities of Northside."

50. Clara Rabinowitz, "I. Therapeutic Work," *Children*, January–February 1956, 3–8; Olivia Edwards, "II. Helping Their Parents," *Children*, January–February 1956, 9–12.

51. Bernard, interview, 14 December 1990.

52. "Minutes," Joint Meeting of Association Members and Advisory Committee, NCCD, 12 June [1947]; "Meeting of Advisory Committee of Northside Center," 5 November 1947; box NCCD, folder "Professional Advisory Committee Minutes, 1947, 1950–51, 1956–57," Bernard Papers.

53. NCCD, "Re—Dispensary License," KBC MSS.

54. Minutes, "Professional Advisory Committee Meeting," NCCD, 15 December 1950, box NCCD, Bernard Papers.

55. Minutes, "Professional Advisory Committee Meeting," NCCD, 2 March 1951, Bernard Papers.

56. Chess, untitled, 16 February 1951, Bernard Papers.

57. Minutes, "Professional Advisory Committee Meeting," NCCD, Bernard Papers; see also MPC to George Gardner [president, AAPCC], 23 May 1951, Bernard Papers.

58. Justine Wise Polier, "The Non-Conforming Adolescent," in round table, chaired by KBC, "Desegregation: Its Implications for Orthopsychiatry," *American Journal of Orthopsychiatry* 26 (July 1956), 473–75.

59. Mrs. Max Ascoli to Francis Carmody [Avalon Foundation], 31 January 1956, box NCCD, Bernard Papers; Marion Ascoli to Bernard, 15 March 1956, Bernard Papers.

60. Minutes, Professional Advisory Committee, NCCD, 16 April 1956, Bernard Papers.

61. Minutes, Professional Advisory Committee, NCCD, 19 October 1956 and Exie Welsch, "Plan for Exploratory Study at Northside Center," Bernard Papers.

62. MPC to Exie Welsch, 4 December 1956, NCCD MSS; MPC to Marion Ascoli, 3 December 1956, NCCD MSS.

63. KBC to Dr. Exie Welsch, 4 December 1956, NCCD MSS.

64. MPC to Exie Welsch, 26 April 1957; NCCD, Professional Advisory Committee, "Minutes," 15 March 1957, box NCCD; MPC to Viola Bernard, 2 May 1957; Exie Welsch to MPC, 14 May 1957, Bernard Papers; "Heads of Departments," [Chess, Edwards, Carter, Gerbitz, Gruan] to Board, 13 May 1957, NCCD MSS.

65. Exie E. Welsch, "Report of Study on Training Possibilities at Northside Center

for Child Development," May 1957, NCCD MSS; "Report of Staff of Northside Center on Possibilities for Training Psychiatrists," June 1957, NCCD MSS.

66. Marion Ascoli to Viola Bernard, 12 December 1957, box NCCD, Bernard Papers.

67. "Recommendations of the Ad-Hoc Committee," attached to Marion Ascoli to Exie Welsch, 27 January 1958; Stella Chess to Board of Directors, 24 March 1958; "Notes from the Meeting of the Ad Hoc Committee," 6 February 1958, Bernard Papers.

68. Minutes, NCCD, 16 January 1958; Marion Ascoli to "The Psychotherapy Staff of Northside Center for Child Development, Inc.," 20 March 1958, Bernard Papers.

69. Marion Ascoli to Board of Directors, 9 February 1959, Bernard Papers.

70. Minutes, NCCD, 9 April 1959.

71. Minutes, NCCD, 11 June 1959.

72. Chess, interview; Minutes, NCCD, 10 December 1959.

73. Minutes, NCCD, 4 February 1960.

74. Staff—Northside Center for Child Development, Inc., to Mrs. Max Ascoli, 19 February 1960, box NCCD, Bernard Papers.

75. MPC to Marion Ascoli, 19 February 1960, Bernard Papers.

76. Notes on Meeting of Personnel Committee of Staff with Personnel Practices Committee of Board, 3 March 1960, in Minutes, NCCD, 22 March 1960; see also Mrs. Max Ascoli to Viola Bernard, 11 March 1960, box NCCD, Bernard Papers.

77. Friedman, *What Went Wrong?*, documents the often-strained relations between blacks and Jews in the pre–civil rights era.

78. KBC, "Candor about Negro-Jewish Relations," *Commentary*, February 1946, 12–13.

79. Ibid. 9–10. See also KBC, "Jews in Contemporary America," *Jewish Social Service Quarterly* 31 (fall 1954), 12–22; presented at the Annual Meeting of National Association of Jewish Center Workers, 17 May 1954.

80. KBC, "Some Personal Observations Concerning My Association with the Commission on Community Interrelations of the American Jewish Congress," [1945], KBC MSS; "Quote Rabbi Cohen," [handwritten notes], n.d., KBC MSS.

81. [KBC], "Supplementary Report on Meeting at the Offices of the Council for Democracy," 12 February 1945, KBC MSS.

82. Minutes, NCCD, 22 March 1960.

83. KBC, "A Positive Transition," *ADL Bulletin*, December 1957, in KBC MSS.

84. KBC, "A Changing Community: Its Impact on and Challenge to American Jewry," [Mimeo], 27 May 1960, KBC MSS.

85. Stern and Sloan, interview; KBC, interview, 26 June 1992.

86. Saul Scheidlinger, tape-recorded interview with Jonathan Lee, 5 February 1991, OHC; Minutes, NCCD, 26 April 1960.

87. Scheidlinger, interview.

88. Bernard to "Marion, Ken and Mamie, and Fellow Board Members," draft, 5 April 1960, Bernard Papers.

89. Bernard, interview, 13 May 1993.

90. MPC, interview.

91. Minutes, NCCD, 19 May 1960.

92. Marion Ascoli to Pauline Falk, 23 March 1960, NCCD MSS.

93. "An Appeal for Funds for the Relocation of Northside Center for Child Development, Inc. Submitted to the Rockefeller Brothers Foundation," 5 May 1960, series 3, box 83, folder "Northside Center, 1948–1969," Rockefeller Brothers Fund MSS, RFA.

94. Doris Goss and David F. Freeman to Dana S. Creel, Memorandum, 23 May 1960, series 3, box 83, folder Northside Center, 1948–1969, Rockefeller Brothers Fund MSS, RFA; "Docket Memorandum, Rockefeller Brothers Fund, Inc., Executive Committee, Northside Center for Child Development, Inc.," 1 June 1960, series 3, box 83, folder Northside Center 1948–1969, Rockefeller Brothers Fund MSS, RFA; David M. Heyman, President, New York Foundation, to MPC, 13 June 1960, NCCD MSS.

95. James Dumpson, tape-recorded interview with Jonathan Lee, 26 November 1990, OHC.

96. Charles Green and Basil Wilson, *The Struggle for Black Empowerment in New York City* (New York, 1989).

97. "Tammany Picks Negro as Boss, Wagner's Push Puts Jones In," *New York Daily News*, 4 December 1964, 1; KBC, interview, 26 June 1992.

98. Minutes, NCCD, 21 April 1966.

99. Dumpson, interview.

4. Children Apart

1. KBC, "Jews in Contemporary America," *Jewish Social Service Quarterly*, 31 (fall 1954), 12–22 (presented at the Annual Meeting of National Association of Jewish Center Workers, 17 May 1954); Jeanne Karp, telephone interview, 5 May 1991.

2. KBC, untitled oral history, KBC MSS; see, for overviews of the role of social science in challenging segregation, Walter A. Jackson, *Gunnar Myrdal and America's Conscience, Social Engineering and Racial Liberalism, 1938–1987* (Chapel Hill, N.C., 1990), 272–311, and Mark A. Chesler, Joseph Sanders, and Debra S. Kalmuss, *Social Science in Court, Mobilizing Experts in the School Desegregation Cases* (Madison, Wisc., 1988), 19.

3. KBC to Viola Bernard, 15 September 1952, box Racism, Bernard Papers; see also Robert L. Carter to Bernard, 6 October 1952, ibid.

4. KBC, untitled oral history, KBC MSS.

5. "Clark," *Models of Achievement*, 270; *Brown v. Board of Education of Topeka*, 347 U.S. 483, 1954.

6. KBC, untitled oral history, KBC MSS.

7. Quoted in KBC, "The Negro in New York City—The Role of Education," speech for Urban League Dinner, Hotel Theresa, 15 February 1954, KBC MSS; KBC makes the point that in communities throughout the State, this bill was evaded by a state law that allowed communities to establish "separate but equal" schools. This law was repealed

in 1900 by the legislature and signed by Governor Theodore Roosevelt. See also Diane Ravitch, *The Great School Wars, New York City, 1805–1973* (New York, 1974).

8. "The Harlem Riot of 1935," [Reports from the *Amsterdam News*] New York, 1969, 28, 79–82; KBC, "Racial Progress and Retreat," 5.

9. Jeannette Hopkins, interview with authors, Portsmouth, N.H., 16 February 1995.

10. KBC, "The Negro in New York City—The Role of Education."

11. Marjorie Ottinger, "Meeting of the Steering Committee, Intergroup Committee of New York's Public Schools," 17 February 1955, KBC MSS; William Jansen to KBC, 24 February 1954; William Jansen to KBC, 4 June 1954; "School Conditions in Harlem," 26 May 1954, KBC MSS.

12. KBC, "Segregated Schools in New York City," 24 April 1954, KBC MSS; KBC to Conference Participant, 14 April 1954, KBC MSS.

13. "Conference Report 'Children Apart,'" 24 April 1954, Bernard Papers; "Harlem Students Learn Inferiority," *Amsterdam News*, 1 May 1954; "Some City Schools Held Segregated," *New York Times*, 25 April 1954, KBC MSS.

14. Minutes, NCCD, 3 June 1954.

15. "Annual Meeting of Urban League of Greater New York," 21 June 1954, in Rose Bruce to Viola Bernard, 2 July 1954, Bernard Papers.

16. "Will Probe Negro-Area Education," *New York Herald-Tribune*, 15 July 1954, KBC MSS.

17. KBC to Arthur Leavitt, 16 July 1954, KBC MSS; "Clark Cites Several Examples of School Segregation Here," *New York Herald-Tribune*, 21 October 1954, KBC MSS; "Advance Text of Address" by KBC, 18 October 1954, KBC MSS.

18. [KBC], "First Draft Report: Activities of Intergroup Committee on New York's Public Schools—April 1954 to April 1955," KBC MSS; "Education Board Sets a Bias Study," *New York Times*, 9 May 1955, KBC MSS.

19. "The Quality of Education Offered to Majority and Minority (Negro, Puerto Rican) Children in New York City's Public Schools," Report Submitted to the Public Education Association by the Research Center for Human Relations at New York University, August 1955, [typescript], box Racism—Desegregation—Relevant Literature, Bernard Papers.

20. Ibid.

21. Ibid.

22. [KBC], untitled draft, [ca. 1955], KBC MSS.

23. "Segregation, Queens Style," *Amsterdam News*, 13 April 1957, 1; see also *Amsterdam News*, 6 April 1957, 1; 16 March 1957, 18; KBC to Charles Silver, 2 November 1956, KBC MSS.

24. KBC, "Segregation and Desegregation in Our Schools," in Algernon D. Black, Kenneth Clark and James Dumpson, *Ethical Frontiers, The City's Children and the Challenge of Racial Discrimination* (New York, 1958), 18–19.

25. "Teacher Groups Oppose Integrating NY Schools," *Amsterdam News*, 2 February

1957, 5. See also New York Teachers Guild, AFL-CIO, "Helping Solve the Difficult School, Staffing, and Integration Problems," September 1957, KBC MSS, in which a conference of teachers decides that they will not discuss "forced transfers" since that was not a possibility from their point of view.

26. KBC, "Segregation and Desegregation in Our Schools," 20; "Teacher Groups Oppose Integrating NY Schools," *Amsterdam News*, 2 February 1957, 5.

27. High School Teachers Association of New York City, Inc., "News Release," 27 December 1956, KBC MSS.

28. "Jansen, CCNY Prof Clash in Public Over Integration," *New York Post*, 29 November 1956, 14, KBC MSS.

29. Intergroup Committee on New York's Public Schools, "Press Release," 17 January 1957, box 54, folder 15, United Neighborhood Houses MSS, University of Minnesota Social Welfare History Archives.

30. Citizens' Committee for Children of New York, Inc., "Statement by Dr. Roma Gans," 17 January 1957, Citizens' Committee for Children MSS, New York; Hubert Delany to Charles Silver, 21 January 1957, box 54, folder 13, United Neighborhood Houses MSS.

31. Charles Cogan to Hubert T. Delany, 23 January 1957, box 54, folder 13, United Neighborhood Houses MSS.

32. KBC, "The Present Crisis in Race Relations," paper delivered at the Annual Dinner of the Unitarian Service Committee, Inc., 19 May 1956, Boston, NCCD MSS. For an opposing interpretation of the significance of the same speech, see "Segregation End in Five Years Seen," *New York Times*, 20 May 1956, KBC MSS.

33. "Dr. Clark Puts Dr. Jansen on School Carpet," *Amsterdam News*, 10 August 1957, 1, 31; "Don't Forget, N.Y. Has Its Own School Problem," *Amsterdam News*, 28 August 1957, 1, 17.

34. William Jansen, "Report on Integration (Report #1)," 19 September 1957, KBC MSS; Intergroup Committee on New York's Public Schools, "Special Executive Committee Meeting," 30 October 1957, box 54, folder 13, United Neighborhood Houses MSS.

35. "Harlem Talks Bid for School Peace," *New York Times*, 30 January 1959, 16; Kate Clark Harris, tape-recorded interview by Jonathan Lee, 6 May 1991, OHC.

36. "2 Harlem Schools Called Inferior as Court Frees Two in Boycott," *New York Times*, 16 December 1958, 1.

37. HANA, Statement of Support for Justine Wise Polier and opposition to Board of Education, 27 February 1959, NCCD MSS.

38. See, for example, "Historic Decision," *Brooklyn Daily*, 13 January 1959; "Open Letter to the Members of the Board of Education," *New York Age*, 3 January 1959, 8, KBC MSS.

39. KBC, "Present Problems in Public School Desegregation in New York City," in *Harlem Works for Better Schools* (New York, [ca. 1959]), 11–12.

40. The story of these boycotts can be followed in the *New York Times* and the

Amsterdam News September 1959 through June 1960. See, for example, "Harlem Pupils Seek Shift to Riverdale; Boycott is Planned," *New York Times*, 11 September 1959, 1; "Schools Picketed in Queens Again; Sixteen Whites Parade in a New Protest Against Transfer of Negro Children," *New York Times*, 19 September 1959, 26; "Boycott Classes Begun in Harlem," *New York Times*, 22 September 1959, 42.

41. Urban League of Greater New York, "Research Study (A Study of the Problems of Integration in New York City Public Schools Since 1955)," September 1963, box 4, Milton Yale MSS, 41. University of Minnesota Social Welfare History Archives; HARYOU-ACT, Inc., *Youth in the Ghetto, A Summary* (New York, 1964), 5; Jeanne Karp, "Report on Intensive Reading Program, Northside Center for Child Development, Inc.," May 1963, NCCD MSS; [Jeanne Karp], "The Effect of Severe Economic, Social, and Educational Deprivation on Remedial Practice," [January 1965], NCCD MSS.

42. Urban League of Greater New York, "Research Study"; State Education Commissioner's Advisory Committee on Human Relations and Community Tensions, [John H. Fischer, Judah Cahn, KBC], "Desegregating the Public Schools of New York City," 12 May 1964, 27, KBC MSS. See, for example of board of education position, Board of Education, City of New York, "Joint Statement by Mr. Charles H. Silver, President and Dr. John J. Theobold, Superintendent," 31 August 1960, KBC MSS.

43. Gladys Meyer, *Parent Action in School Integration, A New York Experience* (New York, 1961), 8, box 4, Yale MSS.

44. Levison, interview; Elaine Gaspard, tape-recorded interview with Wanda Phipps, 24 February 1991, OHC.

45. Meyers, interview.

46. Hermine Popper, "How Difficult Are the Difficult Schools? A Report" (New York, 1959), 9-10.

47. Ibid.

48. Citizens' Committee for Children of New York City, Inc., "Education Section Report: Delinquency 'Crisis' in the Schools," May 1958, CCC MSS.

49. Harrison E. Salisbury, "Well-run Schools Solving Problems in City 'Jungles'," *New York Times*, 29 March 1958, 1, 20; "Women Disagree on Unruly Pupils," *New York Times*, 29 March 1958, 20.

50. Justine Wise Polier, "Equal Education—Promise and Prospects in New York City," [Speech before Intergroup Committee on New York City's Schools], 14 March 1960, box 46, folder 571, Polier MSS.

51. Quoted in Doug McAdam, *Political Process and the Development of Black Insurgency, 1930–1970* (Chicago, 1982), 215.

52. MPC and Jeanne Gerbitz Karp, "Report on Summer Remedial Programs" (mimeo), November 1959, 1–3, NCCD MSS; [Jeanne Karp], "The Effect of Severe Economic, Social and Educational Deprivation."

53. Levison, interview.

54. "Summer Reading Progress Report" [mimeo, n.d.], NCCD MSS.

55. Jeanne Karp, "Notes on Remedial Program," 14 February 1994, NCCD MSS.

56. Levison, interview.

57. Karp, "Notes on Remedial Program."

58. Ibid.

59. Levison, interview; Karp, interview.

60. Karp, "Notes on Remedial Program."

61. MPC and Jeanne Karp, "A Summer Remedial Program," *Elementary School Journal* 61 (1960), 137–42; KBC, *Dark Ghetto: Dilemmas of Social Power* (New York, 1965), 140; MPC and Karp, "Report on Summer Remedial Programs."

62. "Panel Discussion," *Changing Concepts in Mental Health* (May 1976), 24.

63. KBC, *Dark Ghetto*, 142.

64. "Tentative Proposal for Remedial Project," October–June 1963; "The Proposal for an Expanded Summer Remedial Program to be Phased into Year Round," [1962]; Jeanne Karp, "Report on Intensive Reading Program, Northside Center for Child Development, Inc.," May 1963 [Remedial Staff Beatrice Levison, Edna Meyers, Mary Miller, Harriet Moskowitz, Elaine Asch]. All in NCCD MSS.

65. Karp, "Notes on Remedial Program."

66. Ibid.; [Karp], "The Effect of Severe Economic, Social and Educational Deprivation."

67. "The Spreading Boycott," *Time* 83 (14 February 1964), 40.

68. Memorandum from Norman Wyloge to MPC, re: [student] in MPC to Dr. Nathan Jacobson, Supt. District 5, PS 75, 16 February 1968, KBC MSS; MPC to Jacobson, 16 February 1968, ibid.

69. "A Mental Health Program for Enhancement of the Educational Process in the Public Schools," [ca. 1965], NCCD MSS.

70. Ibid.

71. [Donald Watt], "A Plan for the Application for Professional Mental Health Skills Toward the Improvement of the Educational Process in Schools," 25 February 1965, NCCD MSS; Olivia Edwards to MPC, Re: Dr. Watt's Paper for the PS 192 Project, 13 April 1965, NCCD MSS; "A Mental Health Program for Enhancement of the Educational Process in the Public Schools," [February–March 1965], NCCD MSS.

72. "Minutes, Two-Part Meeting of Project P.S. #192," 15 May 1965, NCCD MSS.

73. Ravitch, *The Great School Wars*, 306; "City's 'Ghetto' Schooling Denounced," *New York Times*, 5 October 1966, KBC MSS.

74. Harlem Parents Committee, *Views*, [October 1966], 2, KBC MSS.

75. [KBC], "Proposal for Educational Excellence for I.S. 201 and Its Feeder Schools," 29 September 1966, KBC MSS.

76. Ravitch, *The Great School Wars*, 312.

77. Ibid., 308–9.

78. Draft of "Introduction by Dr. Kenneth B. Clark to *Community Control and the Urban School*," 24 March 1970, KBC MSS.

79. See Ravitch, *The Great School Wars,* for a comprehensive review of these events.

80. MARC, Transcription, Northside Conference, 10 January 1969.

81. Ibid.

82. Ibid.

83. Memorandum, George Dalley to KBC, Kenneth Marshal, Hylan Lewis and MPC, 30 September 1968, KBC MSS; Memorandum, MARC Subcommittee on Parent Organization to KBC, 24 June 1968, KBC MSS.

84. "Why Don't They Want Our Children to Learn?" *New York Times,* 20 September 1968, 30.

85. MARC, Transcription, Northside Conference, 10 January 1969.

86. MPC, Jeannette Hopkins, and Hylan Lewis, [Report] To the President of MARC and Members of the Advisory Committee on the Union of Concerned Parents, 16 May 1969, KBC MSS. The broader struggle over decentralization became mired in complex political maneuvering. Ultimately, Kenneth Clark believed that the original purposes of the community control effort had been "forgotten." "The purpose was not a struggle for power or control. . . . The purpose was to try to find some way in which the quality of education provided children in a particular school could be increased by more direct monitoring, supervision, more effective teaching accountability." Kenneth Clark faulted local boards for concentrating too much on "power, actions, control of finances" rather than on "methods for raising quality." See "Decentralization of Schools Fails, Kenneth Clark Says," *New York Times,* 8 May 1972, 1; "Clark, in Full About-Face, Calls for a Curb on Decentralization," *New York Times,* 30 November 1972, 1.

87. MARC, Transcription, Northside Conference, 10 January 1969; Union of Concerned Parents, chapter 2, "Minutes of Meeting," 4 February 1969–8 May 1969, KBC MSS.

88. MARC, Transcription, Northside Conference, 10 January 1969.

89. "Fund Backs Controversial Study of 'Racial Betterment,'" *New York Times,* 11 December 1977, 76.

90. KBC and Lawrence Plotkin to Professor Doxie Wilkerson, 26 September 1969, KBC MSS; see also, for MARC's efforts to counteract Jensen, "Minutes of Meeting," 7 November 1969; "Minutes, Meeting of Committee on Genetic Factors and Intelligence (or here we go again group)," 2 November 1970; "Minutes," Committee on Genetic Factors on Intelligence, 4 November 1971, all in KBC MSS.

91. KBC, *Pathos of Power* (New York, 1974), 109–10.

92. Edna O. Meyers, "Is Chile a Food? A Description of Whether or Why Black Children Do Poorly on the WISC," delivered at the American Psychological Association, New Orleans, 2 September 1974, NCCD MSS.

93. Meyers, interview.

94. Meyers, "Is Chile a Food?"

95. Ibid.

96. Edna Meyers, "Do Your Own Think," mimeo, 1976, NCCD MSS.

97. Appendix 2, "Questionnaire From 'Do Your Own Think Program'" Annual Report, Psychology Department, 1 July 1969–30 June 1970, NCCD MSS.

98. Psychology Department, End of Year Report, 1 July 1970–30 June 1971, NCCD MSS.

99. Year End Report, Remedial Department, July 1973, NCCD MSS.

100. "Reading Department Workshop Presentation, 'Clinic-in-the-Classroom,'" 7 May 1976, NCCD MSS; Remedial Department, Annual Report, July 1976, NCCD MSS; Northside Center for Child Development, "Progress Fact Sheet, July 1972 thru June 1973," December 1973, 4, NCCD MSS.

5. "The Child, the Family, and the City"

1. [Daniel P. Moynihan], *The Negro Family: The Case for National Action*, U.S. Department of Labor, Office of Policy, Planning and Research, March 1965.

2. Quoted in "The Child, the Family and the City," Seminar with Children's Hospital and Northside, 21 February 1968, Washington, D.C., NCCD MSS.

3. Lee Rainwater and William L. Yancey, *The Moynihan Report and the Politics of Controversy* (Cambridge, 1967), 27–28.

4. William Ryan, "Savage Discovery: The Moynihan Report," *The Nation*, 22 November 1965, reprinted in Rainwater and Yancey, *The Moynihan Report and the Politics of Controversy*, 463–64.

5. KBC, *Pathos of Power*, 128–29.

6. See chapter 5, "The Pathology of the Ghetto," in KBC, *Dark Ghetto*.

7. KBC, *Pathos of Power*, 128–29.

8. Ibid. He went on: "By their training, their style, their language, they are particularly effective in influencing the opinions of the intellectual and academic communities. . . . Some individuals, such as Daniel P. Moynihan himself, will be flagrant and direct in their for-hire role in exchange for rewards of prestige, publicity and power. Others, such as Jensen, Banfield, Forrester, Armor, and Jencks will be more indirect. Still others, such as Bell and Glazer, will be more subtle and polysyllabic apologists for the status quo."

9. Christopher Lasch, *Haven in a Heartless World* (New York, 1977).

10. Minutes, NCCD, 10 November 1960.

11. Minutes, NCCD, 12 January 1961.

12. [MPC], "Effect of Severe Social and Economic Problems of Child Guidance Practice," [about 1964], handwritten notes, NCCD MSS.

13. Abramovich, interview.

14. [MPC], "Effect of Severe Social and Economic Problems."

15. Ibid.

16. Ibid.

17. Oscar Lewis, *La Vida: A Puerto Rican Family in the Culture of Poverty—San Juan and*

New York (New York, 1966) and *The Children of Sanchez* (New York, 1961), quoted in Michael B. Katz, *The Undeserving Poor: From the War on Poverty to the War on Welfare* (New York: Pantheon Books, 1989), 17.

18. Katz, *The Undeserving Poor*, 37.

19. "Abstract, Northside Center Conference," 1 March 1965, NCCD MSS.

20. "A Model of the Future, Northside Center for Child Development," 13 October 1965, in Minutes, NCCD, 2 December 1965.

21. Minutes, NCCD, for 10 November 1960, 9 February 1961, 9 March 1961, and 11 May 1961.

22. Barbara Rubinstein, "Progress Report," May 1965, NCCD MSS. By the late 1960s, little had changed and when the results were prepared for a paper to be presented for the American Orthopsychiatric Association Meetings in 1968, Barbara Rubinstein said that "classroom observers and teachers note a *trend* toward slightly higher adjustment . . . toward the end of their therapy. This trend does not persist nor is the difference in ratings between experimental and controls at any time statistically significant." Barbara Rubinstein, "PPPG—Summary for Ortho," 23 March 1968, NCCD MSS.

23. See, for example, Preston Wilcox, "Positive Mental Health in the Black Community: The Black Liberation Movement," in Charles V. Willie, Bernard M. Kramer, Bertram S. Brown, eds., *Racism and Mental Health* (Pittsburgh, 1973), 463–524, for a discussion of the impact of separatism on African-American mental-health workers.

24. "Abstract, Northside Center Conference," 1 March 1965.

25. Minutes, NCCD, 14 October 1965.

26. Ibid.

27. Ibid.

28. Ibid.

29. Ibid.

30. Ibid.

31. Carter, interview.

32. Pugh, interview.

33. Victor Carter recalls the educational process that professionals in social work underwent in the 1950s and 1960s: "In social work school . . . you had courses in child welfare and you had courses in community organization, all of that theoretical and its very good. And you can take those theories and concepts and . . . impose it and gain understanding. However, there is no way people in those schools could know what I knew." Carter, interview.

34. "A Model of the Future."

35. Ibid.

36. "Reactions to Planning Committee Meeting, Nov. 12, 1965," NCCD MSS.

37. Minutes, NCCD, 2 December 1965.

38. Cloward and Epstein, "Private Social Welfare's Disengagement from the Poor," 45.

39. Ibid., 53–54.

40. Ibid., 55.

41. Ibid., 49.

42. Clara Rabinowitz, "Editorial: Human Rehabilitation in the Sixties," *American Journal of Orthopsychiatry* 33 (July 1963), 589–90.

43. Minutes, NCCD, 2 December 1965.

44. Ibid.

45. Ibid.

46. Ibid.

47. "A Model of the Future."

48. Memo, MPC to All Staff, 31 January 1966, NCCD MSS.

49. "A Model for the Future."

50. Lisa Paisley-Cleveland, tape-recorded interview with Jonathan Lee, 11 November 1990, OHC.

51. "A Model for the Future."

52. Wyloge, interview.

53. Lombard, interview.

54. Paisley-Cleveland, interview.

55. "A Model for the Future."

56. Ibid.

57. Clara Rabinowitz, "The Caseworker and the Private Practitioner of Psychotherapy," *Jewish Social Service Quarterly* 30 (winter 1953), 13.

58. Victor Carter, "Casework 1969–1970," NCCD MSS.

59. Victor Carter, Jeanne Karp, Barbara Jones, Blanche Pugh, and Sam Walton, joint interview with authors, 2 November 1992, New York.

60. Wyloge, interview.

61. Carter, "Casework 1969–1970."

62. Wyloge, interview.

63. Annual Report, Case Work Department, 1969-1970, NCCD MSS.

64. Psychology Department, "End of Year Report, July 1, 1969–June 30, 1970," NCCD MSS.

65. Ibid.

66. Norman Wyloge, "Total Advocacy: A Changing Concept in Mental Health," 7 May 1976, NCCD MSS.

67. Joel Frader to MPC et al. Re: Mothers' Group, "Notes," [early 1967], NCCD MSS.

68. Paisley-Cleveland, interview.

69. "Minutes for Meeting with Parents," 15 June 1967, NCCD MSS; "Minutes,"[Mothers' Group], 29 June 1967, NCCD MSS.

70. Carter, interview; "35 Mothers April 24, Sunday, to Crystal Caves, Pennsylvania, price: $6.30," *Northside News* 1 (April 1967), 1, NCCD MSS.

71. Carter, interview; *Northside News*, n.d. [mid-1967], NCCD MSS.

72. Carter, interview.

73. Ibid.; see also Victor Carter, [winter 1967-68], "Parents Council," NCCD MSS; *Inside Northside*, March–April 1971; Victor Carter, "Getting Down to Basics," Parents Council of Northside Center; Parents Council, "First Draft Report of Activities," June 1975–July 1976, NCCD MSS.

74. Staff Notes attached to "Parents Council of Northside Center, 'Nutrition Fair Schomburg Plaza,' Sept. 27 and 28th, 1974."

75. Case Work Department, "Summary Statement," 1971–1972, NCCD MSS.

76. Ibid.

77. Walton, Carter, Pugh, Karp, Jones, group interview; "More Help for Those Who Need It Most—A Statement about Northside Center for Child Development Prepared for a Few Select Friends of the Center," January 1974, NCCD MSS.

78. O'Connor, interview.

79. Paisley-Cleveland, interview.

80. Minutes, NCCD, 8 October 1970; see also, "Memorandum," MPC to Board of Directors, 9 July 1970: "Of thirty-three (33) eligible employees: eighteen (18) voted to join the union; one (1) voted not to join and fourteen (14) did not choose to vote," in KBC MSS.

81. Minutes, NCCD, 8 October 1970.

82. Minutes, NCCD, 3 December 1970.

83. Wyloge, interview: "When workers tried to bring in a union Mamie was very angry. And she couldn't understand why Northside would need a union. It was a family and she saw that as a rebellious quality that she didn't take well to."

84. Minutes, NCCD, 3 December 1970; KBC, "Racial Progress," 7.

85. Minutes, NCCD, 3 December 1970.

86. Alexander Thomas to KBC, 15 October 1970, KBC MSS.

87. Ibid.

88. Minutes, NCCD, 6 December 1970; Minutes, NCCD, 7 January 1971.

89. Minutes, NCCD, 4 February 1971.

90. Ibid.; "Statement to the Board of Directors on the Issue of the Union Shop," 4 February 1971, attached to ibid.

91. Ibid.

92. Ibid.; see also Minutes, NCCD, 22 February 1971.

93. Minutes, NCCD, 4 February 1971.

94. Lorna Goodman, tape-recorded interview with Lisa Miller, 8 June 1993, OHC.

95. Minutes, NCCD, 22 February 1971.

96. Ibid.

97. MPC to Board of Directors, 25 February 1971, NCCD MSS.

98. Minutes, NCCD, 14 April 1971.

99. "Report—Case Work Department, 1970-1971," NCCD MSS; Lucienne Numa, M.D., Medical Director, "Annual Report—Therapy Department July 1971," NCCD MSS.

6. Juvenile Delinquency and the Politics of Community Action

1. [KBC], untitled "Rough Draft," [1963], KBC MSS.

2. Judge Robert Carter, tape-recorded interview with Jonathan Lee, 10 January 1991, OHC.

3. Calculated from William Glaser, *A Harlem Almanac* (New York, 1964), 19, 10.

4. HARYOU-ACT, Inc., *Youth in the Ghetto, A Summary* (New York, 1964), 3.

5. Glaser, *Harlem Almanac*, 22.

6. MPC, "Evaluation of the Effectiveness of an Interracial Child Guidance Clinic: Intercultural Factors," [1957, Mimeo], KBC MSS. In 1955, the population at the center was 63 percent Negro; 20 percent Puerto Rican; 16 percent white; 1 percent Asian. NCCD, "Annual Report," 1955, KBC MSS.

7. Minutes, NCCD, 10 November 1960.

8. Minutes, NCCD, 9 March 1961.

9. Minutes, NCCD, 13 June 1963.

10. Paul Benedict, "Memorandum To Board Members," attached to Minutes, NCCD, 9 January 1964.

11. Ibid.

12. Richard A. Cloward, "The Administration of Services to Children and Youth in New York City," Institute of Public Administration, New York, October 1963 in *Mobilization for Youth, A Documentary Record* 1 (August–September 1964), n.p., in possession of authors courtesy of Richard Cloward.

13. Minutes, NCCD, 20 February 1964.

14. Katz, *The Undeserving Poor*, chapter 3.

15. Mercer L. Sullivan, *Getting Paid, Youth Crime and Work in the Inner City* (Ithaca, 1989), 3-4; Nicholas Lemann, *The Promised Land, The Great Migration and How It Changed America* (New York, 1991), 120–21.

16. "Notes on a proposal to amend the Youth Correction Authority Bill so as to give Judges an option of sentencing a convicted youth offender without regard to the Authority Act or of committing the offender to the Authority," record group 2, Welfare Interests—General, box 13, folder Youth Correction Authority Act—New York Legislation, RFA.

17. "Organizing Private Resources for Treatment of Delinquent Youth," 26 March 1942, mimeo, ibid.

18. Leonard W. Mayo to John D. Rockefeller III, 20 September 1940, enclosure, "The Youth Correction Authority Act," record group 2, sub-series Welfare Interests, box 13, folder Delinquency Study—Committee, RFA.

19. New York State Committee on Youth Correction Authority Plan, in MacCormick to Rockefeller III, 7 February 1943, record group 2, Welfare Interests—General, box 13, folder Youth Correction Authority Act—New York Legislation, RFA.

20. Peter Marris and Martine Rein, *Dilemmas of Social Reform, Poverty and Community Action in the United States* (Chicago, 1967, 1973), 20.

21. KBC, "Color, Class, Personality and Juvenile Delinquency," *Journal of Negro Education*, summer 1959, 240, 247.

22. Department of Health, Education and Welfare, Welfare Administration, Office of Juvenile Delinquency and Youth Development, "Policy Guides to the Presentation of Proposals for Funding Under Public Law 87-274," 3 September 1963, Piven Papers.

23. "Community Mental Health Board—Jewish Board of Guardians, New York City Youth Board Pilot Project of Mental Health Services in Support of Street Club Work," [June 1961], NCCD MSS. See also George Gregory Jr. and Emma Penn [of HANA] to MPC, 5 July 1960, NCCD MSS.

24. HANA, "Annual Report," April 1960, 1–2, NCCD MSS.

25. KBC, interview, 7 April 1976.

26. Marion Clark, "Mental Health Committee of the Harlem Neighborhoods Association," 14 June 1961, NCCD MSS.

27. KBC, interview, 7 April 1976.

28. "Presentation for a Community Organization Contract to the New York City Youth Board by the Harlem Neighborhoods Association, Inc.," 18 December 1961, NCCD MSS. See also "A Program for Harlem's Youth," December 1961, NCCD MSS.

29. KBC, interview, 7 April 1976.

30. Minutes, NCCD, 11 January 1962, NCCD MSS.

31. MPC to Eugene Callender, 15 January 1962, NCCD MSS.

32. "Report of the Committee on Appropriate Machinery for Operations of the Youth Services Program," ca. May 1962, NCCD MSS. KBC, Chair. Committee includes Dumpson, Jones, Dr. Edward S. Lewis, Reverend Weston. See also KBC, "First Draft, Planning Youth Services in Harlem, A Proposal for a Federal Planning Grant under Public Law 87-274, Prepared for the Youth Services Proposal and Incorporating Committee of the Harlem Neighborhoods Association, Inc.," 2 May 1962, NCCD MSS; "Tentative Draft," Re Y.O.U. 5 May 1962, NCCD MSS; KBC, "Semi-Final Draft . . . Prepared for Harlem Youth Opportunities Unlimited, Inc., and Harlem Neighborhoods Association," 11 May 1962, NCCD MSS.

33. President's Committee on Juvenile Delinquency and Youth Crime, "Newsletter," 13 August 1962, National Archives, record group 220 (President's Committee on Juvenile Delinquency), box 20, folder Newsletter.

34. "Meeting of the Citizens' Advisory Council of the President's Committee on Juvenile Delinquency," 4 January 1963, folder President's Committee, Piven Papers.

35. "Newsletter: Harlem Youth Opportunities Unlimited," 1, March 1963, NCCD MSS; *Youth in the Ghetto*.

36. "Meeting of the Citizens' Advisory Council."

37. James Hicks, "Another Angle," *Amsterdam News* [ca. Feb. 1963], 11, 36, in NCCD MSS.

38. "Uptown Rallies to Answer Sniping at HARYOU and ACT," *New York Courier*, 23 February 1963, 1, 4.

39. "Publisher's Statement," *Amsterdam News*, 9 March 1963, 1, 10.

40. "Report: Sub-Committee on Agency Opportunity of the Social Agencies Committee," NCCD MSS.

41. MPC to Mrs. Carol Matthew, 22 November 1963, NCCD MSS.

42. Levison, interview.

43. Harlem Neighborhoods Association, Executive Committee Meeting, 22 January 1964, 11, 13, NCCD MSS.

44. Ibid., 15.

45. Harlem Neighborhoods Association, Inc., "Minutes of the Board of Directors Retreat," 1 February 1964, 116, NCCD MSS.

46. Ibid., 103.

47. Harlem Neighborhoods Association, Executive Committee Meeting, 22 January 1964, 7–10.

48. Ibid.

49. KBC and Jeannette Hopkins, *A Relevant War against Poverty: A Study of Community Action Programs and Observable Social Change* (New York, 1970), 181, 248–49.

50. Harlem Neighborhoods Association, Inc., "Minutes of the Board of Directors Retreat," 104–9, 111–12.

51. "Newsletter: Harlem Youth Opportunities Unlimited" 1, March 1963, NCCD MSS; *Youth in the Ghetto*.

52. "Threats Are Laid to Powell Aides," *New York Times*, 15 June 1964, 1, 32.

53. KBC, interview, 7 April 1976.

54. Howard Sloan, "Press Release," 15 June 1964, Office of the Mayor, Assistant to the Mayor, John Carro, 1958-64, box 109077C, folder NCCD, Robert Wagner MSS, La Guardia Archives, Queens, New York.

55. "Dr. Clark Quits, Blasts Powell," *New York Post*, 30 July 1964, 3.

56. Woody Klein, "Defeat in Harlem," *The Nation*, 27 July 1964, 27.

57. "Screvane Links Reds to Rioting," *New York Times*, 22 July 1964, 1.

58. KBC, *Pathos of Power*, 159.

59. "A Model for the Future."

60. "A Model for the Future"; MPC, "The Child, the Family and the City."

61. "A Proposal to Expand the Community Program at Northside Center for Child Development, Inc.," June 1968, KBC MSS.

62. MPC, "The Child, the Family, and the City"; "A Proposal to Expand the Community Program at Northside Center for Child Development, Inc.," June 1968, KBC MSS.

63. Elaine Gaspard, interview.

64. Ibid.

65. *Report of the National Advisory Commission on Civil Disorders*, quoted in Andrew Hacker, *Two Nations, Black and White, Separate, Hostile, Unequal* (New York, 1992), ix.

66. "Summary of Meeting of September 21, 1965," NCCD MSS.

67. "Summary of Meeting with Key People," 30 September 1965, NCCD MSS.

68. KBC, *Pathos of Power* (New York, 1974), 75, 78, derived from an address, "Problems of Power and Social Change: Toward a Relevant Social Psychology," at the American Psychological Association Meeting in Chicago, September 1965.

69. KBC, *Dark Ghetto*, chapter 7.

70. KBC, *Pathos of Power*, 161, 75.

71. MARC, Northside Conference, 10 January 1969.

72. Preston Wilcox, "Positive Mental Health in the Black Community: The Black Liberation Movement," in Charles V. Willie, Bernard M. Kramer, Bertam S. Brown, eds., *Racism and Mental Health* (Pittsburgh, 1973), 482.

73. MARC, Northside Conference, 63, 89.

74. "The Child, the Family and the City."

75. Jeanne Karp, Arlene Richards, and MPC, "A Report to the Greater New York Fund on a Summer Tutorial Program at Northside Center for Child Development," 3 October 1968, NCCD MSS.

76. Chris Iigima, Abby Fyer, [Student Volunteers, Summer Recreation Program Evaluation], 13 September 1968, mimeo, NCCD MSS.

77. Sam Walton, Victor Carter, Blanche Pugh, and Barbara Jones, interview with authors, 2 November 1992, New York.

78. Sam Walton, tape-recorded interview with Jonathan Lee, 24 April 1991, OHC; "We Care Presentation at NCCD Seminar," 7 May 1976, NCCD MSS.

79. Walton, interview; "We Care Presentation at NCCD Seminar"; "The We Care Group," interview with Joyce Cleveland, *Parent to Parent* 1 (November 1969), 5; Walton, Carter, Pugh, Karp, Jones, group interview.

80. "We Care Presentation at NCCD Seminar"; Walton, Carter, Pugh, Karp, Jones, group interview.

81. Victor Carter, interview.

82. "We Care Presentation at NCCD Seminar"; Walton, interview.

83. "We Care Presentation at NCCD Seminar."

84. Case Work Department, "Summary Statement," 1971-1972, NCCD MSS.

85. Ibid. We would like to thank Sam Walton for his generosity in sharing his only copy of the film with us.

86. Walton, interview.

87. "Northside and We Care: An Outreach Program," 7 May 1976, NCCD MSS.

88. NCCD, "Progress Fact Sheet, July 1972 thru June 1973," December 1973, NCCD MSS.

89. Walton, interview.

90. Ibid.

91. *Inside and Outside Northside* 2 (May 1967), NCCD MSS; Olivia Edwards, "Report of Community Department," 1966-67, NCCD MSS; *Northside News* 1 (April 1966), NCCD MSS.

92. Olivia Edwards, "Annual Report—September 1969–June 1970, Community Consultant," NCCD MSS.

93. Ibid; Community Consultation Department, Departmental Report September 1970–June 1971, "Walk-On-In Service Center," NCCD MSS; Annual Report—September 1971–June 1972, Community Consultation Department, NCCD MSS.

94. NCCD, "Annual Report, For the Year Ended August 31, 1955," KBC MSS; MPC to June Christmas, Commissioner, NYC Department of Mental Health and Mental Retardation Services, 26 March 1974, KBC MSS.

95. J. Carolina Quintana, Assistant Director, Social Work Department, Director Walk-In Service, "July 1976 Year-End Report," NCCD MSS; J. Carolina Quintana, "Year-End Evaluation," June 1977, NCCD MSS.

96. Mrs. Max Ascoli to Mrs. Joseph B. Thorman [President, Good Neighbor Federation], 27 May 1952, KBC MSS; "An Experiment with a Group of Adolescent Spanish Speaking Girls," [ca. 1952], KBC MSS.

97. "Staff Development Program," 20 October 1961, KBC MSS.

98. J. C. Quintana, "Summer Project," 14 September 1970, NCCD MSS; J. Quintana, Ms. Salas, and Ms. White, "Confidential Report, Visit to Social Agencies Located in East Harlem Area," 16 October 1972, NCCD MSS; J. C. Quintana to MPC, 10 December 1973, NCCD MSS.

99. Quintana to MPC, "Memorandum of Meeting," 8 January 1974, NCCD MSS.

7. Urban Renewal and Development and the Promise of Power

1. "Integrated Project Planned at Central Park, at 110th St.," *New York World-Telegram and Sun*, 1 March 1965, NCCD MSS.

2. Edgar Tafel, "Memorandum of a Recent Luncheon Meeting Given by Mrs. Helen Kamber at Her Home," 31 December 1964, NCCD MSS.

3. "Meeting at Northside Center for Child Development, Inc.," 15 January 1965, NCCD MSS; Edgar Tafel, architect, two architectural drawings, "Proposed Renewal Project for Frawley Circle, December 1964, NCCD MSS.

4. "Address by Manhattan Borough President Constance Baker Motley at First Borough President's Conference of Community Leaders, September 29, 1965, at City Hall," NCCD MSS.

5. Harlem Neighborhoods Association, Inc., "Statement of David N. Dinkins, Chairman, HANA Housing Committee, to the New York State Joint Legislative Committee on Housing and Urban Renewal," 3 February 1967, NCCD MSS.

6. "Statement to Board of Estimate," 2 August 1967, NCCD MSS.

7. Central Park North Committee Meeting, Minutes, 10 November 1965, NCCD MSS.

8. "New Name Given to 110th St. Area," *New York Times*, 7 September 1965, NCCD MSS.

9. "Text of President's Special Message to Congress on Improving Nation's Cities," *New York Times*, 27 January 1966, 20; "Johnson Sends Congress Plan to Rebuild the Nation's Slums," ibid.

10. "2 Renewal Areas Chosen Under New Policy," *New York Times*, 3 November 1966; "Housing Action System: Central Park North Plan," [1968], NCCD MSS.

11. Minutes, NCCD, 1 June 1967.

12. Ibid.

13. "Housing Action System: Central Park North Plan," [1968], NCCD MSS.

14. MPC to Jason R. Nathan, 20 September 1968, KBC MSS.

15. Louella Jacqueline Long and Vernon Ben Robinson, *How Much Power to the People? A Study of the New York State Urban Development Corporation's Involvement in Black Harlem* (New York, 1971), 45.

16. "Rockefeller Plan for Slums Voted," *New York Times*, 10 April 1968, 1.

17. MPC to Edward Logue, 20 September 1968, NCCD MSS.

18. MPC, interview.

19. MPC to Edward Logue, 20 September 1968.

20. Minutes, NCCD, 19 May 1969.

21. Minutes, NCCD, 16 October 1969.

22. Minutes, NCCD, 14 December 1969.

23. Ibid.

24. "Meeting of U.D.C. and 110th Street Plaza Housing Development Corporation," 1 December 1969, NCCD MSS.

25. "More Help for Those Who Need It Most—A Statement about Northside Center for Child Development Prepared for a Few Select Friends of the Center," January 1974, NCCD MSS.

26. 110th Street Plaza Housing Corp., Minutes, 11 February 1970, NCCD MSS.

27. Gaspard, interview.

28. "A Portrait of East Harlem," January 1960, Union Settlement MSS, Social Welfare History Archives, University of Minnesota, box 3, folder East Harlem Project, Proposals and Descriptions; Department of City Planning, City of New York, "Harlem—Public Improvements" [street map], 31 July 1959, Union Settlement MSS, box 2, folder Housing and Redevelopment, General.

29. "Statement Before the City Planning Commission at Hearing," 21 June 1961, Union Settlement MSS, box 2, folder Housing and Redevelopment, General.

30. United Residents of Milbank–Frawley Circle, East-Harlem Association, *Press Release*, [ca. November 1967]; Julio Sabater to Cora T. Walker, 20 November 1967; Julio Sabater to William Ward, 9 November 1967, NCCD MSS. See also Ellen Perry Berkeley, "Vox Populi: Many Voices from a Single Community," *Forum*, May 1968, 60–62.

31. "Negro-Latin Feud Hurting Harlem," *New York Times*, 25 February 1968, 45.

32. MPC, interview.

33. Minutes, 110th Street Plaza Housing Corp., 26 June 1970, NCCD MSS.

34. MPC to 110th Street Plaza Corp., Confidential Memorandum, re: 9 July 1970 meeting, NCCD MSS.

35. MEND, Minutes of Housing Information Meeting, 5 February 1973, NCCD MSS.

36. Young Lords Organization, "Borinqueños: Defend Your Home and Stores," [April 1970], NCCD MSS.

37. Minutes, NCCD, 16 April 1970; P. Cotto to MPC, 15 April 1970; Minutes, 110th Street Plaza Corp., 24 April 1970. NCCD MSS.

38. 110th Street Plaza Corp., "Fact Sheet," 15 April 1970, NCCD MSS.

39. Robert M. Litke to Herbert Tessler, 22 July 1970; MPC to 110th Street Housing Development Corp., 8 October 1970. NCCD MSS.

40. MPC, interview.

41. Carter, interview.

42. Blanche Pugh, interview.

43. MPC to Harold Dolly, 28 January 1971, NCCD MSS.

44. Minutes, 110th Street Plaza Housing Development Corp., 24 June 1971, 15 September 1971, 26 October 1971, and 14 December 1971, NCCD MSS.

45. MPC to Harold Dolly, 1 April 1971; Minutes, 110th Street Plaza Corp., 14 May 1971 and 26 October 1971; "Milbank-Frawley Emergency Meeting," [leaflet], 15 May 1972. NCCD MSS.

46. "UDC Is Gyping in Harlem Project," *Amsterdam News*, 12 February 1972, NCCD MSS.

47. Gaspard, interview.

48. Edward J. Logue to Directors of the Urban Development Corp., 22 July 1970, NCCD MSS.

49. "Fact Sheet," [ca. 1971], NCCD MSS.

50. Minutes, Northside, UDC, and Castro-Blanco, Architects, 2 July 1970, NCCD.

51. Minutes, 110th Street Plaza Housing Corp., 19 April 1972, NCCD.

52. "Minority Contractors in the Construction Industry, the Harlem Plan," in Abraham Isserman to John L. Jenkins, 27 September 1972, NCCD MSS.

53. "UDC Can't Find Black Workers," *Amsterdam News*, 5 February 1972, A11; Minutes, 110th Street Plaza Housing Corp., 19 April 1972, NCCD MSS; Abraham Isserman to Mamie Clark, 1 May 1972, NCCD MSS.

54. Press release, "Lindsay, Sutton, Schomburg Relatives Participate in Housing Ceremony," 17 May 1973, NCCD MSS; "Did You Know That," *Twilight*, 26 May 1973, NCCD MSS; "Schomburg Plaza Dedication Is Set for Thursday, May 17," *Amsterdam News*, 12 May 1973, B13; "Housing Ceremony," *The Black American*, 1–8 June 1973, NCCD MSS; "Harlem Group Launches 600-Unit Housing Plan," *Washington Afro-American*, 29 May 1973, NCCD MSS.

55. "Spanish Residents of El Barrio," leaflet, [ca. summer 1972] NCCD MSS.

56. Charlayne Hunter, "Hopes and Fears on Rise with New Harlem Skyline," *New York Times*, 20 November 1973, 41, 50. See also George M. Brooker to Ron Clare, UDC, 3 October 1973, NCCD MSS.

57. Minutes, 110th Street Plaza Housing Corp., 12 December 1972, 7 February 1973, and 10 September 1973, NCCD MSS.

58. "Profile of First 179 Families Being Considered for Schomburg Plaza," in 110th Street Plaza Housing Corp., Committee on Tenant Profile, 26 September 1973, NCCD MSS.

59. George M. Brooker to Marion Scott, UDC, 29 July 1974, NCCD MSS.

60. Minutes, 110th Street Plaza Housing Development Corp., 11 December 1973 and 24 January 1974, NCCD MSS.

61. George M. Brooker to Ronald J. Clare, UDC, 27 March 1974; George M. Brooker to Marion Scott, UDC, 29 July 1974, NCCD MSS.

62. George M. Brooker to Jane McGrath, UDC, 20 September 1974, NCCD MSS.

63. Minutes, 110th Street Plaza Housing Development Corp., 25 September 1974 and 20 November 1974, NCCD MSS.

64. "Calls New Complex Rebirth For Harlem," *Daily News*, 18 December 1974, NCCD MSS.

65. Press release, "Official Opening of Schomburg Plaza, Building B," 17 December 1974, NCCD MSS.

66. Charlayne Hunter, "Housing Is Dedicated at Schomburg Plaza," *New York Times*, 18 December 1974, 47.

67. Press release, "Northside Center's New Facilities Offer Expanded Health Services," [ca. December 1974], NCCD MSS; Dora Johnson, interview with authors, 14 December 1992; Abramovich, interview.

68. Minutes, NCCD, 6 February 1975.

69. Memorandum, MPC to Staff, 4 March 1974 and 2 April 1974, NCCD MSS.

70. Jeanne Karp, "Appendix A: Clinic-in-the-Classroom, Progress Report, October 1975–June 1976," NCCD MSS.

71. Anne Switzer and Jeanne Karp, "Creative Classroom Program, Language Arts, Summary Report, September, 1976–June, 1977," June 1977, NCCD MSS.

72. Teodora Abramovich, "Problems of Children and Parents Referred to Northside," 7 May 1976, NCCD MSS.

73. Annual Remedial Department, Summary, September 1977–June 1978, NCCD MSS.

74. Minutes, NCCD, 10 April 1975 and 5 June 1975.

75. Remedial Department, Annual Report, July 1976, NCCD MSS.

76. "Annual Remedial Department Summary," Sept 1978–July 1979, NCCD MSS; NCCD, "A Special Campaign to Enable Us to Meet Community Needs Effectively and Creatively as We Enter a New Decade of Services," June 1979, Rockefeller Brother Fund MSS, series 3, box 383, RFA.

77. "Memorandum #1," MPC to All Staff, 6 June 1975, NCCD MSS.

78. Minutes, NCCD, 4 December 1975; Barbara Jones, tape-recorded interview with Jonathan Lee, 17 December 1990, OHC; Minutes, NCCD, 5 February 1976.

79. Remedial Department, Annual Report, July 1975, NCCD MSS.

80. Remedial Department, Annual Report, July 1976, NCCD MSS.

81. Jeanne Karp, "Appendix A: Clinic-in-the-Classroom, Progress Report, October 1975–June 1976"; "Year-End Report, Casework Department 1974–75," NCCD MSS.

82. Alexander Thomas in Conference Proceedings, Thirtieth Anniversary Conference, 7 May 1976, *Changing Concepts in Mental Health: A Thirty Year View* (New York: NCCD, 1976), NCCD MSS.

83. Antonio Parras, M.D., "Year-End Psychiatric Report (1975)," NCCD MSS.

84. J. Carolina Quintana, "Casework Department, Year-End Report 1977–78," NCCD MSS.

85. Victor Carter, "Annual Report, July 1976–June 1977," NCCD MSS.

86. "Annual Report, Casework Department, 1978," NCCD MSS.

87. Victor Carter, "Year-End Summary—Casework Department, July, 1976," NCCD MSS.

88. James Dumpson in Conference Proceedings, Thirtieth Anniversary Conference, 7 May 1976, *Changing Concepts in Mental Health: A Thirty Year View.*

89. Alexander Thomas in Conference Proceedings, Thirtieth Anniversary Conference, 7 May 1976, ibid.

90. Norman Wyloge, "Total Advocacy: A Changing Concept in Mental Health," 7 May 1976, ibid.

91. Ibid.

92. Victor Carter, "Annual Report, July, 1976–June, 1977," NCCD MSS.

93. Walton, Carter, Pugh, Karp, Jones, group interview; Adrienne Meyers, Lou Gugglimi, Dr. Egbal Basith, Gwen Cafe, Norman Wyloge, Lisa Paisley-Cleveland, Bea Levison, interview with authors, 16 November 1992, New York.

94. Casework Department, "Year-End Report, 1979," NCCD MSS.

95. Dora Johnson, tape-recorded interview with Lisa Miller, 3 June 1993, OHC.

96. Meyers, Gugglimi, Basith, Cafe, Wyloge, Paisley-Cleveland, Levison, group interview.

97. Ibid.

98. Reception in honor of Dr. Thelma Dye, Museum of the City of New York, 13 December 1994.

99. Gertrude Samuels, "Where Troubled Children Are Reborn," *New York Times Magazine*, 13 June 1954, KBC MSS.

100. Ibid.

Index

Page numbers in italics refer to illustrations.